Eisenhower Center Studies on War and Peace
Stephen E. Ambrose and Günter Bischof, Editors

CONDITIONAL PARTNERS

CONDITIONAL PARTNERS

Eisenhower, the United Nations,
and the Search for a Permanent Peace

CAROLINE PRUDEN

Louisiana State University Press *Baton Rouge*

Copyright © 1998 by Louisiana State University Press
All rights reserved
Manufactured in the United States of America
First printing
07   06   05   04   03   02   01   00   99   98   5   4   3   2   1

Designer: Michele Myatt Quinn
Typeface: Granjon
Typesetter: Wilsted & Taylor Publishing Services
Printer and binder: Thomson-Shore, Inc.

The author wishes to thank John S. D. Eisenhower for permission to publish excerpts from
the writings of Dwight D. Eisenhower housed in the Dwight D. Eisenhower Library, Abilene,
Kansas; and the Estate of C. D. Jackson, administered by Chemical Bank, for permission to
reproduce excerpts from the C. D. Jackson Papers. Grateful acknowledgment is also made
to the following collections and repositories for permission to reproduce small portions of
unpublished materials: Sherman Adams Papers, Baker Memorial Library, Dartmouth College;
the Dulles Oral History Collection and the Papers of Allen W. Dulles, John Foster Dulles, and
Emmet Hughes, Seeley G. Mudd Manuscript Library, Department of Rare Books and Special
Collections, Princeton University Libraries; Christian A. Herter Papers, Houghton Library,
Harvard University; Henry Cabot Lodge, Jr., Papers, Massachusetts Historical Society,
Boston; Oral History Project Collection, Columbia University, New York.

Library of Congress Cataloging-in-Publication Data
Pruden, Caroline, 1962–
        Conditional partners : Eisenhower, the United Nations,
    and the search for a permanent peace / Caroline Pruden.
            p.   cm.   —   (Eisenhower Center studies on war and peace)
        Includes bibliographical references and index.
        ISBN 0-8071-2204-1 (c : alk. paper)
        1. United States—Foreign relations—1953–1961.   2. Eisenhower,
    Dwight D. (Dwight David), 1890–1969.   3. United Nations.
    4. Security, International.   I. Title.   II. Series.
    E835.P78   1998
    327.73—dc21   97-43275
                                                            CIP

For Bill, Cathleen, and Andrew

CONTENTS

Contents

Preface

The increased prominence of the United Nations has been among the most intriguing developments of the early post–cold war period. UN participation in recent attempts to resolve crises in the Persian Gulf, Somalia, and Bosnia-Herzegovina has propelled the body back into the international spotlight after decades in the wings. The reemergence of the organization as a leading actor on the world stage has sparked renewed scholarly interest in the United States' current relationship with the organization.[1]

These recent developments highlight the value of reexamining the history of American involvement with the United Nations. It is particularly instructive to explore the United States' use of the United Nations in the 1950s, for the Eisenhower administration assumed office at a critical point in the development of the U.S.-UN relationship. Eisenhower took the helm predisposed to seek collective security whenever possible by working in concert with the UN. Although in operation only seven years, the organization had established itself as a force in the international community. These factors converged to offer the prospect of a partnership with the potential to secure both

1. For a brief history of academic interest in the United Nations, see J. Martin Rochester, "The Rise and Fall of International Organization as a Field of Study," *International Organization,* XL (1986), 777–89. On the renewed interest in the United Nations among world leaders, see, for example, Edward C. Luck, "Making Peace," *Foreign Policy,* LXXXIX, (1993), 156–74; and Boutros Boutros-Ghali, "Empowering the United Nations," *Foreign Affairs,* LXXI (1993), 89–102.

Eisenhower's and the UN's paramount goal—a lasting international peace. And during that decade, despite the constraints of the cold war, the UN served as an important instrument with which the Eisenhower administration sought to advance the nation's foreign policy interests. Yet despite the wealth of literature on the administration's foreign policy, on President Dwight D. Eisenhower, and on Secretary of State John Foster Dulles, little attention has been paid to the administration's interaction with the United Nations.

Examining the United States' relationship with the United Nations provides a fresh perspective from which to evaluate the Eisenhower administration's foreign policy. Since World War II, the United States has been compelled to formulate global foreign policy and practice global diplomacy in its effort to become and remain a hegemonic power. A thorough critique of Eisenhower's foreign policy thus requires an assessment of American actions not only in Europe, but also in Asia, Africa, and Latin America, for in addition to maintaining U.S. supremacy over the Soviet Union and its allies in the cold war, the United States had two other goals: retaining its leadership position among its European and Asian allies, and gaining the support of the increasingly significant Third World. The United States faced the challenge of managing its relations with all three of these groups directly and simultaneously in the universal multilateral organization of the United Nations. Moreover, the United Nations considered the full range of issues on the international political scene during the 1950s and attempted to resolve a series of crises throughout the decade; hence the United States' status as one of the principal members of the United Nations necessitated its taking a public stand on innumerable issues and crises.

During the 1950s the two most important international struggles—those between East and West and North and South—competed for center stage at the United Nations. The former conflict, evident in the superpower cold war, and the latter, manifested most prominently in decolonization and the growing demands of the Third World, also dominated the American foreign policy agenda. In addition, tensions within the Western alliance, particularly as a result of the United States' attempt to balance its traditional anticolonial rhetoric with the demands of NATO allies that were the embattled colonial powers, surfaced periodically at the UN.

As the decade progressed, however, the struggle between the Third World and the developed nations increasingly overshadowed the U.S.-Soviet conflict in the UN forum. In this regard, the UN merely reflected the most significant systemic transformation of the 1950s—the impact of decolonization, the increasing diversity of claimants in the world arena, and the resulting shift of the focus of the cold war. As the European theater of the cold war settled along an essentially fixed front, new, more active theaters appeared elsewhere, particularly in Asia and Africa. At the same time, the relative salience and priority of issues on the international agenda changed. Therefore the UN became the central multilateral body where both the troubling issues that plagued the post-war world and the crises that punctuated the decade—those emanating from the superpower cold war, those spawned by decolonization, and those inextricably linked to both struggles—had to be addressed.

Study of American interaction with the United Nations provides insights not only into the ends toward which American policy was directed, but also into the manner in which policy was formulated and the means by which it was pursued and implemented at the height of American influence in the UN. It also raises questions about the degree to which those ends constituted an attempt simply to maintain an appearance of cooperation with and support for the UN and the degree to which it represented genuine, substantive support for multilateral diplomacy. The rhetoric of support for the UN was ever-present, but less clear is the extent to which the administration actually relied on the concept of universal collective security to maintain international peace and security during the decade.

The United Nations thus provides a window through which it is possible to obtain a distinctive view of almost the entire spectrum of American foreign policy. Looking through this window we can see the myriad competing demands upon the United States, the Eisenhower administration's efforts to weigh these demands and prioritize them, the extent to which the administration was successful in protecting and forwarding U.S. interests, and how well international peace and security fared.

More specifically, and of particular pertinence to the revisionist debate, Eisenhower's role in shaping U.S. policy toward the UN illustrates another dimension of his presidential leadership. His command of the foreign-policy-making machinery on this issue has much to tell us about his presidential leadership in a variety of situations. In what ways and to what extent was he an activist president on the question of the nation's relationship with the United Nations? Did his leadership ultimately result in wise and effective policies? It is in answering such questions that we will throw the most light on the Eisenhower years and find lessons that may apply in the years ahead.

With the completion of this book comes the pleasant opportunity to thank those who have helped me in so many ways. This project would not have been possible without the intellectual and practical guidance of Thomas Schwartz. He pushed me to take a critical look at my assumptions and has been an unfailing source of wise counsel and moral support at every stage of this project. I owe special thanks to Dewey W. Grantham for his judicious, responsive, and ever-gracious supervision of this work in an earlier form. His meticulous reading immeasurably strengthened the final product. Samuel T. McSeveney, Paul K. Conkin, and Harry Howe Ransom also read an earlier draft and offered thoughtful criticism, professional advice, and kind support. Bill Brands and Günter Bischof read a more recent version and furnished necessary and constructive criticism as well as timely encouragement. I owe an intellectual debt to Alan Henrikson of The Fletcher School of Law and Diplomacy at Tufts University, and to Martin Sherwin, also of Tufts University, both of whom inspired my initial interest in diplomatic history.

My research was facilitated by the dedicated archivists and staffs of the Dwight D. Eisenhower Library, Abilene, Kansas; the National Archives, Washington, D.C.; the Seeley G. Mudd Library, Princeton University; the Massachusetts Historical Society, Boston; the Baker Memorial Library, Dartmouth College; the Houghton Library, Harvard University; the United Nations Archives; the Jean and Alexander Heard Library, Vanderbilt University; and the D. H. Hill Library, North Carolina State University. Dwight Strandberg of the Eisenhower Library, Virginia Smith of the Massachusetts Historical Society, and Ben Primer of the Mudd Library deserve special mention for their enthusiastic and efficient assistance in guiding me through the rich collections in their care.

I am immensely grateful to Vanderbilt University and to the Dwight D. Eisenhower Foundation for their generous financial assistance during this project.

I would like to thank the staff of Louisiana State University Press, particularly Executive Editor John Easterly and Freelance Coordinator Catherine Kadair, for patiently shepherding this manuscript through the publication process. I am especially grateful to Eivind Allan Boe, whose expert copy-editing markedly improved the quality of this work.

Finally, this study could not have been completed without the support of my family. My husband, Bill, made this book possible with his selfless willingness to share his remarkable knowledge of American history and politics, his unquestioning faith in my abilities, and his inexhaustible encouragement and love. My daughter, Cathleen, who was born midway through the writing of this book, learned to walk and talk before I had completed it. Indeed, one of her first full sentences was, "My mommy write history book on Ike and UN." My son, Andrew, who was born while I was awaiting the galley proofs, wailed his way through my review of them, making this final stage of the project truly joyful and memorable. It is to them that I dedicate this book in gratitude for the happiness they have brought to my life.

Abbreviations Used in Notes

AWF	Ann Whitman File
COHP	The Oral History Project of Columbia University
DDE	Dwight D. Eisenhower
EL	Dwight D. Eisenhower Library, Abilene, Kansas
EP	Dwight D. Eisenhower Papers as President of the United States, 1953–1961
ER	Dwight D. Eisenhower Records as President, 1953–1961
FRUS	*Foreign Relations of the United States* (followed by the year span)
HCLP	Henry Cabot Lodge II Papers
MHS	Massachusetts Historical Society, Boston, Massachusetts
MTCD, MTCH	Paul Kesaris and Joan Gibson, eds., *Minutes of Telephone Conversations of John Foster Dulles and Christian Herter, 1953–1961* (microfilm)
NA	National Archives, Washington, D.C.
RG	Record Group
ROPOS	Records of the Office of Public Opinion Studies, 1943–1965
SISS Hearings	U.S. Congress, Senate, *Hearings Before the Subcommittee to Investigate the Administration of the Internal Security Act and Other Security Laws of the Committee on the Judiciary—Activities of United States Citizens Employed by the United Nations*

1

FROM ELECTION TO EXECUTION
The Eisenhower-Dulles-Lodge Team Takes Shape

On November 4, 1952, Dwight D. Eisenhower won the election for the thirty-fourth president of the United States with 55 percent of the popular vote and a decisive 442 electoral votes. Although a newcomer to national politics, the president-elect lost little time in choosing his foreign policy team. Within days he had tapped John Foster Dulles—the preeminent Republican foreign policy expert—for the post of secretary of state. Shortly afterward, on November 21, Eisenhower asked Henry Cabot Lodge, Jr., to serve as the U.S. representative to the United Nations. The president-elect had considered Lodge for chief of staff, but after consultation with Dulles had concluded that "Cabot's qualifications seemed almost unique" for this post "of vital importance."[1] This trio—Eisenhower, Dulles, and Lodge—became the core of the foreign-policy-making team on matters involving the United Nations.

Although Lodge lacked diplomatic experience, Eisenhower might have enumerated any of a host of qualifications the Massachusetts senator possessed. The ambassador-designate was highly regarded for his political savvy, acquired indirectly growing up under the tutelage of his politically powerful grandfather and namesake, Senator Henry Cabot Lodge, and directly from service in the Massachusetts legislature (1933–1936) and United

1. Dwight D. Eisenhower, *Mandate for Change, 1953–1956* (Garden City, 1963), 89, Vol. I of Eisenhower, *The White House Years.*

States Senate (1937–1944, 1947–1953). In addition, seven years as a journalist, first for the Boston *Transcript* and then the New York *Herald Tribune,* had heightened his sensitivity to public opinion. Lodge was also an impressive public speaker. He had developed his debating skill while in elective office and had recently honed it campaigning simultaneously for Eisenhower and, unsuccessfully, for his own reelection to the Senate. Eisenhower hoped that Lodge's forensic abilities would provide an immediate counter to the vicious verbal assaults of the Soviet representatives. Indeed, Lodge's fluency in French would enable him to tackle the Soviet propaganda machine bilingually, with added prestige and power.

The president and his UN representative came from markedly different backgrounds. Yet in a very short time Eisenhower, with his humble roots, had developed respect and even warmth for the Boston Brahmin with the Harvard degree. Cementing this developing bond was Eisenhower's special debt to Lodge for his being one of the earliest and most active organizers of the Eisenhower-for-president movement. A tireless advocate for creating a more modern Republican party during his thirteen years in the Senate, Lodge by the late 1940s viewed the domestic political situation with considerable alarm.[2]

On June 9, 1950, Lodge had visited Eisenhower at Columbia University, where the former general was president. Emphasizing the very real possibility that a Republican party led by Senator Robert A. Taft of Ohio would take an isolationist turn, Lodge skillfully played upon Eisenhower's sense of duty in urging him to protect the nation's international interests and preserve the vitality of the two-party system. In July, 1951, with the political winds blowing even more strongly in Taft's direction, Lodge again approached the general, who, having come out of military retirement to command the North Atlantic Treaty Organization, was in Paris. In a three-hour discussion on July 10, Lodge painted a bleak picture of the domestic political situation, with Senator Joseph R. McCarthy and his anti-Communist crusade on the horizon and the specter of a resurgence of Republican isolationism looming large. Lodge once more concluded his visit by imploring the general "to en-

---

2. For a fuller exposition of Lodge's views, see Henry Cabot Lodge, "Modernize the G. O. P.," *Atlantic Monthly,* March 23, 1950, pp. 23–28; and Henry Cabot Lodge, "Eisenhower and the GOP," *Harper's,* CCIV (May, 1952), 34–39.

ter politics to prevent one of our two great parties from adopting a disastrous course."[3] The senator returned to Washington reasonably confident that although Eisenhower would not actively campaign for the nomination, he would respond positively to a draft.

The Initial Advisory Group was established to engineer just such a draft. Composed of Herbert Brownell, Jr., New York State governor Thomas E. Dewey, General Lucius D. Clay, and Arthur H. Vandenberg, Jr., among others, the group named Lodge campaign manager on November 10, 1951. For the next twelve months and at great risk to his own career, Lodge devoted his attention to shepherding his initially absent candidate through the primary elections, obtaining the nomination for him in a hard-fought battle at the Republican national convention in Chicago in July, and campaigning for him before the general election. Indeed, in his effort to elect Eisenhower, Lodge neglected his own political backyard and lost his bid for reelection to an up-and-coming young Democrat named John F. Kennedy. Lodge's task was immeasurably complicated by both Eisenhower's continued absence (not until June 3 did the general return from Europe) and the candidate's stubborn insistence upon protecting his credibility as a military spokesman above partisan concerns. The former Allied commander's concern for collective security transcended political ambitions. "I have no right whatsoever to say or do anything that could possibly tend to divide along partisan lines American thinking toward the job of producing collective security," the general apologetically wrote Lodge in December, 1951.[4]

Upon being elected, Eisenhower quickly demonstrated his confidence in Lodge's political and administrative skills. Prior to nominating Lodge to head the U.S. mission to the UN, Eisenhower drafted him to assume control of all aspects of the presidential transition, except for those dealing with the budget. In his workings with his new chief, Lodge affected a demeanor of complete deference. At the same time, he derived great satisfaction from guiding the ostensibly politically naïve president-elect through the labyrinth of transition politics in Washington, D.C. Lodge recorded smugly in his

3. Henry Cabot Lodge, *The Storm Has Many Eyes: A Personal Narrative* (New York, 1973), 79.

4. Eisenhower to Lodge, December 29, 1951, in Louis Galambos *et al.,* eds., *NATO and the Campaign of 1952* (Baltimore, 1989), 829, Vol. XII of Alfred D. Chandler *et al.,* eds., *The Papers of Dwight D. Eisenhower;* Lodge, "Eisenhower and the GOP," 34–39.

journal that Eisenhower insisted upon having him at his side whenever they encountered newsmen in the capital.[5]

Lodge gratefully accepted Eisenhower's offer of the UN post. He believed the president-elect's promises to increase the prestige and prominence of the United Nations. Moreover, he hoped that the position would prove a stepping-stone to the secretary of state post he coveted. According to Lodge, Eisenhower had suggested during their November 21 conversation at the Commodore Hotel that the position would give him "another 'gob' of experience," prepare him "for even higher work," and put him "in the reserve for secretary of state." After the animosity toward Lodge among the right-wing members of the Republican party abated in twelve to eighteen months, it might be possible for him to succeed Dulles at the helm of the State Department.[6]

As evidence of his apparent intention to increase the importance of the representative to the UN, Eisenhower made the position a cabinet-level appointment. Lodge welcomed this move, for cabinet membership would give him additional standing in the UN. Still, he remained extremely sensitive about his status as a cabinet member. He carefully noted in his journal that in the first informal meeting of the cabinet, Eisenhower announced, "This group here in my mind is the Cabinet, no matter what the law says." Defending his membership in his memoirs, Lodge cites both the observation of political scientist Richard Fenno, Jr., that the cabinet is an "extralegal creation" of the president, and a letter from Maxwell M. Rabb, secretary of the cabinet, in which Rabb stated that "the Cabinet is created by the President and consists of whoever he wants to appoint to it."[7]

Lodge's confidence in his relationship with Eisenhower was well founded. Eisenhower thought highly of his ambassador. In a May, 1953, diary entry, the president described Lodge as "well-educated, widely experienced, quick, shrewd, and possessed of a fine personality." Although Lodge's extensive political experience sometimes meant that his judgments were

5. Journal entry, November 18, 1952, in folder marked "T-E: 1952–1953," Box 71, HCLP, MHS.

6. Journal entry, November 21, 1952, in folder marked "T-E: 1952–1953," Box 71, HCLP, MHS; Lodge, *The Storm Has Many Eyes,* 129.

7. Journal entry, January 13, 1953, in folder marked "T-E: 1952–1953," Box 71, HCLP, MHS; Lodge, *The Storm Has Many Eyes,* 129.

"colored by political considerations," he was nonetheless "by instinct and up-bringing, an honorable man—and remains so even in political argument and discussion." Though he never ceased to view politics with some distaste, Eisenhower so valued Lodge's political expertise that from time to time he contemplated bringing him onto the White House staff as either "man without portfolio" handling public relations needs or a political strategist. The president also approved of the effort in November, 1954, to persuade Lodge to accept the chairmanship of the Republican National Committee, a position the ambassador refused.[8] Citing "the suspicions and emotions" that he thought meddling in the business of all departments would generate, Lodge declined the formal political-strategist title. But he did agree to become the "Special Adviser to the President" in November, 1953, and was even provided with space in the Executive Office Building.[9]

Regardless of his official title, Lodge freely counseled Eisenhower on domestic issues as well as foreign policy. He offered advice on matters ranging from appointments to farm strategy to the response to the Soviet *Sputnik* launch in October, 1957. Eisenhower appears genuinely to have welcomed and even solicited Lodge's opinion on domestic political questions. In particular, Lodge provided a steady stream of advice on the president's participation in the 1954 midterm congressional elections. He also analyzed Eisenhower's performance in television appearances, congratulating the president for being "on top of this new medium." Eisenhower welcomed this praise from "one of my friendliest and yet most severe critics." Lodge was equally involved, though generally behind the scenes because of the essentially nonpartisan nature of his position at the UN, in the presidential election of 1956. Having read one of Lodge's campaign speeches in July, Eisenhower wrote

8. Robert H. Ferrell, ed., *The Eisenhower Diaries* (New York, 1981), 238–39; Memorandum of Telephone Conversation between Eisenhower and Dulles, November 16, 1953, in folder marked "Phone Calls: July–December 1953 (1)," Box 5, DDE Diary Series, EP, AWF, EL; Lodge to Eisenhower, November 8, 1954, in folder marked "Henry Cabot Lodge: 1954 (3)," Box 24, Administration Series, EP, AWF, EL; Eisenhower to Lodge, November 10, 1954, in folder marked "Henry Cabot Lodge: 1954 (3)," Box 24, Administration Series, EP, AWF, EL.

9. Lodge to Eisenhower, March 22, 1954, in folder marked "Henry Cabot Lodge: 1954 (7)," Box 24, Administration Series, EP, AWF, EL; Henry Cabot Lodge, *As It Was: An Inside View of Politics and Power in the '50s and '60s* (New York, 1976), 123–25.

him, "I feel about some of your points, as I do about many of the things you write, an inclination to plagiarism."[10]

Lodge's close relationship with the president gave him an unprecedented and unsurpassed degree of independence as the U.S. ambassador to the UN. According to Lodge, Eisenhower personally assured him that "whenever I thought I should have direct access to him, I should talk to him directly—man to man. I was to be the judge of whether to see him or not." The ambassador took the president at his word. During almost eight years at the United Nations, Lodge received about 150 letters from the president and wrote to the president many more than that. Communication by telephone was even more frequent. Trips to Washington—for the weekly cabinet meetings whenever possible, private consultations with the president, and social events at the White House—further increased the frequency of contact. On average, Lodge recalled in 1977, he breakfasted with Eisenhower twice a month, usually immediately before the Friday morning meetings of the cabinet. Lodge also established and assiduously maintained additional lines of contact and influence with Eisenhower. For example, acting on his strong recommendation, Eisenhower appointed Lodge's former administrative assistant in the Senate, Maxwell Rabb, to be cabinet staff secretary.[11]

The appointment of Lodge, a central figure in the emerging administra-

---

10. On the 1954 election, see, for example, Lodge to Eisenhower, April 7, 1954, in folder marked "Henry Cabot Lodge: 1954 (6)," Box 24, Administration Series, EP, AWF, EL; Eisenhower to Lodge, April 9, 1954, same folder; Lodge to Eisenhower, July 30, 1954, in folder marked "Henry Cabot Lodge: 1954 (1)," same box; Lodge to Eisenhower, September 22, 1954, in folder marked "Henry Cabot Lodge: 1954 (4)," same box; Eisenhower to Lodge, September 25, 1954, in folder marked "Henry Cabot Lodge: 1954 (4)," same box; Lodge to Eisenhower, September 28, 1954, in folder marked "Henry Cabot Lodge: 1954 (4)," same box; Lodge to Eisenhower, September 30, 1954, in folder marked "Henry Cabot Lodge: 1954 (4)," same box; Lodge to Eisenhower, October 4, 1954, in folder marked "Henry Cabot Lodge: 1954," same box; Memorandum for the Record, January 21, 1954, Reel 17, HCLP, MHS. On the 1956 election, see, for example, Eisenhower to Lodge, July 9, 1956, in folder marked "Henry Cabot Lodge: 1956 (1)," Box 24, Administration Series, EP, AWF, EL; Lodge to Eisenhower, August 27, 1956, same folder; Lodge to Eisenhower, October 9, 1956, same folder; Lodge to Eisenhower, July 20, 1956, in folder marked "Platforms (1)," Box 67, HCLP, MHS; Eisenhower to Lodge, July 20, 1956, same folder.

11. Seymour Maxwell Finger, *American Ambassadors at the UN: People, Politics, and Bureaucracy in Making Foreign Policy* (New York, 1988), 72–73.

tion, indicated that the U.S. ambassador to the UN might play an important role in the formulation of American foreign policy. Lodge insisted from the beginning on participating in the policy-making process. Although aware that in New York he could not see the big picture as it appeared in Washington, he asserted that at the UN he had access to information often unavailable in the State Department. Furthermore, because of his past experience in the Senate and on the Foreign Relations Committee he possessed valuable insights into the foreign policy views of the U.S. Congress and the public. Secure in his understanding of the president's views, Lodge felt comfortable acting without instructions in the infrequent instances when there was insufficient time for the State Department to draft them. Lodge believed that Dulles too wanted him to exercise a large degree of independence in New York. According to Lodge's account, at a meeting in early 1953, Dulles mocked the Truman administration's practice of providing detailed instructions to the U.S. mission at the UN, even to the point of dictating former ambassador Warren R. Austin's apparel for social functions. The secretary "had enough to do without my pestering him about such details." Lodge recounted that "if the question was not important enough to go to an Assistant Secretary, I should decide it myself."[12]

Lodge's independence, whether real or perceived, inevitably tangled the lines of authority between the State Department and the U.S. mission in New York. For while independent decision making in New York was rare, at least the potential for conflict was readily apparent. Indeed, critics charged that during Lodge's tenure the U.S. mission to the UN (USUN) became "the other State Department." However, the permanent mission in New York was an embassy, though the sole one located on American soil. Like embassies worldwide, it was responsible to the appropriate division of the State Department—in its case, the Office of United Nations Affairs (renamed the Bureau of International Organization Affairs in August, 1954).[13]

12. Journal entry, January 7, 1953, in folder marked "T-E: 1952–1953," Box 71, HCLP, MHS.

13. Arnold Beichman, *The "Other" State Department, The United States Mission to the United Nations: Its Role in the Making of Foreign Policy* (New York, 1967). For a more detailed exposition of the operation of USUN in the 1950s, see Chadwick F. Alger, *United States Representation in the United Nations* (New York, 1961); Channing B. Richardson, "The United States Mission to the United Nations," *International Organization,* VII (1953), 22–34; William

The U.S. permanent representative to the UN technically was nominally subordinate to the assistant secretary of state for international organization affairs. In spite of that, Lodge's status as a cabinet member, his superior personal prestige, and his connections with the president gave him more latitude and enabled him, at least in theory, to bypass the Department of State when he so chose. Moreover, as a participant in the virtually continuous process of negotiation and diplomacy at the UN, he acquired an expertise in procedural matters and occasionally in intelligence that often was not shared by the bureau. This too gave him leverage in determining the American position. Lodge's ability to challenge the State Department also rested to some extent on the public delegates to the General Assembly, including the two congressional representatives, who could exert influence on a department dependent on congressional appropriations.

Still, Lodge estimated that 90 percent of the questions with which he dealt were determined by the "regular policy-making machinery." He insisted that "there was never any conflict or trouble." He firmly denied allegations that USUN and the White House made foreign policy without consulting the State Department, dismissing such accusations as "the most fantastic fairy story that I have heard since I have been in the Executive Branch." But clearly there was room for trouble, and, in fact, it soon surfaced.[14]

Lodge got off to a rocky start in his relations with the Office of United Nations Affairs and its director, Robert Murphy. Unfortunately, Murphy viewed the UN with ill-concealed disdain. In his memoirs he explains that "personally I never regarded the UN as a divine machine from which happy solutions to our problems would miraculously flow. Nor have I feared the

---

Sanders, "Assignment to the United Nations," *Foreign Service Journal,* XXX (1953), 24–27, 62–64. For an explanation of policy formulation in the State Department on UN issues, see James N. Hyde, "United States Participation in the United Nations," *International Organization,* X (1956), 22–34; Lincoln P. Bloomfield, "How the U.S. Government Is Organized to Participate in the U. N. System," *Department of State Bulletin,* September 17, 1956, pp. 435–42; and Richard F. Pedersen, "National Representation in the United Nations," *International Organization,* XV (1961), 256–66.

14. Finger, *American Ambassadors at the UN,* 74; Lodge to Henry A. Byroade (assistant secretary of state for Near Eastern, South Asian, and African affairs), April 20, 1954, Reel 2, HCLP, MHS; Lodge to David McKendree Key (assistant secretary of state for United Nations affairs), April 14, 1954, in folder marked "United States General Assembly—1954," Box 78, HCLP, MHS.

consequences if the UN should collapse utterly." According to Murphy, early in Lodge's tenure the ambassador voted contrary to instructions he had received on a resolution concerning Korea. When Murphy called for an explanation, Lodge countered that as a member of the cabinet he was accountable only to the president and was not bound by State Department instructions. Murphy responded that all ambassadors took their instructions from the secretary of state. He was told by Lodge that a discussion with Dulles would set him, Murphy, straight on this point. After doing so, Murphy learned that he was not to question Lodge's autonomy in the New York embassy.[15]

Murphy's account may not be wholly accurate. Nevertheless, it makes the valid point that while Lodge accepted the vast majority of instructions with good grace, he was hesitant to follow the dictates of some "faceless bureaucrat" on important issues when they were contrary to his judgment. When a decision had been made by high-level administrative figures, however, Lodge executed it loyally regardless of his personal beliefs.

Nevertheless, relations between USUN and the Eisenhower State Department became more harmonious after Murphy's departure in October, 1953. A relieved Lodge suggested Murphy's successor—David McKendree Key, a retired foreign service officer—and Dulles agreed. Eighteen months later, Francis O. Wilcox replaced Key. Lodge's ties to Wilcox dated back to his service as a junior member of the Senate Committee on Foreign Relations when Wilcox was the committee's chief of staff. Indeed, Wilcox had been instrumental in having Lodge, despite his relative lack of seniority, appointed to the General Assembly delegation in 1950. Wilcox obligingly sought Lodge's advice on policy matters. Throughout, relations were smoothed by David W. Wainhouse, a Harvard classmate of Lodge's and a fellow native of Massachusetts, who served first as director of the Office of United Nations Political and Security Affairs and then, beginning in February, 1954, as deputy assistant secretary of state for United Nations affairs.[16]

Lodge organized a high-quality, tightly run, and efficient staff at USUN. For his deputy, he chose James J. "Jerry" Wadsworth, a friend since childhood, because of Wadsworth's administrative ability (he was then serving as

15. Robert Murphy, *Diplomat Among Warriors* (Garden City, 1964), 363, 367.

16. *MTCD,* Reel 1, Dulles and Lodge, October 21, 1953; Memorandum of Conversation with Francis Wilcox, April 27, 1955, in folder marked "Memos of Conversation—General T through Z," General Correspondence and Memoranda, John Foster Dulles Papers, EL; Linda Fasulo, *Representing America: Experiences of U.S. Diplomats at the UN* (New York, 1984), 47.

acting director of civil defense), his familiarity with the legislative process (acquired in the New York legislature), and his ability to get along with people. The position had first been offered, at Eisenhower's request, to Dr. Ralph J. Bunche, the African American Nobel Peace Prize winner and assistant secretary-general at the UN, who was a Democrat; but Bunche had declined. Rather than using Wadsworth as an operating executive, Lodge tended to employ him as something of a troubleshooter, assigning him to particular issues, such as disarmament. Lodge thus served as his own operating executive, with the assistance, beginning in June, 1955, of the minister counselor, James Barco, who was in charge of daily operations. Neither particularly skilled at nor very interested in the management aspects of the large mission in New York, Lodge relied heavily upon Barco and Charles Cook, the deputy counselor, who likewise assumed the post in June, 1955.[17]

One of Lodge's first moves, as he happily crowed to the cost-conscious Eisenhower, was to reduce the size of the staff. By 1953 the USUN staff had grown to 180 people, including 25 from the U.S. Atomic Energy Commission (AEC) and a few Central Intelligence Agency (CIA) officers. During the first year, Lodge cut the staff to 115, eliminating all AEC positions and 40 others. By May, 1954, the staff was down to 102. In an effort to handle the volume of work, even the CIA officers became involved in regular mission business—resulting in reprimands from their superiors for neglecting their intelligence duties. Lodge also arranged for a corresponding decrease of 25 percent in the size of the square footage rented by USUN at 2 Park Avenue.[18]

The strong influence of domestic politics on the administration's approach to the UN surfaced early in the selection of its first UN delegation. Each delegation consisted of five representatives and five alternates. The five representatives usually included the permanent representative, deputy permanent representative, deputy to the Security Council, and, at times, the representative to the Economic and Social Council—all of whom had ambassadorial rank. Seeking to build public support for the UN, the adminis-

---

17. Lodge to Sherman Adams, January 25, 1953, Reel 1, HCLP, MHS; The Reminiscences of James J. Wadsworth, April 24, 1967, p. 65, COHP, Butler Library, Columbia University, New York; *MTCD,* Reel 4, Lodge and Dulles, May 19, 1955; *MTCD,* Reel 4, Lodge and Dulles, May 24, 1955.

18. Statement before the House Appropriations Committee, January 28, 1954, in folder marked "Speeches and Press Releases," Box 112, HCLP, MHS; Lodge to Eisenhower, August 3, 1954, in folder marked "Henry Cabot Lodge: 1954 (3)," Box 24, Administration Series, EP, AWF, EL.

tration made two decisions: first, to follow the precedent set by the Truman administration with regard to appointing two members of Congress (drawn from the Senate in even years and the House in odd years); and second, to open the remaining spots to people prominent in other, nongovernment walks of life, such as business, labor, and the arts. In what would become an annual ritual, in choosing these prominent Americans the administration attempted to achieve a balance among the often conflicting demands imposed by the politics of party, race, gender, ethnicity, religion, age, and region. The limited number of spots made it impossible to satisfy every interest group every year; the competition for the delegate seats thus was intense.

Dulles and Eisenhower professed a desire not to politicize the selection process. The secretary of state maintained that as an instrument for the implementation of U.S. foreign policy, the delegation required members with certain qualifications. It was not a prize to be distributed equally among the nation's myriad special interest groups. The delegation ought not "to become like the NY State slate where a Protestant, a Catholic, a Jew, and an Italian were on everything," he declared. But in practice, Dulles proceeded to operate largely on that basis. For example, in 1954 the secretary conducted a fairly extensive search for an Irish Catholic from New York City. Eisenhower, too, insisted that he did not "like its [the selection of delegates] being handled politically." Yet the president was not above permitting political considerations to influence his decisions on nominees. He wanted to ensure, for example, that nominations would help build Republican popularity in key states.[19]

The administration's foremost concern was to achieve a measure of bipartisanship on the delegation. In their quest for a nationally prominent Democrat, the obvious first choice was the Democratic presidential candidate whom Eisenhower had defeated, Adlai E. Stevenson. Senators Taft and Lyndon B. Johnson of Texas, the majority and minority leaders of the Senate, respectively, gave their approval, and the State Department approached

19. *MTCD,* Reel 2, Dulles and Sherman Adams, July 20, 1953, White House Telephone Calls; *MTCD,* Reel 2, Dulles and Adams, July 16, 1954; Memorandum for the Secretary, July 21, 1954, in folder marked "O'Connor-Hanes Chronological: July 1954 (3)," Box 7, Special Assistants Chronological Series, Dulles Papers, EL; Memorandum from Eisenhower to Sherman Adams, August 19, 1954, in folder marked "SA 2 Appointments," Box 31, Sherman Adams Papers, Baker Memorial Library, Dartmouth College, Hanover; *MTCD,* Reel 8, Dulles and Eisenhower, August 19, 1954, White House Telephone Calls; *MTCD,* Reel 8, Dulles and James C. Hagerty, August 20, 1954, White House Telephone Calls.

Stevenson through private channels. He declined. Despite Lodge's misgivings, Dulles next offered the position to former secretary of state James F. Byrnes, then Democratic governor of South Carolina, after clearing him with the congressional leadership.[20]

Of only slightly less importance in 1953 was the selection of an African American delegate. During a campaign speech in Cleveland, Eisenhower had promised that, if he found one, he would appoint a qualified black to the cabinet. Six months into his term, however, he had yet to do so. Nor had he even appointed an African American to a high office. Hoping to fulfill this campaign promise, Chief of Staff Sherman Adams led the effort to nominate a black to the delegation. The administration's first choice was Jessie Matthews Vann, the wife of Pittsburgh *Courier* founder and publisher Robert L. Vann, and a prominent Republican in her own right. She rejected the offer. Tired of unfounded publicity, first that she would be named ambassador to Haiti, then predicting her early appointment as a full delegate, Vann did not want to be the subject of yet another media barrage when it was announced that she would serve only as an alternate.[21]

Vann's refusal opened the field to a variety of candidates. These included Zelma Watson George, the dean of women at Tennessee State College, and Archibald J. Carey, Jr., a minister from Chicago, each of whom had advocates within the black community. The final selection of Carey pleased few in the administration. Adams voiced a widespread concern that the outspoken minister would not follow instructions. Rather than using the appointment "as a benefit to his race," he would "be a martyr," complaining that he had not been appointed as a full delegate.[22]

For the next seven years, the choice of an African American delegate proved particularly difficult and controversial. The administration sought both to please the various constituencies in the black community and to

---

20. Telegram from Dulles to the U.S. embassy in Belgrade, June 29, 1953, in folder marked "June 1, 1953 (1)," Box 3, Chronological Series, Dulles Papers, EL; Memo for the President from Dulles, June 29, 1953, in folder marked "John Foster Dulles: July 1953," Box 1, Dulles-Herter Series, EP, AWF, EL; *MTCD,* Reel 2, Dulles and Byrnes, July 20, 1953.

21. *MTCD,* Reel 2, Dulles and Vann, July 13, 1953; *MTCD,* Reel 8, Dulles and Adams, July 14, 1953, White House Telephone Calls.

22. *MTCD,* Reel 8, Adams and Dulles, July 8, 1953, White House Telephone Calls; Memorandum of a Telephone Conversation between Adams and Dulles, July 22, 1953, in folder marked "May–December 31, 1953 (2)," Box 10, White House Telephone Calls, Dulles Papers, EL.

name a nationally known person. Additional, private desiderata further complicated the decision. For example, the administration wanted to appoint a dark-skinned delegate with distinctly African American facial features in order to derive as much public relations benefit as possible with regard to Third World delegations. Thus, Secretary to the Cabinet Robert Gray wrote Lodge in 1960 that Frederick Morrow should receive careful consideration for a slot on the U.S. delegation not only because he was "an articulate Negro and Presidential assistant" but also because "he *looks* like a Negro." The administration's concerns extended to the delicate question of determining the issues for which the black delegate would be responsible. Dulles grumbled bitterly in October, 1953, that the UN Affairs Office had assigned Carey to both the genocide and human rights items. "No one could be so stupid as to put a colored man on two such explosive items," Dulles thundered to Lodge.[23]

Generally, government officials filled the full delegate slots, while the cross section of American citizens drawn from the private sector served as alternates. As a general practice the administration wanted only eminent people or those with diplomatic experience as full delegates. In the opinion of Dulles, few black Americans had achieved such distinction. A further impediment to appointing a black person was that blacks were often hampered by "doubtful records" because of the racism that pervaded J. Edgar Hoover's FBI. Moreover, administration officials believed that if a black was appointed as a full delegate, Governor Byrnes, fearing political repercussions in his home state, would refuse to serve on the same delegation. (African American groups and newspapers in turn opposed Byrnes's appointment and lobbied the Senate Foreign Relations Committee to vote against him. Despite Byrnes's unreconstructed racism, disqualifying Byrnes proved to be an impossible task, in light of the governor's past Senate, State Department, and Supreme Court service and confirmations.)[24]

The remaining appointments in 1953 were less contentious. In keeping

23. Robert Gray to Lodge, March 4, 1960, in folder marked "UNGA 1960," Box 78, HCLP, MHS; Memorandum of a Telephone Conversation between Dulles and Lodge, October 7, 1953, in folder marked "JFD Chronological: October 1953 (5)," Box 5, Chronological Series, Dulles Papers, EL.

24. *MTCD,* Reel 8, Dulles and Adams, July 17, 1953, White House Telephone Calls; *MTCD,* Reel 8, Dulles and Adams, July 20, 1953; Memorandum for the Secretary by John W. Hanes, Jr., July 29, 1953, in folder marked "O'Connor and Hanes: July 1953 (1)," Box 3, Special Assistants Chronological Series, Dulles Papers, EL.

with the precedent set under Truman, the Eisenhower administration appointed two members of the House of Representatives to the 1953 delegation. It chose Frances P. Bolton (R-Ohio), partly to include a woman, and James P. Richards (D-South Carolina). Seeking religious balance, Dulles wanted a Jew and a Catholic. He nominated James D. Zellerbach, the Jewish chairman of a paper and paper products company who had a history of involvement in international labor and business organizations, but the choice of a Catholic was not so easy. It came down to either J. Peter Grace, Jr., a New York shipping executive and chairman of W. R. Grace and Company, or Henry Ford II, president of Ford Motor Company, both of whom were young, up-and-coming leaders. Dulles ultimately chose Ford, largely because his being from Michigan provided more geographic diversity. Desirous of including another woman on the delegation, the administration considered Iphigene Ochs Sulzberger (wife of the New York *Times* publisher Arthur Sulzberger and a leader in the National Federation of Women's Clubs) before finally deciding upon Mary Pillsbury Lord (the Pillsbury heiress, who was actively involved in Republican politics and New York charities). At the urging of Lodge, who believed that it would be extremely effective at the international level, the administration also considered a Hispanic representative, Governor Luis Muñoz Marín of Puerto Rico. Questionable results from the FBI investigation doomed his nomination.[25]

With the able assistance of his wife, Emily, Lodge simultaneously tackled the social challenges of running an embassy from their apartment on floor 42-A of the Waldorf Towers. Lodge was occasionally handicapped by his patrician bearing and a self-assurance that not infrequently bordered on arrogance. Yet at the same time, the ambassador usually displayed a genuine concern for the people with whom he worked, demonstrating a practical political awareness and a sense of humor that made him a favorite even among UN interpreters, receptionists, and doormen. He exuded personal charm and social confidence, derived perhaps from his childhood association with such literary and political luminaries as Henry Adams, President Theodore Roosevelt, and, of course, the paternal grandfather he adored. These qualities stood him in good stead in the often dizzying environment of the UN.

25. *MTCD,* Reel 8, Dulles and Frances P. Bolton, July 11, 1953, White House Telephone Calls; *MTCD,* Reel 8, Dulles and Adams, June 23, 1953; *MTCD,* Reel 8, Dulles and Adams, July 20, 1953; *MTCD,* Reel 2, Dulles and Adams, June 23, 1953; *MTCD,* Reel 2, Dulles and Adams, July 20, 1953; Lodge to Dulles, June 24, 1953, Reel 4, HCLP, MHS.

They enabled him to inspire great personal loyalty in many of his subordinates, and respect, bordering on awe, on the part of many of his diplomatic peers. Photogenic good looks, an invaluable asset at the dawn of the television age, completed the picture of a man at ease with himself and his surroundings.

Lodge fully recognized the importance of hospitality in the diplomatic environment of the United Nations. He invited the ambassadors of the nations represented at the UN to dine at the American embassy, and attended as many of the foreign countries' social events as possible. At embassy events, the American delegation often relied on music to create a more convivial atmosphere. Wadsworth was an accomplished musician, and even Lodge himself occasionally sang. As he recalls in his memoirs, he could "render a simple ditty entitled 'You Can Easily See She's Not My Mother'" in five languages.[26]

With the United Nations team firmly in place, the next step in the administration's preparation for policy making was to enunciate a coherent foreign policy blueprint and determine what role the United Nations would play in American foreign policy. That process, while not a formal one, would entail drawing upon the diverse experiences, ideas, and philosophies of the UN policy-making trio—Eisenhower, Dulles, and Lodge.

26. Lodge, *The Storm Has Many Eyes,* 147.

2

Philosophical Foundations

The Roots of the Administration's Relationship with the UN

Since the creation of the United Nations in 1945, American presidents have offered up a steady stream of rhetorical support for the international organization. Their actions, however, have rarely matched their public pronouncements. Frequently cited as the "cornerstone" of American foreign policy in public avowals of commitment, the United Nations appears instead to have been used as a stepping-stone—that is, when it has not been ignored altogether. Nevertheless, it remains valuable to probe the written and spoken word in search of insights into the views on international organizations, and specifically the UN, of the key foreign policy makers in the Eisenhower administration.

More than many of the post-war presidents, Eisenhower was acutely aware of the psychological dimensions of diplomacy. He understood the importance of symbols and appearances, and he sensed that the United Nations had become a symbolic promise of a better, more peaceful world. As a result, both the international and domestic audiences expected at least his rhetorical support for the UN. It was an expectation he was quite willing to fulfill.

Dwight D. Eisenhower embarked upon his presidency with more international experience than any of his predecessors. As supreme commander of the Allied forces in Europe in World War II, army chief of staff, president of Columbia University, and supreme commander of the North Atlantic Treaty Organization, he had become acquainted with the leaders who had created the post-war world. This familiarity, joined with his intimate role in shaping America's post-war security alliances and a universal collective security system, led Eisenhower to develop a personal interest in policy in this critical area. Thus, at the time of his election in 1952, Eisenhower already held a comprehensive and integrated set of beliefs about American foreign policy and the role of the United Nations.

Eisenhower's years on the periphery of the Washington foreign policy establishment from 1945 to 1952 coincided with the formative years of the United Nations organization and the origins of the cold war. The confluence of these factors shaped the future president's views on the UN's role in a world divided by conflicting ideologies, on the organization's potential position in a world community united in support of international peace with justice, and on the appropriate relationship between the United States and the UN. As he observed and reflected upon the changing international situation from 1945 to 1952, Eisenhower's views gradually shifted from whole-hearted approval to something resembling cautious support. In the early post-war period, however, he embraced the concept of a universal security organization, and supported its apparent realization in the form of the United Nations. At no point, however, did he endorse any of the various plans to surrender national sovereignty to a world government or system of federalism.[1]

When the United Nations Conference on International Organization was held in the spring of 1945, General Eisenhower shared the American delegates' confidence that the organization they were creating would be the cornerstone of a new world order. This optimism generally reflected the Allied success in the war, and specifically Eisenhower's success as a coalition warrior. The general's experience at the helm of a multinational fighting force had convinced him that concerted action by the Big Five—the United States, the Soviet Union, Great Britain, France, and China—and enhanced international understanding were not only attainable, but also powerful instruments in the effort to achieve peace. Eisenhower thus initially endorsed the UN in the expectation that it would nurture Great Power cooperation and international understanding. When differences arose among nations, the UN could provide a location as well as the procedures for their peaceful resolution. Indeed, in an address at the state fair in Lincoln, Nebraska, in

1. Eisenhower to Edward John Berminghan, February 28, 1951, in Galambos, ed., *NATO and the Campaign of 1952,* XII, 75.

September, 1946, the former rural Kansan described the United Nations as integral to "the promotion of neighborly virtues among all nations, great and small." Playing down conflicts of interest among nations, the general once again emphasized the ties that bind.[2]

Eisenhower believed that the establishment of the UN represented a significant advance in the quest to eliminate the threat of war. In an address to the American Newspaper Publishers' Association in April, 1946, he listed three means of achieving a just and lasting peace—"organized international cooperation, mutual international understanding, and progressive international disarmament." Since the United Nations embodied the goal of international cooperation, the former supreme commander of the Allied forces maintained that an effective UN could eliminate one of the most frequent causes of war—the violation of a nation's rights by another nation.[3]

General Eisenhower believed that the United States must lead the UN's effort to establish a just and enduring world order. In the new atomic age, American security, he argued, was inextricably linked to the state of the world as a whole. Eisenhower thus wanted the United States to translate the promises of the UN Charter into reality, even in such areas as atomic science and military power. Testifying before the House Military Affairs Committee in November, 1945, he proclaimed his hope that the United Nations could so foster international trust that the United States could safely share its atomic knowledge. As army chief of staff, he joined in the Pentagon's deliberations about the composition of the American forces detailed to the UN for peacekeeping duty. Eisenhower urged the assignment of the best officers, men, and equipment. "We must make this organization work," the general insisted. "Any officers who do not think it is going [to] work are subject to export."[4]

2. Address to the State Fair in Lincoln, Nebraska, September 26, 1946, in Allan Taylor, ed., *What Eisenhower Thinks* (New York, 1952), 147; Address at Norwich University, June 9, 1946, in Rudolph L. Treuenfels, ed., *Eisenhower Speaks: Dwight D. Eisenhower in His Messages and Speeches* (New York, 1948), 113.

3. Address to the American Newspaper Publishers Association, April 26, 1946, in Taylor, ed., *What Eisenhower Thinks,* 94.

4. Memorandum to Joint Chiefs of Staff, December 15, 1945, in Louis Galambos *et al.,* eds., *The Chief of Staff* (Baltimore, 1978), 635, Vol. VII of Alfred D. Chandler *et al.,* eds., *The Papers of Dwight David Eisenhower;* Peter Lyon, *Eisenhower: Portrait of a Hero* (Boston, 1974), 366.

Unfortunately, the international political realities of the cold war prevented the realization of such optimistic expectations. With the marked deterioration of Soviet-American relations, and the attendant dissolution of unity among the Big Five between 1945 and 1947, a staunch cold warrior gradually replaced the Wilsonian internationalist. In September, 1947, Eisenhower lamented in his diary that Soviet "obstructionism" threatened the organization. He believed that the division of the world into democratic and totalitarian camps, and the aggressive intent of the latter, had invalidated the principle of Great Power cooperation upon which the organization was premised.[5]

Still, Eisenhower continued to believe that the United States must not abandon the organization. In his final report as chief of staff in February, 1948, he considered the long-term implications of the United Nations. The organization faced an uphill battle in its quest to earn international acceptance. Since the UN represented a fundamental innovation in the traditional practice of international relations, "a long period of trial and error, of test and experiment, may be necessary before the concept is proved and accepted by all states without reservation." He predicted that during this period, which might last for as long as a century, "threats of secession and boycott by aggrieved disputants" would plague the organization and perhaps even tear it asunder. Eisenhower urged the Truman administration to remain steadfast in its support, for eventually the United Nations would become an "effective international instrument" welcomed by all nations as an unimpeachable arbiter of international justice and the unchallenged guarantor of international welfare.[6]

Eisenhower continued to emphasize the possibility of international cooperation through the UN in his 1948 memoirs of World War II. The general claimed that international unity required nations to transfer a degree of their power to a central organization authorized to make and enforce decisions for all. He noted that, if the Great Powers had applied this lesson to the post-war question of international organization, they might have been able to establish "some form of limited, federated world government." However, he clearly understood that this was "politically unacceptable to any of the

5. Ferrell, ed., *The Eisenhower Diaries,* 143; Address at the American Legion Convention, August 29, 1947, in Treuenfels, ed., *Eisenhower Speaks,* 250.

6. Final Report of the Chief of Staff to the Secretary of the Army, February 7, 1948, in Treuenfels, ed., *Eisenhower Speaks,* 294.

great nations concerned." Citing the most obvious manifestation of this reluctance—the Great Powers' insistence on possession of veto power—Eisenhower regretted that the Big Five had returned to "the traditional but obsolete concept that international purposes could be decided only by unanimous action in committee." It was imperative, he asserted, for people to accept the fact that absolute national sovereignty was anachronistic in the postwar, atomic world.[7]

An international judicial power alone, however, would not suffice to ensure world peace. If even one nation retained a military force capable of offensive operations, then this threatened peaceful nations everywhere. Eisenhower therefore concluded that international disarmament would have to be the first step on the road to a lasting peace. When and if the world achieved disarmament, the United Nations then would need to acquire a police power that commanded universal respect. Yet UN forces should not have the right to intervene in the domestic affairs of member nations, so no nation would surrender or compromise its national sovereignty.[8]

Thus, by the time he delivered his inaugural address on January 20, 1953, Eisenhower had devoted considerable thought to the concept of a collective security system and to the United States' responsibilities within such a system. He was surprised and disappointed that so few of his countrymen appeared to have given it the same attention.[9] Eisenhower's views changed only slightly during his eight years in office. Typical of his moderate Republicanism, he had positioned himself roughly in the political center, between the Roosevelt Democrats' wholehearted and virtually unqualified support for the UN and the Taft Republicans' distrust and disparagement of the organization.

As president, Eisenhower's support for the United Nations rested on a pair of strongly held convictions. First was his belief that the United States could not exist in isolation in the post-war world. To return to a fortress-America mentality would jeopardize the nation's economy and its national

7. Dwight D. Eisenhower, *Crusade in Europe* (Garden City, 1949), 459, 477; Martin J. Medhurst, *Dwight David Eisenhower: Strategic Communicator* (Westport, 1993), 13.

8. "World Peace—A Balance Sheet," Address at Columbia University, March 23, 1950, in Dwight D. Eisenhower, *Peace with Justice: Selected Addresses of Dwight D. Eisenhower* (New York, 1961), 18–19.

9. Eisenhower to Lucius DuBignon Clay, March 30, 1951, in Galambos, ed., *NATO and the Campaign of 1952*, XII, 171.

security. Most Americans shunned the role of world policeman, and Eisenhower agreed that the United States should not attempt to impose a Pax Americana. Instead he believed that the nation could ensure its long-term security best by working with a collective security system. After all, the United States and the United Nations shared the same paramount goal —the achievement of a lasting international peace with justice. Second, Eisenhower believed that cooperation and compromise were the essential lubricants of the stable and just "corporate commonwealth," to use Robert Griffith's apt conceptualization, that the president so ardently wished to create on the international as well as domestic level. Friction was inevitable in international politics. But cooperation and compromise among nations could prevent this friction from creating the sparks that, with the advent of atomic weapons, might ignite a fatal global war.[10]

The general had embraced the original United Nations, as conceived in 1945. However, he was realistic in assessing its potential and early achievements. The UN clearly was not a supergovernment or a superstate. Unlike those who idealistically viewed it as a panacea for the world's ills, Eisenhower fully understood that the organization was only a "mechanism." Although it was productive in its ability to churn out resolutions and documents, he realized that such productiveness in and of itself was worthless: "a fervent speech, or a painstakingly written document, may be worth no more than the good will and patient cooperation of those who say they subscribe to it." As such, the organization's success would hinge upon neither the quality of its procedures nor the diplomatic skills of member delegations, but rather upon international realities.[11]

As he entered the White House, Eisenhower knew that the United Nations was a casualty of the cold war. Rather than becoming a dynamic leader

10. Annual Message to the Congress on the State of the Union, January 6, 1955, *Public Papers of the Presidents: Dwight D. Eisenhower, 1955* (Washington, D.C., 1959), 10; Press Conference Transcript, March 7, 1957, in Box 5, Press Conference Series, EP, AWF, EL; *Legislative Meeting Series, 1952–1960* (Frederick, 1980) Reel 1, Notes on Special Legislative Conference, June 2, 1953; Robert Griffith, "Dwight D. Eisenhower and the Corporate Commonwealth," *American Historical Review,* LXXXVII (1982), 87–122.

11. Address before the Convention of the Veterans of Foreign Wars, September 3, 1946, in Treuenfels, ed., *Eisenhower Speaks,* 130; Dwight D. Eisenhower, *At Ease: Stories I Tell to Friends* (Garden City, 1967), 99; Address at Freedom House Anniversary Dinner, New York, October 7, 1945, in Treuenfels, ed., *Eisenhower Speaks,* 47; Press Conference Transcript, July 7, 1954, in Press Conference Series, EP, AWF, EL.

in the international community, it had become the victim of increasing tensions between its two most powerful members. His endorsement of the concept of the UN, therefore, did not imply an unqualified endorsement of the organization as it was actually functioning. To be effective, a universal collective security organization required the firm support of all the Great Powers, including the Soviet Union. Far from supplying firm support, the USSR had broken the pledges it had made at the San Francisco Conference in June, 1945. It manipulated the organization to serve its own ends and violated the spirit and principles of the Charter. The Kremlin had shunned the collective security provisions of the UN, built up its conventional armed forces to menacing levels, and threatened world peace by acting aggressively to advance the cause of international communism. Eisenhower found it particularly exasperating that because "the Soviets were scornfully contemptuous of any kind of power except materialistic," they were unmoved by the United Nations' unique position in the world community—its status as a moral force.[12] Until the Soviet Union drastically altered its behavior, the United Nations could "always be helpful, but it cannot be a wholly dependable protector of freedom." Eisenhower thus blamed an inhospitable international environment, and specifically the Soviet Union, for the UN's inability to fulfill its mandate. Neither the United States nor the UN's fundamental concept or procedures bore responsibility for its lack of success.[13]

Despite the daunting problems, Eisenhower firmly believed that the United States should not forsake the organization. The nation had made a grievous mistake in refusing to join the League of Nations. He espoused the widely accepted thesis—some would say the myth—that U.S. support for the League would have prevented both World War II and the cold war. Consequently, Eisenhower was committed to support the League's successor despite its early setbacks. Comparing the United Nations to a research labora-

---

12. Eisenhower, *Mandate for Change,* 137; Cabinet Meeting Notes, January 12, 1953, in Box 1, Cabinet Series, EP, AWF, EL.

13. Special Message to the Congress on the Situation in the Middle East, January 5, 1957, in *Public Papers of the Presidents: Dwight D. Eisenhower, 1957* (Washington, D.C., 1958), 10; Eisenhower to Marguerite Courtright Patton, August 27, 1952, in Louis Galambos, *et al.,* eds., *NATO and the Campaign of 1952* (Baltimore, 1989), 1340, Vol. XIII of Alfred D. Chandler *et al.,* eds., *The Papers of Dwight David Eisenhower;* Address at the American Legion Convention, Washington, D.C., August 30, 1954, in *Public Papers of the Presidents: Dwight D. Eisenhower, 1954* (Washington, D.C., 1960), 786.

tory, he noted that neither scientists searching for a cure for cancer nor UN diplomats seeking a cure for war had been successful. Just as these scientists had not abandoned their quest, so the UN had to persevere and the United States had to renew its commitment to the organization. Enlightened self-interest dictated American support. According to his press secretary, James C. Hagerty, Eisenhower considered the organization to be "about the last call to breakfast for this crazy world."[14]

In 1953 it was impossible for the United Nations to operate as originally intended. Nonetheless, the new president wanted to guarantee its continuation until the international environment would allow it to flourish. Eisenhower appears to have wanted to place the United Nations in protective storage until a thaw in the cold war would let the organization assume its rightful place under the sun. He specified two preconditions for its revival. First, nations must agree to reduce their military forces to a level consistent with the maintenance of only internal security. Second, nations must agree to abide by international opinion, as reflected in UN decisions.[15]

Eisenhower never clearly articulated the notion that the United Nations was "still in a state of evolution." This idea, however, sustained his hopes for the future of the organization despite its impotence in the cold war. He also judged it not only possible, but likely, that over time the UN would develop new techniques for handling problems so that it might become more effective even without substantive changes in the international political situation.[16] Since the United Nations had emerged as a functional response to the

14. The Reminiscences of James C. Hagerty, January 31, 1968, p. 365, COHP, Butler Library, Columbia University; Eisenhower to Richard M. Nixon, October 1, 1952, in Galambos, ed., *NATO and the Campaign of 1952,* XIII, 1371; Robert H. Ferrell, ed., *The Diary of James C. Hagerty: Eisenhower in Mid-Course, 1954–1955* (Bloomington, 1983), 200; Press Conference Transcript, February 23, 1955, in Box 11, Press Conference Series, EP, AWF, EL.

15. Remarks to the National Council of the League of Women Voters, May 1, 1957, in *Public Papers of the Presidents: Dwight D. Eisenhower, 1957,* 316; Message to the Congress Transmitting the 11th Annual Report on United States Participation in the United Nations, January 14, 1958, in *Public Papers of the Presidents: Dwight D. Eisenhower, 1958* (Washington, D.C., 1959), 87.

16. Annual Message to the Congress on the State of the Union, January 7, 1954, in *Public Papers of the Presidents: Dwight D. Eisenhower, 1954,* 9; Message to the Congress Transmitting the Tenth Annual Report on United States Participation in the United Nations, July 19, 1956, in *Public Papers of the Presidents: Dwight D. Eisenhower, 1956* (Washington, D.C., 1958), 605–606.

demands of the modern-state system, it was only natural that it would adapt to that system's changing conditions and needs.

The president argued, however, that the United Nations would not be able to assume its rightful place in this future world unless the United States enabled the organization to maintain its credibility. Credibility was, in Eisenhower's opinion, a critical component of international diplomacy, not only for nation-states, but also for international organizations. The U.S. government, he announced in his inaugural address, therefore had a responsibility to direct its policies toward transforming the body from primarily "an eloquent symbol" into "an effective force." Since compromise was the *sine qua non* of any lasting joint enterprise, the United States would have to be more willing to make compromises and perhaps even accept occasional defeats in the General Assembly. After all, he reassured himself, the General Assembly had never yet acted in a manner contrary to American vital interests, and by its use of the veto the United States could prevent the Security Council from ever doing so. Of course, the Great Powers' possession of the veto had made the UN impotent against the USSR, but Eisenhower appears never to have grappled with this contradiction. In fact, in an interesting omission, the president never seems to have considered how the nation should respond if the United Nations did take contrary action on a matter vital to American national security.[17]

Eisenhower believed the United Nations was playing an important role even in the cold war world. Perhaps most significant, the organization was "the living sign of all peoples' hope for peace." Furthermore, the UN served as a constant reminder of the higher standard of international relations toward which all nations must strive. In particular, the UN Charter provided a telling measure of how far the USSR had strayed from the ideals to which it had been an original signatory.[18]

17. Inaugural Address, January 20, 1953, in *Public Papers of the Presidents: Dwight D. Eisenhower, 1953* (Washington, D.C., 1960), 6; Press Conference Transcript, August 11, 1954, in Box 2, Press Conference Series, EP, AWF, EL; Press Conference Transcript, May 28, 1953, Box 1, Press Conference Series, EP, AWF, EL; *Legislative Meeting Series,* Reel 1, Notes on Special Legislative Conference, June 2, 1953; Eisenhower to Nixon, June 1, 1953, in folder marked "Richard Nixon (5)," Box 28, Administration Series, EP, AWF, EL; Eisenhower, *Mandate for Change,* 215.

18. Inaugural Address, in *Public Papers of the Presidents: Dwight D. Eisenhower, 1953,* 6; Eisenhower to Nikolai Bulganin, January 28, 1956, in *Public Papers of the Presidents: Dwight D. Eisenhower, 1956,* 209–10.

In the context of day-to-day operations, the president believed that the United Nations was the only world forum in which nations had an opportunity to debate, presenting their views to an international audience and challenging the presentations of others. As such, it represented a profound improvement over traditional means of diplomacy. Convinced that domestic public opinion as well as world opinion were potent factors even in Communist nations, Eisenhower embraced the UN as the most powerful shaper of world sentiment. In an oft-repeated phrase, he argued that the United Nations "still represent[ed] man's best organized hope to substitute the conference table for the battlefield."[19]

Eisenhower also believed that, even in the midst of the cold war, situations might arise in which the UN's members would agree to "take collective action for peace and justice." Citing the UN's response to the North Korean invasion of South Korea in 1950, Eisenhower maintained that even a hobbled United Nations could play a critical role in the maintenance of world peace. He particularly valued the United Nations' potential in facilitating decolonization. If nations entrusted the decolonization process to the Trusteeship Council, then the transition from colony to trust territory to independent state would take place peacefully. (Indeed, in June, 1946, Eisenhower had urged Truman and Secretary of State Byrnes to place the nation's Pacific territories under the trusteeship system.) As for the newly independent countries, the UN could provide them an unprecedented degree of security. Rather than relying on large armed forces to defend themselves, they could turn to the United Nations. Finally, Eisenhower suggested that the public tended to undervalue the organization because its results usually were not readily apparent; "because the things it has prevented have not happened, we sometimes overlook them."[20]

Eisenhower still qualified his support. Although the organization had

19. See, for example, Remarks to the Members of the United States Committee for United Nations Day, September 23, 1953, in *Public Papers of the Presidents: Dwight D. Eisenhower, 1953,* 605.

20. Annual Message to the Congress on the State of the Union, January 7, 1954, *Public Papers of the Presidents of the United States: Dwight D. Eisenhower, 1954,* 9; Remarks at the 42nd Annual Meeting of the United States Chamber of Commerce, April 26, 1954, in *Public Papers of the Presidents: Dwight D. Eisenhower, 1954,* 423; Memorandum to the Joint Chiefs of Staff, June 4, 1946, in Louis Galambos *et al.,* eds., *The War Years* (Baltimore, 1970), 1097–99, Vol. II of Alfred D. Chandler *et al.,* eds., *The Papers of Dwight D. Eisenhower;* Memorandum of Conversation, Dwight D. Eisenhower and the King of Saudi Arabia, January 31, 1957, in folder marked "Diary—January 1957," Box 21, DDE Diary Series, EP, AWF, EL.

uses even in the cold war world, this should not give the United States a false sense of security. Until the United Nations became an effective guarantor of international peace, the United States had to rely primarily upon its armed forces and its regional alliances. These regional alliances, particularly NATO, were more effective multilateral instruments because they were not paralyzed by the veto of "hostile groups."[21]

Yet Eisenhower was sensitive to the criticism that the administration's worldwide network of regional defense pacts undermined the UN. In an attempt to refute this charge of "pactomania," he frequently cited Article 52(1) of the UN Charter, which sanctioned regional arrangements that shared the universal organization's principles and goals. Furthermore, the president maintained that as long as the provisions of regional and bilateral security pacts neither violated the UN Charter nor superseded any legal actions of the Security Council, they reinforced the global organization. Indeed, he argued that the regional and universal security organizations were tied together so closely that the collapse of the UN would result in the destruction of NATO. When, and if, the UN truly provided consistently effective universal collective security, then Eisenhower would be ready to see it rather than the bilateral and regional organizations assume primary responsibility for such.[22]

Eisenhower believed that ultimately the United Nations would need to have some type of military force at its disposal. Nations would not always comply voluntarily with UN resolutions; the UN would need troops to enforce its decisions. But a relatively independent UN military force would have to follow more fundamental changes in international politics, specifically an easing of cold war tensions. Until then, the president favored merely the establishment of a UN military staff to coordinate the occasional peacekeeping missions.[23]

---

21. Robert Griffith, ed., *Ike's Letters to a Friend, 1941–1948* (Lawrence, 1984), 82. See also Press Release, June 7, 1956, in folder marked "Press Conference—June 6, 1956," Box 5, Press Conference Series, EP, AWF, EL.

22. See, for example, Eisenhower to Marguerite Courtright Patton, August 27, 1952, in Galambos, ed., *NATO and the Campaign of 1952*, XII, 1340; Inaugural Address, January 20, 1963, *Public Papers of the Presidents: Dwight D. Eisenhower, 1953*, 6.

23. Address to the Third Special Emergency Session of the General Assembly of the United Nations, August 13, 1958, in *Public Papers of the Presidents: Dwight D. Eisenhower, 1958*, 610; Address Before the 15th General Assembly of the United Nations, September 20, 1960, in *Public Papers of the Presidents: Dwight D. Eisenhower, 1960–1961* (Washington, D.C.,

Dwight Eisenhower's overall stance toward international organization thus reflected a mix of vague, liberal internationalism, Wilsonian idealism, and practical realism. Like Woodrow Wilson, he believed that cooperation among the Great Powers could prevent another world war and could secure a just and enduring international peace. This required them to support self-determination, democratic government, the peaceful resolution of disputes, and collective security against aggression. As the guardian of such "basic and universal values," the United States, in Eisenhower's opinion, had a responsibility to see that these Wilsonian principles formed the foundation of the post-war international system.[24]

Eisenhower was realistic, however, in his effort to realize this goal. He would not repeat Wilson's mistake of asking the American people to dedicate themselves to "make the world safe for democracy." Nor did he want the United States to impose such an international system through a unilateral display of its superior military force. Rather, he believed that the nation could achieve its goals by working within the collective security system. Since the UN Charter largely reflected American principles and aspirations and the United States had the votes in the General Assembly, the nation would actually be acting in its self-interest if it supported the United Nations.[25]

Although John Foster Dulles came to share Eisenhower's realistic appraisal of the United Nations, his history of involvement with the concept and the reality of the United Nations was quite different. Dulles's role in the creation of a successor to the League of Nations dated to late 1940. Active as a layman in the Federal Council of Protestant Churches, he was in December of that year named to head the council's newly formed Commission on a Just and Durable Peace. Like Eisenhower, Dulles too had played a role on the periphery of the foreign policy establishment. But in contrast to his future chief, Dulles developed a more complex and theoretical set of ideas about the organization and its role in a new post-war world order.

1961), 713–14; Press Conference Transcript, August 20, 1958, in Box 7, Press Conference Series, EP, AWF, EL.

24. Dwight D. Eisenhower, "Our Quest for Peace and Freedom," Address reprinted in the *Department of State Bulletin,* April 30, 1956, p. 700.

25. Eisenhower to Martin Withington Clement, January 9, 1952, in Galambos, ed., *NATO and the Campaign of 1952,* XII, 865–69; Dwight D. Eisenhower, "Fundamentals of U.S. Foreign Policy," rpr. in the *Department of State Bulletin,* December 14, 1953, p. 811.

Not surprisingly, Dulles's initial vision of a new organization, embodied most completely in a March, 1943, commission report entitled *Six Pillars of Peace,* had a highly religious tone. He called upon religious Americans to support the mission to create a world organization—"a moral mechanism" to promote peaceful change—and proclaimed the need to apply Christ's teachings to the establishment of intellectual, political, and economic liberties.[26]

Dulles presented the commission's report to President Franklin D. Roosevelt in an appointment at the White House on March 26, 1943. However, the study did not have the impact that Dulles had anticipated. Indeed, the draft UN Charter subsequently produced at the Dumbarton Oaks conference in August, 1944, was inadequate, in Dulles's estimation, because it failed to embody the flexible arrangements, limited goals, and moral precepts outlined in the report and instead relied too heavily on the collective use of force.[27]

Dulles became more deeply involved in the creation of the United Nations in the spring of 1945. Seeking some measure of bipartisanship in an effort to avoid the League of Nations' fate in the Senate, Roosevelt appointed Dulles an adviser to the U.S. delegation to the Conference on International Organization in April, 1945. Although his role in San Francisco was limited to policy execution rather than formulation, his sharp legal mind propelled him to the forefront of the delegation. Perhaps most important, he worked closely with Republican senator Arthur H. Vandenberg of Michigan to realize the senator's vision of the General Assembly as the "Town Meeting of the World," a forum for the expression of world opinion.[28]

Though in his more inspired moments Dulles was capable of comparing the completed UN Charter to "a Magna Carta for the world," in general his realist nature prevailed. After eight weeks in San Francisco, Dulles had concluded that the Charter "of itself . . . assures nothing, but at least it is an inspiring document which starts off with a good spirit behind it, and it will afford mankind an opportunity if it really wants one." The UN was only a device; it was incumbent upon member nations to make the device work as well as it could. Dulles had consistently opposed more utopian schemes for

26. John Foster Dulles, "What Shall We Do with the U.N.?," *Christian Century,* September 3, 1947, p. 1041.

27. John Foster Dulles, *War or Peace* (New York, 1950), 36.

28. *Ibid.,* 38. For a detailed account of Dulles's service on the delegation, see Ronald W. Pruessen, *John Foster Dulles: The Road to Power* (New York, 1982), chapter 10.

world government, dismissing them as at best fanciful, and at worst dangerous in their tendency to raise public expectations to heights that could not be
matched by achievement. "The World Federalists are, in the main," he believed, "somewhat unrealistic idealists."[29]

Dulles wholeheartedly supported the United Nations despite his recognition of the organization's inherent weaknesses. His commitment stemmed
from his long-standing search for a means to effect orderly, consensual, and
constitutional change. By the mid-1930s, Dulles had become convinced of
the necessity for some means of changing the status quo peacefully so that
disaffected people could be dissuaded from using war as an instrument of
policy. It was imperative, he believed, to concentrate less on the sovereign–
nation-state system and more on institutions that could foster interdependence among nations.[30]

The United Nations, Dulles hoped, might serve to address this need. He
firmly believed that the UN might encourage sufficient cooperation in the
economic and financial areas to establish a basis for eventual political cooperation. The immediate need, he testified before the Senate Foreign Relations
Committee in July, 1945, was to find "new, compelling tasks to pursue in
common." If the fledgling organization could address successfully any of
a number of the social welfare and economic problems that transcended
national boundaries, the spirit of cooperation might spill over into the
strengthening of political bonds. Expounding upon this functionalist approach to creating a new world order, Dulles wrote in November, 1945, that
"the theory of the General Assembly is that if the peoples of the world come
to work together on great social and economic tasks for human betterment,
in the process they will be drawn together in fellowship; they will come to
know each other better; come to trust each other more, and that will create the foundation upon which a more adequate political structure can be
erected."[31]

---

29. Dulles, quoted in Pruessen, *John Foster Dulles,* 255; Dulles, quoted in John F. Landenburger, "The Philosophy of International Politics of John Foster Dulles, 1919–1952" (Ph.D.
dissertation, University of Connecticut, 1969), 159; Dulles, quoted in Michael A. Guhin, *John
Foster Dulles: A Statesman and His Times* (New York, 1972), 81–82.

30. For the most detailed elucidation of Dulles's views in this regard, see John Foster
Dulles, *War, Peace, and Change* (New York, 1939).

31. Dulles, quoted in Pruessen, *John Foster Dulles,* 300–301, 407. See also John Foster
Dulles, "A First Balance Sheet on the United Nations," *International Conciliation,*

Dulles's belief in the possibility of functionalism on a universal level waned and finally all but disappeared during the second half of the 1940s. Personal experience at the United Nations (service on the U.S. delegation in 1946, 1947, 1948, the spring of 1949, and 1950) convinced him that the organization was still too primitive and the bureaucratic hurdles to obtaining a consensus too formidable to permit the body to effect significant change. Moreover, critical international political developments rendered his earlier hopes obsolete. As the Soviet Union shunned cooperation even in functional agencies and on social and economic matters, it became clear that the essential foundation for closer ties in the political realm was not being established. As he witnessed firsthand the impact of the cold war on the United Nations, his conception of that body's potential role in the post-war world order was shattered.[32]

Dulles responded to the changing international climate by rethinking his conception of the functions and purposes of the United Nations. He began to deemphasize both the functionalist possibilities of the organization and its role in maintaining international peace and security. Instead he emphasized the UN's potential as the voice of world opinion, which, he asserted, had "the possibility of exerting a profound influence upon the conduct of nations." Too, he stressed its usefulness in exposing Soviet hypocrisy and in trumpeting the superiority of democracy and capitalism. Though he appears to have come to this conclusion separately, the Truman administration's strategy was developing along similar lines.[33]

Dulles had an opportunity to put his views to the test during the next three years. As a member of the U.S. delegation, he participated in Ameri-

---

CDXXVIII (1946), 177–82; John Foster Dulles, "Thoughts on Soviet Foreign Policy and What to Do About It," *Life,* June 10, 1946, p. 127; Ole Holsti, "The 'Operational Code' Approach to the Study of Political Leaders: John Foster Dulles' Philosophical and Instrumental Beliefs," *Canadian Journal of Political Science,* III (1970), 132.

32. Dulles, *War or Peace,* 137; Congress, Senate, *Hearing Before a Subcommittee of the Committee on Foreign Relations on Proposals to Amend or Otherwise Modify Existing International Peace and Security Organizations, Including the United Nations,* 83rd Cong., 2nd Sess., Dulles testimony on January 18, 1954, p. 4; Richard D. Challener, "Dulles: Moralist as Pragmatist," in Gordon A. Craig and Frank Loewenheim, eds., *The Diplomats, 1939–1979* (Princeton, 1994), 138.

33. John Foster Dulles, "The Future of the United Nations," *International Conciliation,* CDXLV (1948), 581, 587.

can efforts to use the UN as a cold war propaganda weapon on issues ranging from disarmament to the Berlin blockade to the division of Korea. Moreover, since the General Assembly, the most representative of the UN's organs, reflected world opinion (and at least for the moment, U.S. opinion) more accurately than the Security Council, Dulles increasingly sought to shift attention and power from the latter to the former. For example, in an effort to circumvent Soviet obstructionism in the Security Council, he sought and acquired in 1950 an enlarged role for the General Assembly with the Uniting for Peace resolution. In addition, to make the town-meeting concept more of a reality, he advocated finding means to break the membership deadlock that had already taken hold by 1950.[34]

Dulles lamented that the UN still could not serve even as a moral force or as the world's conscience. Before it could do so, it had to achieve a broader consensus about the acceptable behavior of states. "The first step," the international lawyer informed his fellow citizens, "is to develop common customs and practices which public opinion supports. Out of that, definite rules of conduct gradually emerge which become law—common law or statute law." Ideally, General Assembly debate would yield agreement on a written body of legal principles and common international law. This international law, Dulles asserted, must not be a static body emanating from governments and designed to protect the status quo. It must advance and protect individual liberties and encourage peaceful change. Once international law had been codified and member nations had consented to trust their fate to impartial justice, then the Security Council would be able to make decisions on the basis of common standards and the UN would become a government of laws, not potentially despotic men. The UN's military force could then enforce international law and punish transgressors. Unfortunately, the Communists continued denial of "the existence of a moral law or a natural law" rendered such a consensus impossible for the time being.[35]

While the United Nations was not yet capable of maintaining international peace, Dulles still believed that long-term American national security was to be found only in close association with other nations. Collective secu-

34. Dulles, *War or Peace,* 40, 188–91; Landenburger, "The Philosophy of International Politics of John Foster Dulles, 1919–1952," 148–49.

35. Dulles, "What Shall We Do with the U.N.," 1041; Dulles, *War or Peace,* 187, 199.

rity, ultimately on a universal level but for the time being on a regional scale, was indispensable in the post-war world. Until the UN functioned effectively as a collective security organization, the United States had the right and responsibility to protect its national interests through regional mechanisms. Moreover, Dulles claimed, reliance on regional organizations might eventually achieve the goal of "security through interdependence" on a universal level, even if the world arrived at it "through the back door."[36]

Thus between 1943, when he assumed chairmanship of the Commission on a Just and Durable Peace, and January, 1953, when he ascended to the office of secretary of state, Dulles had thought deeply about the theory of international organization. He had amassed an encyclopedic knowledge of the UN Charter, and had experienced firsthand almost every aspect of the United Nations. Although involvement with the UN at no point during that decade dominated either his activities or his thinking, it had been a consistent, even if relatively minor, concern.

By 1953 the new secretary of state had developed a balanced view of the United Nations and the appropriate United States relationship with the organization. He combined a still occasionally idealistic view of the UN's potential in a changed world with a fundamentally realistic appraisal of its flaws, a minimal set of expectations for its usefulness during the cold war, and a pragmatic approach to the use of the organization in the present. Dulles had suggested in 1950 that "every instrument has its own distinctive possibilities and in order to get the best results, has to be used with skill."[37] It remained to be seen how skillfully he would use the organization when, as secretary of state, he became the creator rather than simply an executor or spokesman for American policy.

The third member of the triumvirate, Henry Cabot Lodge, remained his grandfather's philosophical grandson throughout the 1920s and 1930s. Dur-

36. Speech to the American Association for the United Nations, March 2, 1953, in folder marked "United Nations 1953," Box 77, John Foster Dulles Papers, Seeley G. Mudd Manuscript Library, Department of Rare Books and Special Collections, Princeton University Libraries (hereinafter J. F. Dulles Papers, Mudd Library); John Foster Dulles, "Challenge and Response in U.S. Policy," *Foreign Affairs,* XXXVI (October, 1957), 25–43; Anthony Clark Arend, *Pursuing a Just and Durable Peace: John Foster Dulles and International Organization* (New York, 1988), 155–59.

37. Arend, *Pursuing a Just and Durable Peace,* 41.

ing his seven years as a newspaper reporter, Lodge opposed membership in the World Court and the League of Nations. He had dismissed the Kellogg-Briand Pact of 1929, which called upon nations to "renounce war as an instrument of national policy," as mere rhetoric. Though a staunch isolationist, he was an equally outspoken advocate of military preparedness. In *The Cult of Weakness,* written in 1931, he urged Americans to face up to international military realities. In editorials for the New York *Herald Tribune* he repeatedly called for building up the U.S. Army and Navy. Elected to the Senate in 1936, Lodge continued to seek to distance the United States from the war looming in Europe, while simultaneously supporting American military preparedness. Once war erupted in 1939, he strongly advocated American neutrality. As danger approached American shores, Lodge voted for the Lend-Lease Act, while also supporting presidential requests to increase defense appropriations and personally serving in the army active reserve. In January, 1944, he became the first senator since the Civil War to resign his seat in order to volunteer for active duty. After service in France (including a stint on General Eisenhower's staff), he won a bid for election to the Senate in November, 1946.

Lodge returned to the Senate a changed man. World War II had transformed the former isolationist into an ardent internationalist. By 1947, he was convinced that the United States had become "the world's greatest power, even if we elected to do nothing whatever, we would be inextricably involved in everything that takes place in the world." Consequently, Lodge joined Vandenberg in marshaling Republican support for Truman's internationalist policies, including aid to Greece and Turkey, the Truman Doctrine, the Marshall Plan, and NATO. Support for the United Nations became an integral part of his new internationalism. "We must in every possible way strengthen the UN," he proclaimed in a speech to young Republicans.[38]

At the same time, the senator argued that the young organization could not be expected to do too much. Early in 1947, for example, he opposed a movement to deposit the question of aid to Greece and Turkey in the UN. The UN, he insisted, was not "set up to deal with situations of this character." If the United States "sought to impose upon it functions which are clearly beyond its present powers to discharge," he cautioned his fellow sena-

38. Lodge, quoted in Alden Hatch, *The Lodges of Massachusetts* (New York, 1973), 230; *Congressional Record,* 79th Cong., 2nd Sess., vol. 92, pt. 10, p. A2475.

tors, the United States would "swamp," rather than strengthen, the organization.[39]

Lodge also supported measures aimed at enabling the United States to participate in the United Nations more effectively. In October, 1949, he spoke on behalf of an amendment to the UN Participation Act of 1945, which provided the U.S. mission more flexibility and clarified the president's authority to contribute American military personnel and equipment to UN operations. Lodge argued that the United States needed to view the UN as "a permanent institution" and U.S. participation in it as "a long-range affair." It should staff the mission accordingly and make the necessary changes in American defense logistics.[40]

Lodge's support, however, was not unqualified or unquestioning. Service on the U.S. delegation in the fall of 1950 reinforced the Massachusetts senator's realistic assessment of the organization's limited potential in the midst of the cold war. Too, by 1951 he had grown frustrated by the UN's prosecution of the war in Korea. He joined the chorus of Americans charging that other members of the organization were not bearing their fair share of the load, in both monetary and manpower terms. The United Nations, Lodge complained, produced too much talk and too little action. And the United States, because of its "tendency to believe we have accomplished something in international affairs merely by uttering words and then proclaiming our agreement with them," was failing to hold the organization accountable.[41]

Partially to remedy the situation, he advocated holding a special session of the General Assembly to amend the UN Charter and endorse the Vandenberg resolution. Passed by the Senate in June, 1948, the Vandenberg resolution had reaffirmed the United States' commitment to cooperating with collective security organizations. At the same time, it had also reiterated the nation's readiness to protect its national interests, as it interpreted them, either by itself or in concert with other nations, in accord with Article 51 of the UN Charter. Through such action, Lodge asserted, the United States "might actually profit by the bitter experiences which we have recently had,

39. *Congressional Record,* 80th Cong., 1st Sess., vol. 93, pt. 3, p. 3483.
40. *Congressional Record,* 81st Cong., 1st Sess., vol. 95, pt. 11, p. 139834.
41. Henry Cabot Lodge, "To Regain the Peace Initiative," New York *Times Magazine,* April 8, 1951, pp. 14, 26, 28, 30.

and thus build a truly effective organization which is based on realities and which cannot be paralyzed by members who actually want to destroy it."[42]

Thus, by the time he assumed his duties at the U.S. mission in 1953, Lodge had at least a minimal acquaintance with the United Nations. He had developed realistic views about the organization that reflected his experiences as a journalist and a politician. Unfortunately, the United Nations, Lodge realized, was plagued by unreasonable expectations. "Exaggerated claims for it led to exaggerated disappointments," he warned, for the American people had been given to believe erroneously that the UN would be "a panacea." It was not an "automatic device for peace. If the United Nations is as automatic as a burglar alarm it is doing well. But what happens after the bell rings is up to the members and you will get results solely in proportion as you contribute."[43] Still, Lodge believed that it served important functions as a developer and disseminator of public opinion and an informal forum for settling disputes. The UN, the ambassador stated, "is primitive; it is evolutionary; it had not brought—and will not bring—the millennium," but it was "an intelligent first step."[44]

Of the three men who would work together to create American foreign policy, Dulles had the most experience in diplomatic circles and thus possessed a more carefully articulated view of the role of international organization in the world community. Yet Dulles's views had evolved and developed considerably over the years, and consequently there were no guarantees about how he would envision the role of the fledgling United Nations once he bore responsibility for the formulation and execution of American policy. In contrast, while the president's primary field of expertise was not in the diplomatic arena, his experiences in World War II had left him with definite ideas about the need for effective international cooperation and about the nature of the organization that could achieve it. Lodge, the most highly skilled and

---

42. *Ibid.,* 30.

43. Gordon C. Hamilton, "Don't Sell the U.N. Short," *Newsweek,* October 12, 1953, p. 42; Congress, Senate, *Hearing Before the Committee on Foreign Relations,* 83rd Cong., 1st Sess., Lodge testimony on July 23, 1953, pp. 7–8.

44. Lodge testimony, *Hearing Before the Committee on Foreign Relations,* 8; "What the United Nations Means to the United States," Lodge address before the Virginia House of Burgesses on January 30, 1954, *Department of State Bulletin,* February 15, 1954, pp. 252–56.

effective political operator, had the least international experience of the tri-umvirate. But his experience in the world's greatest deliberative body, the United States Senate, and that body's Foreign Relations Committee left him with a distinctive, if limited, set of views about how the United States could best utilize the UN in its foreign policy. It remained to be seen how effectively Eisenhower, Dulles, and Lodge would translate these views into American policy from 1953 to 1961.

3

SECURING THE COLD WAR BATTLEFIELD
The Loyalty and Security Program

By January, 1953, many Americans had come to believe that the United Nations posed a threat to the nation's security. Charges that the UN provided a haven for Communist spies and saboteurs had first acquired an aura of legitimacy during the 1949 trial of Alger Hiss, a key participant in the preparatory work for the UN and a provisional secretary-general at the San Francisco Conference. Subsequent attacks by anti-Communist conservatives (particularly Senator Joseph R. McCarthy), isolationists, and unilateralists further eroded American support.

The nation's fears escalated during 1951 and 1952 in concert with the increasingly strident charges of the ambitious Republican senator from Wisconsin. Congressional committees intensified their investigations of the United Nations, and even the Democratic administration of Harry S. Truman seemed to view the organization with newfound suspicion. These investigations revealed the apparent inability of the United States to prevent subversives from obtaining employment at the UN. Although the State Department and not the UN itself bore the brunt of public, press, and congressional criticism, diminished trust in the UN was an inevitable by-product of the attacks. As Eisenhower assumed the presidency, the United States' commitment to the United Nations seemed destined to become the latest victim of McCarthyism unless the State Department could demonstrate its willingness and ability to purify the organization, ridding it of its allegedly subversive elements.

Eisenhower had to act if he wanted to avoid a return to isolationism and make the United Nations an effective instrument in his cold war foreign policy. The widespread anger over the UN's employment of purportedly disloyal Americans and the fear that the organization was endangering national security had to be addressed directly and put to rest. The State Department's close monitoring of press, radio, and public opinion had revealed that a majority of Americans were aware of the charge that the UN employed disloyal Americans.[1]

Administration officials devised a two-track plan to restore public confidence in the UN and the State Department's relationship with the organization. First, they sought to remove actual or potential American subversives from the staffs of both the U.S. mission and the UN Secretariat. Second, they improved security measures at USUN and tightened security restrictions on foreign delegations, foreign employees, and representatives of nongovernmental organizations (NGOs) in an attempt to foil Communist efforts to use the UN complex on New York City's East River as a base for spying in the United States. Throughout, the administration sought to balance security needs with domestic political pressures and international opposition.[2]

The Eisenhower administration raised security standards for American citizens employed by the United Nations to unprecedented levels. But the nation's violation of the letter and spirit of the UN Charter in regard to personnel matters began under the Truman administration. Article 100 of the UN Charter empowers the secretary-general to recruit and dismiss UN employees and expressly states that in so doing he "shall not seek or receive instructions from any government." Under Byrnes, the State Department, seeking to avoid even the appearance of impropriety, initially refused requests from Secretary-General Trygve Lie to recommend candidates for Secretariat posts.

1. Memorandum, n.d. (*ca.* January 20, 1953), in folder marked "UN Misc. 1953," Box 24, ROPOS, RG 59, NA; "The United Nations: A Review of Developments, December 16, 1952–January 15, 1953," in folder marked "UN Monthly Reports (Permanent Copies) 1953," Box 21, ROPOS, RG 59, NA; "Popular Attitudes Toward the United Nations," March 11, 1953, UN Misc. 1953, Box 24, ROPOS, RG 59, NA.

2. Many of the Eisenhower revisionists, most notably Fred I. Greenstein in *The Hidden-Hand Presidency: Eisenhower as Leader* (New York, 1982), cite the president's handling of Senator McCarthy as an example of this hidden-hand leadership style in operation. Recent works, including Richard M. Fried, *Nightmare in Red: The McCarthy Era in Perspective* (New

By the late 1940s, however, escalating fears of Communist infiltration led the administration to reverse its position. Meeting in the fall of 1948, representatives of the Truman administration and the secretary-general's office reached a confidential agreement that the State Department would screen American incumbents and candidates for Secretariat positions to ascertain whether they had a "police record" or possessed a "political affiliation or sentiment" which made them a security risk. The department would then inform the secretary-general of the existence, but not the exact nature, of any derogatory information uncovered. The State Department screened 1,846 Americans between 1948 and 1952 and sent comments on 40 of them to the secretary-general. It even supplied the Secretariat with advice on the matter of promotions. Despite some misgivings, Lie, a staunchly anti-Communist Social Democrat from Norway, largely acquiesced to the demands of the host nation, which was providing 40 percent of the UN's budget.[3]

The politics of the upcoming presidential election fueled attacks on the United Nations in 1952. Both the Senate Internal Security Subcommittee (SISS) of the Committee on the Judiciary, chaired by Patrick A. McCarran (D-Nevada), and a federal grand jury of the Southern District of New York, led by Roy M. Cohn, the special assistant to the attorney general, focused their attention on alleged subversive activity at the UN. In December, 1952, the SISS discovered and publicized the secret agreement. This further legitimized charges that, although the Democratic administration had been aware of the UN's role in fostering internal subversion, it had failed to respond sufficiently.

Earlier actions by the grand jury and the Internal Security Subcommittee, however, had already taken a critical toll on American support for the New York–based international organization. The investigating committees subpoenaed a total of seventy-seven American employees of the UN. Twenty-

---

York, 1990), and Jeff Broadwater, *Eisenhower and the Anti-Communist Crusade* (Chapel Hill, 1992), challenge aspects of this interpretation.

3. *SISS Hearings,* "Arrangements with U.N. for the Provision of Information on U.S. Nationals" (1952), 82nd Cong., 2nd Sess., Appendix, 415; Raymond N. Habiby, "Problems of Loyalty of United Nations Personnel" (Ph.D. dissertation, University of Minnesota, 1965), 249; New York *Times,* August 9, 1949, p. 12; New York *Times,* August 19, 1949, p. 3; United Nations, Secretariat, "Report of the Secretary General to the General Assembly," Doc. A/2364, VII Sess., January 30, 1953; Trygve Lie, *In the Cause of Peace: Seven Years with the UN* (New York, 1954), 386–405.

three who testified before the SISS and "over a score" of those who came before the grand jury invoked the Fifth Amendment when questioned about their past or present membership in the Communist party. Although the grand jury presentment of December 2, 1952, contained no figures, names, or indictments to substantiate its claims, it nevertheless concluded that there was "infiltration into the United Nations of an overwhelmingly large group of disloyal United States citizens."[4] Lie dismissed the American employees who had pleaded the Fifth Amendment. The consequences of his action would haunt the new administration, for the dismissed employees appealed to the Administrative Tribunal of the General Assembly for reinstatement and/or compensation.

On January 9, 1953, the executive branch rather belatedly joined the fray when Truman issued Executive Order No. 10422. Following the recommendations of the grand jury presentment, the order created procedures to determine whether "there [was] a reasonable doubt as to the loyalty of the person involved to the Government of the United States." It essentially applied the regulations concerning the investigation of the loyalty of federal employees to present and prospective American employees of the United Nations. It stipulated that the Civil Service Commission should conduct a preliminary screening of all U.S. citizens employed by the UN, to be followed by an FBI full-field investigation of all Americans offered a professional post or one open to international competition. The Civil Service Commission would then transmit its findings to one of its Regional Loyalty Boards, which would offer the accused individual a hearing if derogatory information had been discovered. The Regional Loyalty Board, or the Loyalty Review Board in the case of an appeal, was then to communicate its conclusions to the secretary-general "in as much detail as security considerations permit."[5]

It was a situation increasingly in need of new leadership when Eisenhower took the oath of office. In fact, however, even before the inauguration the president-elect and his UN representative–designate had begun to formulate a moderate response. On this, as on most of the other salient campaign issues, the Eisenhower Republicans carefully staked out a position be-

4. *SISS Hearings,* "Presentment of the Federal Grand Jury on Disloyalty of Certain United States Citizens at the United Nations," 82nd Cong., 2nd Sess., Appendix B, pp. 407–408; David Caute, *The Great Fear: The Anti-Communist Purge Under Truman and Eisenhower* (New York, 1978), 326–27.

5. *Codification of Presidential Proclamations and Executive Orders, April 13, 1945–January 20, 1989* (Washington, D.C., 1989), 385.

tween that of the liberal Democrats and that of the conservative wing of the Republican party. They conceded the least-damaging accusation—that the UN had employed Americans who, because of past or present Communist party sympathies, were not wholly loyal to their government. But they stood firm against the potentially more threatening charge that the organization was a hotbed of subversion and espionage on American soil. Consequently, the new officials castigated the previous administration for its perceived laxity in uncovering and removing American Communists. At the same time, hewing to their moderate position, they resisted strident demands from the conservative Taft–William F. Knowland–McCarthy forces to withdraw from the United Nations.

The responsibility for articulating the administration's middle-of-the-road position and defending it from critics on both flanks fell logically to the new representative to the United Nations. Lodge knew that the UN was commonly described as a "glass house," not only because of the architectural style of its Manhattan riverside complex, but also because of the public nature of its proceedings. He patiently but firmly explained again and again that the United States transmitted no secret or classified information to the UN. For example, the UN received only the same information—a brief sheet—on military operations in Korea that the Pentagon released to the press. There was simply nothing to spy on at UN Headquarters. To underscore this point, Lodge frequently noted that no American employee had ever been charged with espionage. Nevertheless, he insisted that the United Nations still should not employ American Communists. In sharp contrast to isolationist and unilateralist Republicans, however, he did not justify this position on the grounds of national security. Rather, he maintained that the issue was one of justice: "When we have so many good Americans to choose from, why should we give the job to an American Communist[?]"[6]

The administration's first priority was to defuse the hysteria surrounding the proceedings of the various investigating committees. After his electoral

---

6. Congress, House, *Hearings Before the Subcommittee on International Organizations and Movements of the Committee on Foreign Affairs,* 83rd Cong., 1st Sess., February 2, 1953, pp. 12 (quotation), 2–3, July 8, 1953, p. 90; Congress, Senate, *Hearing Before the Committee on Foreign Relations; Testimony of Ambassador Henry Cabot Lodge, Jr., The United States Representative to the United Nations, and Representative in the Security Council,* 83rd Cong., 1st Sess., July 23, 1953, pp. 5, 15; "The United Nations: A Place to Promote Peace," Lodge speech to the Women's National Press Club on April 15, 1953, *Department of State Bulletin,* May 4, 1953, pp. 659–60; Hamilton, "Don't Sell the U.N. Short," 42.

victory, Eisenhower reportedly sent an unofficial envoy to request that Senator McCarran moderate his subcommittee's denunciations of the United Nations, promising that the new administration would remedy the errors of the previous administration. McCarran apparently complied. Shortly thereafter the subcommittee shifted the direction of its inquiries.[7]

A second task was to formulate procedures for screening all government employees. From the outset, Lodge took a firm stand. He strongly urged Eisenhower to screen all employees in sensitive agencies, to set a date for the completion of the process, and to allocate the manpower and financial resources necessary to meet this self-imposed deadline. Lodge championed his approach as "utterly practical, factual, and without demagoguery." The political veteran from Massachusetts advised the political novice from Abilene that unless the executive branch took prompt and decisive action congressional demagogues would "make political capital" of the issue as they had under Truman and would further "prolong the hysteria for years on end."[8]

Lodge outlined a proposal for a loyalty program in early January, 1953. He broached the idea, which he may have gotten from Truman's deputy undersecretary of state for security, of establishing a twelve-member committee. Modeled on the Hoover Commission on Governmental Reorganization (1947–1949), it would conduct a thorough, secret investigation of American personnel in sensitive agencies, including the UN. Such a commission, Lodge insisted, would avoid the pitfalls of both a congressional investigation, "which destroys sources of information and tends to besmirch innocent people," and the loyalty boards within departments, which were not always sufficiently independent and objective. Although nothing came of the proposal, Lodge immediately began to work with Assistant Secretary of State for United Nations Affairs John D. Hickerson to establish a screening process for Americans employed by USUN or the UN.[9]

The specific loyalty measures ultimately adopted by the administration reflected its temperate stance. Although President Eisenhower set forth

7. Habiby, "Problems of Loyalty," 259; New York *Times,* November 14, 1952, p. 1.

8. Memorandum, Lodge to Eisenhower, n.d., in folder marked "Henry Cabot Lodge: 1952–1953 (1)," Box 23, Administration Series, EP, AWF, EL.

9. Carlisle H. Humelsine to Dulles, January 2, 1953, 315.3, in Box 1253, RG 59, NA; Journal entries, January 3, 7, 1953, in folder marked "T-E, 1952–53," Box 71, HCLP, MHS; Diary entry, January 7, 1953, in folder marked "Diary—Copies of DDE personal: 1953–1954 (3)," Box 9, DDE Diary Series, EP, AWF, EL; *MTCD,* Reel 1, Dulles and Lodge, October 7, 1953.

more stringent security standards for other governmental employees with the issuance of Executive Order No. 10450 on April 27, 1953, Truman's Executive Order No. 10422 remained the basis of the loyalty program for American employees of USUN and the United Nations. Executive Order No. 10450 replaced the previous standard of reasonable doubt as to loyalty with a requirement that an individual's employment be "clearly consistent with the interests of the national security." But the UN was neither a government nor a "sensitive" agency, so employees were not privy to classified defense information. Consequently, they were not in a position to endanger national security. The new "security" standards of Order No. 10450 therefore were not applicable. The loyalty standards remained the only reasonable basis for evaluation.[10]

However, in a move pertaining directly to Americans employed by the UN, on June 2, 1953, Eisenhower issued Executive Order No. 10459. The order, which amended No. 10422, established an International Organizations Employees Loyalty Board (IOELB) in the Civil Service Commission. This board was to evaluate the findings of the commission and FBI investigations, conduct hearings, determine whether there was "a reasonable doubt as to the loyalty of the person involved," and communicate any derogatory information to the secretary-general "in as much detail as the Board determines that security considerations will permit." Clearly, as the State Department's UN Affairs Planning Staff conceded in its 1953 review, the cold war (and the domestic political exigencies of McCarthyism, it might more honestly have noted) had convinced the administration that it was first necessary to have satisfactory proof of allegiance to the United States "as the foundation for any attachment to a 'general interest' symbolized by international organization." Yet the administration sought to revise the order in a manner that would avoid jeopardizing the nation's long-term interest in maintaining an independent Secretariat. State Department officials thus accepted advice from both Lodge and the new secretary-general, Dag Hammarskjöld, who had assumed office in mid-April, about the wording of the new order.[11]

10. *Codification of Presidential Proclamations and Executive Orders, April 13, 1945–January 20, 1989,* 1055, 47–53, 383–87; Congress, House, *Hearings Before the Subcommittee on International Organizations and Movements of the Committee on Foreign Affairs,* 83rd Cong., 2nd Sess., February 2, 1953, p. 3; Press Meeting, January 26, 1953, in folder marked "Speeches and Press Releases: 1953," Box 109, HCLP, MHS.

11. "The 1953 Review: Organization of United States Participation in the United Nations System," State Department United Nations Affairs Planning Staff, Bureau of United Nations

Ideally the implementation of the new loyalty program at the UN should have been the result of a coordinated interdepartmental effort. On paper the key participants would have been Dulles, Attorney General Herbert Brownell, Jr., chairman of the Civil Service Commission Philip Young, and FBI director J. Edgar Hoover, with Lodge coordinating the execution of the plan. Yet the reality was quite different. Secretary of State Dulles provided only limited assistance and direction. Although he remained abreast of key developments and even reviewed the most important cases, Dulles did not participate in the daily business of putting the new regulations in place. The secretary delegated primary responsibility for personnel matters to Donold Lourie, president of Quaker Oats Company at the time of his appointment as undersecretary of state for administration. It was an unfortunate choice. A political novice, Lourie was virtually paralyzed in the face of McCarthyism and his own virulently anti-Communist assistant, R. W. Scott McLeod. The naïve Lourie selected McLeod for the post of administrator of the Bureau of Security and Consular Affairs largely because of his experience as an FBI agent and as administrative assistant to Senator Styles Bridges of New Hampshire. McLeod proved to be a poor administrator who was handicapped by "a very black and white kind of approach to things."[12] Meanwhile, Brownell, Hoover, and Young, deluged by departmental requests for personnel security investigations, did not make the UN cases a top priority.

Lodge presented a stark contrast to the inexperienced and ideologically isolated Lourie and McLeod in the State Department and the less personally involved directors of the various investigatory bodies. He was above all an eminently pragmatic politician. From the beginning, his ultimate goal was clear—to quickly cleanse the American delegation to the UN and American employees of the organization of the taint of communism with a minimum of political fallout. The path to its achievement, however, was fraught with obstacles. Right-wing anti-Communists presented a constant threat on the

---

Affairs, n.d., in *FRUS, 1952–1954,* III, 159; Telegram from Lodge to Dulles, April 13, 1953, 315.3/4–1353, in Box 1254, RG 59, NA; Telegram from Lodge to Dulles, May 25, 1953, 315.3–2553, in Box 1254, RG 59, NA. See also Brian Urquhart, *Hammarskjöld* (New York, 1972), 62.

12. John W. Hanes, oral history (January 29, 1966), Dulles Oral History Project, Mudd Library, Princeton University; Press Conference, March 9, 1953, in folder marked "United Nations: 1953," Box 77, J. F. Dulles Papers, Mudd Library; Allen W. Dulles, oral history (June 3, 1964), Dulles Oral History Project, Mudd Library; Townsend Hoopes, *The Devil and John Foster Dulles* (Boston, 1973), 152–53.

homefront, while cold war conflicts and differences with the nation's traditional allies presented challenges on the international scene.

The practical business of implementing these new regulations dominated Lodge's first days in office. Indeed, his first official act was to request on January 25 and 26 of FBI director Hoover that his agency begin an investigation of all American personnel at the United Nations and USUN, respectively. Presenting his credentials to Lie on January 27, Lodge emphasized the gravity of the personnel issue and urged the secretary-general to give it his immediate attention. The following day Lodge returned to Lie's office, this time accompanied by an official from the Civil Service Commission with 2,000 questionnaires and fingerprint charts. The fingerprinting began later that same day in the basement of the UN building, and the FBI continued to work out of the UN Headquarters until Hammarskjöld requested it to leave the premises in November.[13]

Following the advice he had given the president, Lodge set a target date of September 1 for completing the process. By February 7, having forwarded 1,200 completed forms to the State Department, he was already pressing Brownell to speed the investigation. The attorney general professed his desire to cooperate, but blamed the absence of sufficient funds to begin the investigations immediately.[14] It was only the first of many such exchanges.

The mechanics of establishing a loyalty program was relatively easy compared to the far more difficult task of convincing Congress that the executive branch had the situation under control—this despite the fact that the American press and public appear to have been reasonably reassured by the administration's prompt action. Conservative congressmen had their own ideas. On January 7, Pat McCarran, chairman of the SISS, introduced a bill that would make it a criminal act punishable by a $10,000 fine for an American citizen to accept UN employment without first obtaining a security clearance. The State Department ultimately intervened to prevent its pas-

13. Lodge to Hoover, January 25, 26, 1953, in folder marked "Speeches and Press Releases: 1953," Box 109, HCLP, MHS; Urquhart, *Hammarskjöld,* 64; Lodge to Donold B. Lourie, April 7, 1953, in folder marked "UN—Loyalty Program for Personnel," Box 79, HCLP, MHS; Lodge to Lie, January 29, 1953, in folder marked "UN—Loyalty Program for Personnel," Box 79, HCLP, MHS.

14. Lodge to Brownell, February 7, 1953, in folder marked "UN—Loyalty Program for Personnel," Box 79, HCLP, MHS; Brownell to Lodge, February 13, 1953, Box 79, HCLP, MHS.

sage, arguing that other nations might follow the United States' example, depriving the UN of the services of many employees (particularly escapees from the Communist bloc) who zealously supported the United States.[15]

Desperate to persuade the Senate that legislative action was unnecessary, Lodge worked assiduously to keep key congressmen informed of his progress in implementing the new security provisions. The former three-term senator communicated with the chairmen of the Senate's Committees on the Judiciary, Foreign Relations, Appropriations, and Rules and Administration, and the Senate's Permanent Investigating Subcommittee; with the chairmen of the House Committee on Foreign Affairs, Appropriations Subcommittee on State Department Appropriations, and Committee on Un-American Activities; and with other members of the House and Senate who made inquiries. McCarthy, Styles Bridges, Alexander Wiley, and Harold H. Velde all praised his handling of the situation. Indeed, Bridges deemed Lodge's efforts "one of the most heartening taken by the new administration," while Wiley and Velde expressed their appreciation of his efforts "to clean up" the U.S. representation in the United Nations.[16]

Lodge was justifiably satisfied with the fruits of his first attempt to cultivate congressional support. The response, he proudly reported to Lourie, had been "extremely favorable." Lodge also spread his gospel of progress in personal meetings. By April 22, he had already entertained over 150 members of Congress. By late September he had testified before the New York grand jury, the SISS, the Senate Committee on Foreign Relations, and twice

15. "The United Nations: A Review of Developments, January 16–February 14, 1953," in folder marked "UN Monthly Reports (Permanent Copies) 1953," Box 21, ROPOS, RG 59, NA; "Popular Attitudes Toward the United Nations," March 11, 1953, in folder marked "UN Misc., 1953," Box 24, ROPOS, RG 59, NA; "Interview with Henry Cabot Lodge, Jr.," *U.S. News & World Report,* November 26, 1954, p. 98; Thruston B. Morton to William Langer, April 9, 1953, p. 8, 315.3/2–1453, in Box 1253, RG 59, NA.

16. Journal entry, January 3, 1953, in folder marked "T-E 1952/53," Box 71, HCLP, MHS. For copies of the congressional correspondence, see Lodge to Styles Bridges, January 31, 1953; to William Langer, January 31, 1953; to John Taber, January 31, 1953; to Alexander Wiley, January 31, 1953; to Robert B. Chiperfield, February 2, 1953; to Cliff Clevenger, February 2, 1953; to William Jenner, February 2, 1953; to Joseph McCarthy, February 2, 1953; to Chauncey W. Reed, February 2, 1953; to Harold H. Velde, February 2, 1953; McCarthy to Lodge, February 6, 1953; Bridges to Lodge, February 6, 1953; Chiperfield to Lodge, February 9, 1953; Velde to Lodge, February 13, 1953; Wiley to Lodge, February 4, 1953, all in folder marked "UN—Loyalty Program for Personnel," Box 79, HCLP, MHS.

before the House Subcommittee on International Organizations and Movements.[17]

While Lodge's efforts at romancing the Congress allowed the administration to extend the traditional honeymoon period, the international community was less accommodating. Bowing to pressure from the General Assembly, the secretary-general thrust the issue into the international limelight with the presentation of his personnel report on January 30, 1953. Lie's report met American demands by stating that "the Secretary-General should not retain a staff member in the employment of the United Nations if he has reasonable grounds for believing that that staff member is engaging or is likely to engage in subversive activities against the government of any member state." Furthermore, Lie asserted that a refusal to answer questions about Communist party membership or subversive activities constituted a breach of staff conduct regulations that warranted dismissal because it cast suspicion on the Secretariat as a whole.[18]

While not completely satisfied, the State Department welcomed the proposal as "a feasible" means of meeting American objectives without unduly compromising the Secretariat's independence. The department instructed the American delegation to seek early General Assembly approval of Lie's report in order to resolve this awkward issue prior to the arrival of Lie's successor. Dulles directed American embassies worldwide to inform the governments to which they were accredited of the importance of the removal of "subversive United States nationals" from the UN and of U.S. support for Lie's proposal as a means of accomplishing this objective.[19]

The primary responsibility for marshaling this international support fell to the U.S. delegation in New York. By the end of February, Lodge or a member of the USUN staff had met at least once with representatives of

17. Lodge to Donold Lourie, April 7, 1953, in folder marked "UN—Loyalty Program for Personnel," Box 79, HCLP, MHS; Lodge to Eisenhower, April 22, 1953, Reel 28, Box 79, HCLP, MHS; Congress, House, *Hearings Before the Subcommittee on International Organizations and Movements,* February 2, July 8, 1953; *SISS Hearings,* 83rd Cong., 1st Sess., September 24, 1953.

18. UN Doc. A/2364.

19. Position Paper, "Report of the Secretary General on Personnel Policy," February 18, 1953, in Box 15, Lot 82 D 211, RG 59, NA; Telegram from Dulles to USUN, February 12, 1953, 315.3/2–953, in Box 1253, Lot 82 D 211, RG 59, NA; Circular airgram from Dulles, February 5, 1953, 315.3/2–553, same box.

most friendly nations.[20] Most expressed similar opinions. They viewed Executive Order No. 10422 as an essentially internal American matter. Yet in an ironic twist, these foreigners questioned the constitutionality of dismissing an employee simply on account of a refusal to testify. Moreover, they doubted the United States' ability to determine accurately an individual's likelihood of engaging in subversion in the future. The American embassy in Ottawa, in conveying its perception of the attitude of the Canadian government, perhaps best articulated the emerging international consensus. American views on the loyalty of UN personnel had "strong elements of unreality" because there was nothing to spy on at the United Nations. The Canadians understood, however, that it had become a domestic political problem of such magnitude as to necessitate taking steps to appease the host country. Though critical of U.S. actions, Canada and the nation's other traditional allies agreed to endorse Lie's proposal.[21]

Consequently, the Western Big Three—the United States, Great Britain, and France—submitted a joint resolution on March 28. The resolution expressed approval of the secretary-general's personnel report, recalled the international character of the UN staff, and called on the incoming secretary-general to report on the status of the personnel situation to the present, eighth session of the assembly six months hence.[22] The Arab-Asian bloc (which consisted of the Arab countries of Africa and Asia plus other Asian countries) objected. It put forth a two-part proposal to appoint a fifteen-member committee to study the question and to instruct the secretary-general to cease any further dismissals until this committee had reported. The motion was ultimately defeated by a vote of 21 to 29, with 8 abstentions.

The American delegation wholeheartedly approved Lie's proposal.

20. Telegram from Dulles to USUN, February 9, 1953, 315.3/2–953, in Box 1253, RG 59, NA; Telegram from Lodge to Dulles, February 9, 1953, 315.3/2–953, same box; Telegram from Lodge to Dulles, February 9, 1953, 320/2–953, in Box 1287, RG 59, NA; Telegram from Dulles to USUN, February 12, 1953, 315.3/2–1253, in Box 1253, RG 59, NA; Telegram from USUN to State Department, "Daily Classified Summary," February 19, 1953, 310.5–1-1953, in Box 1249, RG 59, NA.

21. Telegram from the U.S. embassy in Ottawa to the State Department, February 13, 1953, 315.3/2–1353, Box 1253, RG 59, NA; Telegram from USUN to State Department, "Daily Classified Summary," February 24, 1953, 310.5/2–2453, in Box 1249, RG 59, NA; Telegram from USUN to State Department, "Daily Classified Summary," February 17, 1953, 310.5/2–1753, same box.

22. United Nations, General Assembly, UN Doc. A/L 146, VII Sess., March 28, 1953.

Speaking in the General Assembly on March 28, Lodge supported Lie's actions as essential to rebuilding American support for the organization. Noting that many Americans advocated withdrawal, he warned that the United Nations could fall apart over this "essentially administrative problem." Lodge pledged that the U.S. government would provide the Secretariat with the results of its loyalty reviews "only as advice." The secretary-general would still be responsible for the final decisions. Sensitive to charges that it was impossible to judge an individual's future loyalty, Lodge maintained that close examination of a person's past record would result in reasonable judgments. The American position prevailed. On April 1 the General Assembly passed the American, French, and British resolution by a vote of 41 to 13, with 4 abstentions.[23]

Lodge's description of the situation as an "essentially administrative problem" was disingenuous. At the very least, it was an administrative problem that stemmed from fundamental political and philosophical questions about international organization. The American demands cut to the heart of the principle of international loyalty upon which the UN Secretariat was based. Such challenges were not new. Traditionally, many nations had worried that their citizens might transfer allegiance from their respective nation-states to the concept of a greater international good that transcended national interests. In fact, Communist nations, insisting that national loyalty took precedence over international loyalty, regularly sought to retain control over their nationals employed by international organizations. However, the Eisenhower administration's position presented a new twist, in which ideological rather than national allegiance became the key issue. The United States wanted to prevent the employment of its citizens who were suspected of loyalty to an opposing ideological system—communism. Lodge, Eisenhower's "special political adviser," clearly understood that the problem transcended administrative concerns, but he also recognized the political realities of the situation. In his desperation to disperse the cloud that covered his office and turn his attention to more substantive matters, his pressing objective was to dispose of the issue.

The administration thus did not provide the measure of support one

---

23. "Maintaining Charter Standards for International Civil Servants," Lodge statement on March 28, 1953, in the General Assembly plenary session, *Department of State Bulletin,* April 27, 1953, pp. 620–23.

would have expected given its rhetoric trumpeting the UN as an essential force for world peace. Compelled to pick its battles by domestic political pressures and a finite amount of presidential capital, it understandably chose not to make the principle of international allegiance a top priority. The continued onslaught of McCarthyism, the introduction of the Bricker Amendment, and unexpected attacks on the now Republican-led State Department had taken too heavy a toll. Still, the administration did not leave the secretary-general alone to confront congressional demands to "clean up" the UN. Instead, administration officials worked with him to design a program that both held congressional critics at bay and allowed for the maintenance of essential Secretariat independence.

The installation of a new secretary-general on April 10, 1953, introduced another variable in the equation for the United States. As the State Department noted, Lie's behavior had "at times caused us some unhappiness," but he had "been sound on the basic proposition" of screening American nationals.[24] Dag Hammarskjöld, however, was an unknown quantity. The U.S. delegation immediately set out to secure his support. In a meeting on April 22, Lodge stressed that the administration's aim was to "restore the good name of [the] UN." Hammarskjöld, according to Lodge, announced his determination to "clean up" the situation.[25] In late August, anticipating that new problems would arise shortly with the announcement of the Administrative Tribunal's decision, he even petitioned Lodge for a meeting with Attorney General Brownell, asserting that "it might be of great value to all parties concerned to establish a direct contact and have a chance of talking matters over freely and frankly." Hammarskjöld sought closer contact at least in part because of his determination to provide the "maximum legal protection to staff members" and maintain the "independence of the United Nations."[26]

Meanwhile, USUN pressured the government to complete the employee investigations by September 1, before the Ninth General Assembly con-

24. Memorandum for the President, April 29, 1953, 315/1–650, in Box 1251, RG 59, NA.

25. *Ibid.;* Lodge to Dulles, April 23, 1953, 315.3/4–2353, in Box 1254, RG 59, NA; Lodge to Herbert Brownell, May 26, 1953, Reel 2, HCLP, MHS.

26. Hammarskjöld to Lodge, August 27, 1953, Reel 6, HCLP, MHS; Record of the Secretary-General's Private Meetings, August 28, 1953, File 1, Box 2, Series 1.1.3, The Executive Office: Office of the Executive Assistant (1946–1961), Office of the Secretary-General, UN Archives, New York.

vened. Lodge knew that only completion of the process would quiet the international furor. As his frustration with the snail's pace of the security bureaucracy mounted, he began a one-man lobbying campaign in Washington, D.C. Like a broken record, he constantly repeated his theme—prompt clearance was imperative to restore American confidence in the UN—to any and all in the State Department, the cabinet, the Executive Office, Congress, the FBI, and the Civil Service Commission who might be able to speed the process.[27]

It was not to be. Insufficient funding and confusion over the application of successive executive orders thwarted Lodge's hopes for an early completion of the investigations. As Philip Young explained in mid-April, the screening was delayed while the commission awaited a new executive order that would entail new procedures. Lodge justifiably complained that delay was unnecessary. Executive Order No. 10422 was adequate, and, more important, the secretary-general's office already had been "educated" and was functioning smoothly under that order.[28] On August 20, McLeod delivered the anticipated bad news, notifying him that a lack of funds and personnel to conduct the overseas investigations necessary for most employees of international organizations made the September 1 deadline unattainable. Even a last-minute intervention by Dulles, in the form of a telegram to American embassies in Europe instructing them to give priority to the security clearances for UN employees, was not sufficient to overcome the early delays.[29]

Lodge's initially cordial relations with the other departmental representatives on this issue began to show signs of strain. He faulted Lourie's office for timid requests for the necessary financial resources from Congress and failing to keep USUN informed of its progress. He even intimated that the gla-

27. Lodge to Eisenhower, January 29, 1953, Reel 28, HCLP, MHS; Lodge to Donold Lourie, April 20, 1953, 315.3/4–2053, in Box 1254, RG 59, NA; Cabinet Meeting Notes, October 9, 22, 1953, in Box 2, Cabinet Series, EP, AWF, EL; *MTCD,* Reel 1, Lodge and Dulles, October 7, 1953.

28. Lodge to Young, April 15, 1953, in folder marked "UN—Loyalty Program for Personnel," Box 79, HCLP, MHS; Young to Lodge, April 13, 1953, same box; Lodge to Herbert Brownell, March 1, 1953, in folder marked "Henry Cabot Lodge, Jr.: 1953," Box 72, J. F. Dulles Papers, Mudd Library.

29. Lodge to Brownell, February 7, 1953, in folder marked "UN—Loyalty Program for Personnel, Box 79, HCLP, MHS; Brownell to Lodge, February 13, 1953, same box; McLeod to Lodge, August 20, 1953, 315.3/8–2053, in Box 1254, RG 59, NA; Telegram from Dulles to U.S. embassies in Paris, London, Rome, and Bern, August 14, 1953, 315.3/8–1453, same box.

cial pace of the process resulted from "an unwillingness on the part of people to face up to difficult issues."[30]

By November, Lodge had succeeded in conveying his concern to Eisenhower. Responding to yet another Lodge missive, Eisenhower agreed that it might be necessary to "do something more drastic" to resolve the continuing questions about personnel security. But he ignored Lodge's advice to intervene personally in order to give the issue the visibility it deserved. Consequently, the investigatory agencies did not clear all USUN employees until late April, 1954. The completion of the process for the American employees at the UN took even longer.[31]

By the time it concluded its investigations in December, 1954, the IOELB had reviewed almost four thousand cases. On the whole, it accomplished its unenviable task with remarkable circumspection. According to attorneys who handled cases before it, the board "was aware of the limitations of anonymous accusations, and understanding of the changes in the political climate since the 1930s." Despite its efforts to conduct the hearings without a media circus, a few cases, most notably a twelve-hour hearing for Ralph Bunche, who was then serving as director of the Department of Trusteeship and Information for Non-Self-Governing Territories, became public. The administration handled even these cases with reasonable moderation. Both Lodge and Dulles personally examined the FBI's file on Bunche. Claiming that it would be virtually impossible for black Americans to "come through an FBI check lily white because all of their organizations had been infiltrated at one time or another," Dulles advocated clearing Bunche and others in a similar position.[32]

Late in August, 1953, the Administrative Tribunal delivered a devastating blow to the administration's efforts to shift attention from the loyalty is-

30. Lodge to Eisenhower, December 2, 1953, Reel 28, HCLP, MHS; Lodge to Brownell, March 31, 1953, in folder marked "Henry Cabot Lodge, Jr.," Box 72, J. F. Dulles Papers, Mudd Library; Lodge to Donold Lourie, April 20, 1953, 315.3/4–2053, in Box 1254, RG 59, NA.

31. Lodge to Eisenhower, December 2, 1953, June 3, 1954, Reel 28, HCLP, MHS. See also New York *Times,* April 27, 1954, p. 21.

32. Ralph S. Brown, Jr., *Loyalty and Security: Employment Tests in the United States* (New Haven, 1958), 79; *MTCD,* Reel 1, Dulles and Leonard Hall, May 6, 1953; *MTCD,* Reel 1, Dulles, Allen Dulles, Lodge, and Wilbur, June 29, 1953; *MTCD,* Reel 1, Dulles and Lodge, August 28, 1953; Caute, *The Great Fear,* 331; New York *Times,* May 26, 1954, p. 9; New York *Times,* May 29, 1954, p. 1.

sue. The tribunal announced that it had reversed Lie's decisions in eleven of the dismissals of American employees. When Hammarskjöld declined (after meeting with Wadsworth) to reinstate them, it awarded compensation that totaled almost $180,000.[33]

The United States denounced the decision. The State Department insisted that the secretary-general and not the Administrative Tribunal had the power to establish staff standards of conduct and criticized the tribunal's failure to verify the dismissed employees' charges. Moreover, in a move that illuminated its primary concern, the administration asserted that the tribunal should have based its decision primarily on an assessment of the "political advisability" of reinstating the employees rather than on a legal evaluation. Left unarticulated, but clearly implied, was the belief that had the tribunal considered the political ramifications of its judgment on American public opinion, it would have upheld Lie's decision.[34] Interestingly, in espousing a political argument to denounce the decision, the administration had swung 180 degrees from Lodge's earlier description of the issue as "merely an administrative question." At the very least, it appears that in the spring of 1953 the State Department had formulated its policy without adequate consideration of its long-term strategy in the event of an adverse Administrative Tribunal ruling.

Once again, Ambassador Lodge served as the administration's point man on this issue. Following the basic lines of the State Department arguments, Lodge too attacked the decision on both legal and political grounds. He noted that the tribunal did not include an American jurist and questioned the propriety of having justices unfamiliar with American law ruling on a case about the Fifth Amendment of the U.S. Constitution. To permit individuals under congressional investigation to plead the Fifth Amendment, Lodge lectured the General Assembly, would undermine the congressional power of investigation upon which the federal system was based. Ominously injecting domestic politics into the heated situation, the former senator

---

33. *MTCD*, Reel 1, Dulles and Lodge, September 3, 1953.

34. Telegram from Dulles to USUN, November 25, 1953, in *FRUS, 1952–1954*, III, 375; Circular telegram from Dulles, October 30, 1953, in Box 32, Lot 82 D 211, RG 59, NA; Position Paper, "Statement of Alternative United States Positions on Problems Arising from Administrative Tribunal Decisions," October 16, 1953, in *FRUS, 1952–1954*, III, 356–57; Telegram from Dulles to the U.S. embassy in the United Kingdom, November 25, 1953, in *FRUS, 1952–1954*, III, 374–75.

warned that neither Congress nor the American people would countenance the allocation of tax money to indemnify those who sought to subvert the U.S. government. Consequently, Lodge asserted, the General Assembly could and should overrule the tribunal. The General Assembly should be mindful that it was not simply deciding the fate of "a few obscure and largely clerical former employees," but was playing with American public opinion, the alienation of which "could maim and very possibly destroy the United Nations."[35]

When the General Assembly discussed the matter in November, 1953, the United States refused to vote appropriations to pay the staff. Presenting the U.S. position, Congressman James P. Richards seconded Lodge's criticism of the decision in a November 19 speech in Committee V (Administrative and Budgetary). Richards contended that the Administrative Tribunal had overstepped its authority and had impinged on the secretary-general's discretionary power in staff matters. Because the tribunal was subordinate to the secretary-general, it should not have overridden two secretaries-general's decisions. He urged the assembly to refuse to dispense the indemnities.[36]

The State Department dissected the decision in search of a legal loophole and pressured its Western European allies to overturn the decision in the General Assembly. Reminding France's minister of foreign affairs, Georges Bidault, that the United States frequently supported unpopular French positions, especially on colonial questions, Secretary Dulles made it clear that he expected a "sympathetic attitude" from the French delegation.[37] He also sent a circular telegram directing U.S. officials to request the governments to

35. "Administrative Tribunal Speech, Draft #3," n.d., p. 11, in folder marked "UN—Loyalty Program for Personnel," Box 79, HCLP, MHS; *SISS Hearings,* 83rd Cong., 1st Sess., pt. 3, September 24, 1953, pp. 497–98; Memorandum of Conversation, November 4, 1953, in *FRUS, 1952–1954,* III, 365–66.

36. "Personnel Policy in the United Nations," James P. Richards statement on November 19, 1953, *Department of State Bulletin,* December 21, 1953, pp. 874–75.

37. Telegram from Dulles to the U.S. embassy in Paris, October 21, 1953, in folder marked "October 1953 (3)," Box 5, Chronological Series, Dulles Papers, EL; Telegram from Dulles to the U.S. embassy in the United Kingdom, November 3, 1953, in *FRUS, 1952–1954,* III, 361–63; Telegram from Dulles to the U.S. embassy in France, November 4, 1953, in *FRUS, 1952–1954,* III, 363–64; Telegram from Dulles to the U.S. embassy in France, November 13, 1953, in *FRUS, 1952–1954,* III, 369; Memorandum of Conversation, November 19, 1953, 313.2/11–1953, in Box 1250, RG 59, NA; Memorandum of Conversation, November 25, 1953, 320.15/11–2553, in Box 1295, RG 59, NA.

which they were accredited to support the American refusal to pay the awards, though he conceded that he expected it to do little good and thought the five-thousand-dollar charge a waste of money.[38]

And a waste of money it was. The nation's Western European allies and even many Latin American nations insisted that the tribunal had the authority to make such a decision.[39] Hammarskjöld agreed, telling his staff it would be "inappropriate for the General Assembly to revise the decisions of a tribunal it had itself constituted."[40] On December 17, 1953, the General Assembly voted to pay the compensation, and the United States threatened to withdraw. Dulles determined to take the question of whether the General Assembly could override the tribunal to the International Court of Justice. In an effort to obtain American approval, the General Assembly changed the Rules of the Administrative Tribunal to allow appeals to the ICJ for an advisory opinion. But on July 13, 1954, the Court ruled 9 to 3 in support of the tribunal's right to make the final judgment.

38. Circular telegram from Dulles, November 2, 1953, 315.3/11–253, in Box 1255, RG 59, NA; *MTCD,* Reel 1, Dulles and Lodge, October 31, 1953. See also "Written Statement of the United States of America on the Questions Submitted to the ICJ by the United Nations General Assembly by Resolution Dated December 9, 1953, Relating to the Power of the General Assembly Regarding Awards of Compensation Made by the United Nations Administrative Tribunal," n.d., in Box 50, Lot 82 D 211, RG 59, NA; Telegram from the State Department to the U.S. embassy in Paris, November 9, 1953, in Box 32, Lot 82 D 211, RG 59, NA.

39. Telegram from Lodge to Dulles, "USUN Information Digest," October 29, 1953, 310.5/10–2953, in Box 1249, RG 59, NA; Telegram from Lodge to Dulles, October 30, 1953, 310.5/10–3053, same box; Telegram from Lodge to Dulles, November 4, 1953, 310.5/11–4531, same box; Telegram from Penfield (James Kedzie Penfield, U.S. chargé d'affaires in London) to the Department of State, November 9, 1953, in *FRUS, 1952–1954,* III, 366; Telegram from Achilles (Theodore Carter Achilles, chargé d'affaires in Paris) to the Secretary of State, November 17, 1953, in *FRUS, 1952–1954,* III, 369–70; Telegram from Lodge to Dulles, "USUN Information Digest," November 18, 1953, 310.5/11–1853, in Box 1249, RG 59, NA; Memorandum of Conversation, November 19, 1953, 313.2/11–1953, in Box 1250, RG 59, NA; Telegram from Achilles to the Department of State, November 23, 1953, in *FRUS, 1952–1954,* III, 371–72; Telegram from Lodge to Dulles, "USUN Information Digest," November 24, 1953, 310.5/11–2453, in Box 1249, RG 59, NA; Memorandum of Conversation, November 25, 1953, 313.2/11–2553, in Box 1295, RG 59, NA; Telegram from Alger (Frederick M. Alger, U.S. ambassador in Belgium) to the Department of State, November 27, 1953, *FRUS, 1952–1954,* III, 372–73.

40. Record of the Secretary General's Private Meetings, October 23, 1953, in File 1, Box 2, Series 1.1.3, The Executive Office: Office of the Executive Assistant (1946–1961), Office of the Secretary General, UN Archives, New York.

In the final skirmish of this two-year conflict, the administration sought both to prevent paying the awards with American taxpayer money and to avoid charges "of flouting an advisory opinion of the Court." Although it had lost the war, the administration won this final battle. The United Nations paid the awards in January, 1955, through a Special Indemnity Fund financed by taxes on UN staff salaries.[41]

The second facet of the administration's plan to restore American trust in the United Nations addressed the ostensible threat to national security posed by foreign representatives and staff in New York City. These suspicions were captured by a reporter at the UN who asserted that "a spy sent here with diplomatic credentials by a foreign power to steal military or defense secrets can take refuge behind the ramparts of the UN." Critics believed that the Soviet mission served as Moscow's "high command post." It was "the nerve center on this side of the Atlantic Ocean for almost every phase of the Kremlin's subversive activities in North and South America."[42]

The Subcommittee to Investigate the Administration of the Internal Security Act and Other Internal Security Laws kept the matter on the domestic political agenda. In March, 1954, it reported "the existence of a 'fifth-column' in the Secretariat," including citizens from the United States and other non-Communist countries. Furthermore, it charged the Soviets with using their diplomatic privileges to conceal espionage and subversive activities. Senator William E. Jenner warned that if the UN could not ensure that its staff would not "be used as a beachhead for the advance of Communist power," congressional reconsideration of U.S. financial support for and membership in the international organization would be in order.[43] The administration responded to this alarm, anger, and frustration by revising the existing security measures at the offices of the U.S. mission. It also placed

41. Memo to Acting Secretary of State Walter Bedell Smith from David McKendree Key, September 7, 1954, 320/9–754, in Box 1290, RG 59, NA; Position Paper, "Administrative Tribunal Awards: Advisory Opinion of the International Court of Justice," September 9, 1954, in Box 32, Lot 82 D 211, RG 59, NA; Telegram from Dulles to Certain Diplomatic Missions, December 11, 1954, in *FRUS, 1952–1954,* III, 409–11.

42. Pierre J. Huss and George Carpozi, Jr., *Red Spies in the U.N.* (New York, 1965), 10, 11.

43. *SISS Hearings,* "Activities of United States Citizens Employed by the United Nations," 83rd Cong., 2nd Sess., March 22, 1954, p. 49; Jenner to Lodge, July 16, 1954, in *FRUS, 1952–1954,* III, 400–402.

new restrictions on foreign delegations, foreign nationals employed at the UN, and representatives of nongovernmental organizations who wished to attend UN meetings.

The first order of business was to evaluate and if necessary upgrade the security of the U.S. mission. Unlike UN Headquarters, USUN did have classified information and sensitive intraoffice records. In addition, confidential consultations were held on the premises, several floors of an office building at 2 Park Avenue. Although the security measures included thrice-yearly checks of the building, thorough briefings on security precautions, and the maintenance of proper facilities for burning secret papers, Lodge was not satisfied.[44]

Lodge quickly decided that security requirements necessitated the relocation of USUN to a separate building. The ambassador's determination to enhance the prestige of the U.S. mission and his own office of U.S. representative undoubtedly influenced his decision. Nonetheless, his security concerns were well-founded. A State Department survey concluded that housing USUN in a commercial building was "a serious and major security deficiency" that "constitute[d] a risk to the national security more than is calculated and beyond a reasonable degree of safety." Armed with official confirmation, Lodge requested the services of U.S. Marines in guarding the existing offices, asserting that the security officers supplied by the General Services Administration did not provide adequate protection. To bolster his case he noted that USUN was the only American embassy not under guard by the Marines.[45]

Careful enforcement of the existing security regulations and the institution of new measures met the immediate dangers. Still, the administration seriously considered relocating USUN to a federal government office building, before rejecting the idea because of the prohibitive cost of the remodeling that would have been necessary to meet USUN needs. Lodge also began a quest for congressional approval of a new building solely for the U.S. mis-

44. Journal entries, January 26, 27, 1953, Reel 17, HCLP, MHS; *Hearings Before the Subcommittee on International Organizations and Movements of the Committee on Foreign Affairs,* July 8, 1953, p. 15; Lodge to Samuel D. Boykin (director, Bureau of Security and Consular Affairs), January 25, February 24, 1953, 315/1–650, in Box 1251, RG 59, NA.

45. "Memorandum Re: Security Survey of USUN" by Scott (probably Walter Kenneth Scott, deputy assistant secretary of state), February 25, 1953, 315/1–650, in Box 1251, RG 59, NA; Lodge to Lourie, April 30, 1953, 310.3/7–150, in Box 1238, RG 59, NA.

sion. His efforts did not come to fruition until 1959, when construction began on a new headquarters—a fifteen-story building located at First Avenue and East Forty-fifth Street, directly across the avenue from the General Assembly building.[46]

Lodge was far less successful in his simultaneous effort to acquire better personal accommodations. He asserted that the representative's current residence in a suite at the Waldorf Astoria Hotel raised security concerns. Although his fears were perhaps exaggerated, there was an element of truth in the ambassador's warning that "hotel servants and hotel accommodations are a prolific source of clandestine information and are a happy hunting ground for those who wish to place microphones in places where secret conversations are being conducted." Moreover, Lodge maintained that it was virtually impossible to create the proper atmosphere for diplomatic entertaining "in a large, impersonal commercial establishment." Larger dining facilities also were essential to entertain more than forty people at a time—the maximum capacity of the Waldorf Astoria apartment. Lodge therefore sought, unsuccessfully, to relocate the official residence to a private home.[47]

The administration next turned its attention to a series of far more controversial matters—the establishment of security measures to be applied to non-Americans. The first priority was to limit, if it could not prevent entirely, the Soviet Union's use of the UN as a base for spying. By controlling the issuance of visas, the administration attempted to impose restraints on the movements of Communist-bloc nationals, keeping them within the UN Headquarters District and the immediate vicinity.

The Justice Department initiated this effort. It argued that Communist-owned properties such as the Soviet estate on Long Island gravely hindered its espionage investigations. Early in February, 1953, the department requested the Interdepartmental Committee on Internal Security to issue special visas to Communist personnel. In a *quid pro quo* in light of the restrictions imposed

---

46. Lodge to Joseph M. Dodge (director, Bureau of the Budget), May 27, 1953, 310.311/5–2753, in Box 1238, RG 59, NA; Lodge to Henderson, September 9, 1955, 310.311/9–955, in Box 1241, RG 59, NA; Henderson to Lodge, September 19, 1955, 310.311/9–955, same box; New York *Times,* April 25, 1953, p. 8, May 9, 1953, p. 8; Lodge to Henderson, September 1, 1958, in folder marked "US-UN Bldg: 1956–60," Box 79, HCLP, MHS.

47. Lodge to Lourie, May 27, 1953, 310.311/2753, in Box 1238, RG 59, NA; Lodge to Dulles, March 14, 1957, Reel 5, HCLP, MHS; Statement before the Senate Appropriations Committee, May 1, 1957, in folder marked "1957: Statements and Letters," Box 113, HCLP, MHS.

upon U.S. diplomats in the USSR, the special visas would permit them to reside or travel only within the borough of Manhattan of the City of New York. Violation of these limits would constitute grounds for deportation. The State Department, though apprehensive about the impact on American relations with UN members, agreed to support the move if the Justice Department believed that it was imperative for national security purposes.[48]

Lodge had misgivings. He feared that in combating a relatively minor threat the administration might do greater harm to American foreign policy. The freedom of the American press and the travel permission granted to representatives of Communist nations in Washington, D.C., Lodge pointed out, already provided the Communists with more information than they could possibly acquire at the UN. Moreover, Lodge noted that the Soviet Union had not filled its quota of UN employees, an action it would have taken if it viewed the UN as a valuable command post for espionage. He cautioned that restrictions might alienate support for the United States, especially at a time when tensions were already high because of the loyalty investigations. Furthermore, restrictions might negate the propaganda advantage inherent in the image of the United States as a land of freedom in contrast with the closed society of the Soviet Union, and might give the Soviets "an opportunity to play the martyrs" if they were forbidden to use their Long Island estate. Finally, a tightening of security procedures might undermine the conciliatory tone of Eisenhower's April 16 "Chance for Peace" speech.[49]

Despite Lodge's opposition, beginning early in 1955 the administration quietly moved to confine Communist-bloc delegates to the area within a twenty-five-mile radius of Columbus Circle, in midtown Manhattan. Permission was required for travel outside this area. The State Department justified the restrictions as a response to corresponding restrictions on U.S. diplomatic personnel in Communist countries.[50] Clearly, in this case the United

48. "Memorandum for the Standing Committee" by the Interdepartmental Committee on Internal Security, February 10, 1953, in *FRUS, 1952–1954,* III, 237–39; Acting Secretary of State Walter Bedell Smith draft letter to Attorney General of the United States (Brownell), March 6, 1953, in *FRUS, 1952–1954,* III, 241.

49. Memorandum, Lodge to Hickerson, April 28, 1953, in *FRUS, 1952–1954,* III, 269–70; *Hearing Before the Committee on Foreign Relations,* July 23, 1953, p. 15; Lodge to Brownell, February 9, 1953, in folder marked "UN—Loyalty Program for Personnel," Box 79, HCLP, MHS.

50. Summary of Major Decisions, July 19, 1954, Reel 86, State Department Microfilm, J. F. Dulles Papers, Mudd Library; *MTCD,* Reel 3, Lodge and Dulles, December 22, 1953.

States went beyond safeguarding its national security and sought an unfair advantage from its position as host country. Indeed, neither the international agreements establishing the UN Headquarters in the United States nor customary international law sanctioned such actions. Legally, retaliatory restrictions could be imposed only on delegations in Washington, D.C.

The administration also considered means of exerting greater control over non-Communist foreign employees of the United Nations. Unlike the diplomatic personnel of member delegations, these foreigners had not been investigated by their governments. In this instance, Lodge did not dismiss the SISS charge of a "fifth column" in the UN. Indeed, he felt the committee's concern about foreign employees was "legitimate." Lodge worried that these Communist sympathizers had access, at least theoretically, to the diplomatic pouches of the UN and their own nations and enjoyed opportunities to travel and conceivably even transport espionage material in their baggage. Lodge recommended that the New York customs authorities check the baggage of these employees and that the federal government place limits on their freedom of movement. Furthermore, he suggested that U.S. investigatory agencies supply non-Communist governments with any information they possessed on the loyalty of their nationals and urge these countries to check the background of their citizens employed by the UN.[51]

Finally, the administration prescribed new security measures for the representatives of nongovernmental organizations. It attempted to eliminate a security risk altogether by denying any type of visa to objectionable NGO representatives. The first case involved Margarette Rae Luckock, a Canadian representing the Women's International Democratic Federation (WIDF), who sought to attend a meeting of the Economic and Social Council's (ECOSOC) Commission on the Status of Women. The Justice Department refused entry to Luckock on the grounds that, as a supporter of Ethel and Julius Rosenberg and the representative of a Communist-dominated organization, she "would probably engage in subversive activities after entry into the U.S."[52] Other cases soon followed.

The United Nations vigorously protested the new visa policy. ECOSOC debated the issue, called on the secretary-general to investigate, and placed the issue on its next agenda. Predictably, Communist nations denounced the

---

51. Lodge to Dulles, April 29, 1954, Reel 4, HCLP, MHS.
52. Telegram from Lodge to the Department of State, March 25, 1953, in *FRUS, 1952–1954*, III, 250–51.

action, charging the United States with a violation of Section 11 of the Headquarters Agreement, which stated that the federal government could not impede the transit of representatives of recognized NGOs to UN Headquarters. The Departments of State and Justice maintained that the United States had accepted the Headquarters Agreement subject to the provisions of Public Law 357, a joint resolution of the Eightieth Congress stipulating the right to protect American national security. The United States therefore had the authority to decide that aliens excluded under the Immigration and Nationality Act also could be excluded under the U.S. reservation to the Headquarters Agreement. The UN Legal Department, contending that the reservation was invalid, insisted that the dispute should be referred to negotiation as outlined in Section 21(a) of the Headquarters Agreement.[53]

Anxious to avoid a debate on the question by ECOSOC or the General Assembly, the Eisenhower administration sought to resolve the matter privately with the secretary-general. Lodge agreed, eager to minimize negative repercussions with friendly delegations and to protect the most effective weapon in the United States psychological warfare arsenal—its reputation as a free society. Also important was his desire to obtain a more significant role in the decision-making process. The former senator was too sensitive about his place on the bureaucratic ladder to tolerate being a mere operative of the State Department. He argued that it was impossible for him to respond promptly to Soviet attacks if the State Department did not keep him fully apprised of its reasons for denying visas to NGO representatives. And being apprised, he could in turn inform Hammarskjöld, which was essential if the United States desired the secretary-general's cooperation.[54]

---

53. Telegram from Lodge to the Department of State, March 16, 1953, in *FRUS, 1952–1954*, III, 247; Telegram from Lodge to the Department of State, March 18, 1953, in *FRUS, 1952–1954*, III, 249; "Admission of Representatives of Non-Governmental Organizations Enjoying Consultative Status," in *FRUS, 1952–1954*, III, 257–60; United Nations, Economic and Social Committee, Doc. E/2397, VII, April 10, 1953. For a legal analysis of the administration's actions, see Memorandum by Meeker (Leonard C. Meeker, assistant legal adviser for United Nations affairs), Part I, April 15, 1953, and Part III, April 15, 1953, in *FRUS, 1952–1954*, III, 262–68; Memorandum Prepared Jointly by the Department of State and the Department of Justice, May 4, 1953, in *FRUS, 1952–1954*, III, 275–78; Leo Gross, "Immunities and Privileges of Delegations to the United Nations," *International Organization,* XXX (1976), 483–520.

54. Telegram from Smith to USUN, April 10, 1953, 340/4–1053, in Box 1314, RG 59, NA; Telegram from Lodge to Department of State, April 23, 1953, in *FRUS, 1952–1954,* III, 268–69; Hammarskjöld to Lodge, June 22, 1953, same volume, 293–95; Lodge to Hammarskjöld,

The Department of State and the secretary-general agreed that a "practical working solution" for this messy legal conflict was the only realistic option. An interdepartmental meeting led by Brownell, Lodge, and Lourie hammered out such a *modus vivendi,* though noting that it was to remain in effect only for the duration of Lodge's and Hammarskjöld's tenures in office. The administration decided that in order to avoid the often arbitrary decisions of consular officers, the denial of a visa would require the personal approval of the secretary of state. Questionable aliens granted visas would be restricted to the area within the boundaries of 9th Avenue, 98th Street, Franklin D. Roosevelt Drive, and 24th Street, and subject to deportation if they engaged in activities outside the scope of their official duties. Lodge also secured his key point. In future cases he would be kept informed and would have the discretionary authority to share this information with Hammarskjöld. Conceding that as the host country the United States had a special right to deny visas to those who might plot against it, Hammarskjöld acquiesced in what he described as a "gentlemen's agreement."[55]

This "gentlemen's agreement" did not still the furor. As the March, 1954, meeting of the Economic and Social Council approached, the United States and the Communist bloc prepared to do battle over this developing cold war issue. Lodge, in particular, believed that further visa delays or denials would leave the United States vulnerable to a Soviet propaganda attack that might alienate the secretary-general and jeopardize Secretariat support for the administration's more comprehensive loyalty and security program. The Soviet "psychological offensive" would be premised, Lodge advised Dulles, "on the theory that our laws were so rigid and our administration of them so unimaginative that they could easily maneuver us into a position whereby we would look both stupid and cowardly by refusing to admit representa-

July 2, 1953, same volume, 296; Lodge to Lourie, July 7, 1953, same volume, 296–97; Hammarskjöld to Lodge, July 3, 1953, same volume, 297–98; Telegram from Wadsworth to Lourie, July 9, 1953, same volume, 298–300; Memorandum from Meeker to Wadsworth, July 22, 1953, same volume, 300–302; Telegram from Lodge to the Department of State, July 24, 1953, same volume, 302–304; Lodge to Lourie, May 19, 1953, 315.3/5–1953, in Box 1255, RG 59, NA; Memorandum, Lodge to Brownell and Lourie, May 19, 1953, in *FRUS, 1952–1954,* III, 278–83.

55. Hammarskjöld to Lodge, July 8, 1953, in *FRUS, 1952–1954,* III, 298–99; Memorandum, Lourie to Lodge, May 29, 1953, same volume, 287–88; Memorandum for the Files, by Harris H. Huston (special assistant to the undersecretary of state for administration), June 1, 1953, same volume, 288–90; Lodge to Lourie, June 1, 1953, same volume, 290–93.

tives of organizations which are entitled to attend meetings of the United Nations."[56]

The administration prepared to preempt a Soviet propaganda attack by assuming the offensive. Lodge became the driving force behind a "concerted program" by the State and Justice Departments, the USUN Public Affairs Office, and C. D. Jackson's Psychological Warfare staff to prepare and disseminate counterpropaganda outlining the Soviet Union's far more egregious violations of cultural and information freedom. Warning of the "obvious intent [of the] Soviets to launch [a] propaganda offensive" and the absence of support for the American position, USUN urged the State Department to admit two Communists representing the World Federation of Trade Unions. The government granted a visa to one of the representatives, Jan Dessau, but denied the request of the second, Iraj Eskandary, because he had been convicted of murder. Lodge successfully defended the decision. He vowed indignantly that the United States could never safely allow the Headquarters Agreement "to be used as a device to permit the importation into the United States of desperados and trigger men." By associating the Communist cause with a criminal, Lodge put the Communists on the defensive, quieted opponents of the "gentlemen's agreement," and helped defuse the controversy for six years.[57]

The Eisenhower administration's loyalty program for American employees at the United Nations thus was motivated by a confluence of factors. It attempted to remedy the perceived laxity of the preceding Democratic administration, to quiet domestic critics, and to restore the public's confidence in the UN. Administration officials did not act out of a genuine belief that Americans (or even American Communists) on the staffs of the United Na-

56. Lodge to Brownell, February 1, 1954, in folder marked "United Nations (1)," Box 99, Confidential File, ER, EL; Lodge to Dulles, March 31, 1954, Reel 4, HCLP, MHS; *MTCD,* Reel 2, Lodge and Dulles, March 20, 1954.

57. Lodge to Brownell, February 1, 1954, in folder marked "United Nations (1)," Box 99, Confidential File, ER, EL; Telegram from Wadsworth to the Secretary of State, March 4, 1954, 340/3–454, in Box 1316, RG 59, NA; Lodge to Dulles, March 31, 1954, Reel 4, HCLP, MHS; Brownell to Lodge, n.d., in folder marked "United Nations (1)," Box 99, Confidential File, ER, EL; Lodge to Lourie, February 12, 1954, in folder marked "United Nations (1)," Box 99, Confidential File, ER, EL; Telegram from Wadsworth to the Secretary of State, March 12, 1954, in Box 1316, RG 59, NA.

tions or the U.S. mission posed a genuine threat to national security. Rather, the establishment of the loyalty program was a calculated political move, in Francis O. Wilcox's opinion one that was "designed to reassure the American people that any confidence they wanted to place in the United Nations and in the State Department were [*sic*] not in fact misplaced."[58]

The administration considered the threat presented by foreign nationals to be more serious. By 1953 heightened cold war tensions had raised the stakes for international espionage. Foreigners posed at least a latent threat that the administration felt it could ignore only at the risk of compromising national security and, of perhaps more immediate concern, invoking the wrath of the conservative wing of the Republican party. Eisenhower was no gambler. Anxious to reunite the divided Republican party and build bipartisan support for his foreign policy, he followed the only logical path. He sought to minimize the risks by designing and implementing a moderate loyalty and security program.

Little evidence thus exists to indicate that Eisenhower used a "hidden-hand" style of leadership to combat the McCarthy forces' assaults on the UN. Although he ultimately proved willing to risk his public popularity to defend the U.S. Army from McCarthy's attacks, the president chose not to do so to defend the United Nations. Domestic political imperatives proved to be of greater import to Eisenhower than individuals' civil liberties or the concept of an international civil service.

As a result, the administration gravely compromised the concept of an international civil service process by the screening and often the actual selection of candidates that occurred during the remainder of the decade.[59] Moreover, the establishment of restrictions on some foreign delegations, UN staff members, and NGO representatives represented a disproportionate response to the actual threat. Overall, the attempt to impose standards of ideological purity on a universal international organization set a dangerous precedent and raised troubling questions about the degree to which the United States would attempt to manipulate the organization.

Perhaps most important, the administration's preoccupation with what were essentially personnel issues (though admittedly complicated by their

58. The Reminiscences of Francis O. Wilcox, April 3, 1972, pp. 29–30, COHP, Butler Library, Columbia University.

59. Edwin H. Fedder, "United States Loyalty Procedures and the Recruitment of International Personnel," *Western Political Quarterly,* XV (1962), 705–12.

cold war implications) prevented it from aggressively pursuing solutions to grave problems in a host of substantive areas. Pressing questions and problems, ranging from formulating a strategy to meet the Soviet propaganda challenge in the United Nations to negotiating an armistice in Korea, demanded attention. But having put its house in order, the Eisenhower administration began to devote more attention to these matters.

4

INFLUENCING INTERNATIONAL OPINION
Psychological Warfare at the UN

Before it made a decision about the extent to which it would enter into a partnership with the United Nations, the Eisenhower administration had to determine whether the UN was capable of advancing American goals in the cold war. The new administration fully appreciated the UN's unique potential for allowing the United States to do battle with its ideological foe in a war of words and to avoid using atomic bombs. Particularly from 1953 to 1955, the period in which the cold war propaganda battle between the United States and the USSR dominated Security Council meetings and UN business in general, the UN would become a forum to present the nation's policies to an international audience and build worldwide opposition to the policies of the Communist bloc.

Eisenhower opposed communism and hoped to liberate those held in its clutches. At the same time, he insisted upon somehow keeping the costs incurred in pursuit of these objectives at manageable levels. Early in his presidency he organized "Operation Solarium." This strategic-planning project was to take a new look at how to achieve national security while balancing the nation's interests and threats and, more specifically, holding the military budget in check. In October, 1953, the National Security Council approved NSC 162/2, which was an outgrowth of this project. Articulating the basic premises of the New Look, NSC 162/2 endorsed a reduction in conventional military forces and approved a shift to less costly alternatives, namely heavier reliance on American atomic superiority as well as covert action, alliance diplomacy, negotiation, and psychological warfare. This endorsement of the nuclear alternative gave rise to the concepts of massive retaliation and brinksmanship which are so closely identified with the Eisenhower-Dulles effort to eliminate "atheistic communism." Far less attention, however, has been paid to the other dimensions of the New Look, particularly the administration's increased interest in psychological warfare, a tactic that Eisenhower viewed as rich with intriguing possibilities.

As President Eisenhower formulated the nation's strategy for waging this new type of cold war, he recognized the need for new weapons and tactics. Indeed, as a military man whose career had spanned the development of the nation's arsenal from cavalry to tanks to atomic bombs, Eisenhower was not one to dismiss out of hand any new weapon, however unorthodox it might appear on first appraisal. He firmly believed that American power emanated not only from the nation's superior military, economic, and political strength, but also from such psychological factors as public opinion and public morale. Driven by this belief in the psychological nature of diplomacy as well as his fiscal conservatism, the new president enthusiastically embraced the concept of psychological warfare as a potentially valuable and relatively inexpensive weapon in the American cold war arsenal. He even appointed a special assistant on psychological warfare to his White House staff. According to this special assistant, Charles Douglas "C. D." Jackson, Eisenhower believed that psychological warfare was "just about the only way to win World War III without having to fight it."[1]

The administration never developed a consensus definition of the term *psychological warfare*. In general it referred to the attempt to create the best possible image of the United States abroad and to exploit events and policies that reflected negatively on Communist nations. All governmental policies, particularly in the fields of defense, economy, politics, and diplomacy, were viewed as potential "weapons." Psychological warfare, Eisenhower wrote, encompassed anything "from the singing of a beautiful hymn up to the most extraordinary kind of physical sabotage."[2]

Propaganda was at the center of the psychological warfare effort. Propo-

1. Blanche Wiessen Cook, *The Declassified Eisenhower: A Divided Legacy* (Garden City, 1981), 177. See also Eisenhower to Gordon Gray (director, Psychological Strategy Board), September 11, 1951, in Galambos, ed., *NATO and the Campaign of 1952,* XII, 533.

2. Quoted in John Lewis Gaddis, *Strategies of Containment: A Critical Appraisal of Postwar American National Security Policy* (New York, 1982), 155.

nents viewed it as the key to winning the battle for the hearts, minds, and ideological allegiance of the world's people, the struggle that was at the core of the cold war. The UN, in turn, assumed a new importance for devotees of psychological warfare. Lodge pointedly observed that "since the United Nations is the place where a great deal of world opinion is made, it is of great psychological value to us." The organization's broad membership, open meetings, and extensive press coverage made it a singular forum for the dissemination of propaganda and the mobilization of world opinion. The United States could use the UN to explain its policies, spotlight communism's failings, emphasize the aggressive nature of the Soviet threat, and build support for the U.S.-led battle against communism. Voting majorities in support of United States positions and opposed to Communist ones became a way to score points in the gamesmanship of the cold war. Success at the UN would prove, to observers both at home and abroad, that the United States was "right" and would thereby provide the national credibility the president, and most Americans, craved.[3]

The Eisenhower administration's decision to use the United Nations as a forum for its cold war propaganda represented a fairly substantial change from the practice of the Truman administration. For the past seven years the Soviet Union had been far more adept at using the United Nations, especially the General Assembly, to spread its propaganda. The Republicans were determined to reverse that trend.[4] Soviet propaganda would no longer go unchallenged. The administration set out to intensify the practice, first begun in a far more limited form after the outbreak of the Korean War, of using the General Assembly "as an instrument of active propaganda."[5]

The State Department's UN Affairs Planning Staff outlined a new ap-

3. "The United Nations and the Cold War," Address to the Inland Daily Press Association, May 25, 1954, in Box 52, HCLP, MHS. The administration operated with a broad definition of propaganda. The State Department's United Nations Affairs Planning Staff defined it as an attempt "to influence the attitudes of others by communicating to them (through either words or actions) broad ideas or concepts." "Propaganda in the United Nations," United Nations Affairs Planning Staff, n.d., in *FRUS, 1952–1954,* III, 106.

4. Elderly and frequently ill, Warren R. Austin, Truman's ambassador to the UN, had failed to press the United States' case with enthusiasm and vigor, and the administration appeared to lack any coherent plan for using the UN in the propaganda battle.

5. Memorandum, "The 1953 Review: Principal Stresses and Strains Facing the United States in the United Nations," United Nations Planning Staff to the Planning Adviser, Bureau of United Nations Affairs (William Sanders), July 27, 1953, in *FRUS, 1952–1954,* III, 86.

proach. Its report identified five general tactics with which the United States could meet the Soviet propaganda threat and also derive greater propaganda benefits. The U.S. delegation should use its speeches in the General Assembly to emphasize the contrast between the United States' positive role in international affairs and the Soviet Union's negative approach; take advantage of the extensive UN press coverage to highlight American positions; "dress up" substantive policies to impress particular audiences; raise nonsubstantive issues that were intended primarily for "winning cold war propaganda advantages with little or no expectation that their ostensible purpose would be achieved directly or within a reasonable time"; and engage in personal diplomacy.[6]

Eisenhower believed that a new approach was not sufficient. It must be accompanied by a restructuring of the national security system. He considered the existing organizational structure for waging the cold war in general, and psychological warfare in particular, to be inadequate, largely because it was too compartmentalized. The president was convinced that the National Security Council had not functioned as a policy-making body, and the Psychological Strategy Board (PSB), established by President Truman in June, 1951, to coordinate the activities of the State and Defense Departments in implementing NSC decisions, had been ineffective because of the absence of close interdepartmental coordination and involvement by senior staff members. "We must," Eisenhower demanded, "bring the dozens of agencies and bureaus into concerted action under an overall scheme of strategy and we must have a firm hand on the tiller to sail the ship along a consistent course."[7]

In January, 1953, Eisenhower established the International Information Activities Committee to determine how to achieve this "concerted action" in integrating psychological warfare into the national security structure. Following the recommendations of the Jackson Committee (named informally after its chair, William H. Jackson), Eisenhower abolished the PSB in September, 1953, and replaced it with an Operations Coordinating Board (OCB) to coordinate the various departments in implementing NSC policies and coordinating psychological strategy. In addition to the members of the

6. "Propaganda in the United Nations," United Nations Affairs Planning Staff, n.d., in *FRUS, 1952–1954,* III, 106, 109–10.

7. Quoted in Robert L. Ivie, "Eisenhower as Cold Warrior," in Martin Medhurst, ed., *Eisenhower's War of Words: Rhetoric and Leadership* (East Lansing, 1994), 12.

PSB (deputy secretary of defense, director of the Mutual Security Administration, undersecretary of state, and the director of the CIA), the OCB would include the director of the Foreign Operations Administration, and the president's special assistant on psychological warfare (whose title was changed to special assistant for cold war planning).[8]

C. D. Jackson provided the "firm hand on the tiller." Whatever his official title, Jackson was a dynamic proponent of the concept of psychological warfare. His boundless energy, supreme faith in his mission, and extensive background in the advertising industry and the press (most recently as a *Time* executive) made him uniquely qualified for this novel post. He soon discovered that in approaching problems from a new perspective he confronted formidable obstacles, including tradition-bound minds and bureaucratic fears of encroachment. Nevertheless, he was convinced that the president's support for his objective and the inextricable linkages between diplomatic, economic, and military policy in the post-war world had created "The Great Opportunity" to inaugurate a new era in American foreign policy.[9]

The president's special assistant on psychological warfare found a willing ally in the new U.S. representative. Lodge believed that the Soviet Union was vulnerable to an American propaganda attack at the United Nations. He considered the UN to be, in the words of Jerry Wadsworth, "the one big hole in the Iron Curtain that they [the Soviets] can't plug up." Lodge embraced the use of psychological warfare as a possible means to widen this hole. He believed that the UN could become "a place in which we can take the Big Truth in order to expose the Big Lie." By demonstrating the fallacy of Soviet charges in an international arena, the United States could unite the free world in the battle against communism.[10]

8. Eisenhower to Dulles, November 26, 1952, in folder marked "Confidential—Memos and Letters (3)," Box 8, Subject Series, Dulles Papers, EL; Memo, "Appraisal Survey of Our Cold War Effort," November 26, 1952, same folder. See also Anna Kasten Nelson, "The 'Top of Policy Hill': President Eisenhower and the National Security Council," *Diplomatic History,* VII (1983), 307–26.

9. Cook, *The Declassified Eisenhower,* 177; Lodge to Jackson, March 9, 1953, Reel 7, HCLP, MHS.

10. "Mobilizing for a Just and Lasting Peace," Wadsworth address to the American Association for the United Nations on March 2, 1953, *Department of State Bulletin,* March 16, 1953, p. 418; Remarks to Conference for Representatives of Non-Governmental Organizations, December 19, 1953, in folder marked "Speeches and Press Releases 1953," Box 109, HCLP, MHS.

Jackson and Lodge were the central figures in the administration's effort to use the United Nations for propaganda purposes. Eagerly following Eisenhower's instructions to place the UN "at the heart of" the psychological warfare operation, they set to work. Their fundamental goal, according to Lodge, was "to take the psychological offensive and have people ask: 'What is the United States going to do?,' instead of asking, as they have in the past: 'What are the Russians going to do?'" Through private meetings and correspondence as well as weekly meetings of the PSB/OCB Committee on the UN, Lodge and Jackson began planning a twofold "fall campaign." The first part of this campaign was to counter Soviet propaganda that arose in the General Assembly. This was to be accomplished through immediate responses to Soviet charges against the United States and a project to use the Soviet propaganda to discredit the USSR. The second part of the campaign consisted of instituting an active anti-Soviet propaganda offensive. This offensive was referred to as the Lodge Human Rights Project, or simply the Lodge Project.[11]

Successful implementation of the campaign demanded broad interagency cooperation. The operational plan was for Jackson, working largely behind the scenes with his staff, the PSB/OCB, and the State Department's intelligence unit to coordinate strategy and tactics and supply Lodge with the "ammunition" he needed on the front lines of the battle at the United Nations. This ammunition would consist of "bullets" (short points to be used in rebuttals), "juicy, 500-word, newsworthy excerpts" that could be used in brief speeches, and sufficient new information to issue "three or four sizzling press releases a week" while the General Assembly was in session.[12] It was

11. Lodge to Jackson, April 23, 1953, Reel 7, HCLP, MHS. Unfortunately, almost all of the information on the Lodge Human Rights Project remains classified. A second project, named "cosmos," was also designed by the PSB and used by Lodge. Very little information on cosmos has been declassified, but it appears to be similar in content to the Lodge Project. See, for example, Memorandum, Twentieth Meeting, OCB Committee on the 8th General Assembly, December 14, 1953, in folder marked "OCB 334 UN (File #1) (4)," Box 102, OCB Central Files, NSC Staff Papers, EL.

12. Lodge Project, n.d. (probably December, 1953), in folder marked "Project Notes (1)," Box 7, C.D. Jackson Records, 1953–1954, EL; Lodge to Jackson, March 9, 1953, Reel 7, HCLP, MHS; Memorandum of PSB Committee on the 8th General Assembly, Sixth Meeting, July 10, 1953, in folder marked "PSB 334 UN (4)," Box 23, Psychological Strategy Board Central Files Series, White House Office: National Security Council Staff Papers, 1948–61, EL; Memorandum, Wallace Irwin, Jr., (Office of Evaluation and Review) to the PSB Com-

hoped that the public information staff at USUN could be enlarged during the General Assembly session to provide on-site assistance with support from an "interdepartmental backstopping committee" in Washington. Specifically, staff was needed to "whip all the less startling material into shape as connected narratives . . . at a level that will appeal to intellectuals." Both groups would benefit from access to the intelligence units at the State Department and Central Intelligence Agency.[13]

Lodge executed the administration's quick-response strategy brilliantly. He determined never to permit Soviet propaganda salvos to go unanswered. If a Soviet representative attacked the United States, a member of the American delegation would respond that same day. A Soviet thrust would be met by an American parry. Under Truman, the State Department had maintained that responding to scurrilous and ludicrous charges only legitimized them. Lodge thought this policy a mistake. Acutely aware of the importance of timing, the former newspaperman argued that only by responding instantly could the United States "top their story by our story, and try to take the headlines away from them." The new U.S. representative also pledged to follow Eisenhower's more general advice to avoid "the blustering and the yelling and screaming in public," and instead adopt a "smiling, polite, clever, firm" demeanor.[14]

Lodge did not worry unduly that he might misspeak during these rebut-

---

mittee on the 8th General Assembly, July 14, 1953, in folder marked "PSB UN (5)," Box 23, Psychological Strategy Board Central Files Series, NSC Staff Papers, EL.

13. Memorandum by Charles I. Norberg (acting deputy assistant director, Office of Coordination), "Program for psychological support for Ambassador Lodge during the 8th session of the General Assembly," April 20, 1953, in folder marked "PSB 334 UN (1)," Box 23, Psychological Strategy Board Central Files Series, NSC Staff Papers, EL; Memorandum, Irwin to George A. Morgan, July 30, 1953, in folder marked "Amb. Henry Cabot Lodge," Box 4, Jackson Records, EL; Memorandum, Irwin to Morgan, May 29, 1953, in folder marked "PSB 334 UN (2)," Box 23, Psychological Strategy Board Central Files Series, NSC Staff Papers, EL; Memorandum for the Record by Irwin, May 22, 1953, in folder marked "Ambassador Henry Cabot Lodge," Box 4, Jackson Records, EL.

14. "The United Nations and the Cold War, Projects," January 1953, Reel 17, HCLP, MHS; Journal entry, January 7, 1953, in folder marked "T-E: 1952–1953," Box 71, HCLP, MHS; Congress, House, *Hearings Before the Subcommittee on International Organizations and Movements of the Committee on Foreign Affairs,* 83rd Cong., 1st Sess., July 8, 1953, p. 91; Smith to Lodge, November 17, 1953, in folder marked "OCB 334.UN (File #1) (2)," Box 102, OCB Central File Series, NSC Staff Papers, EL.

tals. After years in public office and on the campaign trail, he was supremely confident of his parliamentary knowledge and forensic skills. He approached extemporaneous debate with the attitude that "if I don't speak I will always be wrong. I will miss the boat. If I wait three or four days and then make a long legalistic reply I will miss the chance because the correction never catches up."[15]

Lodge did not wait long before unleashing his new weapon. He made his first sustained rebuttal on March 1 in response to an oration by Andrei Vishinsky, the Soviet representative, who accused the U.S. Army of exacting reprisals on Korean and Chinese prisoners of war. Lodge indignantly reminded Vishinsky that the U.S. Army in Korea was essentially the same force that had fought alongside the USSR in World War II. Soviet fears of attack were baseless, for neither the United States nor more specifically its army had changed since 1945. Rather, the Soviet government's apprehensions emanated from the rampant fears that flourished within its tyrannical system. Lodge's defense evoked praise from the commander in chief. Eisenhower lauded Lodge's rebuttal as "a grand effort," which did "not surrender to the Russians the advantage of an exclusive day in the papers."[16]

The project to use Soviet propaganda to discredit the Soviets also came into play quickly. By documenting the falsity of selected charges and depicting them as representative of a larger pattern of deceit, the administration hoped to convince the world that the Communists were liars and prevaricators. The United States directed its counterattack at what was referred to as the "Soviet item." The item was a perennial fixture on the General Assembly agenda; the exact nature of the item changed from year to year, but it always involved some type of allegation of U.S. aggression. In 1953 and 1954 the Soviet item included charges that the United States engaged in subversion and espionage in Communist nations, used bacteriological weapons in Korea, monopolized world trade, and conducted piratical raids on shipping in the China Sea. The administration's response to the first item it faced established a successful pattern of action, which it followed for the remainder of its tenure.

In the spring of 1953, the General Assembly considered an item entitled "Prohibition of Propaganda in Favor of a New War" sponsored by the

15. "How to Handle the Communists," August 21, 1954, p. 3, in Box 78, HCLP, MHS.
16. Eisenhower to Lodge, April 24, 1953, Reel 28, *ibid.*

Czechoslovakian delegation. The item denounced the U.S. Mutual Security Act (MSA), alleging that its $100 million appropriation was targeted for subversion and espionage activities in Communist nations. The State Department directed the U.S. delegation to deny the charge and explain that only $4 million of the fund was allocated to assist escapees from behind the Iron Curtain. Furthermore, the department advised Lodge to shift attention from American to Communist actions by describing why thousands were fleeing and by stressing that the MSA was a necessary response to Soviet aggression, not a belligerent move. Lodge emphatically insisted that the Soviet Union and not the United States was the guilty party. The USSR had spent billions of dollars on propaganda; overthrown legally constituted governments, including Czechoslovakia's in 1948; and oppressed its own citizens. The United States won a resounding victory, turning the "Soviet item" into a resolution criticizing Communist barriers to the free exchange of information.[17]

The second and ultimately more significant part of the United States' psychological warfare strategy was designed to seize the propaganda initiative. Following the recommendation of the State Department UN Affairs Planning Staff review, USUN attempted to set the General Assembly agenda with both its substantive policy and propaganda items. Lodge's ultimate goal was to expose what he believed to be the biggest lie of all—the hypocrisy of communism. He arranged with the Psychological Strategy Board for the preparation of an academic analysis of the fundamental doctrines of Marxism.[18] Using this critique as a basis for its speeches, USUN intended to dem-

17. Position Paper, "Charges of United States Interference in the Internal Affairs of Other States," February 17, 1953, SD/A/C.1/403, in Box 23, Lot 82 D 211, RG 59, NA; Memorandum, "Suggested lines of counter-attack against Soviet UN charges of US subversion and espionage," March 27, 1953, in folder marked "Amb. Henry Cabot Lodge," Box 4, Jackson Records, EL; "Czechoslovak Subversion Charges Against U.S. Refuted," Lodge statements in Committee I on March 23, 25, 1953, *Department of State Bulletin,* April 13, 1953, pp. 539–46.

18. It appears that such an analysis was indeed produced. Two almost exact copies of a thirty-page document, one of which is entitled "Communism: Promise and Fulfillment," are in the National Security Council Staff papers. See Memorandum, F. Bower Evans (OIR/CPI) to Ed Lilly (PSB), October 9, 1953, in folder marked "Lodge Project—Essays (2)," Box 4, OCB Secretariat Series, NSC Staff Papers, EL; "Communism: Promise and Fulfillment," no author, n.d., same folder. A second critique on essentially the same subject, entitled "White Paper Exposing the Doctrine and Record of Communist Imperialism," apparently was writ-

onstrate that the Marxist-Stalinist ideology was neither scientifically nor intellectually valid. By emphasizing "the worst failures of Marxism and omit[ting] those which held out some hope for humanity," USUN hoped to show that Communist political and economic doctrine was fatally flawed.[19]

In order to expose the hypocrisy of the Communist system, the United States had to show that a gulf existed between Communist doctrine and the reality of Soviet actions. The Lodge Project was designed to do just that—draw international attention to the Soviet Union's violations of internationally recognized standards of human rights and international conduct. It would also be instrumental, Lodge hoped, in "reveal[ing] to the world that the Soviet Union [wa]s on the morally wrong side of every great issue."[20]

Ironically, the propaganda offensive was also aimed at the nation's allies. In May, 1953, the PSB expressed concern that "since the death of Stalin the Soviet 'peace offensive' has already considerably softened the will" of both American allies and neutrals to denounce Soviet aggression and human rights abuses. This "softening process, if unchecked," might encourage "appeasement-mindedness" among those fearful of another world war, place the United States in the uncomfortable position of disagreeing with its allies and thereby imperil its leadership of the free world, and tarnish the American image if it alone continued to criticize the USSR. The Lodge Project thus sought to strengthen the bonds among the nation's allies and stiffen the group's resolve by constant reminders of continued Soviet transgressions. It was imperative to do so early, for a series of upcoming issues—from the political conference on Korea to the recognition of Communist China—might generate further discord and dissension among the Western allies.[21]

---

ten in the fall of 1954 for USUN by a Tom Buchanan in the State Department. However, I have not been able to find a copy of this latter critique. On Buchanan's paper, see Memorandum, Harold W. Moseley to Jackson, December 9, 1954, in folder marked "U. N. Misc., 9th Gen. Assembly 1954 (1)," Box 87, Jackson Papers, EL.

19. "Projects," January, 1953, Reel 17, HCLP, MHS; Jackson to Lodge, March 31, 1953, Reel 7, *ibid.;* John C. Ross (deputy representative in the Security Council) to Wallace Irwin, Jr., May 27, 1953, Reel 7, *ibid.*

20. Telegram from Lodge to Dulles, February 9, 1953, 320/2–953, in Box 1287, RG 59, NA.

21. "Exploitation of Soviet, Satellite, and Chinese Communist Psychological Vulnerabilities Before and During the Eighth U. N. General Assembly," May 28, 1953, in folder marked "Lodge's Human Rights Project (1)," Box 4, White House Office: National Security Council Staff: Records, 1948–1961, EL.

By early spring, the Lodge Human Rights Project included at least twenty possible topics to be used by USUN in exposing Soviet hypocrisy. The National Security Council, Dulles, and members and staff of the OCB all proposed items, but Lodge and Jackson appear to have contributed the majority of the ideas. The resulting list of topics and suggestions for their exploitation was divided into four sections, each of which addressed a different type of Soviet transgression. The first section covered the violation of rights within the Soviet empire. The second group enumerated the diverse types of Soviet external aggression. The third category covered Soviet relations with "the Free World." The fourth category, labeled "the Iron Curtain," focused on the manner in which the USSR had cut the Communist bloc off from access to the international community. According to the administration, the "exploitation of each topic would have the dual purpose of putting pressure on the Soviets to alter their conduct and calling the attention of the free world to the injustices of Soviet actions and the obstacles they place in the path of world peace."[22]

The United States experienced mixed success in its propaganda offensive. When it was well prepared—basing its allegations on incontrovertible evidence and conducting advance consultations with its allies—and tactically flexible, it was able to command convincing majorities. USUN's orchestration of the forced-labor issue provides a textbook example of the advantages derived from thorough preparation. In response to American urging, the General Assembly in 1950 established the UN-ILO (International Labor Organization) Ad Hoc Committee on Forced Labor. The committee's final, six-hundred-page report, released in the spring of 1953, documented the use of forced labor for political punishment and economic gain behind the Iron Curtain. The Department of State was eager to maximize the psychological value of the report, which it described as "one of the most effective propaganda items for the representatives of the free world countries." USUN, however, insisted upon first acquiring the assent of the nation's Western Eu-

22. "List of Soviet Vulnerabilities for Possible Exploitation at the UN," April 30, 1953, in folder marked "Amb. Henry Cabot Lodge," Box 4, Jackson Records, EL; Memorandum, Horace S. Craig to George A. Morgan, April 28, 1953, in folder marked "PSB 334 UN (1)," PSB Central Files Series, NSC Staff Papers, EL; "'Human Rights' Project: Suggested Topics for Intelligence Development," Irwin (PSB), May 19, 1953, in folder marked "Ambassador Henry Cabot Lodge," Box 4, Jackson Records, EL; "Lodge Project," n.d. (probably December, 1953), in folder marked "Project Notes (1)," Box 7, Jackson Records, EL.

ropean allies (some of whom were miffed because the report criticized labor practices in their colonies) before General Assembly consideration of the issue. Assured of allied support, the U.S. delegation made the most of the damaging evidence compiled under international auspices, mercilessly denouncing Soviet hypocrisy in describing the USSR as a "workers' paradise."[23]

In contrast, the Lodge Project was only mildly successful in its attempt to secure General Assembly denunciation of the Communists' alleged perpetration of atrocities against UN prisoners in Korea. In this case, the initiative suffered from hasty presentation, the failure to adequately consult beforehand with U.S. allies, and the absence of corroborating evidence from a neutral investigatory body. On October 30, 1953, Lodge requested that the General Assembly include the item on its agenda. The administration's publicly professed aim was to heighten international outrage to such an extent that the Communists would terminate their mistreatment of prisoners and observe internationally recognized standards of human rights.[24]

But closer analysis belies this declared intent. By October 30 the armistice was in effect and most of the prisoners of war had already been exchanged. Furthermore, neither North Korea nor the People's Republic of China was a member of the United Nations, and as belligerents at war with UN military forces it was highly unlikely that they would comply with General Assembly resolutions. Consequently, the United States could have expected little in the way of substantive positive results. Instead, Lodge and his associates raised the issue for two different reasons. The first, as Secretary Dulles conceded, was "to get a little good propaganda out of it." It was an attractive case from a propaganda perspective because, as C. D. Jackson bluntly noted, it was "new, unique, dramatic, and understandable by the dullest schoolboy."[25]

23. "Position Paper on Forced Labor," March 23, 1954, 340/3–2354, in Box 1316, RG 59, NA; "U.S./U. N. Press Release, August 17, 1953," *Department of State Bulletin,* August 31, 1953, pp. 298–99; Telegram from Smith to USUN, August 8, 1953, 320/8–853, in Box 1289, RG 59, NA.

24. "Inclusion of Atrocities Item on General Assembly Agenda," Lodge statements of November 2, 1953, in the General Committee, *Department of State Bulletin,* November 30, 1953, pp. 757–58.

25. *MTCD,* Reel 8, Dulles and Hagerty, October 29, 1953, White House Telephone Calls; Jackson to Smith, November 10, 1953, in folder marked "OCB Miscellaneous Memos (2)," Box 1, Jackson Records, EL; Telegram from Dulles to USUN, October 31, 1953, in folder marked "Atrocities in Korea," Box 6, Lot 55 D 560, RG 59, NA.

The second reason was ultimately more compelling. The executive branch wanted to quiet the domestic furor over the mistreatment of American soldiers and steal the thunder from imminent congressional consideration of this politically attractive issue. Late in October, the Department of the Army had released, without first informing the State Department, the OCB, or USUN, a statement on the torture of American prisoners. Congress reacted immediately. Senator McCarthy appointed Senator Charles E. Potter (R-Michigan) to chair a special subcommittee to investigate the atrocities, and subcommittee hearings were scheduled to begin in late November. In order to preempt Congress, USUN was forced to submit the issue, an almost purely propagandistic action for domestic consumption, without adequate preparation.[26]

Speaking to the domestic audience as much as to the General Assembly, Lodge on November 30 presented case summaries of Communist atrocities—mass murders in cold blood, forced death marches, and attempted brainwashing. The Soviet representative claimed that the charges, which had been compiled by the Department of Defense War Crimes Division in Korea, were fabricated. Lodge challenged him to support an impartial inquiry by the International Red Cross. He refused, thereby according added credibility to the American indictment. USUN's handling of the item pleased congressional and public opinion. Lodge even received a congratulatory call from Roy M. Cohn, chief counsel to the Subcommittee on Investigations and McCarthy's top aide. However, the administration's actions received only tepid international approval. In contrast to the ringing endorsement of the American position on forced labor, the General Assembly passed a resolution that only mildly decried the violation of standards for the treatment of prisoners and civilians in war, but named no countries in particular.[27]

The Korean atrocities case presents a stark example of the dilemma con-

26. Lodge to Jackson, October 29, 1953, in folder marked "Ambassador Henry Cabot Lodge," Box 4, Jackson Records, EL; Jesse M. MacKnight (P-UNA) to Charles Norberg (OCB), October 30, 1953, in folder marked "Atrocities in Korea," Box 6, Lot 55 D 560, RG 59, NA; Roger M. Keyes to Dulles, November 21, 1953, same folder.

27. Telegram from the State Department to USUN, n.d. (probably November 1 or 2, 1953), in folder marked "Atrocities in Korea," Box 6, Lot 55 D 560, RG 59, NA; Howard Meyers (UNP) to Sneider (UNA), "Section on Atrocities for President's Report," same folder; Telegram from Christopher H. Phillips to Wadsworth, November 24, 1953, same folder;

fronting the administration as it attempted to satisfy multiple audiences. The administration clearly recognized that its delegation's speeches were directed toward a variety of groups, not the least important of which was the American public. The domestic audience, frustrated by its nation's apparent inability to achieve a clear victory over the Soviets, clamored for at least a rhetorical triumph. By catering to domestic public opinion, the administration hoped to increase domestic approval of the UN. However, the administration could not ignore the other audiences at the international organization—the member delegations and international opinion—for international support was essential to achieve American foreign policy goals therein. Speeches aimed solely or primarily at the domestic audience risked alienating segments of this international audience, especially the neutralist Arab-Asian bloc, which Lodge argued could be reached "through the United Nations forum better than we can in any other way."[28]

The difficulty was that the international audience responded to a different type of speech than appealed to the domestic audience. The UN audience, the OCB believed, constituted an "intellectual elite," and could not be addressed solely on the level of the common man. If the United States hoped to educate the "neutralist intelligentsia" and the "crypto-Communists" from the Soviet satellite nations about the hypocrisy of Communism and sway them to the Western cause, it needed to present a "reasoned and rational" case and an alternative world vision based on "positive, progressive principles." The OCB concluded that "bombastic propaganda, even if factual, and even if interesting," would only alienate the increasingly crucial Third World nations.[29]

Particularly in 1953 and 1954 the administration struggled, with reasonable success, to achieve an acceptable balance between the often competing demands of these audiences. It sought to acquire the domestic support for

Speech in Plenary Meeting of the General Assembly, November 30, 1953, in folder marked "Speeches and Press Releases: 1953," Box 109, HCLP, MHS.

28. Memorandum, Wallace Irwin, Jr., to George A. Morgan, July 30, 1953, in folder marked "Amb. Henry Cabot Lodge," Box 4, Jackson Records, EL; Irwin, Memorandum for the Record, "Human Rights," May 22, 1953, same folder.

29. "Lodge project within the United Nations," n.d., in folder marked "Lodge's Human Rights Project (1)," Box 4, OCB Secretariat Series, NSC Staff Papers, EL; Memorandum, Irwin to Morgan, July 30, 1953, in folder marked "Amb. Henry Cabot Lodge," Box 4, Jackson Records, EL.

the UN that was essential if the nation was to have a strong and consistent internationalist foreign policy without simultaneously undermining the organization and the aims it desired to advance.

Lodge and Jackson were rightfully at the heart of the psychological warfare effort. However, the development and implementation of a truly effective program required extensive support from a host of government agencies. Ideally, USUN, the State Department's Office of United Nations Affairs (UNA), and the PSB/OCB should have worked together as a team. Drawing on and coordinating information from other agencies and departments, the team should have provided USUN with strategy, tactics, and information. It also might have followed through by publicizing American propaganda victories at home and abroad through the United States Information Agency, the Voice of America, and American embassies.

But this support was not forthcoming. The new concept of psychological warfare impinged on the sacred ground of foreign policy, zealously protected by the secretary of state. As C. D. Jackson quickly discovered, Dulles brooked no challenge to his status as the president's chief foreign policy adviser. Nor was Dulles alone in desiring to protect State Department turf. Diplomatic traditionalists were equally wary of the concept of psychological warfare, although they did not identify the challenge in such personal terms. Despite Jackson's assurances that psychological warfare and traditional diplomacy worked best in tandem, diplomats feared that psychological warfare would only complicate their mission. The president's special assistant for cold war planning was unable to persuade the diplomatic corps that, while in the short run psychological warfare might make a situation more difficult, in the long run it would create an environment conducive to a diplomatic resolution of problems.[30] Eisenhower must have been aware of this personal and philosophical tension between his secretary of state and his special assistant. Harold Stassen recalled that "from time to time, the President used the words 'psychological and not diplomatic' to shift the play from Foster Dulles and State to C. D. Jackson's Psychological Strategy Board."[31]

30. Memorandum, Mallory Browne to George A. Morgan, April 13, 1953, in folder marked "PSB UN (1)," Box 23, PSB Central Files, NSC Staff Papers, EL; Jackson to Eisenhower, July 10, 1959, in folder marked "Eisenhower Presidential Correspondence: 1957–8–1959 (3)," Box 41, Jackson Papers, EL.

31. Harold Stassen and Marshall Houts, *Eisenhower: Turning the World Toward Peace* (St. Paul, 1990), 155–56.

This distrust of psychological warfare and its practitioners at the apex of the State Department inevitably filtered down through the bureaucratic hierarchy to the working levels. The development of the Lodge Project illuminates these tensions. Lodge's and Jackson's efforts to develop propaganda initiatives on its various topics were hampered by resistance on the part of the UN Affairs Office (UNA) of the State Department. UNA appears to have resented the developing relationship between USUN and the PSB/OCB Committee on the United Nations, even though Lodge himself agreed that the latter should provide help only as UNA needed it. But the UN Affairs Office, which had traditionally backstopped USUN, viewed the PSB/OCB as interlopers on its departmental turf. Assistant Secretary of State for United Nations Affairs Hickerson professed his desire to work with Lodge and Jackson. Hickerson named David W. Wainhouse, still the director of the Office of UN Political and Security Affairs, and Herbert Fierst to represent UNA in its contacts with the PSB and USUN. Wainhouse and Fierst cooperated, but without the enthusiasm necessary to win acceptance for a new approach and program. According to an OCB staff member who worked at USUN during the Eighth General Assembly session, UNA was unwilling to make allowances for "the novelty of the project, the proportional scarcity of really 'shocking' items, the utility of the many less shocking items if properly edited."[32] Given UNA's reluctant support, Lodge and Jackson believed that the "OCB or other suitable extra-departmental watchdog arrangements" were essential. Even a State Department report allowed that the OCB was a necessary coordinating mechanism. USUN could not wage a propaganda war successfully when it received only "fragmentary, loosely connected, classified, and generally useless" information from other departments.[33]

Despite this limited cooperation, Lodge and Jackson gradually built a rel-

32. Memorandum, Irwin to Craig, August 19, 1953, in folder marked "Ambassador Henry Cabot Lodge," Box 4, Jackson Records, EL; Memorandum of Conversation on May 11, 1953, May 12, 1953, same folder; "Lodge Project," n.d., in folder marked "Project Notes (1)," Box 7, Jackson Records, EL; Memorandum, April 1954, in folder marked "Lodge's Human Rights Project (1)," Box 4, OCB Secretary Series, NSC Staff Records, EL.

33. Memorandum, Craig to Jackson, October 20, 1953, in folder marked "Ambassador Henry Cabot Lodge," Box 4, Jackson Records, EL; Memorandum, Colonel P. Corso to Horace S. Craig, October 21, 1953, same folder; "Report of State Department Activities for the OCB Committee on the Eighth General Assembly," December 28, 1953, in folder marked "OCB 334 UN File #1 (5)," Box 102, OCB Central Files, NSC Staff Papers, EL.

atively effective operation that provided USUN with "hard-hitting material on cold war subjects." Forty separate subject folders of material covering the full range of Soviet vulnerabilities were collected for use during the Eighth General Assembly and future sessions. Jackson, a member of the U.S. delegation to the General Assembly in 1954, even claimed with characteristic hyperbole that because of the high quality of expert advice "a deaf-mute stand-in for the Hunchback of Notre Dame" could have served on the American delegation.[34] In April, 1953, the State Department's UN Affairs Planning Staff had demonstrated noteworthy prescience when it warned that if too much importance was placed on propaganda, it might "become the master rather than the servant of policy."[35] By late 1954 the United States appeared to be headed down this path.

However, beginning in late 1954, a variety of factors halted further movement in this direction. Personnel changes, namely Jackson's resignation on March 30, 1954 (and his ultimate departure from the scene in December, 1954, after serving on the U.S. delegation), left the concept of psychological warfare bereft of its most impassioned proponent. An absence of conceptual consensus further clouded the situation. Even as late as May, 1955, the president and his secretary of state did not agree on the definition or purpose of psychological warfare. Dulles perceived it as a propaganda weapon for liberating the satellite countries. Eisenhower had a far broader vision, in which "every economic, security and political policy of the government manifestly is one of the weapons (or should be) in psychological warfare." Organizational weaknesses, particularly the relative impotence of the OCB, also hindered the implementation of psychological warfare programs. The OCB lacked a vigorous executive officer, responsible solely to the president, who possessed sufficient authority to transcend interdepartmental divisions and engage in central planning, and a trained intelligence group able to collect information.[36]

34. Jackson to Lodge, December 16, 1954, in folder marked "Henry Cabot Lodge, Jr.," Box 56, Jackson Papers, EL; "Report of State Department Activities for the OCB Committee on the Eighth General Assembly," December 28, 1953, in folder marked "OCB 334 UN File #1 (5)," Box 102, OCB Central File Series, NSC Staff Papers, EL.

35. "The 1953 Review: Principal Stresses and Strains Facing the United States in the United Nations," in *FRUS, 1952–1954,* III, 112.

36. Eisenhower to Rockefeller, August 5, 1955, in folder marked "SA 2 'Atoms-For-Peace' Program," Box 31, Adams Papers, Dartmouth; Rockefeller to Eisenhower, December

Changes on the international scene, however, had the most significant impact on American propaganda campaigns at the United Nations. The admission of sixteen new nations (many of which were African, Asian, and Arab) in 1955 altered electoral alignments in the organization. Distrustful of the superpowers' preoccupation with cold war propaganda issues, these new members prevented the United States from compiling the overwhelming majorities it had enjoyed in the early part of the decade and attempted to redirect the UN's attention toward the myriad economic and social problems of the Third World. The slight lessening of cold war tension in 1955, manifested in the "Spirit of Geneva," further limited the superpowers' use of the UN as a propaganda forum. As Lodge himself reported to Dulles, the percentage of Soviet speeches characterized by "vitriolic anti-American utterances" had declined from 80 percent in 1952 to 40 percent in 1953 to 16 percent in 1955.[37]

This is not to suggest that the administration abandoned its use of the UN as a forum to present its case against the Soviet Union. However, during Eisenhower's second term, the administration became more reactive. It retreated to defending itself against Soviet charges rather than taking the propaganda offensive. USUN's handling of the U-2 incident in the spring of 1960 provides the most salient example of this trend.

After using its capture in May, 1960, of an American U-2 reconnaissance plane piloted by Francis Gary Powers to scuttle the Paris summit, the Soviet Union sought additional mileage from the incident at the UN. Soviet foreign minister Andrei Gromyko introduced a resolution, accompanied by a series of vituperative speeches, condemning the United States for aggression. The United States' response was carefully planned by the State Department, the White House, and USUN. Indeed, Eisenhower personally edited Lodge's speech. Lacking a strong legal defense, since it conceded the illegality of the U-2 flights, the administration counterattacked. Lodge asserted

---

22, 1955, same folder; OCB Staff Study, "Proposed Reorganization of the Operations Coordinating Board," same folder; Memorandum, Corso to Craig, October 21, 1953, in folder marked "Amb. Henry Cabot Lodge," Box 4, Jackson Records, EL; Jackson to Dulles, February 9, 1959, in folder marked "Strictly Confidential: I–K (2)," Box 2, General Correspondence and Memoranda Series, Dulles Papers, EL.

37. Lodge to Dulles, August 24, 1955, Reel 4, HCLP, MHS. See Robert E. Riggs, *US/UN: Foreign Policy and International Organization* (New York, 1971), chapter 2, for a quantitative analysis of the decline of the use of the UN as an instrument for cold war legitimization.

that the Soviet Union had engaged in even more duplicitous intelligence activities against the United States. Soviet espionage activities had made it essential, he claimed, for the United States to respond in kind in order to protect its national security and that of the free world.[38]

Lodge provided stark evidence to substantiate his charge. During Security Council debate on May 26, he unveiled a plaque of the Great Seal of the United States that had been presented to the U.S. embassy in 1945 as a token of esteem from the Soviet-American Friendship Society. Lodge showed that inside the eagle's beak was a microphone sensitive enough to hear everything that transpired in Ambassador George Kennan's office. To Eisenhower's great pleasure, Lodge succeeded in his attempt "to advertise Soviet espionage." Moreover, he put the ball back in the USSR's court by suggesting that the UN begin universal fly-over patrols—the "Open Skies" concept—in order to free the entire world from the fear of surprise attacks. Following Lodge's speech, the Security Council defeated the Soviet resolution by a vote of 7 to 2 with 2 abstentions.[39]

On the whole, and particularly during its first two years in office, the administration became proficient at countering Soviet propaganda in the UN. Although rarely personally involved in its implementation, Eisenhower provided the essential directives to launch the new program and welcomed the results. Lodge, the principal spokesman, proudly boasted that "when the Reds start trouble we never run away from it; whenever they hit us we always aim to hit them harder. In the war of words and propaganda we use every parliamentary device the law allows and push them just as hard as possible. We are legal, but we are very firm and sometimes we are rough."[40] In

38. "Draft statement for Ambassador Lodge," May 22, 1960, in folder marked "Christian Herter: May 1960 (2)," Box 10, Dulles-Herter Series, EP, AWF, EL; Memorandum of Conference with the President, May 23, 1960, in folder marked "Staff Notes: May 1960 (1)," Box 50, DDE Diary Series, EP, AWF, EL; Memorandum of Conference with the President, May 26, 1960, in folder marked "Staff Notes: May 1960 (1)," Box 50, DDE Diary Series, EP, AWF, EL.

39. Lodge to Eisenhower, May 28, Reel 29, HCLP, MHS; *MTCH,* Reel 11, Herter and Lodge, May 10, 1960; Eisenhower to Lodge, May 31, 1960, Reel 29, HCLP, MHS; Memorandum for the Files, June 1, 1960, Reel 29, HCLP, MHS; Lodge, *The Storm Has Many Eyes,* 143–44.

40. "How to Handle the Communists," p. 18, August 24, 1953, Reel 28, HCLP, MHS.

addition to this defensive response, the new administration also attempted to seize the initiative with the Lodge Project. It succeeded. In 1953 and 1954, the United States skillfully used the UN to legitimize its cold war policies.

But this American success was hardly an unmitigated positive. First, the psychological warfare offensive was poorly timed. It moved into high gear just as Stalin's death (on March 5, 1953), the termination of the Korean War, and the opening of disarmament and atomic energy discussions held forth the possibility of an easing of cold war tensions. Instead of exploring this possibility, the Psychological Strategy Board focused on checking the antici- pated "softening process" among U.S. allies by stepping up its psychological warfare campaign.[41] The emphasis on psychological warfare therefore may have discouraged more pacific tendencies in the Soviet Union. It thus bears at least some responsibility for contributing to the "lost opportunity" to im- prove relations between the superpowers.

Second, by focusing on points of political conflict rather than possible areas of cooperation, the United States retarded the UN's potential develop- ment as an agent of peaceful social and economic change. As some involved in policy making at the time recognized, the psychological warfare cam- paign detracted from more substantive actions to acquire and retain support from allies and neutral nations. It might well have lent credence to the allied belief that the United States had "a distorted and even a hysterical attitude" about the Soviet threat. Moreover, it failed to address a whole range of issues, from colonialism to economic aid, that were of greater importance to many nations.[42]

Even more important, this emphasis upon political propaganda victories undermined the UN's ability to serve as a forum for negotiation. As the United States consistently garnered overwhelming voting majorities and racked up a seemingly uninterrupted series of propaganda victories, it occasionally was guilty of indulging in unbecoming displays of self-congratulation. Such actions inevitably served to alienate further the Communist bloc and, more significantly, in the long run, put off many neutral nations as well. It became

41. Memorandum by Charles Norberg, "Program for Psychological Support for Ambas- sador Lodge During the 8th Session of the UN General Assembly," April 10, 1953, in folder marked "PSB 334 UN (1)," Box 23, Psychological Strategy Board Central Files Series, NSC Staff Papers, EL.

42. Memorandum, Arthur M. Cox to Browne, June 2, 1953, in folder marked "PSB 334 UN (2)," Box 23, Psychological Strategy Board Central Files Series, NSC Staff Papers, EL.

increasingly unlikely that the USSR would bring East-West issues to a hostile UN environment for negotiation or abide by resolutions voted by an openly antagonistic majority. To the extent that the United Nations was perceived, both at home and abroad, as a mouthpiece for American propaganda, it lost a measure of the worldwide respect—its most powerful weapon— that it desperately needed to fulfill its fundamental mandate of maintaining international peace and security.

The psychological warfare operation at the UN clearly arose from one of the Eisenhower administration's less well grounded conceptions of international diplomacy. It flourished in large part due to the journalistic mindsets and public relations mentality of Lodge and Jackson. The operation led to an overemphasis on what were essentially matters of perception rather than reality. Placing a premium on short-term gains rather than long-term accomplishments, the Eisenhower administration, in its preoccupation with the war of words, at times lost sight of the greater goal of attaining a lasting peace. Indeed, the Eisenhower administration's early emphasis on using the UN to wage psychological warfare influenced its relationship with the organization in dealing with threats to international peace and security in Korea, Indochina, and Guatemala during 1953 and 1954.

5

RESPONDING THROUGH THE UN?
The Search for Peace and Security in Korea, Indochina, and Guatemala

During its first eighteen months, the Eisenhower administration dealt with issues directly related to international peace and security in Korea, Indochina, and Guatemala. The United Nations, the basic function of which is the maintenance of international peace and security, would appear to have been an ideal forum in which the administration could shape its response to these challenges. Although the particular circumstances differed in each situation, all three cases provided President Eisenhower and his foreign policy team with opportunities to forge a strong partnership with the United Nations in their shared quest for international peace.

When Eisenhower took the reins as commander in chief, the United States had been embroiled in the Korean War for almost two years.[1] Sixteen

1. For comprehensive secondary accounts of American involvement in the Korean war, see Bevin Alexander, *Korea: The First War We Lost* (New York, 1986); Ronald J. Caridi, *The Korean War and American Politics: The Republican Party as a Case Study* (Philadelphia, 1968); Rosemary Foot, *The Wrong War: American Policy and the Dimensions of the Korean Conflict, 1950–1953* (Ithaca, 1985); Rosemary Foot, *A Substitute for Victory: The Politics of Peacemaking at the Korean Armistice Talks* (Ithaca, 1990); Callum MacDonald, *Korea: The War Before Vietnam* (New York, 1986); Burton L. Kaufman, *The Korean War: Challenges in Crisis, Credibility and Command* (Philadelphia, 1986); Leland Goodrich, *Korea: A Study of U.S. Policy in the United Nations* (Westport, 1979); Peter Lowe, *The Origins of the Korean War* (New York, 1986); William Stueck, *The Road to Confrontation: American Policy Toward China and Korea, 1947–1950* (Chapel Hill, 1981); and Bruce Cumings, *The Origins of the Korean War* (Princeton, 1981).

of the sixty members of the UN had ultimately sent forces, but the United States provided the vast majority of armed forces, matériel, and money. Furthermore, while the multinational force may have fought under the UN flag, the United States dominated the military command. The United States' preeminence on the battlefield continued at the truce table in Panmunjom. Armistice talks, begun in July, 1951, remained deadlocked in January, 1953, primarily on the question of the repatriation of prisoners of war.

The Communist Chinese and North Koreans argued that in accord with the Geneva Conventions of 1949 all prisoners of war must be returned to their country of origin. The United States and the Republic of Korea insisted on nonforcible repatriation. Frustrated by this stalemate, the General Assembly had passed an Indian proposal to resolve the dilemma during its fall, 1952, session. The Indian resolution recommended that a repatriation commission comprising members from four neutral nations be authorized to assume control of all the prisoners. This commission would arrange the immediate release of those prisoners who chose to return home. Those who refused would be held for an additional ninety days, during which period both sides would have an opportunity to speak with them. The fate of those who still had not chosen to return would be decided by a political conference held after the ceasefire. The United States added an amendment to ensure that the remaining prisoners would not be held indefinitely, and the assembly passed the amended resolution, which the president-elect also approved, on December 3 by a vote of 54 to 5, with 1 abstention.[2]

Despite the General Assembly resolution, negotiations at Panmunjom remained at a standstill when Eisenhower entered office in January, 1953. Few expected the standstill to continue for long. During his campaign, the military hero of World War II had promised that if elected he would "go to Korea," a pledge he had redeemed with a secret three-day trip in December, 1952. Increasingly weary of the prolonged "police action" in Korea, Americans looked to their new president to devise an honorable solution to the conflict. Unhappily, Eisenhower, the skilled military commander, had no magic formulas for the essentially political and diplomatic issues that deadlocked negotiations.

2. On the American position, see, for example, "U.S.S. R. Offers Nothing New on Korea," Lodge statements in Committee I on March 2, 1953, *Department of State Bulletin,* March 16, 1953, pp. 419–20. On Eisenhower's support, see Peter Lowe, "The Settlement of the Korean

Indeed, Eisenhower faced a cacophony of conflicting diplomatic and political opinions on whether he should even continue to negotiate. Led by
Taft, Knowland, and McCarthy, the powerful right wing of the party advocated terminating the talks and expanding the war into China. Eisenhower
himself, during the recent campaign, had criticized Truman's willingness to
negotiate. Secretary of State Dulles too evinced a reluctance to negotiate except from a position of strength, and the obstreperous South Korean leader,
Syngman Rhee, decried any type of compromise, calling for a clear-cut victory. On the other hand, America's key European allies urged Eisenhower to
compromise. It was imperative, they argued, to resolve this situation on the
periphery of the cold war and refocus their attention on the most important
threats, those emanating directly from the Soviet Union and Communist
China.

Those who had hoped that the incoming administration would offer bold
new peace initiatives in the General Assembly were disappointed. The new
administration largely continued its predecessor's policy on the key issue of
the prisoners of war. Staunchly supporting nonforcible repatriation, it was
willing to accept a resolution along the lines of the Indian proposal, but
would compromise no further. The State Department feared, however, that
when the General Assembly resumed its seventh session, on February 24, it
might compromise or even abandon these fundamental principles in a desperate effort to stop the bloodshed in Korea. The department therefore directed USUN to prevent the introduction of resolutions that proposed new
formulas for a settlement of the prisoner-of-war situation or any alterations
to the Indian resolution. From the outset, the new administration thus
sought to exert maximum control over the pace and direction of the negotiations.[3]

While it conducted what was essentially a diplomatic holding action at
the United Nations, the administration explored a wide variety of unilateral

---

War," in John W. Young, ed., *The Foreign Policy of Churchill's Peacetime Administration, 1951–
1955* (Leicester, 1988), 223.

3. Telegram from Hickerson to U.S. embassy in New Delhi, January 28, 1953, 795.00/1–
2853, Reel 20, LM 81, RG 59, NA; Position Paper, "The Korean Question," February 13,
1953, SD/A/C.1/407, in Box 23, Lot 82 D 211, RG 59, NA; Telegram from Lodge to the Department of State, February 5, 1953, in *FRUS, 1952–1954,* XV, 733–35; Telegram from
H. Freeman Matthews (acting secretary of state) to USUN, February 6, 1953, same volume,
741–42.

means to end the war. With Eisenhower in firm control at the helm, the National Security Council considered the full range of military and political options, including the use of tactical nuclear weapons, at a series of meetings held from January to June, 1953. Ultimately, the commander in chief decided to continue the truce negotiations at Panmunjom under the basic framework established by Truman. But Eisenhower was not willing to accept the seemingly endless stalemate that had plagued the armistice effort. If the Communists delayed the negotiating process, or would not agree to a satisfactory armistice, the United States would fight to win. It would attack beyond the Yalu River and employ tactical atomic weapons against targets in Manchuria and China.[4]

The administration thus unilaterally made plans to terminate the conflict. Practicing brinksmanship, it even warned Peking of its intention to use atomic weapons if an acceptable resolution of the POW issue was not forthcoming. There is some question, however, about how unambiguous the warnings were and whether they had a decisive impact on subsequent Communist decisions.[5]

The first significant movement in the new year occurred on March 28, when the Chinese and North Koreans accepted a UN offer to exchange all seriously sick and wounded prisoners. Suspecting a propaganda ploy, Eisenhower and Dulles feared that the acceptance would provoke a General Assembly stampede for a settlement, on virtually any terms. While the administration waited for the Communists to fulfill their pledge, it struggled to keep the locus of decision making and negotiation at Panmunjom. Panmun-

4. For the most accessible copies of the minutes of the National Security Council meetings, see the following: Memorandum of Discussion at the 131st Meeting of the National Security Council on Wednesday, February 11, 1953, in *FRUS, 1952–1954,* XV, 769–72; Memorandum of Discussion at a Special Meeting of the National Security Council on Tuesday, March 31, 1953, same volume, 825–27; NSC 147, "Analysis of Possible Courses of Action in Korea," April 2, 1953, same volume, 839–40; Memorandum of Discussion at the 143rd Meeting of the National Security Council, Wednesday, May 6, 1953, same volume, 975–78; Memorandum of Discussion at the 144th Meeting of the National Security Council, Wednesday, May 13, 1953, same volume, 1012–17. See also Edward C. Keefer, "President Dwight D. Eisenhower and the End of the Korean War," *Diplomatic History,* X (1986), 267–89, *passim.*

5. Dulles may have conveyed the ultimatum to the Communists through Indian prime minister Jawaharlal Nehru during a meeting between the two men on May 21, 1953, in *FRUS, 1952–1954,* XV, 1068, 1071. See also Roger Dingman, "Atomic Diplomacy During the Korean War," *Diplomatic History,* XIII (1989), 50–91; Foot, *A Substitute for Victory,* 165–83.

jom was to be the center ring; the General Assembly was to be at most a side-show, a relatively innocuous diversion from the main event. The General Assembly's consideration of the latest move at such an early stage, Dulles professed, might "foul it up."[6]

The transfer of sick and wounded prisoners began on April 20, 1953, and armistice negotiations at Panmunjom resumed six days later. However, the United States continued its efforts both to restrict participation in the negotiations in Korea and to prevent further consideration of the issue by the General Assembly. The administration's perception of power politics and its assessment of the UN's ability to end the war shaped its course of action. As U. Alexis Johnson (deputy assistant secretary of state for Far Eastern affairs) bluntly explained to the Joint Chiefs of Staff, "The real question is one of how much political power we can wield in the U. N." The answer was self-evident. The administration wielded more power at Panmunjom than in New York.[7]

Nor did the administration have confidence in the UN's ability to arrange an armistice. Dulles even asserted that the "only chance in getting an armistice is to keep the UN in the background." The administration therefore resisted pressure from Britain and India to reconvene the General Assembly. It also failed to keep the UN Secretariat informed of its actions; Hammarskjöld complained that Dulles treated Korea as "a pure U.S. business." Not until mid-July, when the negotiations had almost concluded, did the United States accord Hammarskjöld the courtesy of informing him of the progress to that point.[8]

Finally, on June 8, 1953, both sides signed a prisoner-of-war repatriation agreement, one that was strikingly similar to the General Assembly resolution of December 3. Still, the United States struggled to balance the compet-

6. *MTCD,* Reel 1, Lodge and Dulles, March 31, 1953; *MTCD,* Reel 1, Lodge and Dulles, March 30, 1953; Lodge and Dulles, March 28, 1953, in folder marked "Telephone Memoranda (excepting to or from White House), January 1953–April 1953 (1)," Box 1, Telephone Conversation Series, Dulles Papers, EL; Memorandum of Conversation, March 31, 1953, 795.00/3–3153, Reel 20, LM 81, RG 59, NA; Circular Airgram from Dulles, March 31, 1953, 795.00/3–3153, Reel 20, LM 81, RG 59, NA; Telegram from Dulles to USUN, April 2, 1953, in *FRUS, 1952–1954,* XV, 837–38.

7. Memorandum of the Substance of Discussion at a Department of State–Joint Chiefs of Staff Meeting, May 18, 1953, in *FRUS, 1952–1954,* XV, 1045.

8. *MTCD,* Reel 1, Lodge and Dulles, June 25, 1953; Hammarskjöld, quoted in Urquhart, *Hammarskjöld,* 87.

ing demands of its European allies, the United Nations, and Rhee, who had critical support from some within the administration and Congress. Just as a peaceful resolution appeared imminent, Rhee threatened to shatter the fragile agreement. On June 18, he ordered the release of twenty-five thousand prisoners being held by the South Korean army. The prisoners promptly disappeared into the South Korean civilian population, escaping repatriation. This attempt to sabotage the negotiations was initially successful; the Communists walked out. But Rhee's triumph was short-lived. Employing a combination of personal persuasion, concessions, and coercion, the administration finally compelled the recalcitrant South Korean leader to cease obstructing the peace process.

With the prisoner-of-war issue resolved, progress toward an armistice was relatively rapid. The Armistice Agreement, signed on July 27, 1953, established a cease-fire line that ran roughly along the 38th parallel. It thereby achieved the UN's military goal—restoration of the pre-war boundaries of the Republic of Korea. The political goal—the reunification of Korea—remained elusive. The Armistice Agreement stipulated that a political conference to consider this latter question would be called within three months. However, the agreement left the specific arrangements to the General Assembly, which had been scheduled to reconvene in a special session on August 17.

The State Department was determined to select the participants, choose the location and dates, and set the agenda for the political conference. Lodge shared the department's desire "to play the leading role" in the General Assembly's deliberations. However, he believed that it would be preferable to do so while working primarily behind the scenes. He asked Dulles: "Should this be a leading role in the open, or should we let other people get out in front while we actually do the hard work? I believe that one of our greatest weaknesses in diplomacy is being heavy-handed and giving [the] appearance of throwing our weight around and gaining our ends by main strength and awkwardness. It should be possible to work through others, letting them get credit and letting us avoid blame."[9]

Dulles's answer was clear. In a letter listing "principles" for Lodge's guidance, he insisted that the United States must not only control every feasible

9. Telegram from Lodge to Dulles, June 12, 1953, 795.00/6–1253, Reel 21, LM 81, RG 59, NA.

aspect of the conference, but also guarantee that it "would be entitled to act for itself, in the protection of its own interests, and would not have any representative responsibilities to others or be bound by the vote or recommendation of others." Otherwise, it was prepared to refuse to participate. Sensitive to Will Rogers' witticism that the United States had never won a peace conference, Dulles declared his intention to prove Rogers wrong, even if it meant writing the rules so as to rig the game's outcome.[10]

Of primary importance was the matter of determining what nations would attend. Lodge and Dulles ideally wanted only the United States, South Korea, North Korea, and the People's Republic of China to participate. A large UN delegation would, Dulles claimed, cause "untold trouble and confusion." Although he understood that such a limited conference was out of the question, Dulles still argued that the United States deserved "greater independence of position than would be reflected by our being one of many" on the UN side at the conference. Lodge concurred, suggesting that political power be divided in direct proportion to each nation's troop contributions.[11] The United States, accustomed to the luxury of single command on the battlefield, desired a similar status at the conference table.

The administration sought to reinforce its position as the *de facto* leader of the UN side before the General Assembly reconvened on August 17. USUN and the State Department drafted two resolutions (one called for a political conference and one offered tribute to the UN forces in Korea), and presented them to the group of sixteen for their advance approval. Dulles and Lodge also traveled to Korea to urge an increasingly fractious Rhee to participate.[12] At the same time, by aggressively taking command of the situation, the administration deliberately prevented the UN Secretariat from

10. Dulles to Lodge, August 13, 1953, in *FRUS, 1952–1954*, XV, 1492–93; *MTCD*, Reel 1, Dulles and Lodge, August 14, 1953.

11. *MTCD*, Reel 2, Lodge and Dulles, July 24, 1953; *MTCD*, Reel 1, Dulles and Lodge, June 20, 1953; *MTCD*, Reel 1, Dulles and Lodge, June 20, 1953; *MTCD*, Reel 1, Lodge and Dulles, August 12, 1953; Telegram from Dulles to Lodge, July 22, 1953, 795.00/7–2253, Reel 23, LM 81, RG 59, NA.

12. *MTCD*, Reel 2, Dulles and Lodge, July 24, 1953. On the contact with other delegations see, for example, Telegram from Dulles to Lodge, July 22, 1953, 795.00/7–2253, Reel 23, LM 81, RG 59, NA; Memorandum of Conversation, August 8, 1953, 795.00/8–753, same reel; Telegram from Dulles to Lodge, August 12, 1953, 795.00/8–1253, same reel; Memorandum, Durward V. Sandifer (deputy assistant secretary of state for United Nations affairs) to Dulles, August 18, 1953, 795.00/8–1853, same reel.

fulfilling its rightful role as the organizing agent for the conference. Hammarskjöld agreed to an American request to serve as a "letter-box" through which the United States could communicate indirectly with Peking and North Korea, but the UN Secretariat did little else.[13]

The question of a Korean political conference was the General Assembly's primary order of business when it reconvened. Lodge announced that the United States would insist upon strict adherence to paragraph 60 of the Armistice Agreement, which stated that the conference should be composed of representatives of "the governments of the countries concerned on both sides." Thus, only nations with troops in Korea could attend.[14]

The American proposal encountered immediate opposition. Many nations sought broader conference participation, with a role for neutrals. Australia and New Zealand urged that the Soviet Union be added to the list of participants. Others wanted to include India, since this increasingly prominent neutral and Asian power had served as a mediator at various points during the Panmunjom negotiations. The administration was willing to have the USSR attend as an invitee of North Korea and Communist China. The USSR's presence was justified because of its involvement, albeit indirect, in the conflict. Furthermore, Soviet attendance might enable the United States to hold the USSR accountable for its future actions in Korea.[15]

The prospect of Indian participation evoked a far different response. The administration ardently hoped to create a situation in which the nations of the free world would confront the Communist aggressors across a two-sided table. A roundtable conference would accommodate neutrals, but it would not provide a symbolic and dramatic illustration of the division between the free world and communism. Dulles's personal and philosophical aversion to neutralism, as well as public, congressional, and South Korean opposition to

---

13. Urquhart, *Hammarskjöld,* 88. It even appears that Dulles would have preferred to communicate with Peking through the Swedish embassy rather than the secretary-general. Memorandum of Conversation, September 1, 1953, 795.00/9–353, Reel 23, LM 81, RG 59, NA; Telegram from Wadsworth to Dulles, August 4, 1953, 795.00/8–453, same reel.

14. Lodge statements in Committee I on August 18, 19, 1953, *State Department Bulletin,* August 31, 1953, pp. 284–87. The administration's position and presentation were closely and carefully coordinated between Dulles and Lodge. In fact, they spoke five times in less than three hours on August 12. *MTCD,* Reel 1, Lodge and Dulles, August 12, 1953.

15. Memorandum, Hickerson and Walter S. Robertson (assistant secretary of state for Far Eastern affairs) to Dulles, June 8, 1953, in *FRUS, 1952–1954,* XV, 1155.

Indian participation, reinforced the administration's determination to stand firm on this point.[16]

The American position prevailed. On August 28 the General Assembly approved the resolutions naming the fifteen nations contributing troops in Korea to the political conference and calling for the Soviet Union's participation if desired by the other side. These resolutions became General Assembly Resolution 711, under which the United Nations sanctioned participation in a future Korean Political Conference.[17]

The Eisenhower administration also was determined to serve as the soloist for the UN chorus of sixteen on the questions of an agenda, participants, site, and time for the conference. In an effort to unify the group behind American leadership, Dulles moved quickly to "bring the action back to Washington," where differences could be resolved in a series of pre-conference consultations safely beyond the glare of the General Assembly spotlight. Assured of group support, the administration sent Arthur H. Dean, an international lawyer and one of Dulles's former partners in the firm of Sullivan and Cromwell, to Panmunjom late in October to negotiate with his North Korean and Communist Chinese counterparts. Although Dean remained until December 12, the negotiators failed to reach an agreement. Meanwhile, the administration continued to oppose concurrent General Assembly consideration of the issue.[18]

The Berlin Conference of Foreign Ministers finally concluded arrangements for the political conference, agreeing to all of the U.S. demands. Meet-

16. *MTCD,* Reel 1, Dulles and Lodge, August 14, 1953; Telegram from Dulles to Lodge, August 14, 1953, 795.00/8–2453, Reel 23, LM 81, RG 59, NA; Henry Cabot Lodge, "Statements in Committee I on August 18 and 19, 1953," *Department of State Bulletin,* August 31, 1953, pp. 284–87; Henry Cabot Lodge, "Statements in Committee I on August 25, 26, 27, and 28, 1953," *Department of State Bulletin,* September 14, 1953, pp. 361–66; Kaufman, *The Korean War,* 342.

17. Henry Cabot Lodge, "Statements in the General Committee of the General Assembly on September 22, 1953," *Department of State Bulletin,* October 5, 1953, pp. 469–70; Memorandum, Dulles to Eisenhower, October 9, 1953, in folder marked "UN Matters: 1953–1954 (3)," Box 7, Subject Series, Dulles Papers, EL.

18. *MTCD,* Reel 1, Lodge and Dulles, August 28, 1953; Memorandum, Murphy to Dulles, August 31, 1953, 795.00/8–3153, Reel 23, LM 81, RG 59, NA; Telegram from Smith to USUN, December 6, 1953, in *FRUS, 1952–1954,* XV, 1646–47; Telegram from Dulles to USUN, January 12, 1954, same volume, 1719–21; Telegram from Wadsworth to the Secretary of State, January 21, 1954, 320/1–2154, in Box 1291, RG 59, NA.

ing from January 24 to February 18, 1954, the Soviet Union, the United States, Britain, and France accomplished what they had been unable or unwilling to achieve under the auspices of the General Assembly or in direct talks between the principal belligerents at Panmunjom. The four powers agreed to hold a conference in Geneva, Switzerland, beginning on April 26, 1954, with the objective of creating a unified and independent Korea. In an attempt to reduce tension throughout Asia, the conference also would address the ongoing conflict in Indochina.

The administration evinced little enthusiasm as it developed its strategy for the Geneva Conference. The State Department acted more from a sense of international obligation and a recognition of the potential political opportunities than from an expectation of diplomatic success. Commitments to allies, the Armistice Agreement, and General Assembly resolutions all obligated the United States to pursue a political resolution to the Korean problem. In addition, the conference provided an opportunity to demonstrate to the American public the depth of its government's commitment to seeking peace. Fully appreciating the domestic political import of the situation, Lodge suggested that if the administration "pulled this conference off Gen-[eral] Eisenhower would never be put out of office." Moreover, a credible American performance promised to yield dividends in the international realm, demonstrating the U.S. commitment to a non-Communist Southeast Asia.[19]

Not anticipating great success, and anxious to guard against being blamed for the more likely failure, the administration adopted conservative tactics and set limited goals for the conference. While it would present genuine proposals with room for trades and concessions, under no circumstances would it compromise the basic principles for which it had fought in Korea. Perhaps most important, in the event that the conference failed, the onus must rest solely with the Communists. The State Department resolved that the United States must, at a minimum, emerge with its moral and political standing intact, and ideally, even enhanced.[20]

After the prolonged wrangling over the arrangements, the Geneva Con-

19. *MTCD,* Reel 1, Dulles and Lodge, August 31, 1953; Telegram from Dean to the Department of State, December 1, 1953, in *FRUS, 1952–1954,* XV, 1629–32.

20. See, for example, Position Paper, "General United States Views on Korean Phase of Geneva Conference," April 14, 1954, in *FRUS, 1952–1954,* XVI, 97–99; Memorandum of Conversation by Brown, April 20, 1954, same volume, 119–24.

ference itself proved to be something of an anticlimax. The Korean phase began first and quickly stalemated when the two sides proposed plans for the reunification of Korea that differed little from their pre-war positions. Little effort was made to resolve these differences, and the talks ended on June 15 with an exchange of hostile statements.

Nevertheless, the United States achieved its two goals. It maintained unity with and among its allies, though at times it was, according to delegation leader Undersecretary of State Walter Bedell Smith, "like herding a flock of rabbits through a hole in a fence." Second, it succeeded in keeping the "UN symbol . . . to the forefront" in its public statements. The administration had justified American casualties for the principle of collective security, and it feared that "those representations [would] sound hollow" if it did not publicly proclaim continued loyalty to this principle. The American-backed statement, the "Declaration of Sixteen," consequently insisted that progress was impossible as long as the Communists refused to accept UN supervision of elections in Korea and, by extension, the concept of collective security.[21]

Neither side was willing to risk its gains in an all-Korean election. The principal belligerents wanted reunification only if they could be sure that their side would emerge as the dominant power. By bypassing the UN at the Berlin and Geneva Conferences, the United States had achieved control of its allies' forces. Ironically, in doing so it had damaged the very prestige of the UN that might have encouraged the Communists to entrust the organization with the supervision of elections in Korea. At least to a limited extent, the administration therefore had brought this situation upon itself.

The conclusion of the Geneva Conference effectively ended serious consideration of the issue of Korean reunification. As required by General Assembly Resolution 711, the fifteen member nations of the UN presented their report (essentially a restatement of the Declaration of Sixteen) to the Ninth General Assembly on November 11, 1954, and the assembly approved it. The State Department then endeavored to avoid any further debate or ac-

21. Telegram from Smith to the Department of State, June 16, 1954, in *FRUS, 1952–1954,* XVI, 389; Telegram from Murphy to Smith, June 1, 1954, 795.00/6–154, Reel 27, LM 81, RG 59, NA; Memorandum of Conversation, May 3, 1954, in *FRUS, 1952–1954,* XVI, 182–83; Telegram from Murphy (acting secretary) to the U.S. delegation, May 31, 1954, in *FRUS, 1952–1954,* XVI, 326–27; "Declaration by the Sixteen," June 15, 1954, in *FRUS, 1952–1954,* XVI, 385–86.

tion. The U.S. delegation voted against an Indian resolution that proposed a continuation of the negotiations. Merely changing the venue from Panmunjom or Geneva to New York, USUN protested, would not in and of itself alter Communist opposition to free elections. Left largely unarticulated was the fear that the United States might not be able to control the actions of the international body.[22]

As a civilian, Dwight Eisenhower had supported the UN's initial intervention in Korea in the belief that it would provide the UN with "a real test of its viability." When the Armistice Agreement was signed, President Eisenhower commended the United Nations for meeting aggression in Korea "not with pathetic words of protest, but with deeds of decisive purpose."[23] Dulles echoed his praise, claiming that "we have established the fact that 'collective security' is not just an ideal" but something that works. Lodge too emphasized the value of collective action in easing the nation's military burdens. UN contributions, he contended, had permitted the United States to send two fewer divisions to Korea and saved over $600 million.[24]

In reality, however, the administration's actions failed to match its rhetoric. By the time Eisenhower assumed office, the United States so dominated the military, diplomatic, and economic command as to render the term "collective security" almost meaningless. Despite his proclamations of support for the UN, the new president did nothing to help the organization reassert control over the conduct of the war or the negotiation of the peace. Instead, Eisenhower continued Truman's basic policy of waging the war and negotiating a peace more as a U.S.-commanded alliance operation—sixteen mostly Western nations contributing troops in an effort to resist Communist aggression—than as a collective security action controlled by the international organization. The president skillfully used the UN to legitimize the alliance

22. Memorandum, David McK. Key to Smith (acting secretary), September 7, 1954, 320/9–754, in Box 1290, RG 59, NA; Memorandum of Discussion at the 213th Meeting of the National Security Council, September 10, 1954, in folder marked "213th Mtg. of NSC—September 9, 1954," Box 6, NSC Series, EP, AWF, EL; H. Alexander Smith statement in Committee I on December 20, 1954, *Department of State Bulletin,* December 20, 1954, pp. 955–56.

23. Eisenhower, *Mandate for Change,* 82; Radio and Television Address to the American People Announcing the Signing of the Korean Armistice, July 26, 1953, in *Public Papers of the Presidents: Dwight D. Eisenhower, 1953,* 521.

24. "U.N. Achievements in Korea," Dulles remarks to the Boys Nation and the Department of State, July 27, 1953, *Department of State Bulletin,* August 10, 1953, p. 175; "Don't Sell the U.N. Short," *Newsweek,* October 12, 1953, p. 42.

operation by contributing its flag and credibility while deferring to the senior partner's desires. Although Eisenhower announced that it was essential for the United States to make compromises, his actual willingness to do so was minimal.[25] During both the war and the armistice, the key decisions emanated from the White House and the State Department, and were simply echoed in the halls of the UN.

Led by Eisenhower, the Big Four—the United States, Britain, France, and the Soviet Union—both literally and symbolically distanced themselves from the authority and influence of the United Nations when they moved the negotiations from New York to Panmunjom and finally to Geneva. This was unfortunate, for the Korean negotiations was one case in which the objectives of the UN and the United States coincided almost completely. Including the United Nations more fully in the negotiations might have meant additional work for the State Department, but it would have earned the United States tremendous goodwill and set a better tone for the future. In an almost pathetic attempt to put the best face on an awkward situation, the secretary-general maintained that since the Geneva Conference was being conducted in general conformity with the "main terms" of the General Assembly's August resolutions, it represented a victory for collective security. In actuality, the use of outside arrangements, even in pursuit of the UN's principles and objectives, inevitably weakened the organization and undermined its credibility in dealing with future crises.[26]

The situation in Indochina offered another opportunity for Eisenhower to work with the United Nations in the search for international peace. After almost a century of French colonial rule, by 1953 the tide of sentiment appeared to be moving inexorably toward independence. Nevertheless, the French were fighting the tide, waging a desperate struggle against the nationalist forces of the Vietminh, led by Ho Chi Minh. The Eisenhower administration, concerned about the cold war implications of the struggle in Indochina, increasingly turned its attention to that corner of Southeast Asia.[27]

25. Press Conference, May 28, 1953, in Box 1, Press Conference Series, EP, AWF, EL.

26. "Big Four Decision Is Hailed at U.N.," New York *Times,* February 19, 1954, p. 2.

27. For comprehensive accounts of American involvement in Indochina, see William J. Duiker, *U.S. Containment Policy and the Conflict in Indochina* (Stanford, 1994); George McT. Kahin, *Intervention: How America Became Involved in Vietnam* (New York, 1986); Lloyd C. Gardner, *Approaching Vietnam: From World War II Through Dienbienphu, 1941–1954* (New

The Eisenhower administration was determined to keep Indochina non-Communist. Economic and security reasons dictated this stance, as did the belief that the "loss" of any more Asian territory to communism would damage American credibility as the leader of the free world. Eisenhower's and Dulles's firm commitment to the European Defense Community (EDC) also shaped their handling of the situation. They believed that France would not be able to participate in the EDC at anticipated levels if it was still engaged in a war in Southeast Asia, and it might be unwilling to participate at all if defeated.[28] As a result, the administration slowly assumed financial responsibility for the situation, bankrolling approximately 70 percent of the French war effort. Yet the administration remained at odds with France about how best to defeat the nationalist forces.

The Vietminh invasion of northern Laos in April, 1953, provoked the first disagreement between the new American administration and the French government over the appropriate role for the United Nations in the Indochinese conflict. France refused to bring the invasion of Laos to the attention of the UN. It feared precipitating a lengthy debate on and ultimate condemnation of French colonial practices, and it wanted to avoid establishing a dangerous precedent. If problems arose in its other colonies, the French government did not want to be under any obligation to involve the UN.[29]

The Eisenhower administration disagreed with the French position. Dulles believed that despite a virtually inevitable Soviet veto, an otherwise unanimous Security Council vote condemning the Vietminh aggression would give the French military action a degree of multinational legitimacy. Furthermore, strong Security Council support, Dulles suggested in a moment of remarkable overoptimism, might increase Vietnamese loyalty to their colonial rulers and persuade the American public to support increased

---

York, 1988); George C. Herring, *America's Longest War: The United States and Vietnam, 1950–1975* (New York, 1986); Andrew J. Rotter, *The Path to Vietnam* (Ithaca, 1987); David L. Anderson, *Trapped by Success: The Eisenhower Administration and Vietnam, 1953–1961* (New York, 1991).

28. Lawrence S. Kaplan, "The United States, NATO, and French Indochina," in Kaplan, Denise Artaud, and Mark R. Rubin, eds., *Dien Bien Phu and the Crisis of Franco-American Relations, 1954–1955* (Wilmington, 1990), 235; Denise Artaud, "France between the Indochina War and the European Defense Community," *ibid.,* 251–68.

29. See, for example, Telegram from C. Douglas Dillon (U.S. ambassador to France) to the Department of State, April 30, 1953, in *FRUS, 1952–1954,* XIII, 528–29; Telegram from Dillon to the Department of State, May 3, 1953, same volume, 538–39.

assistance to the French. Still, Eisenhower and Dulles declined to push the French.[30]

Nor did the administration actively pursue other possible avenues to UN involvement during the spring of 1953. In April the Thai ambassador solicited American support for his plan to request the Security Council to send observers from the Peace Observation Commission to the region. The State Department favored such a course, in principle at least. Indeed, Dulles reminded Eisenhower that as a member of the U.S. delegation to the General Assembly in 1950 he had been largely responsible for creating the commission. Nevertheless, the State Department again bowed before French and British opposition; Dulles encouraged Thailand to postpone its request.[31]

Thus, by July, 1953, the administration had shown that it would not compel France to rely upon the UN's negotiation and conciliation mechanisms to bring about a diplomatic resolution of the conflict. Nor did Eisenhower or his Joint Chiefs of Staff advocate military action under the aegis of the UN. The lessons of waging an essentially defensive police action in Korea were painfully fresh.[32]

The administration's position on UN involvement in the Indochinese situation changed little during the following year, as French control collapsed. The crisis occasioned by the impending fall of the garrison at Dien Bien Phu in the spring of 1954 intensified interest in the situation, but produced no significantly new policy. On March 25, 1954, the National Security Council considered and rejected using American ground forces to prevent a Com-

---

30. Memorandum of Conversation by Baker (Office of UN Political and Security Affairs), April 15, 1953, in *FRUS, 1952–1954,* XIII, 468–70; Telegram from Dulles to the U.S. embassy in France, April 29, 1953, same volume, 526–27; Telegram from Dulles to the U.S. embassy in France, May 6, 1953, same volume, 543–44; Memorandum, Charlton Ogburn, Jr. (regional planning adviser, Bureau of Far Eastern Affairs), September 8, 1953, same volume, 762–66; Memorandum, Robertson to Livingston T. Merchant (assistant secretary of state for European affairs), May 8, 1953, 751G.00/5–853, Reel 7, LM 71, RG 59, NA; Memorandum, Hickerson to Dulles, April 28, 1953, 751G.00/4–2853, Reel 7, LM 71, RG 59, NA.

31. Memorandum of Conversation, June 1, 1953, in *FRUS, 1952–1954,* XIII, 588–89; Memorandum of Conversation, July 29, 1953, same volume, 703–704; Minutes of Meeting at the White House, May 7, 1953, same volume, 551–52; Telegram from Wadsworth to Dulles, May 11, 1953, 751G.00/5–1153, Reel 7, LM 71, RG 59, NA; Telegram from Dulles to the U.S. embassy in Bangkok, July 9, 1953, 751G.00/7–953, Reel 8, LM 71, RG 59, NA.

32. Substance of Discussions of State–Joint Chiefs of Staff Meeting, July 10, 1953, in *FRUS, 1952–1954,* XIII, 651–52.

munist victory in Indochina. Seeking an excuse not to act, the president asserted that the United States must obtain prior UN approval before committing troops to defend the Associated States (Vietnam, Laos, and Cambodia). American intervention hence became highly improbable, since Arab-Asian opposition to French colonialism would make a two-thirds vote almost impossible.[33]

At Dulles's request, the Office of UN Political and Security Affairs evaluated less drastic courses of action. Among the options considered were sending a Peace Observation Commission subcommittee to Indochina; lodging a complaint of aggression against the Associated States; developing a plan for the Associated States' independence; establishing a UN commission to negotiate a settlement similar to the armistice in Korea; and even authorizing temporary UN administration of Indochina. Working through the UN would internationalize the conflict and erase some of the colonial stigma associated with the French venture. It might also build American public support for U.S. intervention, enhance the principle of collective resistance to aggression, generate economic and military assistance from other UN members, and cut the free world's losses by helping to establish a new non-Communist and noncolonial status for the region. On the other hand, once the United Nations became involved, the United States might not be able to control its actions. Furthermore, multilateralizing the conflict without French consent might hurt the U.S. relationship with France, jeopardize French control of its North African colonies, and hasten French withdrawal and the Communist takeover of Indochina.[34]

The potential problems of UN intervention discouraged Eisenhower and Dulles from aggressively pursuing that course of action. They were equally determined, however, not to get involved in the Indochina morass without support. As Eisenhower wisely asserted during an April 7, 1954, news con-

33. Memorandum of Discussion at the 190th Meeting of the National Security Council, March 25, 1954, in *FRUS, 1952–1954,* XIII, 1165, 1167; Memorandum of Conversation, April 2, 1954, same volume, 1216; Melanie Billings-Yun, *Decision Against War: Eisenhower and Dien Bien Phu, 1954* (New York, 1986), 55. See Memorandum of Conversation by N. G. Thacher (Office of South Asian Affairs), April 12, 1954, in *FRUS, 1952–1954,* XIII, 1315–17, for an example of the Arab-Asian bloc views.

34. Memorandum, Wainhouse to Dulles, March 26, 1954, in *FRUS, 1952–1954,* XIII, 1174–77.

ference, the Indochina problem was "the kind of thing that must not be handled by one nation trying to act alone."[35]

Consequently, the president and secretary of state instead called for "united action" to meet the Communist threat. They contemplated creating a regional coalition, which might include the United States, Britain, France, New Zealand, Australia, Thailand, the Philippines, and the Associated States of Indochina. This coalition, which Dulles described to the Canadian ambassador as "an *ad hoc* political association somewhat along the lines of the North Atlantic Treaty Organization but limited in purpose," would also have a military component. If necessary, it would undertake collective defense measures to sustain France or perhaps even carry on the effort in the event of French withdrawal. United Action would provide both the legal sanction inherent in intervention as part of a collective effort and protection against charges of anti-colonialism.[36]

The United Action scheme envisioned by Eisenhower and Dulles had only a tenuous connection to the UN. Dulles and Eisenhower eventually conceded reluctantly that before it took any military action a coalition ought first to discuss the situation with the Security Council. Eisenhower's half-hearted endorsement of UN involvement is starkly apparent in an April 4, 1954, letter to Winston Churchill: "I suppose that the United Nations should somewhere be recognized, but I am not confident that, given the Soviet veto, it could act with needed speed and vigor." The president believed that although it was not possible politically, it would be preferable militarily for a coalition to act first, in accordance with Article 51 of the UN Charter, and then report its actions to the Security Council. The chance for a viable coalition died in late April when Britain withheld its support and France contin-

35. Press Conference, April 7, 1954, in *Public Papers of the Presidents: Dwight D. Eisenhower, 1954,* 384–85. See also Memorandum of Conversation, May 11, 1954, 751G.00/5–1154, Reel 11, LM 71, RG 59, NA.

36. Memorandum of Conversation, April 7, 1954, in *FRUS, 1952–1954,* XIII, 1276; George C. Herring and Richard H. Immerman, "Eisenhower, Dulles, and Dienbienphu: 'The Day We Didn't Go to War' Revisited," *Journal of American History,* LXXI (1984), 346–63; George C. Herring, "'A Good Stout Effort': John Foster Dulles and the Indochina Crisis, 1954–1955," in Richard H. Immerman, *John Foster Dulles and the Diplomacy of the Cold War* (Princeton, 1990), 213–33; Gregory James Pemberton, "Australia, the United States, and the Indochina Crisis of 1954," *Diplomatic History,* XIII (1989), 45–66.

ued to dispute the proper relationship between itself and the United States in such a group. Ever tenacious, Dulles still promoted United Action right through the Geneva Conference.[37]

Lodge did not share Eisenhower's and Dulles's views on this question. He understood that Dulles faced conflicting pressures, including the French intimation that they might not participate in the European Defense Community if they were not relieved of their responsibilities in Indochina. Indeed, as early as 1950, then-senator Lodge had urged the Truman administration to ease France's burden in Indochina so that it might contribute more sizably to a Western European armed force. Nevertheless, he wanted to pressure France to turn to the United Nations. The ambassador made his views clear at an NSC meeting on February 11, 1954, advising the participants that he "had a lot of experience in dealing with the French, and that if you get behind them and push hard enough they will do what is required." The decision to handle the matter primarily through bilateral channels, however, relegated Lodge to the periphery of the policy-making process. While the State Department acquiesced in Lodge's plaintive request to be kept apprised of the general developments in Indochina, neither Eisenhower nor Dulles appears to have sought his views.[38]

Regardless, Lodge evidently felt strongly enough about the issue to send both men his unsolicited advice. In an April 27 letter to the president, a copy of which he sent to the secretary of state, Lodge requested an explanation of the rationale for not making greater use of the UN. He marshaled political, military, and moral arguments in an attempt to persuade the president to re-

37. Peter G. Boyle, ed., *The Churchill-Eisenhower Correspondence, 1953–1955* (Chapel Hill, 1990), 137; Memorandum, Charles C. Stelle to Robert Bowie (assistant secretary of state for policy planning), March 31, 1954, in *FRUS, 1952–1954,* XIII, 1195–97; Memorandum of Conversation by Drumright, April 2, 1954, same volume, 1214–17; Memorandum of Conversation, April 4, 1954, same volume, 1231–35; Memorandum of Conversation, April 7, 1954, same volume, 1279–80; Draft Declaration submitted by the U.S. Representatives, April 12, 1954, same volume, 1314–15; Memorandum by Stelle, April 9, 1954, in *FRUS, 1952–1954,* XVI, 508; Geoffrey Warner, "The Settlement of the Indochina War," in Young, ed., *The Foreign Policy of Churchill's Peacetime Administration,* 233–59.

38. Memorandum of Discussion at the 184th Meeting of the National Security Council, February 11, 1954, in *FRUS, 1952–1954,* XIII, 1039; Key to Lodge, April 16, 1954, same volume, 1345–46; Lawrence S. Kaplan, "Prologue: Perception by the United States of Its Interests in Indochina," in Kaplan, Artaud, and Rubin, eds., *Dien Bien Phu and the Crisis of Franco-American Relations,* 6.

consider. He contended that, on the home front, American opinion favored exploring any and all avenues that might bring about a peaceful resolution of the conflict and avoid committing American troops to another land war in Asia. On the battlefields, UN involvement would make the Indochinese soldiers a more effective fighting force by giving them something to fight for—reassurances of eventual independence—and would reduce the manpower burden on France if other nations contributed military units. Finally, a multilateral approach would disprove the Communists' charge that the Indochinese conflict was a colonial war. Lodge insisted that the administration ought to call for a special General Assembly session immediately. Dulles, not Eisenhower, responded on May 10 in a brief letter. The secretary maintained that the administration had not insisted upon UN involvement because "the French have been violent in their opposition." Dulles opined that a UN call for troops was not feasible, but he assured Lodge that he was still contemplating support for a Peace Observation Commission for Laos, Cambodia, and possibly Thailand.[39]

Despite this rebuff, Lodge persisted. Seizing upon the secretary's comment about the possibility of establishing a Peace Observation Commission subcommittee on Indochina, he again urged Dulles to act at once. In addition to expanding upon his earlier arguments, Lodge raised a number of new points. He suggested that a UN commission could validate American claims about Communist intervention in Indochina. Moreover, UN consideration would enhance the nation's moral position by demonstrating that the administration was not bypassing the organization in favor of unilateral or regional collective action. It might also improve American relations with those nations that resented being denied a place at the Korean political conference, and provide an alternative in case the Geneva Conference collapsed. Perhaps in an effort to head off objections, Lodge even outlined a possible strategy, predicting that USUN could garner sufficient votes to establish a Peace Observation Commission subcommittee.[40]

The possible role of the UN in Indochina remained unresolved when the Geneva Conference convened on April 26, 1954. France and Britain con-

39. Dulles to Lodge, May 10, 1954, in folder marked "Henry Cabot Lodge: 1954 (6)," Box 24, Administrative Series, EP, AWF, EL; Lodge to Eisenhower, April 27, 1954, Reel 28, HCLP, MHS.

40. Telegram from Lodge to the Department of State, May 13, 1954, in *FRUS, 1952–1954,* XIII, 1554–57.

tinued to resist UN involvement, fearing that it might set a precedent for international interference in other colonial matters. Nevertheless, perhaps spurred by Lodge's entreaties, the State Department stepped up its efforts to bring the matter before the United Nations while continuing to work on the United Action plan. Dulles asked Prince Wan of Thailand to revive his government's plan to initiate Security Council consideration of the situation. To minimize conflict with the ongoing negotiations in Geneva, the appeal would be limited to Thailand; it would not raise the question of Vietminh aggression in the Associated States.[41]

Having finally resolved to seek at least a limited role for the United Nations, the administration moved forward despite opposition from various quarters. Britain's and France's refusal to support the Thai initiative, though not wholly unexpected, infuriated the secretary of state. If again forced to withdraw its support, Dulles complained, the administration would "appear as totally bankrupt, incompetent and undependable." On a personal level, since Dulles himself had already announced American support for the Thai proposal, he worried that a reversal in policy would "be particularly ignominious." Furthermore, he feared incurring the displeasure of Congress, which was pushing for UN consideration of the issue before authorizing more funds for the French. In light of these factors, Dulles emphasized that "it is difficult to overstate the importance which we attach to proceeding in the UN."[42]

The administration also encountered unexpected resistance from the secretary-general. Resentful that the Thai representative had consulted with the American delegation and not the Secretariat, Hammarskjöld questioned the wisdom of simultaneous consideration of the Indochina question in Geneva and New York. Lodge countered that UN action might serve as the

41. The plan called for Thailand to request the Security Council to dispatch a subcommittee of the Peace Observation Committee to monitor the threat to Thai peace posed by Vietminh troops in Lao and Cambodian territory. Telegram from Dulles to the U.S. Delegation, May 13, 1954, in *FRUS, 1952–1954,* XVI, 790–91; Telegram from Smith to the Department of State, May 16, 1954, same volume, 822–23; Memorandum of Conversation, May 18, 1954, same volume, 846–47; Lodge to Dulles, May 20, 1954, 751G.00/5–2054, Reel 12, LM 71, RG 59, NA.

42. Telegrams from Lodge to Dulles, May 27, 1954, 7:00 P.M. and 10:00 P.M., 751G.00/5–2754, Reel 13, LM 71, RG 59, NA; Dulles News Conference, May 25, 1954, *Department of State Bulletin,* June 7, 1954, p. 863; Telegram from Dulles to the U.S. delegation, May 28, 1954, in *FRUS, 1952–1954,* XVI, p. 964.

"thunder in the distance" necessary to spur the negotiators at Geneva into action. Not entirely convinced, Hammarskjöld discussed the situation with Dulles on June 2. Warned by Lodge that Hammarskjöld had "been off the reservation lately," the secretary of state firmly supported the analysis of his ambassador. Dulles reiterated that since it was increasingly unlikely that the Geneva negotiations would conclude successfully, any progress at the UN would be welcome.[43]

Backed by the United States, Thailand officially lodged a complaint on May 29, 1954. The Thai representative, Pote Sarasin, submitted a letter (written by Lodge and the State Department and approved in advance by Britain and France) to the Security Council in which he asserted that the war in Indochina represented a threat to the security of his country and the maintenance of international peace and security. Pote Sarasin requested the Security Council to send observers to Thailand from the Peace Observation Commission. On June 18 the Council recorded 9 votes in favor and 1 abstention, but a Soviet veto killed the resolution. The Soviet representative insisted, not without some justification, that the Thai request was merely a pretext to facilitate eventual U.S. military intervention.[44]

The UN's involvement ended suddenly in late July. Strongly encouraged by Dulles, the Thai minister for foreign affairs had asked the secretary-general on July 7 to place the issue on the General Assembly agenda.[45] But Thailand proceeded no further with its initiative after the negotiators reached a series of agreements later that month in Geneva. Although the United States refused to sign the Geneva Accords, it declared that in compliance with its obligations under the UN Charter it would not use force to disturb the agreement, and it promised to seek Indochinese unity through free elections supervised by the United Nations. The administration, however,

43. Memorandum of Conversation, May 28, 1954, in *FRUS, 1952–1954,* XIII, 1634; *MTCD,* Reel 2, Dulles and Lodge, June 2, 1954; Memorandum of Conversation, June 2, 1954, in *FRUS, 1952–1954,* XIII, 1658–59; Charles D. Cook to Lodge, July 22, 1954, Reel 6, HCLP, MHS.

44. Telegram from Lodge to Dulles, May 29, 1954, 751G.00/5–2954, Reel 13, LM 71, RG 59, NA; Telegram from Dillon to Dulles, May 30, 1954, 751G.00/5–3054, same reel; *MTCD,* Reel 2, Dulles and Murphy, June 11, 1954, 9:15 A.M.; same reel, Dulles and Lodge, June 11, 1954, 9:35 A.M.; same reel, Dulles and Lodge, June 14, 1954, 11:38 A.M.; "Observation of Thailand Area Proposed," *United Nations Bulletin,* June 15, 1954, p. 434.

45. Telegram from Wadsworth to Dulles, June 9, 1954, 751G.00/6–954, Reel 13, LM 71, RG 59, NA; *MTCD,* Reel 2, Dulles and Merchant, June 18, 1954.

soon turned its considerable energies toward the creation of a collective security treaty for Southeast Asia, SEATO, in order to meet the perceived threat from Communist China, the USSR, and North Vietnam, rather than relying on the UN.[46]

At this relatively early stage of its involvement in the Indochina conflict, the Eisenhower administration thus set a precedent, signaling that it would handle the situation primarily outside of the United Nations.[47] Although Eisenhower and his foreign policy advisers did not use the UN in the manner for which it was intended—as an arena for negotiation—they did not ignore the organization. Instead, they attempted to use the UN as a catalyst for action. Administration officials sought to engineer a show of international support for the free world's objectives in Indochina in order to provide the leverage necessary to extract a negotiated settlement from the Communists outside of the UN forum. In pursuing this course, Eisenhower, Dulles, and Lodge demonstrated an astute recognition of the multifaceted nature of the United Nations and the ways in which it could be used to further American objectives.

Ironically, at the same time that Eisenhower was pledging to abide by the nation's obligations under the UN Charter in Korea, the administration was involved in a covert operation in Guatemala that clearly violated its responsibilities under the Charter.[48] The United States' actions in Guatemala saw the

46. Richard H. Immerman, "The United States and the Geneva Conference of 1954: A New Look," *Diplomatic History,* XIV (1990), 43–66; Gary Hess, "Redefining the American Position in Southeast Asia: The United States and the Geneva and Manila Conferences," in Kaplan, Artaud, and Rubin, eds., *Dien Bien Phu and the Crisis of Franco-American Relations,* 123–48.

47. On the Eisenhower administration's subsequent involvement in Indochina, see Anderson, *Trapped by Success;* George C. Herring, Gary Hess, and Richard H. Immerman, "Passage of Empire: The United States, France, and South Vietnam, 1954–1955," in Kaplan, Artaud, and Rubin, eds., *Dien Bien Phu and the Crisis of Franco-American Relations,* 171–95; David L. Anderson and Daniel P. O'C. Greene, "John Foster Dulles and the End of the Franco-American Entente in Indochina," *Diplomatic History,* XVI (1992), 551–71; Arthur Combs, "The Path Not Taken: The British Alternative to U.S. Policy in Vietnam, 1954–1956," *Diplomatic History,* XIX (1995), 33–57.

48. For comprehensive accounts of American involvement in Guatemala, see, for example, the following: Stephen Schlesinger and Stephen Kinzer, *Bitter Fruit: The Untold Story of the American Coup in Guatemala* (Garden City, 1982); Richard H. Immerman, *The CIA in*

nation working at cross-purposes with the United Nations and raised serious questions about Eisenhower's desire to develop a positive and constructive relationship with the organization.

The United States government had become increasingly concerned about the leftward political trend in Guatemala in the aftermath of the Guatemalan Revolution of 1944. The election of Colonel Jacobo Arbenz Guzmán in November, 1950, and the implementation of Arbenz's far-reaching program of social and economic reform heightened anxiety about the rise of radicalism, nationalism, and even communism in its Latin American neighbor. After only a few months in office, the new administration concluded that the Arbenz government posed a Communist threat to the Western Hemisphere. Eisenhower cited the expropriation of land owned by American corporations and Arbenz's refusal to send Guatemalan troops to join the UN fight in Korea as "proof" of the nation's Communist leanings. Guatemala had also, Eisenhower noted in his memoirs, "accepted the ridiculous communist contention that the United States had conducted bacteriological warfare in Korea."[49] Guatemala's importation of Czechoslovakian weapons in May, 1954, provided the final "evidence" of Communist infiltration necessary to prompt a response from the administration.

Eisenhower, John Foster Dulles, CIA director Allen Dulles, and Lodge all averred that it was imperative for the United States to oust Arbenz. The commander in chief and his key lieutenants believed that a Communist government in Central America would damage American prestige abroad and arouse the political wrath of the McCarthy forces at home. Using Guatemala as a base, the Soviet Union could engage in subversive activities aimed at spreading communism throughout the region. The Dulles brothers, in particular, interpreted the conflict as another in an ongoing series of confrontations between the free world and a monolithic Communist bloc. Lodge had taken a stance against the revolutionary regime as early as 1949, with a speech in the Senate protesting the impact of Guatemala's new labor codes on the United Fruit Company. As a senator from Massachusetts, the home state of the United Fruit Company, he was subject to heavy pressure from company lobbyists. Moreover, his family held stock in the corporation, as did

---

Guatemala: The Foreign Policy of Intervention (Austin, 1982); Piero Gleijeses, *Shattered Hope: The Guatemalan Revolution and the United States, 1944–1954* (Princeton, 1991).

49. Eisenhower, *Mandate for Change,* 422; Telegram from Dulles to USUN, April 27, 1953, 330/4–153, Box 1306, RG 59, NA.

the Dulles family. These personal and political factors most likely only reinforced Lodge's already strong disposition against Communist influence in Guatemala. Still, he had been among the first in Congress to denounce Guatemalan actions against United Fruit.[50]

In June, 1954, the United States was at the height of its power in the Security Council. The six elected members—Brazil, Colombia, Denmark, Lebanon, New Zealand, and Turkey—were all basically supportive of the United States. Furthermore, during that month Lodge was president (a position that rotated monthly among the permanent members). Nevertheless, the administration does not appear to have given a moment's thought to using the UN to meet this ostensible threat. It believed that concerted Great Power action to eliminate a Communist threat was simply not possible in the cold war environment of 1954. The ongoing difficulties encountered in preserving a UN coalition to repel a clear-cut case of military aggression in Korea had convinced the administration that it would be impossible to use the UN to fight the more insidious form of Communist expansionism allegedly taking place in Guatemala. Nor did the administration have any confidence in the ability of the Organization of American States (OAS) to eradicate communism in Latin America. Thus, the administration never seriously considered pursuing its objectives in Guatemala through either universal or regional multilateral organizations.[51]

Instead of seeking his objectives in an international public forum, Eisenhower turned to covert intervention. After the CIA's recent success in bringing down the ostensibly Communist-leaning premier of Iran, Eisenhower embraced covert intervention as the most efficacious means of eliminating the objectionable regime in Guatemala. The CIA launched a covert operation, named Operation Pbsuccess, aimed at turning the Guatemalan army against Arbenz, suggesting that an overwhelming insurrectionary force was invading, and forcing Arbenz to flee. Propaganda broadcast into Guatemala City laid the groundwork by spreading misinformation about the invading forces. Finally, on June 18, 1954, a small group of 150 exiles led by an

50. Allen Dulles, *The Craft of Intelligence* (New York, 1963), 234–36; Eisenhower, *Mandate for Change,* 421–26; Immerman, *The CIA in Guatemala,* 116; Gleijeses, *Shattered Hope,* 132.

51. For a thorough analysis of the relationship between the UN and the OAS during the Guatemalan crisis, see Aida Luisa Levin, "Regionalism and the United Nations in American Foreign Policy: The Peace-Keeping Experience of the Organization of American States" (Ph.D. dissertation, Columbia University, 1971).

American-selected, right-wing colonel, Carlos Castillo Armas, invaded from Honduras. Armas' poorly organized force progressed barely beyond the border. But aircraft supplied by the United States dropped bombs on targets in San José and Guatemala City, spreading panic. Having allied himself too closely with the Guatemalan Communist party to expect assistance from the American-dominated OAS, Arbenz turned to the United Nations for protection. On Saturday, June 19, the Guatemalan foreign minister, Guillermo Toriello, requested the Security Council and the Inter-American Peace Committee (IAPC) of the OAS to convene immediate meetings.

Guatemala's appeal to the UN came as no surprise to the State Department. As early as May, 1953, the department had noted that to "counterbalance its isolation in Central America it [Guatemala] will seek political support elsewhere, particularly in the United Nations." Indeed, in April, 1953, the Guatemalan government had notified the secretary-general and the General Assembly that subversive activities by American citizens in Guatemala were threatening the nation's sovereignty.[52]

The Eisenhower administration was compelled to hide United States complicity in the Guatemalan rebellion from UN scrutiny, and to do so without appearing to show a callous disregard for the organization's prescribed role in the peaceful resolution of threats to international peace. The administration determined to refer the matter to the OAS, where the United States could exert greater power, to bury it or at least control an investigation. OAS deliberation would forestall UN involvement.[53]

The U.S. effort provoked an uproar. It brought to the surface a latent jurisdictional conflict over whether the UN or a regional organization had precedence, in the first instance, in handling a local threat to international peace. Invoking Article 52(2) of the UN Charter, which stated that nations "shall make every effort to achieve pacific settlement of local disputes through such regional arrangements or by such regional agencies before re-

52. National Intelligence Estimate, "Probable Developments in Guatemala, May 19, 1953, in *FRUS, 1952–1954*, IV, 1063; Telegram from Wadsworth to Dulles, April 15, 1953, 330/4–1553, in Box 1306, RG 59, NA; Telegram from Dulles to USUN, April 27, 1953, 330/4–153, in Box 1306, RG 59, NA.

53. The administration decided upon this course despite the objections of some officials in the State Department. For example, the U.S. ambassador to the OAS, John Drier, cautioned that the enforcement of an OAS decision required Security Council concurrence. Minutes of a Meeting, "OAS Action Against Communism in Guatemala," May 10, 1954, in *FRUS, 1952–1954*, IV, 1105.

ferring them to the Security Council," Lodge emphatically insisted that the proper procedure was referral to the OAS. The secretary-general responded with a defense of the UN's right to original jurisdiction. Hammarskjöld reminded Lodge that the final paragraph of Article 52 declared that this "article in no way impairs the application of Articles 34 and 35." Since Article 34 authorized the Security Council to "investigate any dispute . . . likely to endanger the maintenance of international peace and security," while Article 35 stipulated that UN member nations could bring any such dispute to the attention of the Security Council, the UN was fully entitled to investigate the situation. Thus, the secretary-general argued, in a conflict between a regional organization and the international organization, the UN was paramount. Lodge and Hammarskjöld had only exchanged the opening salvos in the debate.[54]

In his role as Security Council president, Lodge initially called a meeting for Monday morning, June 21, 1954. Discovering that the Soviets intended to complain that he should have called an earlier emergency session, and that others believed that the actual fighting mandated an immediate session, he rescheduled the meeting for Sunday, June 20. Lodge and key members of his staff spent a sleepless night at the offices of the U.S. mission preparing for the 3:00 P.M. meeting.[55]

Debate on Sunday afternoon quickly focused on the fundamental question. Was the OAS or the Security Council the proper body to handle the conflict in Guatemala? The absence of definitive legal guidelines enabled both sides to invoke the UN Charter to support their positions. After opening remarks by Lodge, who informed the council that Brazil, Colombia, and Cuba had already requested that the matter be submitted to the OAS, the Guatemalan envoy, Eduardo Castillo-Arriolla, presented his case. Refusing the OAS offer to investigate, Castillo-Arriolla instead petitioned the Security Council to call upon Honduras and Nicaragua to capture the expeditionary force and to send a peace commission to Guatemala to verify his account of the events. While acknowledging that Articles 33 and 52 of the UN Charter enjoined the "parties to a dispute" to settle their differences directly or through the offices of a regional organization before bringing the matter to the Security Council, Castillo-Arriolla insisted that the situation in Guate-

54. Urquhart, *Hammarskjöld,* 90; Summary of Major Decisions, July 7, 1954, Reel 86, State Department Microfilm, J. F. Dulles Papers, Mudd Library.

55. Memorandum of Telephone Conversation, June 20, 1954, 330/6–2054, in Box 1306, RG 59, NA; "How to Handle the Communists," August 21, 1954, in Box 78, HCLP, MHS.

mala was not a "dispute" or a civil war. It was a case of naked aggression. As such, it deserved to be dealt with according to the provisions of Chapter VII of the Charter, which outlined the Security Council's actions in handling such acts.

Lodge countered that the situation was an internal conflict between Arbenz and Armas. Consequently, the obvious procedure was for the matter to be referred to the OAS, where it could be handled "most expeditiously and most effectively." The American representative claimed that it was ludicrous for anyone to suspect the United States of intervention, for Eisenhower "abhor[red] all forms of imperialism." Rather, a Soviet veto of the resolution to refer the matter to the OAS, he claimed, would lead "unbiased observers throughout the world [to] come to the conclusion that the Soviet Union has got designs on the American Hemisphere." As the five-and-one-half-hour meeting neared its conclusion, Lodge, playing to the extensive radio and television coverage, wagged his finger at Semyon Tsarapkin and sternly warned: "I say to you, representative of the Soviet Union, stay out of this hemisphere and don't try to start your plans and your conspiracies over here."[56]

The subsequent vote confirmed the divisions apparent during debate. Brazil and Colombia offered a resolution written by the State Department that asked the Security Council to refer the matter to the OAS. This resolution, amended by a French proposal calling for "the immediate termination of any action likely to cause further bloodshed," received ten affirmative votes. Ambiguity about the composition of the forces and past OAS success in resolving regional conflicts enabled the United States to persuade a strong majority to place the matter in the hands of the OAS. Nevertheless, a Soviet veto killed the resolution. French representative Henri Hoppenot then reintroduced his amendment as a separate proposal. The council unanimously passed the French resolution, with Lodge hesitantly voting in favor, for he realized that the resolution left the door open for renewed consideration.[57]

The Arbenz government quickly seized this opportunity. On June 22 the

56. Lodge statement before the Security Council on June 20, 1953, *Department of State Bulletin,* July 5, 1954, pp. 27–28; Andrew Boyd, *Fifteen Men on a Powder Keg: A History of the U. N. Security Council* (New York, 1971), 165; Immerman, *The CIA in Guatemala,* 171.

57. Telegram from Murphy (acting secretary) to USUN, June 20, 1954, 1:05 P.M., 714.00/6–2054, in Box 3244A, RG 59, NA; Telegrams from Lodge to the Secretary of State, June 20, 1954, 7:04 P.M. and 8:39 P.M., 714.00/6–2054, same box; Memorandum of Conversation, June 20, 1954, 714.00/6–2054, same box; Memorandum of Conversation, June 21, 1954, 714.00/6–2154, same box.

Guatemalan representative requested another meeting of the Security Council on the grounds that the aggressors were ignoring the resolution of June 20. Lodge denounced the request as "a carefully planned Communist plot." For Guatemala to insist upon raising the issue again, after the Security Council's resounding 10 to 1 decision that the matter belonged in the OAS, suggested that the Arbenz government was only "a cat's paw of the Soviet conspiracy to meddle in the Western Hemisphere."[58]

But the Guatemalan representative was not a lone voice crying in the wilderness. In addition to the Soviet Union, Britain and France supported Guatemala's request for another meeting. Maintaining that the OAS did not have mandatory jurisdiction, they too favored a Soviet proposal to send a UN peace commission to the region to investigate. It was necessary, British foreign secretary Anthony Eden argued, to "act on principle . . . and treat the plight of unfriendly and unpleasant Guatemala in the same way we would treat a friendly state." New Zealand, Denmark, and Lebanon concurred.[59]

The stance of the U.S. allies put the U.S. delegation in a difficult position. As Lodge explained to the interdepartmental (the CIA–State Department– Defense Department–United States Information Agency) "Guatemalan Group" on June 23, he might have to vote to send UN observers unless he could report that the OAS had already dispatched observers of its own. State Department officials therefore urged "speedy OAS consideration" to at least "buy us [the United States] a little time."[60]

The attitude of Britain and France infuriated Eisenhower, Dulles, and Lodge and threatened to create a serious rift between the United States and its two most important allies. Eisenhower ranted that the United States had been "too damned nice to the British on this" issue. Taking a hard-line attitude, he told Dulles that "the British expect us to give them a free ride and side with them on Cyprus and yet they won't even support us on Guatemala.

58. *MTCD,* Reel 2, Dulles and Lodge, June 22, 1954; "Statement of June 20, 1954," Lodge statement before the Security Council, *Department of State Bulletin,* July 5, 1954, p. 28.

59. Eden, quoted in Sharon Meers, "The British Connection: How the United States Covered Its Tracks in the 1954 Coup in Guatemala," *Diplomatic History,* XVI (1992), 419; Telegram from Lodge to Dulles, June 24, 1954, 330/6–2454, in Box 1306, RG 59, NA.

60. Key to Holland (Henry F. Holland, assistant secretary of state for inter-American affairs), June 22, 1954, 714/00/6–2254, in Box 3244A, RG 59, NA; Notes of a Meeting of the Guatemalan Group, June 23, 1954, in *FRUS, 1952–1954,* IV, 1178; Meers, "The British Connection," 418–19.

Let's give them a lesson." To teach this "lesson," the president on June 24 authorized Lodge to exercise the United States' first veto in the Security Council if necessary. Eisenhower and Dulles had concluded that the principle at stake, the prestige of the inter-American system, was important enough to sacrifice one of the nation's most valuable propaganda assets in the UN—that only the USSR used its veto power.[61]

Dulles readily followed Eisenhower's lead. The secretary of state directed the U.S. ambassador in France to convey his conviction to Prime Minister Pierre Mendès-France that Hoppenot's insistence on presenting his resolution at the June 20 meeting was inexcusable, for the "matter was of no direct interest to them and of vital concern to us." Dulles was particularly galled by the French attitude because he believed it was undeserved. The United States had backed France loyally during debate on the colonial questions in past General Assembly sessions. Even more recently, the United States had agreed to its ally's request not to bring the question of Indochina to the UN. France had claimed that as a civil war, the conflict did not fall under UN jurisdiction. Surely, Dulles maintained, it should now accept the same line of reasoning by the United States.[62]

Dulles echoed the same refrain in direct talks with Churchill and Eden. When the British leaders arrived in Washington, D.C., on June 25 for consultations about the Geneva conference, the secretary wasted no time in raising the matter of Guatemala. Beginning the discussion on the car ride from the airport, Dulles insisted that the Security Council ought not to adopt a provisional agenda that included the Guatemalan question. When the meeting continued at the White House, Eisenhower joined Dulles in talking "cold turkey" to the British leaders. In order to obtain American support on a variety of other pressing issues, such as the EDC, Egyptian claims to the Suez Canal, and the ongoing Geneva negotiations on Indochina, Eden finally agreed to direct his representative to abstain and encourage France to do so as well.[63]

---

61. Ferrell, ed., *The Diary of James C. Hagerty,* 74; *MTCD,* Reel 2, Dulles and Lodge, June 24, 1954; Gleijeses, *Shattered Hope,* 330–31.

62. Telegram from Dulles to the U.S. embassy in France, June 23, 1954, in *FRUS, 1952–1954,* IV, 1183; *MTCD,* Reel 2, Dulles and Lodge, June 22, 1954; Memorandum of Conversation, June 24, 1954, 330/6–2454, in Box 1306, RG 59, NA.

63. Ferrell, *The Diary of James C. Hagerty,* 78; *MTCD,* Reel 2, Dulles and Lodge, June 25, 1954; Memorandum of a Meeting, June 25, 1954, in *FRUS, 1952–1954,* IV, 1075–76; Meers,

Meanwhile, Lodge communicated the administration's hard-line attitude to the British and French delegations in New York. On June 24, Eisenhower instructed Lodge to inform them that the United States would not tolerate interference in affairs in the Western Hemisphere. While their governments were free to take whatever positions they chose on Guatemala, if they declined to follow the U.S. lead, the administration would feel free to act independently on controversial colonial questions such as Egypt, Cyprus, and North Africa. Lodge welcomed this possibility. Frustrated by how the nation's defense of its colonialist allies handicapped efforts to court the Third World, he optimistically opined to Dulles that "if this releases us to do what we want in the colonial question, it's not a bad deal."[64] This news was not to be presented, Eisenhower emphasized, as "a threat." Rather, he wanted a "clear understanding" that a refusal to back one's allies on unpopular issues was a "two-way street." The pronouncement, Lodge reported to Dulles, was "received with great solemnity."[65]

Lodge could not postpone indefinitely another Security Council meeting. However, he used his prerogatives as president to delay the meeting until Friday, June 25, while the State Department and USUN lobbied for support from Britain, France, China, Colombia, and Nicaragua. The administration also carefully planned its tactics. Lodge and Dulles decided to put forth a procedural motion as a test vote in order to get an estimation of their strength in the council. The United States would oppose the first order of business—the usually *pro forma* motion to adopt the provisional agenda.[66]

Eisenhower played no appreciable role in determining the tactics for the Security Council meeting. According to Lodge, however, the president was "intensely interested in all the details" of American maneuvering after the fact. Informed that U.S. tactics had been similar to those employed in pass-

---

"The British Connection," 121, 125. See also Immerman, *The CIA in Guatemala,* 172, and Cook, *The Declassified Eisenhower,* 282.

64. *MTCD,* Reel 2, Dulles and Lodge, June 25, 1954; Summary of Major Decisions, June 24, 1954, Reel 86, State Department Microfilm, J. F. Dulles Papers, Mudd Library.

65. Memorandum of Conversation, Dulles and Lodge, June 24, 1954, in *FRUS, 1952–1954,* IV, 1184; Telegram from Lodge to Dulles, same volume, 1185.

66. *MTCD,* Reel 2, Dulles and Lodge, June 25, 1954; Memorandum of Conversation, June 25, 1954, 330/6–2554, Box 1306, RG 59, NA; Memorandum of Conversation, June 25, 1954, 714/00/6–2554, in Box 3244B, RG 59, NA.

ing the fair-play amendment at the Republican National Convention in 1952, Eisenhower "laughed and said that he understood."[67]

According to a prearranged plan, the representative from Brazil objected to the adoption of the agenda and was seconded by the representative of Colombia. Others followed. Once he became aware of what was happening, the Soviet representative was forced to put forward a motion calling for its adoption. Lodge countered with a speech written largely by Dulles in which he maintained that the United States was "legally and as a matter of honor" bound to insist upon OAS consideration of the Guatemalan question in the first instance. To move to the Security Council first, would "create international anarchy rather than international order" by setting "a chain of disastrous events" in motion. Security Council consideration would culminate, Lodge predicted, in "a catastrophe of such dimensions as will gravely impair the future effectiveness both of the United Nations itself and of regional organizations," and consequently "the United Nations will have destroyed itself in 1954."[68]

After Lodge's apocalyptic speech, the motion was put to a vote. The U.S. position prevailed, with four nations voting in favor of adopting the agenda, five opposed, and two (Britain and France) abstaining. No Soviet veto was possible, because U.S. tactics had placed the burden on the Soviets to get the seven affirmative votes required to adopt the agenda. Instead, the U.S. delegation had adeptly wielded what political scientist John Stoessinger has termed its "hidden veto," the use of the nation's "considerable influence to persuade members of the Council to form a negative majority for its position," thus making a U.S. veto unnecessary.[69]

Security Council action or inaction became a moot point shortly thereafter. Conclusive American intervention obviated further consideration of the issue. On June 27 Arbenz capitulated and the new Guatemalan government informed the Security Council that its assistance was no longer required.

67. Memorandum of Conversation, Lodge and Winston Churchill, June 26, 1954, Reel 3, HCLP, MHS; Telegram from Dulles to Lodge, June 24, 1954, Box 1306, RG 59, NA.

68. Lodge statement of June 25, 1954, *Department of State Bulletin,* July 5, 1954, pp. 30–31.

69. John G. Stoessinger, *The United Nations and the Superpowers: United States–Soviet Interaction at the United Nations* (New York, 1965), 14–15.

The United States had succeeded in circumventing the Soviet veto and achieved its primary goal—the elimination of the Arbenz government. The American victory, however, had cost both the UN and the OAS dearly in terms of lost prestige. Contrary to its public pronouncements, the Eisenhower administration had not sought to refer the Guatemalan matter to the OAS because the regional organization could handle the situation "most expeditiously and most effectively," or because it was anxious to fulfill its obligations under the OAS Charter, or because it desired to avert "international anarchy." Rather, knowing that the Security Council might sustain the Arbenz regime, the administration had used OAS consideration as a pretext to obstruct UN intervention while it achieved its politico-security objectives by unilateral action. The administration accurately concluded that in this situation the OAS would be more responsive to American demands than the United Nations and more likely to supply a modicum of multilateral legitimacy to the United States' essentially unilateral move.

The administration apparently gave little thought to the long-term impact of its actions on its relationship with the UN. Rather, its *ad hoc* response to the exigencies of this particular set of circumstances in Guatemala reflected a determination to reassert American hegemony in Latin America. The administration failed to heed the warning of a member of the State Department's Policy Planning Staff that "concentration on what appears to be a local emergency may result in inadequate attention to larger considerations that are not local or short-range."[70]

The administration also violated, in spirit at least, the UN Charter's provisions for members to receive a hearing and an on-the-spot investigation of a complaint. It thereby undermined the UN's potential as a force for the preservation of international peace and security. In insisting upon the primacy of regional organizations, the administration also set a dangerous precedent. Surely Eisenhower and Dulles would not have desired the League of Arab States to handle a volatile situation in the Middle East before referring it to the UN. Moreover, the United States' position further jeopardized relations with the secretary-general, who viewed the American action as a grave threat to the United Nations and its future "constitutional development."

70. Memorandum, Louis J. Halle, Jr., to Bowie, May 28, 1954, in *FRUS, 1952–1954,* IV, 1139.

Continued American action along these lines would, he said, force him to reconsider whether he would continue in his post.[71]

The administration's behavior in these three situations raised troubling questions about its relationship with the United Nations and its basic conception of the organization's role in the international community. President Eisenhower's actions in Korea, Indochina, and Guatemala belied his rhetorical support of the international organization. During both the final months of the Korean War and the prolonged period of the armistice, the United States usurped virtually all control and power from the UN. Later, American policy makers at first discouraged UN involvement in Indochina and then advocated only a limited role—as a neutral observatory and fact-finding body—for the organization. Correctly convinced that a majority would condemn American intervention in Guatemala, the administration made every possible effort to prevent the UN's examination of the situation. In all three cases, the organization was left watching the action from the wings, while the United States not only took center stage but also directed the show, relegating the UN and even important U.S. allies to limited supporting roles. The administration had demonstrated conclusively that the United Nations could function effectively as a collective security organization only when the United States was willing to allow it do so, under the guise of a collaborative effort.

Despite the obvious implications of these rather extensive, perhaps even blatant, power plays, the administration appeared in mid-1954 to be reasonably satisfied with the way in which the United Nations had functioned as a pliable instrument of American policy. And indeed, the administration had reason to be satisfied. Eisenhower had skillfully used the organization to provide multilateral legitimacy to an operation of anti-Communist allies in Korea. Only French resistance prevented him from using the organization in a similar fashion in the Indochina situation. When the United Nations posed a potential roadblock to the United States' pursuit of its objectives in Guatemala, the administration exerted its power and influence to prevent, albeit by a narrow margin, such international intervention.

71. Memorandum, Charles D. Cook to Lodge, July 22, 1954, Reel 6, HCLP, MHS; Urquhart, *Hammarskjöld,* 92.

In all three cases, Eisenhower established the broad direction of American policy, and set the tone for the administration's dealings with the United Nations and foreign nations. In these first opportunities to exercise presidential influence and authority on the international front, Eisenhower showed his pragmatic willingness to use all available options to achieve what he deemed to be the short-term interests of the United States. What was less clear, especially in the cases of Indochina and Guatemala, was whether this approach would prove equally successful over the long term.

6

Parting the Bamboo Curtain
The United States and Communist China

The second front in the cold war extended along the perimeter of the People's Republic of China (PRC) in the Far East. There too the Eisenhower administration used the United Nations in a variety of ways to advance its cause in the ongoing struggle against communism. The UN came into play most prominently in the effort to resolve two conflicts with Communist China—the imprisonment of U.S. airmen captured during the Korean War and the Communists' periodic threats to "liberate" islands off the mainland in the Straits of Formosa. Further exacerbating Sino-American hostility during the Eisenhower era was the administration's vigorous effort to prevent the United Nations from admitting the People's Republic of China as the rightful representative of the Chinese people.

The Eisenhower administration had a variety of objectives in its dealings with the PRC. It attempted to isolate and contain the Communist power, to manage its relations with a nation that it did not recognize, and to drive a wedge in the Sino-Soviet relationship. Throughout, the administration recognized the psychological importance of these objectives and worried that failure to obtain them would damage American credibility with both allies and adversaries. Interestingly, in pursuing these often-conflicting aims at the UN, the administration's public posture was one of unyielding opposition to any association with the PRC, while behind the scenes it proved relatively more flexible.

When Eisenhower entered office, the controversy over whether the

People's Republic of China should replace the Republic of China as the representative of the Chinese people in the UN raged unabated. The question was particularly critical for political reasons—domestic, international, and UN. Traditional Republican interest in the affairs of the region and the adamant support provided the Chinese Nationalists by Knowland and McCarthy and their supporters circumscribed Eisenhower's options. Internationally, the issue represented a sharply defined contest between the forces of communism and the forces of anti-communism, with the United States' willingness and ability to assist its anti-Communist allies seemingly at stake. Furthermore, China, as one of the five permanent members of the Security Council, wielded veto power, a veto the United States wanted to remain in the hands of friend, not foe.

The Eisenhower administration thus publicly opposed Communist China's representation even more vehemently than had the Truman administration. It insisted that the Nationalist government was the sole legitimate representative of the Chinese people. Immediately upon entering office, Lodge began compiling material "with good hard-hitting propaganda and publicity value" against the seating of Communist China. Lodge and the State Department developed a thorough case, the basic points of which remained the same throughout Eisenhower's two terms. The administration insisted that Communist China should not be represented, for it did not respect the principles and purposes of the UN. The Peking regime had demonstrated repeatedly that it was not "peace-loving" and would not discharge its international responsibilities. The United Nations itself had branded Communist China an aggressor in the Korean conflict. Further examples of unsatisfactory behavior abounded. The PRC had occupied Tibet, engaged in subversive activity in Southeast Asia, enslaved its own people, violated international agreements, committed atrocities against UN prisoners of war, and participated in the international drug trade. The organization had to show the Communist Chinese that they "could not shoot their way into the UN. If anyone wished to join a club," Dulles advised, "he should not go about it by insulting the members of the Admissions Committee."[1]

The administration feared the results of a successful motion to extend

1. Lodge to Dulles, March 15, 1954, 310.2/3–1544, in Box 1238, RG 59, NA; Memorandum of Conversation, July 1, 1955, in *FRUS, 1955–1957,* II, 626. For a contemporary account of the United States' approach to China at the UN, see Lincoln Bloomfield, "China, the United States, and the United Nations," *International Organization,* XX (1958), 653–76.

representation to the People's Republic of China. The admission of Communist China, it claimed, would weaken the UN's effectiveness as a coalition of free nations. It would enable the PRC to spread its revolutionary program and enhance its influence among African and the other Asian states. In addition, many people would interpret a vote to seat the Communist delegation as *de facto* recognition of the Peking regime, infuriating the Formosa regime of Chiang Kai-shek and the powerful Nationalist China lobby in the United States. Dulles also supported nonrecognition because he believed that it would strain the Sino-Soviet alliance, perhaps to the breaking point, with China demanding Soviet support on this issue.[2]

Moreover, Congress' implacable and vocal opposition to Communist Chinese representation virtually ruled out the possibility of a change in American policy on this issue. Dulles had personally indicated a willingness to consider a two-China policy in the UN as early as 1950. In early 1953 he had requested that John Dickey, an international lawyer, devise a UN Charter amendment that would remove China as a permanent member of the Security Council and seat both Chinas in the General Assembly, where they would have little power. In the summer of 1954, he even presented the idea to British foreign secretary Anthony Eden and Indian prime minister Jawaharlal Nehru. But domestic political realities short-circuited any serious contemplation of a shift in policy. As Vice President Richard Nixon reassured Chiang, the admission of the People's Republic to the UN "would produce violent political repercussions" at home.[3]

---

2. Memorandum, Lodge to Dulles, March 30, 1954, Reel 4, HCLP, MHS. On Dulles's attempt to drive a wedge between the PRC and the USSR, see David Mayers, "Eisenhower and Communism: Later Findings," in Richard A. Melanson and David Mayers, eds., *Reevaluating Eisenhower: American Foreign Policy in the Fifties* (Urbana, 1989), 92–93; John Lewis Gaddis, "The American 'Wedge' Strategy, 1949–1955," in Harry Harding and Yuan Ming, eds., *Sino-American Relations, 1945–1955: A Joint Reassessment of a Critical Decade* (Wilmington, 1989), 168, 171–72.

3. Memorandum of a Conversation, July 8, 1956, in *FRUS, 1955–1957*, III, 399. On Dulles's ideas, see William Snyder, "Dean Rusk to John Foster Dulles, May–June 1953: The Office, the First 100 Days, and Red China," *Diplomatic History*, VII (1983), 86; Wang Jisi, "The Origins of America's 'Two China' Policy," in Harding and Ming, eds., *Sino-American Relations, 1945–1955*, 205; Nancy Bernkopf Tucker, "John Foster Dulles and the Taiwan Roots of the 'Two Chinas' Policy," in Immerman, *John Foster Dulles and the Diplomacy of the Cold War*, 256–57; Robert Accinelli, *Crisis and Commitment: United States Policy Toward Taiwan, 1950–1955* (Chapel Hill, 1996).

Initially, the administration confidently anticipated the defeat of any move to grant representation to the PRC. Dulles emphasized that the United Nations and the specialized agencies had defeated over 150 such proposals in the past. Furthermore, in a departure from Truman's strategy, Dulles announced that the United States considered the question to be of a substantive rather than a procedural nature. Therefore, a two-thirds, rather than a simple, majority in the General Assembly would be necessary to seat the mainland delegation. The secretary of state declared that if the issue arose in the Security Council, the United States "would invoke the veto if necessary" (for the first time) to protect the status quo.[4]

Eisenhower publicly declared his unequivocal opposition to the PRC's representation early in his presidency. Rising international support for seating the Communist delegation and the necessity of winning the votes of key congressmen who opposed the Korean negotiations on the grounds that talks would facilitate subsequent recognition of the PRC prompted his statements. On May 14, 1953, the president announced that he did not believe that Communist China should be admitted to the UN after an armistice in Korea. He added at a cabinet meeting that he did not "like the idea that you're respectable if you stop robbing me—that's not decent."[5] A year later, he remained "completely and unalterably opposed" to Communist China's representation until it had established "a record of deeds that would prove really good faith." Yet Eisenhower refused to use the threat of withdrawal to compel a vote against Communist China, though he did not categorically rule it out. Reluctant to give up on the UN, he insisted that the United States would withdraw only if it served the cause of peace more effectively than remaining in the organization.[6]

Congress, however, still insisted on voicing its opinion. Attention centered on a rider to the Senate appropriations bill for the UN. Introduced by Knowland and passed on May 28, 1953, the rider barred any American contribution to the organization if Communist China was admitted to membership. In a letter to Nixon, undoubtedly written for public consumption,

4. "Chinese Representation in the United Nations," Dulles news conference on July 8, 1954, *Department of State Bulletin,* July 19, 1954, p. 87.
5. Notes of Cabinet Meeting, May 31, 1953, Reel 28, HCLP, MHS; Press Conference, May 14, 1953, in Box 1, Press Conference Series, EP, AWF, EL.
6. Press Conference, July 7, 1954, in Box 2, Press Conference Series, EP, AWF, EL.

Eisenhower explained that such a "hostile, punitive measure" was "unworthy of our responsibilities of leadership and our great traditions." The president insisted that it would be better to "renounce our membership and leave by the front door, rather than default on our obligations as a member and sneak out by the rear door."[7]

Meeting with the legislative leaders on June 2, Eisenhower explained that he opposed the rider for a number of reasons. First, it was not the appropriate means to achieve American goals. Second, the United States needed allies and would have to learn to accept occasional defeats in the UN without shunning the organization that remained "the hope of the world for creating eventually an association in which laws would replace battlefields." Finally, perhaps heeding Lodge's oft-repeated axiom that a politician should never say "never," Eisenhower insisted that the United States should not rule out the possibility that Communist China would reform and become a UN member. In turn, he promised to seek pledges from U.S. allies that they would not use the Korean armistice as a reason to seat the Communists.[8]

Nevertheless, international pressure to support the seating of Communist China increased after the Korean armistice in the spring of 1953. Arguing that bestowing representation would appear to be a reward for simply halting illegitimate aggression, Dulles personally devised the American strategy to prevent such a move. He determined to extend the moratorium arrangement, reached between the United States and Great Britain in June, 1951, to the end of 1953. Under the moratorium, both nations agreed to dispose of the issue on a procedural basis, through a motion to postpone action on the question. Avoiding debate and votes on the substance of the question enabled the United States to obtain the broadest possible support, for it did not force nations to vote directly against the Communists. Dulles saw no reason to abandon this tactic, since it had the support of a majority of even those nations that had recognized the PRC.[9]

Acquiring allies' consent was not easy, however. Britain had made it clear that it intended to abandon the moratorium policy after an armistice. France too indicated that it was prepared to recognize the People's Republic of

7. Eisenhower to Nixon, June 1, 1953, in folder marked "Richard Nixon (5)," Box 28, Administration Series, EP, AWF, EL.

8. *Legislative Meeting Series,* Reel 1, Notes on Special Legislative Conference, June 2, 1953.

9. Telegram from Dulles to USUN, June 18, 1953, in *FRUS, 1952–1954,* III, 677–79.

China if it would help negotiations in Indochina.[10] Reminding Eisenhower and Dulles that the U.S. public, prodded by the China lobby, considered the question of Chinese representation to be the most important issue before the General Assembly, Lodge still implored Eisenhower and Dulles to reach a tripartite agreement to extend the measure. Lodge even requested advance authorization to use the veto in the Security Council if necessary. Dulles granted him "discretion," but insisted that only the president could make the final decision on the use of the veto. Britain finally agreed to extend the moratorium for the remainder of the calendar year, and a U.S. proposal to postpone the issue until 1954 carried by a vote of 44 to 10, with 2 abstentions.[11]

Congressional agitation, spearheaded by Republican leaders Knowland and Representative Walter H. Judd of Minnesota, continued. Acting on behalf of the congressional contingent on the Committee of One Million (a Nationalist China lobbying group), Judd sent Eisenhower a petition in October, 1953. Eisenhower replied in a carefully worded letter in which he agreed that Communist China sought participation in the UN to spread its economic and political doctrines, but did not comment upon the committee's call for a U.S. withdrawal if such an event occurred.[12]

On July 1, 1954, Knowland, long a spokesman of the China lobby, announced that if the UN admitted the PRC, he would resign his leadership

10. Memorandum, Bacon (Ruth E. Bacon, United Nations adviser, Bureau of Far Eastern Affairs) to McConaughy (Walter P. McConaughy, director of the Office of Chinese Affairs), May 26, 1953, in *FRUS, 1952–1954,* III, 641–51; Telegram from Lodge to Dulles, June 3, 1953, same volume, 657–58; Telegram from Lodge to the Department of State, June 9, 1953, same volume, 660–61; Telegram from C. Douglas Dillon (U.S. ambassador to France) to the Department of State, June 15, 1953, same volume, 676; Telegram from Winthrop W. Aldrich (U.S. ambassador to the United Kingdom), July 1, 1953, same volume, 682–83; Memorandum, "Chinese Representation in the Security Council," June 10, 1953, 330/6–1053, in Box 1306, RG 59, NA.

11. Dulles to Lodge, June 19, 1953, in *FRUS, 1952–1954,* III, 679–80; Lodge to Dulles, June 11, 1953, same volume, 667; Telegram from Dulles to U.S. embassies in the United Kingdom and France, June 12, 1953, same volume, 670–71; Lodge to Dulles, June 24, 1953, in folder marked "UN Matters: 1953–1954 (3)," Box 7, Subject Series, Dulles Papers, EL; Telegram from Wadsworth to the Department of State, September 2, 1953, in *FRUS, 1952–1954,* III, 694.

12. Congressional Petition, October 23, 1953, in folder marked "United Nations (1)," Box 99, Confidential File, ER, EL; Walter Judd to Eisenhower, October 22, 1953, same folder; Eisenhower to Judd, October 24, 1953, in folder marked "October 1953 (2)," Box 3, DDE Diary Series, EP, AWF, EL.

position in the Senate and campaign for United States withdrawal. He also called for a congressional resolution requesting that, in the event of Communist China's entry, the National Security Council reappraise American policy toward the UN. Eisenhower pronounced Knowland's resolution to be "just a pitiful act of Congress to get into the act," since he "would have done that [an NSC study] anyway." Dulles pressured Knowland to moderate the language in his resolution and retreat from his call for withdrawal, but he could not convince the senator to abandon his very public interest in the question.[13]

Apprehensive about American prospects in 1954 to defeat a motion to seat the Communist Chinese delegation, Lodge began his quest to extend the moratorium in March. In a remarkable waste of time and political capital, the ambassador developed a detailed campaign strategy, including dinners and receptions to sway friendly delegations and a series of speeches outlining the American position. On a more substantive level, Lodge suggested threatening to alter American policy on colonial issues in an effort to extract British, French, and Dutch pledges to honor the moratorium arrangement for another year. To build support for the contention that the PRC was not "peace-loving," the ambassador issued a press release that listed thirty-nine "warlike acts" committed by the Communist Chinese in the previous four years. Finally, at the opening General Assembly meeting on September 21, he used his superior knowledge of the parliamentary system to outmaneuver the Soviet representative and obtain a vote of 43 to 11, with 6 abstentions, to prohibit consideration of the question during the session.[14] Thus matters stood when Sino-American tensions flared over a potentially far more dangerous situation.

In September, 1954, the People's Republic of China began bombarding three groups of offshore islands, the Tachens, Quemoy, and Matsu, held by

13. *MTCD,* Reel 8, Eisenhower and Dulles, July 8, 1954, Reel 8, White House Telephone Calls; *MTCD,* Reel 2, Dulles and Knowland, July 6, 1954; *MTCD,* Reel 2, Dulles and Knowland, July 8, 1954; Memorandum of Conversation, July 6, 1954, in *FRUS, 1952–1954,* III, 735–36.

14. USUN Press Release no. 1956, September 17, 1954, in folder marked "Speeches and Press Releases: 1954," Box 110, HCLP, MHS; Lodge to Dulles, March 30, 1954, in *FRUS, 1952–1954,* III, 720–23; Telegram from Dulles to the U.S. embassy in Paris, July 30, 1954, 310.2/7–3054, in Box 1238, RG 59, NA; Telegram from John C. Ross (deputy representative to the Security Council) to the Department of State, August 6, 1954, in *FRUS, 1952–1954,* III, 751–52; Telegram from Smith (acting secretary) to Lodge, September 8, 1954, in *FRUS, 1952–1954,* III, 777–79.

the Nationalists.[15] Dulles suspected that the attack was aimed at provoking a U.S. military response and dividing the nation from its allies, particularly Britain and France, which would not go to war over Taiwan. Although the administration recognized the military insignificance of the islands, for political and diplomatic reasons it was not prepared to cede them to Red China. There would be no more territory lost in Asia.

The NSC considered its options at an emergency meeting on September 12. Dulles advised taking the question to the Security Council "with the view of getting there an injunction to maintain the status quo and institute a cease fire in the Formosa Strait. Whether Russia vetoes or accepts such a plan," he posited, "the United States will gain" and the Soviet Union would lose. A USSR veto would negate recent attempts to cultivate a more peaceful image, while a vote in favor would strain the Sino-Soviet relationship. Eisenhower approved the idea, but his assent represented less than total confidence in the UN. As he recalled in his memoirs, he believed that recourse to the UN "could have no harmful results and give us a much better position in convincing other free nations of our sincerity and honesty in the policies we followed in that area."[16]

Dulles developed and Eisenhower approved the plan to submit the question to the Security Council. Both men sought a return to the status quo of the last five years; they did not expect the UN to undertake a collective security action to resolve the conflict. UN involvement relieved the United States of sole responsibility for finding a peaceful settlement. The United States could use Security Council support for a resolution, even if it was vetoed by

15. For more detailed studies of the Offshore Islands Crisis, see Robert Accinelli, "Eisenhower, Congress, and the 1954–1955 Offshore Island Crisis," *Presidential Studies Quarterly,* XX (1990), 329–48; H. W. Brands, "Testing Massive Retaliation: Credibility and Crisis Management in the Taiwan Strait," *International Security,* XII (1988), 124–51; Gordon H. Chang, "To the Nuclear Brink: Eisenhower, Dulles, and the Quemoy-Matsu Crisis," *International Security,* XII (1988), 96–122; Gordon H. Chang and He Di, "The Absence of War in the U.S.-China Confrontation over Quemoy and Matsu in 1954–1955: Contingency, Luck, Deterrence?," *American Historical Review,* XCVIII (1993), 1500–24; Leonard H. D. Gordon, "United States Opposition to Use of Force in the Taiwan Strait, 1954–1962," *Journal of American History,* LXXII (1985), 637–60; Bennett C. Rushkoff, "Eisenhower, Dulles and the Quemoy-Matsu Crisis, 1954–1955," *Political Science Quarterly,* XCVI (1981), 465–80.

16. Record of Actions by the National Security Council, September 12, 1954, in folder marked "Record of Actions by NSC 1954 (3)," Box 1, NSC Series, EP, AWF, EL; Eisenhower, *Mandate for Change,* 464–65.

the USSR, to justify further assistance to the offshore islands. According to Dulles, Eisenhower even asserted that he would consider using military force "if the UN is in it." Moreover, Communist China's violation of a UN resolution might build support for an embargo on certain strategic materials to the mainland.[17]

Later in September, Dulles enlisted New Zealand's assistance in presenting the resolution to the Security Council. As a temporary member of the council and a nation in the region of the conflict, New Zealand was an eminently logical choice for this task. Dulles suggested that its representative request consideration under Chapter VI of the UN Charter (which addresses the pacific settlement of disputes) and recommend the suspension of hostilities on both sides. Only the vehement objections of Chiang Kai-shek, who still hoped for U.S. military assistance in retaking the mainland, postponed implementation of the plan.[18]

At the same time that the United States was laying plans for multilateral action, it also pursued bilateral means to protect Formosa. The State Department negotiated the Mutual Defense Treaty with Nationalist China, in which the United States guaranteed protection for Formosa and the Pescadore Islands, and Chiang agreed to stop Nationalist raids on the mainland. The treaty was an effort, at least in part, to obtain Chiang's consent to American–New Zealand submission of a joint cease-fire resolution to the Security Council. On December 2, 1954, the United States and the Republic of China signed the treaty.[19]

The virtually concurrent escalation of a second crisis with Communist China presented a fresh challenge. On November 23, 1954, the PRC announced that it had tried and convicted thirteen Americans, eleven of whom were crew members of a B-29 bomber shot down during the Korean War in January, 1953. The Peking government claimed that they had been operat-

17. *MTCD,* Reel 8, Dulles and Cutler (Robert Cutler, special assistant for national security affairs), October 7, 1954, White House Telephone Calls; Memorandum, Dulles to Eisenhower, October 19, 1954, in folder marked "John Foster Dulles: October 1954," Box 3, Dulles-Herter Series, EP, AWF, EL.

18. Telegram from Dulles to the Acting Secretary of State, September 29, 1954, in folder marked "John Foster Dulles: September 1954 (1)," Box 3, Dulles-Herter Series, EP, AWF, EL; Sir Leslie Knox Munro, interview on September 10, 1964, Dulles Oral History Project, Mudd Library; Brands, "Testing Massive Retaliation," 131–32.

19. Tucker, "John Foster Dulles and the Taiwan Roots of the 'Two Chinas' Policy," 242.

ing two spy rings for the Central Intelligence Agency. In addition to the B-29 crew and two alleged CIA agents, the Chinese held four other American pilots, also downed during the war. China's bold announcement of this gross breach of the Korean armistice exacerbated the already dangerously high level of Sino-American tension.

Eisenhower denounced the action as "a deliberate attempt . . . to goad us into some impulsive action." The president's concern was well-founded. Public anger at China reached new heights. In Congress, Knowland called for a naval blockade of Red China, while Representative Thomas J. Lane of Massachusetts went so far as to demand the use of force if necessary to liberate the captives. A vigorous presidential response was essential to calm the uproar. Yet the United States had limited means of retaliation at its disposal, for Eisenhower would not even consider turning the cold war into a hot war. "The hard way," he chided Knowland, "is to have the courage to be patient." Dulles also quickly disavowed "war actions" such as a blockade.[20] Economic sanctions were not a possibility because the United States had no trade with China. Nor was a blockade of mainland China an attractive alternative, for such action would harm U.S. allies—including Great Britain—that traded with the People's Republic. Moreover, because the United States had no diplomatic relations with Communist China, it could not even demonstrate its indignation by severing ties. The administration did send letters of protest to the mainland government, but, not surprisingly, Peking ignored them.

In the absence of appealing unilateral or bilateral alternatives, Eisenhower perceived the General Assembly as an increasingly attractive forum in which to press the American case. Indeed, he quickly silenced the objections of his ambassador to the UN. Lodge wanted to adjourn without raising the issue in order to avoid what he feared would be an interminable and ultimately futile debate. An emergency session of the Security Council could be called later if necessary. But the president insisted on turning to the United Nations immediately. He maintained that since the American airmen had been captured while fighting under the UN flag, the organization had responsibility for their welfare. Moreover, while a General Assembly resolution condemning the PRC might not free the prisoners, it would legitimize

20. News Conference of December 2, 1954, in *Public Papers of the Presidents: Dwight D. Eisenhower, 1954,* 1075–76; "Text of Address in Chicago by Dulles Explaining Basic Aims of U.S. Foreign Policy," New York *Times,* November 29, 1954, p. 4.

the American position and provide another reason for denying Red China a seat in the UN. As Dulles explained, by first exhausting all possibilities of collective action, the United States would "be in a good moral position" to proceed unilaterally if necessary. The desire to condemn Communist China, buy time, and legitimize possible unilateral action thus motivated the administration's move to the UN more than any expectation that the organization could successfully negotiate the liberation of the prisoners.[21]

The administration might not have expected the General Assembly to resolve the crisis, but it nevertheless pressured the body to act in some fashion. Eisenhower publicly declared that the UN had to act if it was "to redeem its self-respect" and engage in future collective security operations. Dulles also warned that a refusal to respond would gravely undermine the principles of collective security and civilized warfare, and perhaps even imperil the future of the world organization. The members of the UN faced a simple choice—whether to go "back to the laws of the jungle or . . . take collective action." On December 4 Lodge requested the secretary-general to take prompt action to free the Americans.[22]

The General Assembly began debate on a U.S.-sponsored resolution on December 7. Lodge made two points. First, the prisoners were "United Nations men." Second, every "self-respecting government . . . has the elementary and historic duty to protect its men whom it sends to war." Although the UN was not a government, in conducting a collective security action it had assumed this traditional responsibility for its soldiers. On December 10, the assembly adopted a resolution, by a vote of 47 to 5, that requested the secretary-general to make "continuing and unremitting efforts" to obtain the prisoners' release.[23]

Eisenhower took an active part in setting policy and determining tactics

21. *MTCD*, Reel 3, Dulles and Lodge, December 4, 1954, 12:22 P.M.; *MTCD*, Reel 3, Dulles and Phleger, November 30, 1954, 3:01 P.M.

22. News Conference of December 2, 1954, in *Public Papers of the Presidents: Dwight D. Eisenhower, 1954,* 1076; *MTCD*, Reel 3, Dulles and Phleger, December 2, 1954, 9:38 A.M.; Memorandum of Telephone Conversation between Dulles and Lodge, December 1, 1954, in folder marked "December 1954 (8)," Box 10, John Foster Dulles Chronological Series, Dulles Papers, EL. See also Urquhart, *Hammarskjöld,* 99.

23. "United Nations Condemns Actions of Communist China in Imprisoning American Fliers," Lodge statements in the General Committee on December 6, 1954, and the plenary session on December 8, 1954, *Department of State Bulletin,* December 20, 1954, pp. 932–33, 939.

throughout the deliberations. He made the final decisions on questions ranging from when the General Assembly should adjourn to whether the administration should comment on the situation while Hammarskjöld negotiated
in Peking. In general, Eisenhower and Dulles appear to have followed their
ambassador's counsel in most of these matters, particularly his injunction to
allow Hammarskjöld time to work without comment. But the president and
his secretary of state wisely chose not to follow Lodge's more rash advice.
For example, in the event that Hammarskjöld's mission should fail, Lodge
advocated seeking a UN resolution that would give the United States "a
blank check" to retaliate by blockading traffic between Hong Kong and
Shanghai. Concerned that an aggressive response might provoke war, Dulles
decided instead to seek a resolution condemning the Communist Chinese,
since he correctly doubted that USUN could procure a two-thirds vote for
stronger measures.[24]

The administration and Hammarskjöld worked together closely during
December and early January. Even before the General Assembly requested
him to seek the prisoners' release, Hammarskjöld informed Lodge that he
intended to go to China himself. In turn, a State Department team hand-
picked by Dulles prepared him a briefing book that covered every conceiv-
able legal question involved in the case. Though Lodge offered no specific
suggestions, he urged Dulles to provide Hammarskjöld with "trump cards"
for his trip.[25]

Hammarskjöld met with Chou En-lai in Peking from January 5 to January 10, 1955. The Chinese premier insisted that the question of the imprisoned airmen be discussed only in the context of the broader Sino-American
relationship, including the question of Chinese UN membership. The
secretary-general consequently returned without the prisoners. Nevertheless, Hammarskjöld remained optimistic, believing that the meeting had es-

24. *MTCD,* Reel 3, Dulles and Lodge, January 7, 1955, 2:13 P.M., 3:58 P.M.; Lodge to
Eisenhower, December 11, 1954, Reel 28, HCLP, MHS; Eisenhower to Lodge, December 14,
1954, Reel 28, HCLP, MHS; *Legislative Meeting Series,* Reel 1, Legislative Leadership Meeting, January 11, 1955; Memorandum of a Conversation, January 7, 1955, in *FRUS, 1955–1957,*
II, 6–8.

25. *MTCD,* Reel 3, Dulles and Lodge, December 11, 1954, 10:15 A.M.; *MTCD,* Reel 3,
Dulles and Lodge, December 8, 1954, 12:58 P.M.; Memorandum, Dulles to Phleger (Herman
Phleger, legal adviser of the Department of State), December 10, 1954, in file marked "De-
cember 1954 (7)," John Foster Dulles Chronological Series, Dulles Papers, EL.

tablished the groundwork for an eventual resolution of the problem, as long as the United States continued to show forbearance.[26]

Following Hammarskjöld's return, the administration quickly began to despair of UN success, though it assumed a public attitude of guarded optimism. Eisenhower expressed his disappointment that Hammarskjöld had not secured the prisoners' immediate release, but he maintained that the United States would "support the United Nations in its efforts so long as those efforts hold out any promise of success." Dulles concurred. At the same time, however, the president sought to avoid an official meeting with the secretary-general. For domestic political reasons it was preferable both to avoid the appearance that Hammarskjöld was an intermediary between Eisenhower and Chou En-lai and to see that the United Nations and its Secretariat alone bore the blame for the continued imprisonment of the American servicemen.[27]

Instead, the secretary-general communicated with the administration through Lodge and Dulles. Hammarskjöld met with Lodge on January 13 in New York and with Lodge, Dulles, and Walter S. Robertson (assistant secretary of state for far eastern affairs) in Dulles's office on January 19. What transpired during the latter one-and-one-half-hour meeting remains unclear. Hammarskjöld later maintained that he had explained that the Communist Chinese might use a visit to China by the families of the prisoners as a pretext for the airmen's release. Dulles and Lodge insisted that Hammarskjöld had made no such connection.[28]

In any event, by January 21, when the Peking government made public its

26. *MTCD*, Reel 3, Dulles and Lodge, January 7, 1955, 3:25 p.m.; *MTCD*, Reel 3, Dulles and Lodge, January 10, 1955, 9:44 a.m.; Hammarskjöld to Lodge, January 11, 1955, in folder marked "'U. N. Pioneers' in China," Box 91, HCLP, MHS. For Hammarskjöld's statements on his mission, see Andrew Wellington Cordier and Wilder Foote, eds., *Public Papers of the Secretaries-General of the U. N.*, Vol. II: *Dag Hammarskjöld, 1953–1956* (New York, 1972), 415–59.

27. Statement on United Nations Negotiations with Communist China for Release of American Airmen and Other Personnel, January 14, 1955, in *Public Papers of the Presidents: Dwight D. Eisenhower, 1955*, 86; *MTCD*, Reel 3, Dulles and Lodge, January 12, 1955, 10:17 a.m., 5:37 p.m.; Memorandum of a Conversation, January 17, 1955, in *FRUS, 1955–1957*, II, 34–35.

28. *MTCD*, Reel 3, Dulles and Carl W. McCardle (assistant secretary of state for public affairs), January 28, 1955; Hammarskjöld to Dulles, January 27, 1955, in *FRUS, 1955–1957*, II, 149–51; Dulles to Hammarskjöld, January 28, 1955, in *FRUS, 1955–1957*, II, 160.

offer to permit the families of the airmen to visit, the State Department (over Lodge's objections) had already announced that it would not grant them passports. A frustrated Hammarskjöld sent a personal letter to Dulles in which he asserted that family visits were crucial to a successful resolution of the problem. Dulles privately accused Hammarskjöld of trying to create an "alibi" to excuse his probable failure, while even Lodge suggested that the secretary-general had "delusions of grandeur."[29] Dulles responded testily to Hammarskjöld's letter. He denied a connection between family visits and freedom for the prisoners, and told Hammarskjöld to handle these matters in the future with Lodge, "who has the complete confidence of the President and myself." Even the secretary of state wanted to distance himself from the secretary-general and the prospect of a UN failure.[30]

Renewed hostilities in the Formosa Strait fueled the administration's anger at the People's Republic of China, and indirectly at the UN's apparent inability to resolve any of the multiple conflicts with the Peking regime. On January 10, 1955, the Communist Chinese had launched a new bombardment of the offshore islands. On January 19, the United States announced that it would help the Nationalist Chinese in defending Quemoy and Matsu but would insist upon the evacuation of the Tachens. Eisenhower requested that Congress grant him authority to use American forces to protect Formosa, the Pescadores, and the principal islands. On January 28 the Senate overwhelmingly approved the enabling Formosa Resolution.

The administration moved simultaneously on two fronts. In addition to securing passage of the Formosa Resolution, it revived the New Zealand proposal (code-named "Oracle"). Eisenhower and Dulles calculated the odds at about ten to one that renewed UN consideration of a cease-fire would benefit the Republic of China and the United States. Although the Security Council was unlikely to pass the resolution, council attention was still potentially advantageous. It might strengthen world support for Nationalist China, alleviate European pressure to bring the situation to the UN, temporarily stabilize the situation, divide the Sino-Soviet alliance, keep Chiang

29. *MTCD,* Reel 3, Dulles and Lodge, January 17, 1955, 4:06 P.M.; Telegram from Lodge to the Department of State, January 13, 1955, in *FRUS, 1955–1957,* II, 26–30; *MTCD,* Reel 3, Dulles and Allen Dulles, January 17, 1955; Telegram from Lodge to the Department of State, January 17, 1955, in *FRUS, 1955–1957,* II, 35–37; Ferrell, ed., *The Diary of James C. Hagerty,* 159, 178.

30. Dulles to Hammarskjöld, January 28, 1955, in *FRUS, 1955–1957,* II, 160.

from using the crisis to drag the United States into defending the islands, and perhaps even enhance security for Quemoy and Matsu without a public U.S. pledge of protection. Moreover, if the United States always bypassed the UN, Dulles noted, then the organization "would never grow up to its responsibilities."[31]

The United States, Britain, and New Zealand agreed to a "working party" report that set forth the timing, manner of presentation, and specific resolution to be presented to the Security Council. Still, the administration made its priorities evident when it delayed New Zealand's communication with the Security Council until after the Formosa Resolution had cleared both congressional committees for fear that concurrent UN action might slow the congressional process.[32]

Accordingly, on January 28, 1955, the New Zealand representative, Sir Leslie K. Munro, raised the issue in the Security Council. The council met three days later and voted 9 to 1 (China) with 1 abstention (the USSR) to invite the PRC to participate in the debate. On February 3, the PRC's foreign minister declined the invitation, insisting that the status of the Formosa Strait was a purely domestic matter. The next day Nationalist China began evacuating its troops from the Tachen Islands, thereby eliminating one of the immediate sources of tension. Ironically, as Gordon Chang and He Di note, these diplomatic initiatives persuaded the PRC that the United States was not as determined to enact military deterrence as its rhetoric implied.[33]

The lull in hostilities only increased Anglo-American disagreement about the next step. The British felt that further action might upset the fragile peace. Convinced that they had not exhausted all the possibilities, Eisenhower and Dulles wanted to pursue a cease-fire agreement in the UN. Moreover, they did not want the United States to appear to have backed down in the face of threats from Chou En-lai. Lodge therefore asked Hammarskjöld

---

31. Memorandum of a Conversation, January 25, 1955, in *FRUS, 1955–1957,* II, 121; Memorandum of a Conversation, January 20, 1955, same volume, 55–68; Memorandum of Discussion at the 233d Meeting of the National Security Council, January 21, 1955, same volume, 89–96; Memorandum of a Conversation, January 21, 1955, same volume, 102; Chang, "To the Nuclear Brink," 109–11.

32. Memorandum of Conversation, January 25, 1955, in *FRUS, 1955–1957,* II, 121.

33. Chang and Di, "The Absence of War in the U.S.-China Confrontation over Quemoy and Matsu in 1954–1955," 1515–17.

to make a brief *pro forma* report to the Security Council on the Chinese refusal in order to prevent action from coming to a complete standstill.[34] After an inconclusive discussion, consideration of the resolution ceased on February 14. Recognizing the futility of further attempts, the administration abandoned its efforts at the UN, though it remained prepared to renew them immediately if the Communist attack it believed imminent materialized. Indeed, on March 10 and 11 the NSC even considered using nuclear weapons against Communist China. Eventually, however, tensions subsided in late April, after Chou En-lai's conciliatory remarks at the Bandung Conference, and both sides agreed to ambassadorial-level talks in Geneva.[35]

Hammarskjöld continued his "quiet diplomacy" to free the prisoners, despite the hostile atmosphere created by the Formosan crisis. Seemingly oblivious to the obstacles facing the secretary-general, the administration increasingly disparaged his performance as Peking appeared to ignore Hammarskjöld's communications. By early May, Dulles and Lodge questioned whether Hammarskjöld was too "neutral" even to make a "stiff report" to the General Assembly. Dulles fretted that, given the public's rising impatience, the situation was on the verge of becoming "very ugly." If the Chinese wanted to act without "los[ing] face," they had better do so quickly, for the United States would not put itself "in the position of giving concessions for these men." The United States thus began to consider its next step, recognizing that immediate action was out of the question, since, as Dulles noted, the United States could not "give H[ammarskjöld] a chance to claim that we took back the responsibility before he completed his job."[36]

China's decision to deport the four jet pilots on May 31, 1955, buoyed the

34. For the British position, see, for example, Message from Eden to the Secretary of State, March 25, 1955, in *FRUS, 1955–1957,* II, 397–98. On the administration's views, see Memorandum of a Conversation, February 7, 1955, same volume, 234–38; Memorandum of a Conversation, March 9, 1955, same volume, 344–45; "Alternative Courses in the United Nations on the Off-Shore Islands Problem," February 4, 1955, Reel 7, State Department Microfilm, J. F. Dulles Papers, Mudd Library; Memorandum, Key to Dulles, February 5, 1955, Reel 7, State Department Microfilm, J. F. Dulles Papers, Mudd Library; *MTCD,* Reel 3, Dulles and Lodge, February 7, 1955; *MTCD,* Reel 3, Dulles and Lodge, February 9, 1955; Telegram from Lodge to the Department of State, February 8, 1955, in *FRUS, 1955–1957,* II, 241–43.

35. Memorandum of a Conversation, March 30, 1955, in *FRUS, 1955–1957,* II, 430–31; Chang, "To the Nuclear Brink," 106–108.

36. Dulles and Lodge, May 4, 1955, 12:29 P.M., in folder marked "Telephone Conversations—General: May 2, 1955–August 31, 1955 (8)," Box 4, Telephone Conversation Series,

administration's hopes. Eisenhower counseled continued patience—"a quiet, cagey, ear-to-the-ground approach"—while the nation waited to see if the B-29 crew followed. Acknowledging that "the UN effort has had its results," Dulles believed that it was incumbent upon the United States to see that the United Nations and Hammarskjöld received the credit that was their due.[37] In the meantime, the administration became more careful not to "cross wires" with the secretary-general. Lodge urged the president to meet with Hammarskjöld at the summit conference in Geneva in order to enhance the secretary-general's international prestige, and Eisenhower and Dulles did so on July 18. Even so, the administration still sent out feelers of its own. Indeed, the administration directed Ambassador U. Alexis Johnson to begin talks with the Chinese Communists in Geneva late in July.[38]

The Chinese announced that it had freed the B-29 crew at the commencement of talks with the United States on August 1, 1955. Eisenhower commended the UN and its secretary-general. Lodge offered far more effusive praise. The secretary-general, the U.S. representative proclaimed, had courageously "put his life's reputation as a diplomat on the chopping block" when he offered to go to Peking to fulfill the General Assembly's mandate.[39]

If the imprisonment of the fliers had in fact constituted what *Newsweek* magazine headlined as the "Acid Test for the U. N.," then the organization passed with high marks.[40] The UN had mediated successfully between the

Dulles Papers, EL; *Legislative Meeting Series,* Reel 1, Bipartisan Congressional Leaders Meeting, March 31, 1955; *MTCD,* Reel 4, Dulles and Lodge, May 4, 1955, 6:00 P.M.; Dulles to Lodge, April 1, 1955, in *FRUS, 1955–1957,* II, 442.

37. *Legislative Meeting Series,* Reel 1, Legislative Leadership Meeting, June 1, 1955; *MTCD,* Reel 3, Dulles and Lodge, June 3, 1955, 10:48 A.M.; Memorandum, Hoover (Herbert Hoover, Jr., acting secretary) to the Secretary of State, May 28, 1955, in *FRUS, 1955–1957,* II, 578–80; "Release of Captured U. N. Command Airmen," *Department of State Bulletin,* June 13, 1955, p. 953; Hoover to Lodge, June 2, 1955, in *FRUS, 1955–1957,* II, 585–87.

38. *Legislative Meeting Series,* Reel 1, Bipartisan Legislative Leadership Meeting, July 12, 1955; Lodge to Eisenhower, July 12, 1955, in folder marked "Henry Cabot Lodge: 1955 (2)," Box 24, Administration Series, EP, AWF, EL; Dulles to Hammarskjöld, July 28, 1955, in folder marked "July 1955 (1)," Box 12, John Foster Dulles Chronological Series, Dulles Papers, EL.

39. U.S. Mission Press Release, no. 2178, June 21, 1955, in folder marked "Speeches and Press Releases: 1955," Box 81, HCLP, MHS; Statement Regarding Release of United States Airmen by Communist China, August 1, 1955, in *Public Papers of the Presidents: Dwight D. Eisenhower, 1955,* 746.

40. "Acid Test for the U. N.," *Newsweek,* December 20, 1954, p. 17.

leading nation of the Western world and a Communist power—two countries, moreover, that had no diplomatic relations with each other. Accordingly, its status in the United States and the world received a big boost. Hammarskjöld's success also compelled a reassessment of the secretary-general. Eisenhower, Dulles, and Lodge emerged from the crisis with greatly enhanced respect for his diplomatic abilities and a new recognition of the potential value of the Secretariat in bridging the gap between East and West. This change could not help but affect the way the administration viewed the UN in subsequent situations. In the fall of 1954 Eisenhower and Dulles had been desperately seeking an honorable alternative to the war that some Americans were demanding. The UN provided that alternative, and it was a lesson that would not be forgotten.

The release of the prisoners, however, did not alter the administration's position on the question of the PRC's representation in the UN. In 1955 the administration again sought and ultimately obtained British agreement to extend the moratorium. Britain acquiesced only reluctantly in this show of Anglo-American solidarity. It insisted that such support should not continue for long; the time had come to seat the Communist Chinese. A U.S. motion not to consider the question passed by a vote of 42 to 12, with 7 abstentions, but a State Department report admitted that "in demanding support on this generally unpopular issue, we are draining the reserves of goodwill and solidarity which we would like to have available to us on other matters."[41]

During 1956 the administration attempted to delay consideration of the issue until after the presidential election, lest it prove politically damaging. Once again, Lodge hounded Dulles to pressure Britain to extend the moratorium through the end of the General Assembly session. When the issue did arise on November 14, other events allowed Lodge to move successfully for postponement. He asserted that at "this time of difficulty in world history in Hungary and in the Near East, it is particularly desirable that we should not further divide the United Nations."[42]

---

41. Draft report by Lincoln P. Bloomfield, "Evaluation of Role of US in 10th General Assembly," in *FRUS, 1955–1957,* XI, 57; Memorandum of Conversation, September 9, 1955, 320/9–955, in Box 1257, RG 59, NA.

42. "Question of Chinese Representation in the United Nations," Lodge statement in the General Committee on November 14, 1956, *Department of State Bulletin,* November 26, 1956, p. 855; Lodge to Dulles, January 12, 1956, 310/2/1–1256, in Box 1237, RG 59, NA; Lodge to

As international opposition to the U.S. position grew by 1957, some officials in the State Department advised accepting the inevitable. The United States should agree to seat the PRC in exchange for some type of deal, such as a guarantee for the security of Formosa. Assistant Secretary of State for Policy Planning Robert Bowie argued that American policy had gone "astray" in committing its prestige to the negative goal of isolating mainland China. The United States, Bowie advised, should gradually adopt a two-China policy in the UN.[43] Ultimately, echoed a member of the Policy Planning Staff, it was not in the nation's best interest to use its power as "paymaster of the Free World . . . to dragoon the vote of the supposedly sovereign members of the UN to assure the continuing exclusion of Peking" for another five years or so. Unfortunately, Bowie's memorandum appears to have elicited no response. Once again an American procedural motion to postpone consideration passed, but this time only by 47 to 27, with 7 abstentions.[44]

The Sino-American conflict shifted from New York back to Asia late in August when the Chinese Communists resumed shelling Quemoy and Matsu, now fortified by one-third of the Nationalist army. Once again, the administration considered a variety of possible responses in the UN. Eisenhower suggested "making a great play of this matter in the United Nations" in order to derive the maximum propaganda benefit from the Communist aggression.[45] Lodge worried that the administration would appear foolish in drawing a line over which the Communist Chinese must not cross regarding the virtually indefensible offshore islands. He insisted that the administration ought to seek a cease-fire resolution in order to "provide some justification" if it resorted to military might to protect the islands, retreat to a more defensible position, or seek the secretary-general's assistance in "neutralization" of the islands. Dulles rejected "neutralization," on the grounds that

Dulles, January 23, 1956, 310.2/1–2356, in Box 1237, RG 59, NA; Telegram from Lodge to Dulles, February 1, 1956, 310.2/2–156, in Box 1237, RG 59, NA.

43. Memorandum, Bowie to Dulles, June 19, 1957, in *FRUS, 1955–1957,* III, 545–49.

44. Paper prepared by Robert McClintock of the Policy Planning Staff, December 31, 1957, in *FRUS, 1955–1957,* III, 667; Memorandum, McClintock to Bowie, February 8, 1957, same volume, 470–73; Memorandum of Conversation, March 24, 1957, in folder marked "People's Republic of China," Box 127, J. F. Dulles Papers, Mudd Library.

45. Memorandum of Conference with the President, August 14, 1958, in folder marked "August 1958: Staff Notes (2)," Box 35, DDE Diary Series, EP, AWF, EL.

neither of the Chinese governments would accept such status for the islands. Determined to preserve U.S. freedom of action, he evinced little enthusiasm for a Hammarskjöld mission to Peking.[46]

Instead, Eisenhower and Dulles used the UN indirectly in their effort to avert war in Asia. First, an agreement to suspend shelling for one week was obtained on October 6 in bilateral talks held outside the UN framework. Dulles then directed Lodge to "do some talking [at the UN] which might get back to the Chinese." He was to explain that the United States did not view China's acceptance of a cease-fire as "a sign of physical weakness," and that, if the cease-fire was extended, the administration would "continue actively to try to eliminate the provocations in the situation" on the Nationalist Chinese side. Finally, Lodge could suggest that if the People's Republic broke the cease-fire, the United States would seek a UN resolution of condemnation.[47]

The administration prevented the perilous situation from escalating into war. In exchange for a cease-fire, the United States evacuated some of the Nationalist troops from Quemoy and forced Chiang to renounce the use of force to regain the mainland. When the cease-fire ended, the PRC announced that it would bombard the islands only on odd-numbered days, thus enabling Chiang to resupply his garrisons on even-numbered days. Despite the resulting "Gilbert and Sullivan war," as Eisenhower aptly described the situation, the immediate danger receded.[48] Operating largely through ambiguity and veiled threats, the administration had deterred a Communist assault and simultaneously restrained Chiang. It had used the UN, albeit in a minor role, as one of the channels through which it conveyed its intentions to the People's Republic.

The question of PRC representation remained. Support for the U.S. stand had eroded to such an extent by 1958 that the administration was relegated to beseeching indirect support, such as an "accidental absence" on the day of the vote. During the fall General Assembly session, India presented a

46. Lodge to Dulles, September 18, 1958, Reel 5, HCLP, MHS; Memorandum of Telephone Conversation with Ambassador Lodge, September 23, 1958, in folder marked "Memoranda of Telephone Conversations—General: August 1, 1958 to October 31, 1958 (3)," Box 9, Telephone Conversation Series, Dulles Papers, EL.

47. MTCD, Reel 8, Lodge and Dulles, October 9, 1958.

48. Eisenhower, quoted in Stephen E. Ambrose, *Eisenhower: The President* (New York, 1984), 485.

direct challenge to the U.S. resolution, and even many of the nations that voted with the United States refused to support the American position in debate. Many European nations had come to view "support of the moratorium as merely one of the prices which they must pay for American friendship." Latin American nations claimed that voting with the United States on this question made them look like "U.S. satellites." As Lodge conceded, support for the American position "came almost entirely from loyalty to the US as free world leader. There was no discernible evidence that it was based on the view that our policy was right."[49]

Increasingly apprehensive in light of these ominous views, Lodge redoubled his efforts in 1959. The State Department too began reevaluating the situation. It considered permitting some substantive debate as long as the United States retained "tactical control" of the situation, and it assisted in assuaging the feelings of the Latin American countries that were becoming "restive." Once again, the United States succeeded. But it owed its victory not to more diligent preparation but to renewed questions about the PRC's worthiness for membership in the wake of its resumed shelling of the islands and aggressive incursions into neighboring Tibet.[50]

In 1960, the United States used Communist China's aggression against Tibet and border raids against India and Nepal as evidence that the People's Republic was not peace-loving. India's decision not to introduce a resolution as it had the past three years provided a telling indication of rising neutralist disaffection with Communist China, and immeasurably helped the American cause. Nevertheless, the United States prevailed by its narrowest margin yet—42 to 34, with 22 abstentions.

The outgoing administration thus publicly remained resolute on the question of Red China's admission to the UN. But in private, Eisenhower

49. Circular telegram from Herter (acting secretary) to U.S. embassies, January 2, 1958, in *FRUS, 1958–1960,* II, 2; Memorandum, William T. Nunley (European desk) to Green (Marshall Green, regional planning officer for the Far East), October 17, 1958, 310.293/10–2258, in Box 1238, RG 59, NA; Telegram from Lodge to the Department of State, September 24, 1958, in *FRUS, 1958–1960,* II, 63.

50. Memorandum, Wilcox and J. Graham Parsons (Far Eastern Affairs) to the Acting Secretary, July 24, 1959, 310.2/7–2459, in Box 1241, RG 59, NA; Telegram from Lodge to Dulles, January 5, 1959, 310.2/1–559, in Box 1238, RG 59, NA; Telegram from Herter to USUN, July 7, 1959, same box; Circular instructions from Herter to certain diplomatic missions, August 7, 1959, in *FRUS, 1958–1960,* II, 151–52.

acknowledged that pragmatic acceptance of PRC membership might eventually be necessary. The president cautioned his cabinet that "too many people say never, never. He remarked that never is an awfully long time. And he himself is always very careful: he says that if these people correct three or four of the worst things they are guilty of, we'd have a tough time keeping them out."[51]

The Eisenhower administration used the United Nations in different and, on first appraisal, contradictory ways, in its ongoing struggle with the People's Republic of China. Throughout the decade, the administration sought to isolate the Asian Communist power. Most noteworthy in this regard, at least symbolically, was its effort to exclude it from the UN, the only universal world organization. For eight years the administration succeeded in preventing the expulsion of Nationalist China and the entry of Communist China. But as indicated by the General Assembly vote in 1960, it was only a matter of time before the People's Republic of China would obtain admission and replace the Republic of China as one of the five permanent members of the Security Council. Moreover, it was a costly victory. Although the administration pacified the China lobby, an important consideration in the aftermath of the Korean War, it expended an inordinate amount of international political capital in an effort that was arguably misguided and shortsighted.

Somewhat ironically, at the same time that the administration was working to keep Communist China out of the UN, it used the organization directly and indirectly to achieve its broad foreign policy goals and to resolve conflicts with the Peking regime. It repeatedly attempted to use the question of Chinese membership to exacerbate tensions in the Sino-Soviet relationship. It also turned directly to the United Nations to intervene on behalf of the American servicemen imprisoned on the mainland. In 1950 Dulles had written that "the world organization provides a lap into which even the great powers may choose to drop their disputes."[52] That was exactly what hap-

51. Cabinet Meeting Minutes, October 7, 1960, in folder marked "Cabinet Meeting of October 7, 1960 (1)," Box 16, Cabinet Series, EP, AWF, EL; Telegram from Herter to USUN, April 12, 1960, in *FRUS, 1958–1960,* II, 238–39; Circular telegram from Herter to certain diplomatic missions, August 4, 1960, in *FRUS, 1958–1960,* II, 281–82; Telegram from Wadsworth to the Department of State, October 11, 1960, in *FRUS, 1958–1960,* II, 413–15.

52. Dulles, *War or Peace,* 59.

pened in 1954, when both the United States and the People's Republic, unwilling to negotiate directly, deposited the thorny problem in the lap of the UN. Lacking a more agreeable alternative, the administration permitted and was grateful for the opportunity to allow the UN (in the person of the secretary-general) to adopt the problem and straighten it out.

However, in handling the periodic crises over the offshore island groups, among the tensest Cold War confrontations of the Eisenhower era, the administration made only limited and indirect use of the United Nations. Even here, however, the UN proved useful as a means of establishing channels of communication that pierced the Bamboo Curtain. Given the essentially negative nature of the administration's objectives, it seems unlikely that the United States could have used the organization in a more significant fashion. Intent upon isolating Communist China and supporting the Nationalist Chinese, and constrained by the domestic political situation from retreating from its rhetorical stance, the administration did little to explore a more creative or innovative role for the United Nations in improving its relations with the People's Republic of China during these crises.

7

Rhetoric or Reality?

Eisenhower, the United Nations, and the Struggle to Achieve Arms Control

When Eisenhower assumed office in January, 1953, one of his stated objectives was to achieve disarmament. As he recalled in his memoirs, "Of the various presidential tasks to which I early determined to devote my energies, none transcended in importance that of trying to devise practical and acceptable means to lighten the burdens of armaments and to lessen the likelihood of war." As a hero of the first war whose weapons included nuclear arms, the military man who hated war brought a special determination to the disarmament process. Eisenhower's quest inevitably led him to the United Nations, for in the post-Hiroshima nuclear age the new international organization had become the principal forum for disarmament negotiations.[1]

1. Eisenhower, *Waging Peace, 1956–1961,* 467. On Eisenhower and disarmament, see Richard G. Hewlett and Jack M. Holl, *Atoms for Peace and War, 1953–1961: Eisenhower and the Atomic Energy Commission* (Berkeley, 1989); Richard Aliano, *American Defense Policy from Eisenhower to Kennedy: The Politics of Changing Military Requirements* (Athens, 1975); McGeorge Bundy, *Danger and Survival: Choices About the Bomb in the First Fifty Years* (New York, 1988); Lawrence Freedman, *The Evolution of Nuclear Strategy* (New York, 1981); Raymond L. Garthoff, *Assessing the Adversary: Estimates by the Eisenhower Administration of Soviet Intentions and Capabilities* (Washington, D.C., 1991); Thomas F. Soapes, "A Cold Warrior Seeks Peace: Eisenhower's Strategy for Nuclear Disarmament," *Diplomatic History,* IV (1980), 57–71; Robert A. Strong, "Eisenhower and Arms Control," in Melanson and Mayers, eds., *Reevaluating Eisenhower,* 241–66; Bernard G. Beckhoefer, "The Disarmament Deadlock, 1945–1955," *Social Education,* XXVI (1962), 375–82; Charles Albert Appleby, Jr., "Eisenhower and Arms Control, 1953–1961: A Balance of Risks" (Ph.D. dissertation, Johns

The new administration's first deliberations on disarmament centered on a study commissioned by the Truman administration. In April, 1952, Secretary of State Dean Acheson had appointed a Panel of Consultants on Disarmament, chaired by J. Robert Oppenheimer. Its report, submitted in the final weeks of the Truman administration, was particularly noteworthy in two respects. First, it recommended that the United States should no longer define its ultimate objective as disarmament, because comprehensive schemes for the total elimination of conventional and nuclear weapons were neither feasible nor desirable. Instead, the panel advocated using terms such as arms "regulation" or "limitation." Second, the report advised that the United States "minimize its participation" in disarmament discussions at the UN, for debate on such a complex subject was inevitably "unproductive and even misleading." It either raised unrealistic hopes that the UN could eliminate the world's arsenal or gave the false impression that the United States was "cynical about disarmament" and "merely trying to press for some propaganda advantage." Bilateral discussions with the Soviet Union should replace multilateral negotiation.[2]

In a meeting of the National Security Council, Eisenhower and his advisers gave the report mixed reviews. They agreed that the UN discussions had "become increasingly unrealistic and assumed the character of set pieces in a propaganda morality play." However, they took exception to the recommendation to discontinue the negotiations. Eisenhower set the meeting's tone, questioning the conclusion that for "psychological" reasons the United States should minimize its participation in the talks. Reflecting his interest in psychological warfare, he thought that disarmament initiatives, with their virtually universal appeal, were critical to winning the hearts and minds of millions tired of the cold war. Dulles concurred, insisting that it was "good propaganda" to continue the discussions.[3]

Pending formulation of a new disarmament policy, the administration

---

Hopkins University, 1987); Zachary Shands Davis, "Eisenhower's Worldview and Nuclear Strategy" (Ph.D. dissertation, University of Virginia, 1989); Robert Edward Williams, Jr., "The Evolution of Disarmament and Arms Control Thought, 1945–1963" (Ph.D. dissertation, University of Virginia, 1987).

2. Report by the Panel of Consultants of the Department of State to the Secretary of State, January, 1953, in *FRUS, 1952–1954,* II, 1085.

3. Memorandum by Edmund Gullion (member of the Policy Planning Staff), March 4, 1953, in *FRUS, 1952–1954,* II, 1117; Memorandum of Discussion at the 132d Meeting of the National Security Council, February 18, 1953, same volume, 1107–1108.

chose to temporize in the General Assembly and the Disarmament Commission. It would conduct a "holding operation" until the fall, presenting no new proposals and avoiding further exposition of American views. Following the position taken by Eisenhower in his April 16, 1953, speech, "The Chance for Peace," to the American Society of Newspaper Editors, U.S. delegations insisted that progress on a range of political problems between the superpowers must precede further disarmament. At the same time, the United States encouraged the Soviet delegations to expand on their view of an acceptable disarmament program. Lodge favored this delaying tactic, noting that in a substantive debate the USSR could "keep us on the end of the harpoon concerning our own willingness to accept inspection of atomic facilities."[4]

On September 9, 1953, the National Security Council met to consider whether to present a new disarmament proposal in the UN. Discussion revolved around a report by the Executive Committee on the Regulation of Armaments (RAC) that aptly captured the NSC's skepticism about disarmament and its ambivalence about pursuing it in the UN. The report questioned whether it was technically possible to devise a disarmament system with effective safeguards or to gauge Soviet sincerity and intentions. It declared that "serious negotiations on the subject of disarmament would undoubtedly be more fruitful if they take place in bilateral or multilateral discussion outside United Nations organs."[5]

Yet the committee and the NSC as a whole were loath to abdicate American leadership of the arms control effort. The committee suggested that two reasons—breaking the disarmament deadlock and furthering the nation's international political objectives—could justify new UN initiatives. Any American disarmament program would have to meet three tests. It must have sufficient popular appeal, not raise hopes to the point of weakening the Western coalition's resistance to Soviet aggression, and be a proposal that the administration was genuinely willing to carry out. Nevertheless, the NSC recommended that the U.S. delegation to the fall General Assembly session

4. Memorandum by the Executive Committee on Regulation of Armaments to James S. Lay (executive secretary of the National Security Council), May 26, 1953, in *FRUS, 1952–1954*, II, 1167; Lodge to Dulles, June 5, 1953, same volume, 1177; Dulles to Lodge, June 4, 1953, same volume, 1175–76.

5. Report to the National Security Council by the NSC Planning Board, September 1, 1953, in *FRUS, 1952–1954*, II, 1193; Hewlett and Holl, *Atoms for Peace and War, 1953–1961*, 42–43.

limit its involvement to cosponsoring a resolution that reaffirmed the pertinent sections of Eisenhower's "Chance for Peace" speech.[6]

The American "holding operation" in the United Nations came to an abrupt halt on December 8, 1953. Speaking before a capacity audience of 3,500 in the chambers of the General Assembly, Dwight Eisenhower launched what would prove to be the most significant arms control initiative of his presidency. The president proposed that part of the nuclear stockpiles of the world be donated to an international "bank of fissionable materials" to be used for peaceful purposes such as scientific research and energy production.[7]

The speech, quickly dubbed "Atoms for Peace" by the media, marked the culmination of a seven-month search for a way to educate the American people about the escalating nuclear arms race. Early in April, Eisenhower had commissioned "Operation Candor," a project to draft a presidential speech outlining the issues of the nuclear age for a domestic audience. He assigned the project to C. D. Jackson, Lewis L. Strauss (first his personal adviser on atomic matters and then AEC chairman), and Robert Cutler (special assistant for national security affairs). The early drafts painted such a grim picture of the devastating effects of a nuclear attack that Eisenhower hesitated to make the speech, and Operation Candor languished.

When news of the successful Soviet hydrogen bomb test interrupted his vacation in Denver on August 12, Eisenhower's interest in the project revived. Searching for a way to temper his warning about the nuclear threat with a concrete offer of hope, he hit upon the atomic pool idea. Eisenhower proposed that "the United States and the Soviets . . . turn over to the United Nations, for peaceful use, X kilograms of fissionable material. The amount X could be fixed at a figure which we could handle from our stockpile, but which it would be difficult for the Soviets to match."[8] He requested Jack-

6. Report to the National Security Council by the NSC Planning Board, September 1, 1953, in *FRUS, 1952–1954,* II, 1195; Telegram from Dulles to USUN, September 4, 1953, same volume, 1206–1209; Position Paper, "Report of the Disarmament Commission," September 3, 1953, SD/A/C.1/423, in Box 21, Lot 82 D 211, RG 59, NA.

7. Address Before the General Assembly of the United Nations on Peaceful Uses of Atomic Energy, December 8, 1953, in *Public Papers of the Presidents: Dwight D. Eisenhower, 1953,* 821.

8. Memorandum, Cutler to Strauss and Jackson, September 10, 1953, in folder marked "Atoms for Peace," Box 5, Administration Series, EP, AWF, EL; Hewlett and Holl, *Atoms for Peace and War, 1953–1961,* 41–62.

son and Strauss to incorporate the atomic pool concept into the Candor speech.

Despite widespread resistance within the administration, Eisenhower pushed forward during the next four months. Dulles feared that the atomic pool concept might jeopardize delicate negotiations on the European Defense Community, and he suggested bilateral talks with the Soviet Union instead. Strauss opposed turning over fissionable material to an international body until the United States obtained sufficient intelligence about the size of the Soviet stockpile. Representatives of the Pentagon objected to any wider dispersion of atomic knowledge and materials, especially to the Third World. Some members of Congress shared the Defense Department's qualms; congressional critics derisively referred to the atomic pool proposal as "Watts for Hottentots." Nevertheless, after consulting with Winston Churchill in Bermuda, Eisenhower flew directly to New York to deliver his address to the UN General Assembly.[9]

Critics have charged that Atoms for Peace was designed solely, or at least primarily, as a propaganda measure. Jackson and Eisenhower certainly knew that substantive proposals couched in the form of a public challenge to the USSR made the best propaganda, and the speech undoubtedly contributed to the psychological warfare campaign. As James Hagerty recalled, it captured "the propaganda initiative in the world." The president himself conceded in his diary that "words and protestations, however eloquent or sincere," would not be sufficient to avert nuclear disaster. Moreover, he did not think that the present international situation was conducive to the achievement of a workable system of atomic disarmament.[10]

Even so, Eisenhower believed that his proposal might, in some small way, foster the mutual trust essential for any lasting progress. The president thus

9. Strong, "Eisenhower and Arms Control," 247; Memorandum for the President by Strauss, September 17, 1953, in *FRUS, 1952–1954,* II, 1218–19; Memorandum, Jackson to Eisenhower, October 2, 1953, in folder marked "Atoms for Peace—Evolution (3)," Box 25, Jackson Papers, EL. For a chronology of the development of the Atoms for Peace speech, see Jackson to Strauss, September 25, 1954, in *FRUS, 1952–1954,* II, 1218–19; "Chronology—Candor—Wheaties," September 30, 1954, in folder marked "Atoms for Peace—Evolution (1)," Box 24, Jackson Papers, EL; John Lear, "Ike and the Peaceful Atom," *Reporter,* January 12, 1956, pp. 11–21; Lewis L. Strauss, *Men and Decisions* (Garden City, 1962), 355–61; Hewlett and Holl, *Atoms for Peace and War, 1953–1961,* 41–72.

10. The Reminiscences of James Hagerty, January 31, 1968, p. 89, COHP, Butler Library, Columbia University; Ferrell, ed., *The Eisenhower Diaries,* 262.

viewed Atoms for Peace as a possible "first step" on the long road to disarmament. He would use nuclear power not to wage war but to unite the world in the peaceful pursuit of economic development. As Richard G. Hewlett and Jack M. Holl explain, this idea was indicative of Eisenhower's "basic strategy—to approach world disarmament not in one dramatic proposal, but in small steps in tune with existing realities and simple enough for the public to understand."[11]

The president's actions provide further evidence that the proposal was at least a somewhat sincere attempt to slow the nuclear arms race. Eisenhower contacted the Soviets prior to the speech to alert them that he would be making a major policy statement at the UN. Furthermore, he made a proposal that did not include a requirement for on-site inspection, and he offered to conduct private negotiations.[12]

The initial reception to the speech surpassed the administration's expectations. Lodge reported that the Soviet delegate "applauded with unusual spontaneity." Representatives from the Third World were even more enthusiastic. Their enthusiasm, however, proved to be premature, perhaps even irrelevant, since the USSR quickly raised significant obstacles to the proposal. Maintaining that disarmament and the peaceful use of atomic energy were inseparable, Soviet leaders argued that the prohibition of nuclear weapons would have to precede the implementation of Eisenhower's proposal.[13]

The administration's deliberations about where to conduct negotiations to implement the proposal shed further light on its view of the desired UN role in disarmament. Eisenhower suggested working through the Disarmament Commission, though he also offered to hold bilateral negotiations with the Soviet Union. Dulles, however, asserted that even the twelve-nation Disarmament Commission was too large, although he did admit that it "would probably be necessary to have [the] UN blessing on these talks because of

11. Ferrell, ed., *The Eisenhower Diaries,* 262; Hewlett and Holl, *Atoms for Peace and War, 1953–1961,* 66; Eisenhower to Milton Eisenhower, December 11, 1953, in folder marked "December 1953 (2)," Box 3, DDE Diary Series, EP, AWF, EL.

12. Ferrell, *The Eisenhower Diaries,* 260.

13. "Summary of Reactions to President Eisenhower's Speech Before the General Assembly, December 8, 1953," December 9, 1953, Reel 28, HCLP, MHS; Lodge to Eisenhower, December 10, 1953, same reel; Peter Boyle, "The 'Special Relationship' with Washington," in John W. Young, ed., *The Foreign Policy of Churchill's Peacetime Administration, 1951–1955* (Leicester, 1988), 48; Hewlett and Holl, *Atoms for Peace and War, 1953–1961,* 209–11.

UN interest in the subject." Instead, he maintained that the United States should work with "a small group [ideally just the United States, the USSR, and Britain] in which the U.S. could keep the initiative on the procedures" and prevent a wide-ranging discussion of the broader question of disarmament. Jackson agreed with Dulles, declaring candidly that "to have something as full of dynamite as this pawed over by several uninformed and emotionally opinionated 'foreigners' would tend to confuse rather than clarify." Consequently, the administration presented its proposal for an International Atomic Energy Agency (IAEA) to the Soviet Union through bilateral channels.[14]

The administration's conception of the proposed IAEA's connection to the UN underscored its limited support for placing arms control measures in the hands of the organization. Eisenhower inquired whether "any association of the Agency with the UN was necessary." Dulles also opposed tying the new program too closely to the UN. He worried about congressional criticism that the Communist bloc, because of its UN membership, would benefit from the agency. Dulles therefore advocated making the IAEA a specialized agency with virtually total independence, similar to the World Bank.[15]

Eisenhower's Atoms for Peace proposal was for all intents and purposes moribund by the beginning of the 1954 General Assembly. Ten months of private discussions in Washington and Moscow had yielded no agreement. Nor had the administration carried out the Operations Coordinating Board's plans for domestic and international follow-through on the proposal. The president's continued enthusiasm encountered resistance from officials in the State Department, the AEC, and the Pentagon. Had it not been for the unceasing agitation of Lodge and Jackson (at that time a member of the U.S. delegation to the General Assembly), the proposal would likely have died quietly in the fall of 1954. Jackson bitterly complained that it would be useless as a step toward disarmament or even a psychological warfare measure without subsequent action. Imploring Eisenhower to intervene in order to transform his idea into a reality, Jackson explained that "people have got to feel that you want [the plan] to come off, otherwise it gets frittered away."

14. Memorandum of Conversation, December 24, 1953, in *FRUS, 1952–1954,* II, 1308; Jackson to Eisenhower, December 29, 1953, in folder marked "C. D. Jackson: 1953 (1)," Box 21, Administration Series, EP, AWF, EL; Memorandum of Conversation, January 6, 1954, in *FRUS, 1952–1954,* II, 1324–29.

15. Memorandum of Discussion at the 210th Meeting of the National Security Council, August 12, 1954, in *FRUS, 1952–1954,* II, 1485.

Lodge, too, pressed for authorization to push the plan. State Department officials responded by trying "to keep Senator Lodge within bounds."[16]

Lodge and Jackson received critical administration support in early fall. In a Labor Day speech, Eisenhower announced his determination to proceed with an international agency as well as bilateral agreements. Then, on September 22, the Soviet Union proclaimed its willingness to continue negotiations. The State Department submitted the proposal to the General Assembly as an agenda item, and in a September 23 address to that body, Dulles announced the American intention to create an agency with or without Soviet support. The United States Information Agency showed a film to UN representatives and mounted a one-hundred-foot-long exhibit in the UN building itself that extolled the potential benefits of the peaceful uses of the atom. But there was still dissension in the ranks. Dulles complained that the U.S. delegation was "whooping it up too much," and the AEC continued to seek implementation through bilateral agreements rather than an international treaty.[17]

Eisenhower eventually sided with Lodge and Jackson, acceding to his UN ambassador's plea to authorize the U.S. delegation to pledge a sizable donation of uranium to the agency, if created. Lodge assured the president that such a donation would give the proposal "the kind of U.S. identification, validity, and vitality that it deserves." Consequently, on November 15, Lodge concluded a speech to the First Committee with a pledge to allocate 100 kilograms of fissionable material to serve as fuel in experimental atomic reactors. The announcement, Lodge joyfully reported, had "a cataclysmic effect."[18]

16. Diary entry, August 11, 1954, Box 3, DDE Diary Series, EP, AWF, EL; Memorandum for the Files, by Gerard Smith (consultant to the secretary of state for atomic energy affairs), October 13, 1954, in *FRUS, 1952–1954,* II, 1530; Jackson, "The President's Atomic Proposal Before the UN," December 28, 1953, in folder marked "Atoms for Peace—Evolution (1)," Box 24, Jackson Papers, EL; Memorandum by Richard Hirsch (OCB staff representative, Working Group for Exploitation of President's UN Speech), February 4, 1954, same folder; Jackson, "Follow-Through on the President's U. N. Speech," n.d., in folder marked "John Foster Dulles," Box 40, Jackson Papers, EL; Lodge to Dulles, June 21, 1954, 330.13/6–2154, in Box 1307, RG 59, NA; Memorandum, Lodge to Key and Wainhouse, March 18, 1954, Reel 8, HCLP, MHS; Lodge to Dulles, April 14, 1954, in *FRUS, 1952–1954,* II, 1385.

17. *MTCD,* Reel 2, Dulles and Lodge, October 29, 1954; *MTCD,* Reel 3 Dulles and Lodge, November 1, 1954; Hewlett and Holl, *Atoms for Peace and War, 1953–1961,* 227–28.

18. Lodge to Eisenhower, November 8, 1954, Reel 28, HCLP, MHS; Lodge to Dulles, November 16, 1954, same reel.

Lodge correctly surmised that international pressure and the exigencies of the Soviet "peace offensive" would persuade the Kremlin to support a form of the Atoms for Peace plan. After unsuccessful attempts to undermine support for the proposal and alter its operational structure, by mid-November the Soviets were prepared to vote for a resolution, even if it did not incorporate their suggested alterations. The USSR was "worried to death," according to Lodge, that the IAEA was "a Trojan Horse" for the United States.[19] As he had predicted, the General Assembly unanimously approved a U.S. resolution that called for an international technical conference and expressed the hope that the IAEA would be established without delay. The proposal, Lodge crowed to Eisenhower, had enabled the United States "to dominate this session of the United Nations General Assembly in a way that has never happened before." The USIA exhibit had *"physically"* monopolized the UN's lobby, while the atomic pool concept had dominated the *"minds* of the members."[20]

From January, 1955, until the agency's establishment in late 1957, the United States sought to keep the nations involved in drafting the IAEA statute to a minimum, and deliberately kept the future agency's ties to the UN vague. A twelve-nation working group drafted the charter, relying heavily on an American draft. It submitted a draft statute to a General Conference that opened on October 1, 1957. Although the Soviet *Sputnik* launch and the Little Rock school crisis diverted attention from the conference, the United States prevailed in every respect, and all eighty-two nations voted in favor of the statute. Only U.S. insistence upon the selection of an American, W. Sterling Cole, to be the director-general provoked resentment. According to delegation head Wadsworth, even the United States' closest allies made "sneering reference to U.S. politicians," opposed the salary scale that the U.S. delegation was instructed to seek if Cole obtained the top post, and expressed bitter disappointment that the United States had "brought cold war to the agency."[21]

19. *MTCD,* Reel 3, Dulles and Lodge, November 18, 1954.

20. Lodge to Eisenhower, November 23, 1954, Reel 28, HCLP, MHS.

21. Wadsworth to Lodge, September 16, 1957, Reel 16, HCLP, MHS; "Confidential Report of the U.S. Delegation to the First Meetings of the General Conference and Board of Governors of the International Atomic Energy Agency, October 1–3," n.d., in *FRUS, 1955–1957,* XX, 741–53; The Reminiscences of James Wadsworth, June 2, 1967, pp. 101–105, COHP, Butler Library, Columbia University.

The new agency indeed quickly fell victim to the cold war. Secretary-General Hammarskjöld had voiced his hope that "the Agency would not be considered solely as [a] means to obtain UN blessing for a program of bilateral agreements."[22] But that is almost exactly what happened. Only six months after the U.S. Senate ratified the Statute of the IAEA in June, 1957, the State Department had already concluded thirty-nine bilateral agreements for peaceful atomic cooperation. Thus, despite the administration's central role in establishing the IAEA, the administration almost immediately bypassed the agency, even in its final, truncated form, and used bilateral agreements to arrange for the dispersion of atomic energy materials and knowledge. Reflecting its emphasis upon Europe and NATO, the administration made EURATOM rather than IAEA the focus of the organizational effort.

Meanwhile, the administration had been involved in the ongoing disarmament negotiations in an ever-expanding array of UN forums. In April, 1954, the UN Disarmament Commission reconvened and established a subcommittee consisting of representatives of the United States, the United Kingdom, the Soviet Union, France, and Canada. It authorized this subcommittee—formally called the Subcommittee on Disarmament, though also referred to informally as the Disarmament Subcommittee, the Subcommittee of Five, and the London Subcommittee—to conduct private negotiations and instructed it to report by July 15, 1954. The commission thereby sanctioned extremely limited multilateral discussions, held only marginally within the UN framework.

The Subcommittee of Five met in nineteen sessions at Lancaster House, London, from May 13 to June 22, 1954. The positions taken by the two sides became the focus of disarmament negotiations for the next year. The Soviet Union called for the prohibition of all nuclear weapons prior to the installation of a system of controls. The Western powers countered that such a prohibition must be part of a comprehensive, general disarmament agreement that covered armed forces, atomic and conventional weapons, and a foolproof system of inspection. They laid out their position in two papers, an American paper on an international control organ and an Anglo-French memorandum that outlined the phasing of the various elements of a comprehensive disarmament program.

22. Memorandum of a Conversation, May 11, 1955, in *FRUS, 1955–1957,* XX, 84.

Even in the relative privacy of five-nation negotiations, it proved impossible to reach an acceptable solution. The mutual distrust so evident in the larger UN forums was mirrored in the smaller subcommittee. Indeed, the State Department directed the U.S. delegation to operate on the assumption that the "USSR can be expected to do [nothing] other than distort proposals or possible areas of subcommittee agreement so as to enhance their [*sic*] own global bargaining and power position to serious disadvantages US."[23] Once again the superpowers deadlocked over the issue of a control organ's power to take action if one of the signatories violated the agreement. The Soviet Union insisted that such authority must rest with the Security Council, and thus be subject to a Soviet veto, while the United States sought to empower the control organ to take punitive action.

Announcing a major Soviet disarmament initiative in September, 1954, Soviet representative Andrei Vishinsky proclaimed that the USSR was willing to use the Anglo-French memorandum as a basis for discussion. For the first time the Soviet Union appeared to have accepted, at least in theory, the existence of an international arms control agency with powers of inspection. An intensely skeptical Dulles viewed the announcement as simply part of the post-Stalin "peace offensive." He directed the U.S. delegation to "quickly probe Soviet proposals in order [to] deflate them" and determine whether they were genuine concessions "or only a clever propaganda move." Lodge also judged the Soviet proposal to be just "window dressing," and maintained that the USSR did not want to negotiate seriously.[24]

In keeping with this skepticism, the administration failed to explore the Soviet proposal adequately. Nor could it present a persuasive counterproposal, since it lacked a coherent disarmament policy of its own. A late 1954–early 1955 study starkly revealed the continued absence of consensus within the administration, specifically on the question of whether and how to pursue arms control reduction through the United Nations. The State Department asserted that the current U.S. disarmament plan in the UN was "no longer feasible." It wanted to redefine the objective to be the "reduction of nuclear weapons rather than their elimination," develop a new program, and

23. Telegram from Dulles to Patterson, May 8, 1954, 330.13/5–854, in Box 1307, RG 59, NA.

24. For Dulles's quotations, see Telegram from Dulles to USUN, October 6, 1954, 330.13/10–654, in Box 1307, RG 59, NA. For Lodge, see "Interview with Henry Cabot Lodge, Jr.," *U.S. News & World Report,* November 26, 1954, p. 97.

continue negotiations because they strengthened "the support of our allies for general U.S. policy objectives." The Defense Department, although agreeing that the UN program was no longer realistic, disingenuously professed its support, though it would not implement the plan until the Soviet Union could demonstrate "good faith by other means."[25]

The administration finally decided to follow the traditional American policy, which linked reductions in nuclear weapons and reductions in conventional weapons. It responded to the public clamor to "do something" by agreeing to continued negotiation. But it did not feel compelled to devise a new formula or explore different tactics. Even Lodge predicted that at the London subcommittee talks, scheduled to reconvene on February 25, 1955, the American delegation "would not have to show its hand with respect to a firm U.S. position." The session would be primarily "a cold war exercise."[26]

The Disarmament Subcommittee held twenty-eight further meetings at Lancaster House from February 25 to May 18, 1955. Throughout March and April, the Soviet delegation reverted to its pre-1954 position, demanding a freeze on conventional force levels (an area of clear Soviet superiority), without any attendant reductions in nuclear weapons or conventional armaments. Lodge (who headed the American delegation until mid-March, when Wadsworth replaced him) concluded that the Soviet delegates "knew that they were in a preposterous position . . . that they were proposing a scheme which would really delude no one—a scheme which was not even a clever propaganda scheme." Still the charade continued. According to Wadsworth, Gromyko, the chief Soviet delegate, continued to follow "the tactics of attempting to lead every day's discussion with a concrete Soviet proposal," while the U.S. delegation attempted "to counter this move with further concrete proposals," fully cognizant that its initiatives "will help make the record but will not spell any considerable success for the conference."[27]

25. Memorandum of Conversation by Howard Meyers, November 17, 1954, in *FRUS, 1952–1954,* II, 1565; Memorandum, Cutler to Dulles, Charles E. Wilson (secretary of defense), and Strauss, December 10, 1954, same volume, 1581–82.

26. Memorandum of Discussion at the 236th Meeting of the National Security Council, February 10, 1955, in *FRUS, 1955–1957,* XX, 32–33; Memorandum of a Conversation, February 9, 1955, same volume, 15–20.

27. For Lodge's quotation, see Statement for the Cabinet, March 18, 1954, Reel 4, HCLP, MHS. For the quotations from Wadsworth, see Wadsworth to Lodge, March 23, 1955, Reel 16, HCLP, MHS. See also Lodge to Wadsworth, April 11, 1955, Reel 4, HCLP, MHS.

On May 10, 1955, Jacob Malik, the head of the Soviet delegation, stunned the subcommittee with his announcement of a sweeping new program. Malik agreed to allow Western surveillance posts on Russian territory, offered to exchange information on military establishments and national budgets, suggested a two-year schedule for eliminating overseas bases, and accepted key Anglo-French proposals on the relationship between nuclear and conventional disarmament. Even Dulles admitted that this latest salvo in the "Soviet diplomatic offensive" was "subtly drawn and very cleverly presented to the Western world."[28]

Yet the plan also represented a tremendous substantive shift toward the American position. Distressed that the administration had permitted the Soviet Union to seize the initiative, Lodge complained that he felt "like the man who was lying on the New York Central track, knowing that the express was about to come through—and stays there and is run over." Wadsworth, however, refused to be steamrolled. Insisting that the Soviets had made "tremendous concessions," he argued that it was time "to drop the role of the Guy Who Wants to Go Home" and begin serious negotiations. Most important, Wadsworth beseeched the administration to address the fundamental question "How much do we want to demonstrate willingness to close the cold war and work cooperatively with the Russians for peace?"[29] He never received answers; the administration used the upcoming Geneva summit as an excuse to adjourn.

The attention of the world turned to Geneva, Switzerland, in July, 1955. After the Soviet gesture in London, expectations were high that the heads of state would make further progress toward disarmament. Eisenhower's presentation of his "Open Skies" concept sustained the world's hopes. The president proposed to Soviet premier Nikolai Bulganin that they exchange military blueprints and establish the mutual right to conduct aerial inspection of the other side's territory in order to guard against the possibility of a nuclear surprise attack. Eisenhower thereby met the need, cited by Wadsworth, for the president to have a viable, constructive, proposal. At the same time, it

28. Memorandum of Discussion at the 248th Meeting of the National Security Council on May 12, 1955, in Box 6, NSC Series, EP, AWF, EL.

29. For the quotation from Lodge, see Lodge to Dulles, May 11, 1955, in *FRUS, 1955–1957,* XX, 76. For the quotations from Wadsworth, see Wadsworth to Lodge, May 11, 1955, same volume, 79–81.

provided a public challenge to the USSR and constituted an attempt to regain the psychological warfare initiative from the Soviets, who had been in control since the May 10 proposal.[30]

As he had in his Atoms for Peace plan, Eisenhower adopted a functionalist approach to achieving the goal of arms control. He focused on one small part—the fear of surprise attack—of the far larger and more complex problem and sought to achieve accommodation in this area. Superpower cooperation on this limited question would then, he hoped, develop the habit of cooperation, reduce international tensions, and increase mutual trust to the point where genuine negotiations about comprehensive arms control might be possible.

Eisenhower's decision to make the offer through bilateral channels rather than in the customary UN forums, however, represented a significant departure from tradition. In his wholly symbolic position as the official host for the conference, held at the UN's European headquarters, Hammarskjöld had welcomed Eisenhower to the Palace of Nations. The president reciprocated by inviting Hammarskjöld to lunch at his villa. But the secretary-general played no further role, and UN participation was restricted merely to supplying the building within which the summit took place. Nevertheless, Eisenhower did shift the locus of negotiation back to the world organization when he requested consideration of the proposal at the fall, 1955, General Assembly session and Hammarskjöld supported this move.[31]

In the midst of the London negotiations, Eisenhower had surprised the disarmament policy-making structure by appointing Harold E. Stassen, who had served as an official U.S. delegate to San Francisco in 1945 and was director of the Foreign Operations Administration, to the newly created post of special assistant to the president for disarmament studies. Eisenhower expected Stassen, who quickly acquired the moniker "Secretary of Peace" from the press, to fashion a unified proposal out of the conflicting State, Defense, and AEC positions. Tellingly, Eisenhower announced that Stassen was to "draw on the assistance of Government agencies, the general pub-

---

30. The most detailed work on the development of the Open Skies proposal is Walt W. Rostow, *Open Skies: Eisenhower's Proposal of July 21, 1955* (Austin, 1982).

31. Lodge to Stassen, May 4, 1955, Reel 4, HCLP, MHS; Record of the Secretary-General's Private Meetings, September 9, 1955, File 2, Box 2, 1.1.3, The Executive Office: Office of the Executive Assistant (1946–1961), Office of the Secretary-General, UN Archives.

lic, and even the entire world—without getting into the activities of the United Nations."[32]

This charge was instructive. If Eisenhower genuinely viewed the UN as central to disarmament and the attempt to achieve world peace, Stassen could not possibly have fulfilled his duties as "Secretary of Peace" without being actively involved in the UN effort. Recognizing this, Wadsworth complained that the appointment had "pulled the rug out" from under him and left the United States vulnerable to the charge that it was "scuttling the London SubCommittee exercise."[33]

Stassen soon dramatically altered American arms control policy. In delivering the U.S. response on September 6 to the May 10 Soviet proposal, he announced that in light of a task force's conclusion that it would be impossible to detect concealed nuclear weapons, the United States was reevaluating its pre-Geneva positions. Reflecting the administration's continuing indecision about how best to proceed, the State Department instructed the U.S. delegation to prevent a full-scale debate in the General Assembly until after the fall session of the Subcommittee on Disarmament and the foreign ministers' meeting, scheduled to convene on October 27, had concluded. Only after it first had exhausted the resources of the more restricted multilateral forums would the administration encourage the General Assembly to tackle the disarmament problem again.[34]

Lodge desperately sought to retain the initiative created by the president's address. He urged Eisenhower, Dulles, and Stassen to make the Open Skies concept the centerpiece of a "new World Disarmament Policy" and vigorously push for its adoption. Stassen quickly agreed. Concerned that an American resolution might be amended beyond recognition, Dulles, however, opposed the request. The more politically sensitive Lodge understood that with even a minimum of flexibility—the willingness to mention the ideas of others as long as they were essentially harmless—a U.S. resolution

32. Report of a Conference Between the President and His Special Assistant (Stassen), March 22, 1955, in *FRUS, 1955–1957,* XX, 61. For Stassen's account of his appointment and the difficulties he faced, see Stassen and Houts, *Eisenhower: Turning the World Toward Peace,* 275–91.

33. Wadsworth to Lodge, n.d. (probably March 20, 1955), Reel 16, HCLP, MHS; Lodge to Wadsworth, March 23, 1955, same reel.

34. Position Paper, "Disarmament," August 23, 1955, SD/A/C.1, in Box 1257, RG 59, NA.

would command widespread support. Moreover, Lodge believed that the United States should accept the widespread call to link the Open Skies concept (essentially only an inspection system) with some limited disarmament measure. A resolution in support of Open Skies, he argued, would keep the UN and the United States in the forefront of the search for peace and brand the USSR "as the troublemaker and war-monger of the world" if it refused to implement aerial inspection.[35]

By early December Eisenhower and Dulles had decided, despite Defense Department objections, to support a British resolution that endorsed the plan. Even Dulles now admitted that the United States had "been so evasive re disarmament that we have helped the Soviet propaganda." Some sort of action was imperative. The General Assembly approved Open Skies by a vote of 56 to 7. As he had promised, Lodge used the resounding endorsement to argue that any nation rejecting the plan "lays itself open to grave suspicion." Unfortunately, in the absence of Soviet cooperation, Open Skies proved to be another dead end.[36]

During the winter and spring of 1956, increasingly frustrated advocates of arms control in the administration proposed a variety of unprecedented measures. Some even suggested surrendering part of the nation's sovereign prerogatives to the UN. Lodge suggested that the atomic powers "agree to internationalize the use of atomic weapons under the aegis of the United Nations." Prior to using a nuclear weapon, a nation would have to request permission from the General Assembly. Lodge's idea was not particularly surprising, for in his desire to enhance the status of the UN he had made similarly bizarre proposals before. Dulles too, however, appears to have contemplated a concept similar to Lodge's, at least in the theoretical long term. Although he maintained that "the idea of [nuclear weapons] power in the

35. Lodge to Stassen, August 11, 1955, in *FRUS, 1955–1957,* XX, 170; Lodge to Dulles, October 26, 1955, same volume, 223; Dulles to Stassen, August 15, 1955, same volume, 172–73; Memorandum of a Conversation, September 19, 1955, same volume, 199–202; Lodge to Eisenhower, August 31, 1955, Reel 29, HCLP, MHS; Lodge to Eisenhower, November 28, 1955, Reel 29, HCLP, MHS.

36. *MTCD,* Reel 4, Dulles and Lodge, December 1, 1955, 5:50 and 5:43 P.M.; Lodge to Eisenhower, January 24, 1956, in folder marked "Henry Cabot Lodge: 1956 (3)," Administration Series, EP, AWF, EL; Eisenhower to Lodge, December 1, 1955, in folder marked "Henry Cabot Lodge: 1955 (1)," Box 24, Administration Series, EP, AWF, EL.

United Nations was for the time being quite academic," he professed to believe that "there should be some organic and organizational control of atomic weapons on an international basis." In the meantime, he thought it would be beneficial to obtain "some [UN] sanction for their possession and use."[37] The fact that they even broached such proposals testifies to the chaotic state of American disarmament policy in the midst of the transition from the advocacy of total nuclear disarmament to arms limitation and control.

The idea of investing the UN with more control over the use of existing nuclear weapons soon reached a wider audience. At a May 10, 1956, NSC meeting and in subsequent memoranda, Stassen advanced the idea of an "atoms-for-police" program. He suggested that the atomic powers provide the UN with a small nuclear force. The Defense Department strongly objected, but it was Eisenhower who effectively quashed the idea when he raised a number of pointed questions, ranging from where the weapons would be stored to what bases they would be launched from. It was typical of his role throughout the process. Just as he had forced the opponents of arms control to make concessions, so he now restrained the most outspoken advocates of disarmament.[38]

As these internal debates played themselves out, the United States conducted a holding action during the Disarmament Commission from March to May, 1956. The session ended in stalemate. Eisenhower's ileitis attack in June, the presidential election campaign, and the Suez and Hungarian crises combined to forestall progress on arms negotiations during the fall, despite Lodge's requests to make at least a token effort.[39]

After Eisenhower's reelection, Stassen and the NSC devised a new arms control package with more modest objectives than total nuclear disarma-

37. On Lodge's proposal, see Lodge to Dulles, January 24, 1956, in *FRUS, 1955–1957,* XX, 274. On Dulles's proposal, see Memorandum of Conversation, January 29, 1956, same volume, 305; Dulles to Stassen, February 7, 1956, same volume, 331–33; John Lewis Gaddis, "The Unexpected John Foster Dulles: Nuclear Weapons, Communism, and the Russians," in Immerman, ed., *John Foster Dulles and the Diplomacy of the Cold War,* 53–57.

38. Memorandum of Discussion at the 284th Meeting of the National Security Council on May 10, 1956, in *FRUS, 1955–1957,* XX, 393–400; Memorandum, Stassen to Eisenhower, June 29, 1956, same volume, 406.

39. Memorandum of Discussion at the 275th Meeting of the National Security Council, February 7, 1956, in *FRUS, 1955–1957,* XX, 325–26; Telegram from Lodge to the Secretary of State, September 11, 1956, 310/9–1156, in Box 1231, RG 59, NA.

ment. Lodge presented the new five-point program to the General Assembly on January 14, 1957. The program called for a cessation of nuclear weapons production under international inspection, to be followed by a ban on testing, reductions in conventional armaments and forces, registration of ballistic missile tests and the reservation of outer space for peaceful purposes, and the progressive installation of inspection systems to prevent a surprise attack. During debate it quickly became evident that the General Assembly could not reconcile the U.S. plan with the Soviet Union's insistence on an immediate prohibition of all testing. The General Assembly thus voted to refer all disarmament proposals to the subcommittee.

Pursuant to the General Assembly's recommendation, the UN Disarmament Subcommittee met in London beginning on March 15, for a five-and-one-half-month marathon session. The American delegation, headed by Stassen, presented the arms control package first outlined in January. The Soviet delegation, led by Valerian Zorin, countered with a proposal for the immediate cessation of all tests. Late in April, however, Zorin endorsed the concept of a mutual aerial surveillance system and agreed to permit ground inspection stations. Stassen reported that the Soviets were engaging in "plain talking" rather than "propaganda techniques." He urged Eisenhower to order a test ban as a means of continuing progress and sought specifics upon which to conduct further negotiations. Agreeing on the "absolute necessity of some kind of a halt in the arms race" and eager to cut the defense budget, Eisenhower expressed conditional support for a test ban.[40]

At a meeting of the NSC on May 25, the president authorized Stassen to discuss the implementation of Open Skies and a temporary test ban in exchange for future limitations on nuclear weapons production. However, he stressed that this proposal was to be treated as a "talking paper." Convinced that his own still-festering presidential ambitions were dependent upon the success of the negotiations, Stassen overstepped his authority. He delivered an "informal memorandum" to Zorin that outlined the May decision. The British complained bitterly about this breach of unity among the Western allies, and Eisenhower and Dulles were embarrassed and outraged. Eisen-

40. Memorandum of Discussion at the 324th Meeting of the National Security Council on May 23, 1957, in *FRUS, 1955–1957*, XX, 533–38; Hewlett and Holl, *Atoms for Peace and War, 1953–1961*, 392.

hower unleashed his fabled temper, decrying Stassen's action as "one of the most stupid things that anyone on a diplomatic mission could possibly [do]."[41]

Zorin shrewdly took advantage of the Anglo-American conflict. He declared that the United States and the USSR were close to agreement and announced that the Soviet Union would accept a two- to three-year moratorium on testing and accept international inspection stations on Russian soil. The Soviet announcement and Eisenhower's initially favorable response to the idea of delinking the test ban from the rest of the U.S. arms control package worried opponents of arms control. Strauss and atomic scientists led by Edward Teller dissuaded Eisenhower. They warned that a test ban would prevent the development of "clean" bombs that would significantly reduce radioactive fallout from nuclear explosions. Dulles, too, believing arms limitation "impossible," advised against making any "great political sacrifice" to support a moratorium. From June to August, 1957, both sides traded offers and rejections. Talks recessed on September 6, with no date set for their resumption.[42]

The administration's basic stance remained unaltered during the fall, 1957, General Assembly session, a meeting dominated by the disarmament issue. Speaking before the General Assembly on September 19, Dulles reiterated the August 29 London policy and promised to suspend nuclear tests for one year if the necessary inspections system was implemented. The Western powers set forth a comprehensive package of partial disarmament measures along the lines outlined by Lodge the previous January, and the General Assembly voted overwhelmingly for it. The Soviet Union not only continued to advocate proposals banning both weapons and testing, but also responded on October 28 by demanding parity of representation for East and West in the Disarmament Commission. It insisted that the General Assembly abolish the subcommittee and create a new commission composed of all eighty-two UN members. Opposed on principle to the idea of bloc parity

41. Eisenhower to Jock Whitney (John Hay Whitney, U.S. ambassador to the United Kingdom), June 11, 1957, in *FRUS, 1955–1957,* XX, 616; Informal Memorandum, Stassen to Zorin, May 31, 1957, same volume, 574–83; Telegrams from Dulles to the U.S. embassy in the United Kingdom, June 4, 1957, 5:11 P.M. and 7:59 P.M., same volume, 595.

42. Memorandum of Conversation, July 31, 1957, Reel 227, State Department Microfilm, J. F. Dulles Papers, Mudd Library; Memorandum of a Conference with the President on August 30 and 31, 1957, in *FRUS, 1955–1957,* XX, 717–18.

in any UN body, the United States also resisted expanding the commission to include the entire UN membership. The U.S. delegation did agree to increase the commission to twenty-five members, provided that the main talks remained in the five-member subcommittee. The General Assembly supported the U.S. plan and the Soviet delegation walked out. Five years of effort had led to a negotiating deadlock, a diplomatic stalemate, and a temporary end to negotiations at the UN.[43]

For the next two and one-half years, talks officially took place outside the UN framework, although the participants used UN facilities and services and reported periodically to the organization. Throughout 1958, deliberations about a test ban and the development of a system to prevent surprise attack dominated the agenda. Bulganin made the first move in a late 1957 letter to Eisenhower in which he requested a summit conference and a U.S. pledge for a two- to three-year testing moratorium to begin on January 1, 1958. Stassen and Lodge urged Eisenhower to accept. Asserting that "world opinion blamed" the United States for "the disarmament deadlock" and that the Soviet proposal was only "scenery," Lodge viewed a moratorium as the best way to improve the nation's international standing.[44] But Dulles maintained that "if the Soviets ever wanted to accomplish serious business the best way would be through the method of private talks," not the publicity of a summit. Faced with opposition from his secretaries of state and defense and with his own concerns about the impact on NATO, the president decided to table Stassen's plan and stick to the August 29 proposal.[45]

The Kremlin persisted. On March 31, 1958, the Soviet Union announced a unilateral suspension of nuclear testing and requested the United States

43. "U.N. General Assembly Adopts Western Proposal on Principles of Disarmament; Votes to Enlarge Commission," Lodge statements in Committee I on November 4, 14, 19, 1957, *Department of State Bulletin,* December 16, 1957, pp. 961–65; Staff Notes, October 7, 1957, in folder marked "Toner Notes—Oct. 1957," Box 27, DDE Diary Series, EP, AWF, EL; *MTCD,* Reel 7, Dulles and Lodge, November 5, 1957, 11:48 A.M.

44. Memorandum for the Files, "Remarks at NSC meeting on January 6, 1958," January 7, 1958, Reel 4, HCLP, MHS; Memorandum of a Conversation between Dulles and Lodge, January 7, 1958, in folder marked "Memoranda of Telephone Conversations—General: January 2, 1958–March 31, 1958 (4)," Box 8, Telephone Conversation Series, Dulles Papers, EL.

45. Memorandum of a Conversation, March 21, 1958, in folder marked "Memoranda of Telephone Conversations—General: January 2, 1958–March 31, 1958 (1)," Box 8, Telephone Conversation Series, Dulles Papers, EL; Hewlett and Holl, *Atoms for Peace and War, 1953–1961,* 469–71.

and Great Britain to follow its lead. Lodge encouraged the president to join in declaring a unilateral moratorium. Eager to retain moral leadership of the disarmament effort, but still giving priority to his perception of immediate national security interests, Eisenhower refused, since the United States was about to begin testing a new series—code-named Hardtack—of nuclear weapons, primarily hydrogen bombs. He did, however, agree to tripartite (the United States, the USSR, and Great Britain) talks to discuss the feasibility of detecting nuclear tests. A conference of scientific experts held during the summer concluded that it would be technically possible to police a test-ban treaty. On August 22, Eisenhower pledged an indefinite suspension of American tests beginning on October 31, as long as progress continued on arms control and inspection procedures. This decision stands as one of the major accomplishments in arms control. Unfortunately, a subsequent political conference, the Surprise Attack Conference of 1958, in November and December failed to reach a diplomatic agreement.[46]

The question of arms control remained on the UN agenda, but the administration's use of the UN became increasingly *pro forma*. Even Lodge had become so disillusioned with inconclusive negotiations that he began to adopt the more cynical view espoused by Dulles. "Five years here have convinced me," the ambassador confided to the secretary of state, "that we must proceed on the theory that the Soviets are using disarmament for propaganda purposes without any sincere desire to reach a settlement on the problem itself—except on their terms." Consequently, the United States ought to concentrate primarily on the propaganda aspects of disarmament. The administration, he argued, should go through the motions in the Security Council and the Disarmament Commission, but should pursue opportunities outside of the UN more aggressively.[47]

46. *MTCD*, Reel 7, Dulles and Lodge, March 25, 1958; Memorandum to the President from Lodge, April 8, 1958, Reel 29, HCLP, MHS; Hewlett and Holl, *Atoms for Peace and War, 1953–1961*, 477–80, 546. The most comprehensive account of the test-ban negotiations during the Eisenhower years is Robert A. Divine, *Blowing on the Wind: The Nuclear Test Ban Debate, 1954–1960* (New York, 1978). On the Surprise Attack Conference, see Jeremy Suri, "America's Search for a Technological Solution to the Arms Race: The Surprise Attack Conference of 1958 and a Challenge for 'Eisenhower Revisionists,'" *Diplomatic History,* XXI (1997), 417–51.

47. Lodge to Dulles, March 31, 1958, Reel 5, HCLP, MHS; Dulles and Lodge, March 20, 1958, in folder marked "Jan. 2, 1958–March 31, 1958 (1), Memoranda of Telephone Conversa-

Lodge soon had an opportunity to take "the initiative in the propaganda war." On April 21, 1958, the Soviet Union, claiming that the flight of U.S. planes armed with atomic weapons over the Arctic area posed a threat to its security, lodged a complaint in the Security Council. The council rejected the Soviet resolution on April 29. On the same day, the United States recommended the establishment of a zone of international inspection against surprise attack across the Arctic Circle. As always, Dulles assured Hammarskjöld that the United States was not engaged in "a propaganda exercise."[48]

Dulles's protestations notwithstanding, the American initiative was primarily a propaganda move, albeit one that it would have been willing to see implemented. Believing that a Soviet veto of the U.S. resolution "would permanently spike their [the Soviet] propaganda" campaign, Dulles and Lodge sought and received Eisenhower's permission to counterattack immediately. Dulles carefully orchestrated the plan.[49] The propaganda campaign concluded, successfully for the United States, when the Soviets vetoed the U.S. resolution, effectively ending UN involvement in another area of arms control.

The Soviet Union's proposal of a General Assembly agenda item on the use of outer space generated an American counterproposal. The heightened emphasis on the propaganda aspects of disarmament heavily influenced the U.S. initiative. Fearing that it would not be able to control a discussion on the arms control aspects of outer space, the administration determined to restrict UN consideration to the peaceful uses of the new frontier. The State Department directed USUN to support only the establishment of a temporary committee with a carefully circumscribed agenda.[50]

Typically, the State Department sought to manipulate the UN. It pressed for a committee that would be "heavily loaded in our direction" with "terms of reference" that would limit it to conducting studies and pursuing scientific projects. After prolonged wrangling over its composition, the General Assembly finally established a permanent committee in December, 1959, that would deal solely with the peaceful uses of outer space. The U.S. dele-

---

tions—General," Box 8, Telephone Conversation Series, Dulles Papers, EL; *MTCD,* Reel 8, Dulles and Lodge, October 10, 1958.

48. Lodge to Dulles, March 31, 1958, Reel 5, HCLP, MHS; *MTCD,* Reel 7, Dulles and Hammarskjöld, April 29, 1958.

49. *MTCD,* Reel 7, Dulles and Lodge, April 23, 1958, 12:07 P.M., 12:21 P.M., and 6:58 P.M.

50. Telegram from Herter to USUN, August 18, 1958, in *FRUS, 1958–1960,* II, 863–64.

gation thus managed to prevent debate about outer space in terms of disarmament.[51]

During the fall, 1958, General Assembly session, the administration also reversed its earlier opposition to expanding the Disarmament Commission to include the entire UN membership. Lodge now argued that it would be politically wise for the United States to accede to the pleas of the "little countries" that "want to get in on the act." An enlarged commission might not accomplish anything, but neither had the previous smaller versions. Moreover, it would at least give the UN the "functioning disarmament machinery" lacking since the Soviet boycott. On a more optimistic note, it might "provide an occasion for [the] *ad hoc* corridor meetings on an impromptu basis" where important negotiation actually took place.[52] Despite State Department predictions that a committee of the whole would become a source of "constant meddling" and a "propaganda battle," the United States ultimately supported the enlargement. On November 4, the General Assembly reconstituted the commission to contain the entire UN membership.[53]

Familiar arguments on disarmament echoed in the General Assembly's halls during 1959 and 1960. Nikita Khrushchev issued the clarion call for the Soviets in an address to the General Assembly on September 18, 1959. The Soviet premier presented a "Program of General and Complete Disarmament" that consisted of a four-year plan aimed at achieving total worldwide disarmament under international control. The U.S. delegation responded by reiterating the call for comprehensive, multistage arms control, with verification at each step. Once again, as each side sought a propaganda advantage on the world stage, accommodation, much less progress, proved to be impossible.

In an effort to revive serious negotiations, the two sides decided in August, 1959, to create a Ten Nation Committee on Disarmament. Composed of five nations from the Communist bloc and five nations from the West, the committee would meet the Soviet demand for parity. However, the new

51. Memorandum, Wilcox to Dulles, July 11, 1958, in Box 1232, RG 59, NA; Herter to Dr. James R. Killian, Jr., August 22, 1958, in folder marked "August 1958 (2)," Chronological File, Box 5, Dulles-Herter Series, EP, AWF, EL; Telegram from Lodge to the Department of State, November 20, 1958, in *FRUS, 1958–1960,* II, 874–76; Telegram from Herter to USUN, December 18, 1958, same volume, 880–81.

52. Lodge to Dulles, October 23, 1958, Reel 5, HCLP, MHS.

53. Telegram from Herter (acting secretary) to USUN, October 20, 1958, 320.11/10–2058, in Box 1269, RG 59, NA; Memorandum, Wilcox to the Secretary of State, October 27, 1958, 320.11/10–2758, in Box 1266, RG 59, NA.

body had no representatives from Asia, Latin America, or Africa and therefore was not truly representative of the UN's membership. More important, it was essentially and purposefully outside of the UN.[54]

Neither the Ten Nation Committee on Disarmament that convened on March 15, 1960, nor the abortive Paris summit meeting in mid-May succeeded where negotiations within the UN framework had failed. The shooting down of an American U-2 spy plane over the Soviet Union provoked a Soviet walkout from the Paris summit meeting on May 18, 1960. Meanwhile, at the Ten Nation Committee, the Soviets had reiterated the plan that Khrushchev had presented in September, 1959. The Western nations, in turn, initially proposed creating an International Disarmament Organization, separate from the UN, to oversee the disarmament process. Only after Hammarskjöld objected vociferously did they drop their request and renew their traditional calls for a multiphase plan. On June 27, 1960, the Soviet delegation withdrew from the Ten Nation Committee meeting.[55]

The administration then could have turned to the options provided by the UN proper, requesting an emergency session of the General Assembly or the Disarmament Commission. Despite Lodge's persistent pleas, it rejected this course of action. Secretary of State Christian Herter, who had replaced Dulles after Dulles's resignation due to ill health, opposed handling a complex matter in the eighty-two-member Disarmament Commission, even though Lodge maintained that "it would boil down to the Russians and us" regardless of where negotiations took place. Fearful, like his predecessor, that "some of the little states might get us into a jam," Herter effectively buried the idea of using the UN "in the deep freeze."[56] Not until late July did Eisenhower instruct Lodge to request a meeting of the Disarmament Commission. Even then, Eisenhower did so, he admitted privately, because of "special considerations." The political demands of the presidential election, not a genuine expectation that the UN might succeed, motivated the head of the Republican party.[57]

54. Memorandum by Max V. Krebs, "Secret Attachment," August 21, 1959, in folder marked "August 1959 (1)," Box 7, Chronological File, Herter Papers, EL.

55. Urquhart, *Hammarskjöld*, 324–25.

56. *MTCH*, Reel 11, Herter and Lodge, June 28, 1960; *MTCH*, Reel 11, Wilcox and Herter, July 1, 1960; *MTCH*, Reel 10, Eisenhower and Herter, July 1, 1960, White House Telephone Calls.

57. *MTCH*, Reel 10, Eisenhower and Herter, July 21, 1960, 5:30 P.M., White House Telephone Calls.

Election-year politics prompted a variety of disarmament schemes. Presidential candidate Richard Nixon considered announcing that if elected he would send his vice president, Lodge, to Geneva to conduct the arms control talks. Lodge recommended that Eisenhower call for a resumption of the current session of the General Assembly in Moscow and that Nixon announce his intention to send him to head the U.S. delegation. Holding the General Assembly in Moscow, he averred, would open the Soviet Union to Western ideas and provide greater opportunity for discussion with Soviet leaders. No action was taken. Eisenhower deemed it a "poor idea," and argued that the "timing was wrong now," while Herter bluntly pointed to the obvious problem—"to do it now would look like a political stunt."[58]

Indeed, the administration intended that "nothing of substance" would be discussed at the meeting. Lodge, however, insisted that his address to the Disarmament Committee would look "like forward action" only if it included a new idea. He suggested announcing a cutoff of fissionable-material production for weapons purposes and proposing that the United States and the USSR transfer 30,000 kilograms of weapons-grade uranium 235 to the UN to be used for peaceful purposes. Herter was reluctant to make such a major proposal, but AEC head John McCone enthusiastically backed Lodge, and Eisenhower authorized him to make the offer. The Disarmament Commission subsequently called upon the principal powers to resume negotiations in the Ten Nation Committee, but for all intents and purposes disarmament talks remained "in the deep freeze" for the final months of the administration.[59]

Nuclear technology and, consequently, national defense strategy evolved dramatically during the 1950s. During Eisenhower's two terms in office the arms control strategists and the administration gradually abandoned the goal of total conventional and nuclear disarmament, which had shaped debate on the subject since the days of the League of Nations. In its place they adopted the far more modest and realistic objective of arms control.

58. Memorandum for the Record, October 31, 1960, in folder 1114, bMS Am 1829, Christian A. Herter Papers, Houghton Library, Harvard University, Cambridge, Massachusetts; Herter to Nixon, October 17, 1960, same folder.

59. *MTCH,* Reel 11, Herter and Lodge, August 12, 1960, 11:20 A.M.; *MTCH,* Reel 11, Herter and McCone, August 12, 1960, 12:50 P.M.; *MTCH,* Reel 10, Herter and Eisenhower, August 12, 1960, 2:10 P.M.; White House Telephone Calls.

Given the rapid technological and theoretical arms developments, it is not surprising that there was confusion about whether and how to work with the United Nations. Moreover, as the administration made the transition from seeking disarmament to striving for arms control, it became less willing to work through the UN. It was one thing to discuss utopian schemes for general and complete disarmament in the international body. It was something entirely different to entrust the United Nations with genuine arms control negotiations that might have a very real and immediate impact upon the United States' military capabilities and American national security. The administration was willing to permit the UN to serve as the locus for arms control deliberations, but the real power and ultimately the final decisions must rest solely with the principal nuclear powers.

To the extent that the administration achieved any measurable progress, credit must be given to Eisenhower. The president was unquestionably the guiding force behind arms control policy. It was his Atoms for Peace speech that prompted renewed debate on nuclear issues at the UN. The president showed an admirable willingness to address the difficult moral problems of arms control and nuclear issues and to do so, at least some of the time, in the UN forum.

But it was a constant struggle, one that compelled him to be an activist president in this area. Eisenhower saw the deep philosophical divisions within his administration on this issue and realized that there were significant bureaucratic obstacles present in any interdepartmental endeavor. He understood that these factors posed potentially insurmountable obstacles to the development of a unified American position. As a result, the president attempted to circumvent the traditional bureaucracies at State and Defense by relying on experienced political operators and proponents of psychological warfare, like Stassen, Lodge, Nelson Rockefeller, and Wadsworth, to devise innovative initiatives. These initiatives, like Atoms for Peace and Open Skies, met staunch resistance from the established bureaucracies, but Eisenhower's personal presentation of the proposals emphasized their weight and gave them added credibility.

Although he eschewed theoretical labels and strategies, Eisenhower approached the question of disarmament from an essentially functionalist perspective. He believed that even in the midst of the cold war it would be possible for the United States and its chief antagonist to identify some limited aspects of arms control on which they could agree. Building on the spirit—and ultimately the habit—of collaboration engendered by this first confidence-building measure, the superpowers could gradually extend their cooperation to larger and more complex aspects of the arms control issue. The president clearly shared the tempered optimism of Wadsworth, who recalled that while the negotiations often appeared to be a "hostile minuet," the "public utterances were a great deal more hardened than the private intra-conference remarks."[60]

Lodge never failed to encourage his chief in this regard. Although increasingly pessimistic as the years passed, Lodge remained eager for almost any agreement that might validate the UN. Typically, Dulles was far less optimistic about the chance for even limited arms control measures. Fundamental change in the international situation, he maintained, would have to precede any substantive progress. Dulles nevertheless advocated arms control negotiation. He was fully cognizant of the emotional appeal, both at home and abroad, of the call to disarm, and he understood that continued negotiation was a necessary weapon in the effort to contain the Communist threat. It strengthened cohesion among the United States and its allies and increased international public support for the United States. Eisenhower also appreciated the implications of disarmament negotiations for the nation's expanding system of alliances. Yet, unlike his secretary of state, who valued alliance politics more than progress toward disarmament, Eisenhower at least struggled with the conflict posed by the desire to discuss measures with U.S. allies first and the "mandate from the UN" to negotiate with all parties simultaneously and on an equal basis.[61]

All three men, but especially Dulles, supported continued participation in arms control deliberations because they believed that the process of negotiation was worthwhile regardless of whether the stated objective of arms limitation was achieved. Constructive initiatives, such as Atoms for Peace and Open Skies, served an important function by enhancing the nation's peaceful image and placing the moral onus for continued nuclear tension on the USSR. For Dulles, continuing the process of negotiation at the UN thus became a goal in and of itself.

Despite enthusiastic personal presentations by the president, the adminis-

60. Reminiscences of James J. Wadsworth, June 19, 1967, p. 142, COHP, Butler Library, Columbia University.

61. Diary entry, June 12, 1957, in folder marked "June 1957: Phone Calls," Box 25, DDE Diary Series, EP, AWF, EL.

tration's initiatives generally never made the leap from rhetoric to reality. Eisenhower himself was partly responsible, for he failed to see to it that his proposals received the necessary follow-through. He did not always personally intervene to silence the detractors of arms control within his administration or to see that they loyally followed his directives. This proved to be a major failing, especially in light of the bureaucratic intransigence toward his ideas.

More important, the president's functionalist approach to arms control demanded a consistent long-term policy and strategy in the United Nations if it was to succeed. Functionalism is essentially a slow, incremental process. It would have taken years for the carefully nurtured habit of cooperation to replace the entrenched hostility of the cold war. Eisenhower found himself in a classic catch-22 situation, for he and his administration could devise such a long-term strategy only if they possessed a certain minimal amount of trust in the USSR. However, Eisenhower, no doubt cautioned by Dulles, understandably never overcame his basic distrust of the Soviet Union enough to pursue genuine, sustained negotiations. Perceiving the USSR as an aggressive, imperialistic power, he insisted upon terms of inspection that the Soviets, equally fearful of espionage, would not accept. Eisenhower would not take risks that might jeopardize national security, even in his search for international peace. A stalemate rather than a safer world was the result.[62]

Thus, the story of the Eisenhower administration's relationship with the United Nations in the search for arms control is marked by both serious proposals and shortsighted propaganda battles. Lacking mutual trust among the superpowers and therefore unable to develop a coherent, long-range policy, the administration was itself split over the best approach to pursue. It therefore careened back and forth between UN-sponsored efforts to achieve world disarmament and bilateral or Four Power efforts designed to establish propaganda primacy on the world stage. Even within the UN itself, the United States, according to no less an observer than Wadsworth, was some-

---

62. As his term in office ended, Eisenhower had concluded that the time had come to lift the moratorium and resume underground and outer-space tests. Had Nixon won the election, Eisenhower wrote Herter in June, 1961, he would have issued an announcement to that effect late in 1960. Given the Democratic victory, however, he believed that the decision should be left to the Kennedy administration. Eisenhower to Herter, June 16, 1961, in Folder 176a, bMS Am 1829, Herter Papers, Houghton Library, Harvard; Herter to Eisenhower, June 22, 1961, same folder.

times guilty of a "lack of candor." The administration would "give lip service to disarmament, and then either privately or interdepartmentally say, 'Let's not go too fast.'"[63] The administration gladly used the UN as a forum to expound its views on disarmament, and even to negotiate, but it hesitated to empower the organization to act. Sadly, given Eisenhower's desire to "lighten the burdens of armaments and to lessen the likelihood of war," by the time his presidency came to a close the stockpiles of life-threatening nuclear arms had increased exponentially and the UN, with regard to this critical area, had been marginalized.[64]

63. The Reminiscences of James J. Wadsworth, June 19, 1967, p. 153, COHP, Butler Library, Columbia University.

64. See, for example, David Alan Rosenberg, "The Origins of Overkill: Nuclear Weapons and American Strategy, 1945–1960," *International Security,* VII (1983), 3–71.

8

WALKING THE TIGHTROPE
The Dilemma of Decolonization

While the Soviet-American rivalry remained the focus of American foreign policy throughout the 1950s, decolonization was perhaps the most significant international development of the decade. As the tempo of the transition from colonial status to independence accelerated, decolonization introduced a critical new factor in the cold war equation, with the emerging nations frequently playing the superpowers off against each other in their bids for independence and international legitimacy. Moreover, the decolonization process deeply affected America's staunchest European allies, heightening the complexity of the situation confronting Eisenhower. The administration faced the challenges of coming to terms with the realities of decolonization and then integrating these peripheral nations into the capitalist world economy and the collective security system. The stakes were high, for the United States needed to achieve these objectives in a manner that satisfied its European allies, quieted the political and economic nationalist movements in the Third World, and minimized Communist influence. During the decade, decolonization thus increasingly shifted attention from the European core, which had dominated the early post-war period and with which the Eisenhower administration was most familiar, to the periphery, particularly in Asia and Africa.

The UN General Assembly provided the central stage in this developing drama. Dependent territories and newly independent nations sought to use the international spotlight focused on the UN to advance the anti-colonial

cause. The increasing pressure on this issue made the Eisenhower administration uncomfortable. Its preference was to avoid involvement in the whole
decolonization process, insisting that it was primarily a matter between the
colonial powers and their dependent territories. Such a stance was clearly
impossible. As one of the principal actors at the UN, the United States found
that it could not remain wholly aloof from the decolonization question—at
least as it was manifested at the international organization.

Eisenhower firmly believed that colonialism was dying and ought not to
be revived. At the same time, he was wary of change. The president appreciated the stability provided by the British, French, and Belgian presence in
Africa, the Middle East, and Asia. Moreover, he worried that the collapse of
colonial control might facilitate Communist penetration of the decolonizing
world and deplete the strength of America's crucial NATO allies. While it
was impossible to stem the rising tide of nationalism and the desire for self-
government that was propelling colonies toward independence, Eisenhower
wanted to channel these forces in a pro-Western direction. The United
States and its European allies, Eisenhower wrote Churchill, must direct
decolonization in a way that would "win adherents to Western aims" and
enable the newly independent countries to withstand Soviet imperialism.
Gradual, orderly decolonization, he believed, would best serve the United
States, the European colonial powers, and the emerging nations.[1]

Eisenhower faced a formidable, perhaps impossible, task in seeking to
impose order upon the inherently disorderly process of decolonization. The
issue defied customary regional, political, and ideological patterns. It divided
the "free world" internally, pitting against each other the colonial and the
anti-colonial powers. The United States occupied a precarious position in
the middle of this rapidly widening rift between its European allies and the
anti-colonial forces. Despite its traditional sympathy for self-determination,
the United States had specific geopolitical interests in dependent territories,
as well as responsibilities as an administering power of five non-self-governing territories—Puerto Rico, Guam, the Virgin Islands, Samoa, and the
Trust Territories of the Pacific Islands.[2]

1. Eisenhower to Churchill, July 22, 1954, in Boyle, ed., *The Churchill-Eisenhower Correspondence, 1953–1955*, 163. See also an August 23, 1956, letter from Eisenhower to Swede
Hazlett in Griffith, ed., *Ike's Letters to a Friend, 1941–1958*, 165.
2. "The Colonial Question in the United Nations," United Nations Affairs Planning
Staff, July 27, 1953, in *FRUS, 1952–1954*, III, 96–105.

The Eisenhower administration decided that it had no alternative but to continue the basic middle-of-the-road policy of its Democratic predecessor. In an attempt to differentiate its approach, however, the State Department determined to stress the importance of orderly decolonization. Dulles and Assistant Secretary of State for Near Eastern, South Asian, and African Affairs Henry A. Byroade outlined the nation's basic policy in two speeches in the fall of 1953. In his speech "The World's Colonies and Ex-Colonies: A Challenge to America," delivered before the World Affairs Council of North California on October 30, Byroade explained that the administration's support for the decolonization process was tempered by its recognition that a precipitate rush to independent status might leave the former European colonies vulnerable to Soviet colonialism.

Byroade presented five reasons to support his contention that progress toward independence should be controlled. He maintained that rapid withdrawal of colonial control would foster internal confusion and invite external intervention; the United States desired independence to be genuine and long-lasting; independence would not solve the myriad problems of Asia and Africa; the nation's colonial allies would be economically and politically harmed by an abrupt conclusion to colonialism; and the new states must be prepared to function as responsible members of the international community. Candidly summarizing the American plight, Byroade stated: "It is no secret that these problems confront America with a dilemma. The present situation therefore calls frankly for a middle-of-the-road policy which will permit us to determine our position on practical issues on their merits as they arise." The administration would pursue a reactive rather than a proactive policy.

Dulles reaffirmed Byroade's analysis. Shortly after Byroade's statements, he delivered an address entitled "The Moral Initiative" to the Congress of Industrial Organizations in Cleveland, Ohio. The secretary also stressed the critical importance of effecting an "orderly evolution" from non-self-government to independence in order to prevent Soviet imperial conquest.[3]

To the U.S. mission to the UN fell the responsibility of walking the tightrope between the nation's European allies and the anti-colonial movement in the implementation of this "middle-of-the-road" policy. In addition to

---

3. For Dulles's speech, see the *Department of State Bulletin,* November 30, 1953, pp. 741–44. For Byroade's speech, see *ibid.,* November 16, 1953, pp. 655–60.

Lodge and his deputy, Wadsworth, Mason Sears assumed primary responsibility for handling the colonial issue. Lodge's second cousin by marriage and his former campaign manager, Sears was outspoken, independent, and politically astute. Lodge requested his appointment to the post of U.S. representative to the Trusteeship Council precisely because of his political skills. Lodge was "particularly anxious," he wrote Dulles, "to have someone with political skill in this position" because the colonial issue was such "a hot potato" in the UN.[4]

Lodge, Sears, and the USUN staff loyally attempted to follow the State Department's line. USUN assured the department that it kept "copies of the colonial policy statements" of Dulles and Byroade "constantly at our elbow," and insisted that "we carefully measure our statements and our questions in the Trusteeship Council against these basic documents." Nor was Lodge unsympathetic with the administration's position. Even prior to assuming his post, he had vowed to uphold America's anti-colonial tradition, but also to stress that the UN ought to be concerned first and foremost with maintaining international peace. The organization, he confided to his journal, had not been created to serve as a debating society on colonialism.[5]

At the same time, however, Lodge and USUN lamented the essentially negative character of the U.S. policy. The U.S. mission sought permission to cast the cautious stance in a more positive light by contrasting European colonialism with the more insidious form of Soviet imperialism. The delegation thus attempted to strike a balance between its conflicting objectives. It wanted to encourage colonial devolution while simultaneously counseling patience; emphasize that independence required economic as well as political foundations; and warn that hasty action might in fact not produce independence, but only a transition to satellite status.[6]

The new administration faced its first important test on a colonial matter of direct interest to the United States during the General Assembly session in the fall of 1953. On July 25, 1952, the U.S. territory of Puerto Rico had adopted a new constitution establishing a commonwealth. Citing the island's

---

4. Lodge to Dulles, April 1, 1953, Reel 4, HCLP, MHS.

5. Memorandum, Benjamin O. Gerig (director of the Office of Dependent Area Affairs) to Key, February 17, 1954, in *FRUS, 1952–1954*, III, 1359; Journal entry, January 3, 1953, in folder marked "T-E 1952/53," Box 71, HCLP, MHS.

6. Memorandum by Sears, August 18, 1953, in *FRUS, 1952–1954*, III, 1162–64.

new status, the State Department had informed the secretary-general that the United States intended to cease transmitting to the UN the annual reports on the status of Puerto Rico required of administering authorities by the UN Trusteeship Council. The anti-colonial nations protested. Insisting upon the principle of international accountability, they maintained that the United States could not make such a decision unilaterally. It was the prerogative of the General Assembly, rather than the administering power, to determine the status of each dependent territory.

The U.S. delegation objected. It argued that while the General Assembly could establish guidelines, in the final analysis only the administering authority could determine the constitutional position and status of territories under its sovereignty. The United States eventually succeeded in marshaling sufficient votes to pass a resolution acknowledging the new status of Puerto Rico, but only after exerting a strong effort in New York and capitals abroad. Significantly, in this first case the United States showed that it would not concede jurisdiction to the UN, thereby undermining future exhortations to its Western European allies to do so.[7]

Eisenhower not only set the broad policy on the status of Puerto Rico but also made critical decisions about its implementation. Indeed, Lodge credited him with suggesting that the United States grant Puerto Rico independence any time the commonwealth legislature voted for it, and authorizing Lodge to make an announcement to this effect on the final day of debate. Dulles objected, warning of potentially adverse reactions from congressional leaders, the loyal elements in Puerto Rico, the Puerto Rican community in New York City, and the French. Complaining that Eisenhower and Lodge had discussed this idea at a meeting at which he was not present, Dulles questioned whether the president's decision had been "made after adequate consideration and [the] weighing of relevant facts." Lodge insisted that it had been, describing Eisenhower's idea—somewhat gratuitously, given Dulles's strong opposition—as "a gesture which is typical of the President's political genius and which will help American prestige in quarters where we need it." After the vote, Lodge congratulated Eisenhower on his initiative.

7. Memorandum, United States government to the secretary-general of the United Nations, April 30, 1953, in *FRUS, 1952–1954,* III, 1310–12; Position Paper, September 2, 1953, same volume, 1449–51; Frances P. Bolton (U.S. representative in Committee Four) statement on Puerto Rico, November 3, 1953, same volume, 1456–63.

The announcement, he exulted, had been a "ten-strike" in terms of its impact on the Arab, Asian, and African nations.[8]

The most difficult decolonization questions pitted the nation's Western European allies against dependent territories in strategic areas of Africa and Asia. In such cases, the administration faced conflicting pressures, including the nation's anti-colonial heritage; loyalty to its NATO partners; the national security demands of containing the Communist threat; and the desire to entice the newly emerging nations into the Western camp. The most prominent of such decolonization cases during the Eisenhower era involved the territories of French North Africa—Tunisia, Morocco, and Algeria. This region thus provides a good case study of Eisenhower's decolonization policy at the UN.[9]

Eisenhower, with his wartime experience in North Africa, appreciated the region's geostrategic importance. The National Security Council considered French North Africa to be "of great political and strategic importance because of its geographic position, its sites for military bases, its position with respect to transportation routes, its natural resources, its manpower, its special relationships with the Western powers and the Moslem world, and the possible impact of its problems on the future of the United Nations organization." Moreover, the growing Third World viewed the situation as a test case of U.S. intentions. The NSC therefore recommended that the United States take a "middle-of-the-road" position on North African independence. Most important, it should take no action that might undermine the French position or U.S. security interests in North Africa. To the extent possible, the administration also should strive to minimize alienating the anti-colonial world. Clearly, however, retaining the goodwill of the nation's NATO allies early in Eisenhower's first term took precedence, even if it meant veering off

8. Telegram from Dulles to Lodge, November 24, 1953, in *FRUS, 1952–1954,* III, 1474; Telegram from Lodge to the Department of State, November 25, 1953, same volume, 1475–76; Lodge to Eisenhower, November 28, 1953, Reel 28, HCLP, MHS; *MTCD,* Reel 1, Dulles and Lodge, n.d. (probably November 21–24, 1953).

9. Irwin M. Wall, "The United States, Algeria, and the Fall of the Fourth French Republic," *Diplomatic History,* XVIII (1994), 489–511. See also Brian Urquhart, *Decolonization and World Peace* (Austin, 1989), chap. 3.

the middle-of-the-road course. Wooing the emerging underdeveloped world was a secondary consideration.[10]

The issue of the status of French North Africa first arose in the spring and summer of 1953, when the Arab-Asian bloc attempted to place the question of Morocco on the Security Council agenda. The countries proposing such action argued that French intervention in Morocco and the deposition of the sultan posed a threat to peace and security. The State Department opposed the move. Lodge suggested that the United States object on the grounds that the UN's primary interest at the moment should be the war in Korea. Dulles agreed that the Arab-Asian nations were engaged in a "harassment" operation. Noting that the Korean War was drawing to a conclusion, however, he decided instead to vote against inscription because the situation did not constitute a threat to international peace and security—the precondition for consideration established by Article 34 of the Charter.[11]

Thus, in a dramatic departure from its customary practice, the United States for the first time opposed the inscription of an item on the Security Council agenda. Defending the vote, Lodge employed the rationale he had first outlined in his journal in January. "The surest way to undermine the position of the Security Council," he lectured, "is to divert it from its primary mission of maintaining the peace of the world and use it instead to deal with all sorts of other questions under the pretext of safeguarding international peace and security." The administration thus relied on a legalistic pretext—the unprecedented strict interpretation of Article 34—to limit the UN's role in facilitating the transition to self-government.[12]

The United States continued its pro-colonialist stance during the Eighth General Assembly session in the fall of 1953. Although the administration supported the anti-colonial efforts to inscribe the questions of Tunisia and Morocco on the General Assembly agenda, it voted against the subsequent Arab-Asian resolutions. Lodge professed his government's commitment to

10. Draft policy statement, National Security Council staff to the National Security Council Planning Board, August 18, 1953, in *FRUS, 1952–1954,* XI, 150–52.

11. *MTCD,* Reel 1, Dulles and Lodge, April 9, 1953; Telegram from Lodge to the Secretary of State, April 8, 1953, 330/4–953, in Box 1306, RG 59, NA; Telegram from Dulles to Lodge, April 9, 1953, 330/4–953, in Box 1306, RG 59, NA.

12. "The Moroccan Question," Lodge statement in the Security Council on August 27, 1953, *Department of State Bulletin,* September 7, 1953, pp. 325–26.

the principle of self-government, and expressed the hope that France and its colonies would resolve their differences through direct, bilateral negotiations. He nevertheless deemed UN action inadvisable, since it might hurt the prospects for negotiation. Simultaneously, however, the administration privately began encouraging France to institute real reforms in North Africa.[13]

Pressure on the United States relative to Tunisia eased in July, 1954, when Prime Minister Pierre Mendès-France announced his government's intention to grant Tunisia complete internal autonomy. The U.S. delegation seized on this news during the Ninth General Assembly session to support a resolution postponing consideration of the Tunisian issue. After the negotiation of the Tunisian accords of June 3, 1955, the United Nations conducted no further discussion of the question.

The Moroccan situation proved to be more complex, with French intransigence delaying the independence process. Frustrated by this refusal to negotiate, the anti-colonial powers introduced a resolution calling upon France to initiate talks with Morocco. Dulles and Lodge privately expressed sympathy for the relatively moderate resolution. But the desire to ensure French support for the integration of West German troops into NATO and concerns about upsetting the precarious Mendès-France government persuaded Dulles to instruct Lodge to oppose it. Following a suggestion by Lodge, Dulles exacted a *quid pro quo* from the French. In return for American support on Morocco, France agreed to support a judicial review in the case of the Administrative Tribunal awards against the United States.[14] The commencement of Franco-Moroccan talks in 1955 resulted in an innocuous resolution encouraging continued negotiation. Finally, in March, 1956, Tunisia and Morocco attained independence, effectively ending UN consideration of the issue, much to the relief of the United States.

13. Position Paper, "The Tunisian Problem," in *FRUS, 1952–1954,* XI, 868–79; "U.S. Attitude Toward Moroccan Self-Government," Lodge statement in the Security Council on October 20, 1953, *Department of State Bulletin,* November 2, 1953, p. 610. On the pressure for reforms, see, for example, Telegram from Dulles to the U.S. embassy in France, September 5, 1953, in *FRUS, 1952–1954,* XI, 631–32.

14. *MTCD,* Reel 3, Dulles and Lodge, December 11, 1954; *MTCD,* Reel 3, Dulles and Bonnet, December 11, 1954; Telegram from Dulles to Lodge, December 11, 1954, in folder marked "December 1954 (6)," Box 10, John Foster Dulles Chronological Series, Dulles Papers, EL; *MTCD,* Reel 3, Dulles and Lodge, December 13, 1954; *MTCD,* Reel 3, Dulles and Bonnet, December 13, 1954.

Just as tension subsided over Morocco and Tunisia, France and, more indirectly, the United States faced a new challenge on Algeria. In 1955 the Arab-Asian bloc succeeded in placing the question of Algeria on the General Assembly agenda, and in 1956 sought Security Council consideration of the situation. Once again, the United States supported its ally in seeking to prevent UN involvement. The French delegation, asserting that General Assembly consideration violated Article 2, paragraph 7, of the UN Charter (the domestic-jurisdiction clause), walked out of the assembly in 1955. France insisted that unlike Tunisia and Morocco, which were French protectorates, Algeria had been part of metropolitan France since 1834. Lodge agreed that the situation fell within French domestic jurisdiction, and indeed, Article 5 of the NATO treaty included Algeria as one of the French departments. During the Security Council debate in 1956 the United States again voted with France, declaring that further UN involvement would not be beneficial.[15]

During this same period, Lodge recommended that Eisenhower approve the French request for eighty helicopters and fifty planes to assist in restoring order in Algeria. A staunch advocate of NATO, Lodge was obviously still more than willing to subordinate decolonization to the demands of protecting the Atlantic alliance. The administration obliged, thereby providing France with weapons to fight its war in Algeria.[16]

French foreign minister Christian Pineau continued the same line of defense in 1957, claiming that Algeria was an integral part of the French metropole. He faced an uphill battle, for French standing in the UN had sunk even lower among the African-Arab-Asian nations (that is, the sub-Saharan African countries, the Arab countries, and the countries of south and southeast Asia) after the French use of force in the Suez Canal situation. Lodge yet again firmly defended Pineau in public. He insisted that the situation was covered by the domestic-jurisdiction clause, and warned that UN intervention might not only hinder progress toward a bilateral French-Algerian settlement, but also ultimately destroy the organization. In private, Lodge and Dulles only reluctantly concluded that the United States would have to support France. They ardently wanted to settle the conflict, at least in part

15. "U.S. Views on Consideration of Algerian Question," Lodge statement in the Security Council on June 26, 1956, *Department of State Bulletin,* July 16, 1956, p. 125.

16. Lodge to Eisenhower, March 10, 1956, in folder marked "Henry Cabot Lodge: 1956 (3)," Box 24, Administration Series, EP, AWF, EL.

because nine of the fourteen French divisions that were part of the NATO defensive force had been diverted to Algeria. Eventually, USUN joined a unanimous vote for a relatively mild resolution that expressed concern over the situation and requested that the parties involved seek a solution.[17]

The State Department continued to vacillate in 1958 as the Fourth Republic proved incapable of establishing French control over Algeria. The department equivocated, torn between the nation's ties to France and its growing recognition, signaled by its independent behavior in the Suez Crisis, of the need to improve relations with the anti-colonial world. Upcoming military-base negotiations with Morocco and Libya also encouraged the shift toward anti-colonialism. Convinced that France could not win this war, and determined to establish a bulwark against Soviet intervention in the region, the administration desired to build a positive relationship with the Algerian rebels who, it was hoped, could establish a strong, democratic, pro-Western government. Dulles thus increasingly considered abstaining as the "lesser evil," though he knew that it might simply "annoy both parties."[18]

"The trick," Eisenhower wrote Dulles, was how to "get the French to see a little sense." Lodge adamantly insisted that the French refusal to attend the debate provided a "heaven sent" opportunity to abstain. Ultimately, in an attempt to satisfy both sides, the United States split its vote. The U.S. delegate voted against the anti-colonial resolution in Committee I because of its identification of the nationalist Provisional Government of the Algerian Republic as the negotiating body of the Algerian people. When this reference was removed in the plenary session, the United States abstained.[19]

Continued French intransigence at the UN and France's inability to re-

17. "United States Views on Algerian Question," Lodge statement in Committee I on December 3, 1957, *Department of State Bulletin,* December 30, 1957, pp. 1046–47; *MTCD,* Reel 7, Dulles and Lodge, December 5, 1957; *MTCD,* Reel 7, Dulles and Lodge, December 6, 1957; Wall, "The United States, Algeria, and the Fall of the Fourth French Republic," 495.

18. Telegram from Dulles to USUN, November 21, 1958, 320.11/11–2158, in Box 1269, RG 59, NA; Memorandum, Gerard C. Smith (assistant secretary of state for policy planning) to C. Burke Elbrick (assistant secretary of state for European affairs), September 12, 1958, in *FRUS, 1958–1960,* XIII, 641–42; Wall, "The United States, Algeria, and the Fall of the Fourth French Republic," 508–509.

19. Quoted in Charles G. Cogan, *Oldest Allies, Guarded Friends: The United States and France Since 1940* (Westport, 1994), 105; Telegram from Lodge to the Secretary of State, December 8, 1958, 320.11/12–858, in Box 1266, RG 59, NA; Telegram from Wilcox to USUN, December 12, 1958, 320.11/12–958, in Box 1266, RG 59, NA; Circular telegram from Herter (acting secretary), December 15, 1958, in Box 1266, RG 59, NA.

store order in Algeria prompted a reevaluation of U.S. policy in 1959. Even in the Europeanist-dominated State Department, the tide of opinion was turning against France. Predictably, Lodge led the effort to persuade Eisenhower and Herter that changes in American policy, strategy, and tactics were imperative. He vented his frustration at being caught in the middle between the European colonialists and the anti-colonial forces. Although acknowledging the pressure to "keep faith with our NATO allies," Lodge urged greater sensitivity to the anti-colonial cause.[20]

Lodge insisted that the United States should not take the lead in defending French colonialism if France refused to participate in the debate. "We cannot reasonably be expected to be more French than the French," he insisted. The administration's best option, the ambassador surprisingly suggested, was to announce that it believed that the UN was incapable of handling such matters. Consequently, the United States would refuse to engage in further debate and would simply abstain on all resolutions dealing with Algeria. "The Algerian question," he asserted, could "only be worked out through private and secret negotiations . . . [not] in an open goldfish bowl forum."[21] If the United States continued to participate in UN consideration of the item, Lodge advised taking a firmer stand with France. The Algerian question, he warned, had become "a symbol of the aspirations of Arabs and Moslems to be treated as equals." The United States should, of course, attempt to prevent bad resolutions, but it ought not to present de Gaulle with a "blank check," for the French leader readily would bankrupt the American account with the anti-colonial powers.[22]

Eisenhower agreed that the United States could not provide France with unconditional support. The United States had its own anti-colonial tradition to honor and geopolitical interests to protect and was already too closely identified with colonialism. In addition, the former military leader recoiled at the prospect of defending, even rhetorically, an ally who refused to defend itself.[23]

20. Telegram from Lodge to the Secretary of State, December 15, 1958, 320.11/12–1558, in Box 1266, RG 59, NA; Lodge to Herter, November 13, 1959, Reel 7, HCLP, MHS; *MTCH,* Reel 11, Herter and Lodge, November 12, 1959, 10:30 A.M.

21. Lodge to Dulles, January 12, 1959, Reel 5, HCLP, MHS.

22. Statement at the National Security Council meeting, August 18, 1959, Reel 29, HCLP, MHS.

23. Memorandum of Discussion at the 417th Meeting of the National Security Council, August 18, 1959, in Box 11, NSC Series, EP, AWF, EL.

Eisenhower conveyed his views to Charles de Gaulle in an early September meeting. He had a more receptive audience, for the new president of the Fifth Republic had more liberal views on the question of decolonization. Eisenhower requested that France participate in the UN debate and announce its plans for the political development of Algeria. When later that month de Gaulle declared his intention to grant Algeria independence after a four-year period of pacification, Eisenhower and Herter publicly welcomed the proposal and encouraged the General Assembly to take no action that might prejudice this initiative.[24]

When France still refused to participate, the United States limited its own involvement. Herter seriously considered voting for the African-Arab-Asian resolution, which he deemed "innocuous," partly because of his exasperation with France's refusal to defend itself. The U.S. delegation ultimately abstained, however, with Lodge proclaiming yet again that while the United States supported self-determination, it did not believe that a resolution would help achieve that objective.[25]

The absence of negotiations in the subsequent year meant that the troubling issue remained on the General Assembly agenda during the last months of Eisenhower's tenure. The African-Arab-Asian bloc, emboldened by the admission of sixteen new nations to the UN in the fall of 1960, submitted a resolution calling for a UN-sponsored referendum in Algeria. The State Department urged France to outline its program for the peaceful settlement of the question and indicate its willingness to work with the Front de Libération Nationale (FLN). Otherwise, the department predicted, it would be impossible to replace the resolution with a more moderate measure. Even after years of French obstinance, however, Eisenhower still encouraged the State Department "to find a face-saving device in the UN for the French," a compromise resolution which France could support. Once again, the United States abstained on the final vote. Eisenhower remained

24. Stanley Hoffman, "The Foreign Policy of DeGaulle," in Craig and Loewenheim, eds., *The Diplomats, 1939–1979*, 228–54.

25. *MTCH*, Reel 11, Herter and Amory Houghton (ambassador to France), December 11, 1959; Memorandum, Merchant to Herter, July 10, 1959, in *FRUS, 1958–1960*, XIII, 660–64; Memorandum, Joseph C. Satterthwaite (assistant secretary of state for African affairs) to Murphy, August 13, 1959, same volume, 665–67; Telegram from Herter to USUN, November 19, 1959, same volume, 676–78; Telegram from Herter to USUN, December 1, 1959, same volume, 680–82.

patient, perhaps because de Gaulle was divesting France of its African empire, with eleven former French colonies joining the UN in 1960, even though the French president faced a more politically perilous situation in Algeria.[26]

Thus, the United States' position on the decolonization question changed from 1953 to 1961, but only slightly. At least partly because of the liberating effects of its actions during the Suez Crisis, by the end of the decade the administration had become marginally more likely to abstain on anti-colonial resolutions and apply greater pressure, in private, on France to speed the liquidation of its empire. Still, the administration's basic predisposition toward its NATO allies remained intact. It generally supported the General Assembly's right to discuss the questions of Tunisia, Morocco, and Algeria, but it insisted that such consideration was unwise. The anti-colonial powers requested American support and were rebuffed. The administration maintained that the matters were, if not within French domestic jurisdiction, at least perilously close to being internal matters. Moreover, despite little actual progress on the part of France, the U.S. delegation repeatedly proclaimed its faith in France's willingness to resolve the problem of its own accord. The United States therefore continually reiterated the need to avoid undermining private negotiations, even though little was being accomplished through bilateral channels, and sought desperately to facilitate a dialogue between the two sides. Although Eisenhower and Dulles appreciated the intensity of anti-colonial sentiment and frequently became exasperated with the French, they were unwilling to jeopardize French support for European integration and NATO until the final years of Eisenhower's second term.[27]

Throughout the decade, the administration pursued essentially negative, pro-colonial policies on a host of other issues that came under the umbrella of decolonization. A largely symbolic issue, but one of grave import to the anti-colonial nations, was the participation of inhabitants of the trust territories in the work of the Trusteeship Council. In principle, the United States

---

26. Memorandum of Discussion at the 467th Meeting of the National Security Council, November 17, 1960, in *FRUS, 1958–1960,* XIII, 711; Memorandum, Wilcox to Livingston T. Merchant (undersecretary of state for political affairs), September 7, 1960, same volume, 693–94; Memorandum of a Meeting, September 23, 1960, same volume, 695–97; Message from Herter to de Murville, November 2, 1960, same volume, 702–703.

27. See, for example, Memorandum, William I. Cargo (director, Office of United Nations Political and Security Affairs) to Wilcox, January 9, 1959, in Box 1269, RG 59, NA.

favored greater participation, but it feared detracting from the authority of the administering powers. The administration thus opposed oral hearings of indigenous inhabitants on the grounds that they were too time-consuming and repetitive. Other examples of this pro-colonial bent included a failure to support resolutions requesting administering states to submit political information on their non-self-governing territories and set target dates for independence, and an unwillingness to ask Spain and Portugal, admitted to the UN in 1955, to acknowledge that their territories should be covered by the UN Charter's provisions on dependent territories.

Just as the question of decolonization split the world into new alignments during the 1950s, it also engendered divisions within the Eisenhower administration. The closer administration officials became involved with the colonialism issue at the UN, the more they became frustrated by the constraints of the "middle-of-the-road" policy and eager to embrace the anti-colonial cause. Thus, Mason Sears proved to be the most outspoken proponent of a more independent, anti-colonial attitude. He deeply resented European demands for American support. "This idea of the colonial powers that we should say 'Aye, aye, sir' every time they ask us to reverse a traditional American position in order to take some unpopular stand in their behalf will not help us to make friends—at least in Africa," he complained. On the whole, Sears loyally executed the department's decisions. But he continually pushed to translate U.S. rhetorical support for anti-colonialism into action. Constantly frustrated by the administration's timidity, Sears occasionally overstepped his bounds and advanced views that were out ahead of U.S. policy. Yet the State Department tolerated his transgressions, most likely because, as Donald A. Dumont, the officer in charge of Black African affairs, posited, Sears's actions provided "some evidence" that the nation favored future political independence for colonial territories.[28]

In contrast to Sears's immersion in the colonial question, Lodge's involvement in a broader range of issues moderated his anti-colonial ardor. Yet he too became a vocal proponent of decolonization. As the intermediary between New York and Washington, Lodge gradually took the lead in trying

28. The Bureau of African Affairs provided a natural ally for Sears and the anti-colonial camp at USUN. Sears to Key, January 25, 1955, Reel 4, HCLP, MHS; Reminiscences of Donald A. Dumont, December 28, 1972, p. 32, COHP, Butler Library, Columbia University. See also Sears to Wilcox, April 3, 1956, Reel 14, HCLP, MHS; Lodge to Dulles, February 15, 1955, 350/2–1555, in Box 1344, RG 59, NA.

to persuade Eisenhower of the political necessity of shifting policy first toward a more genuinely neutral position and then toward the anti-colonial camp. As the decade progressed, his initially narrow focus on the cold war broadened. Daily exposure to the UN and the responsibility of obtaining sufficient votes to adopt American policy had convinced him of the critical importance of the growing nonaligned bloc. "At the UNGA," the ambassador wrote, "you see the world as a place in which a large majority of the world is non-white and inclines to feel itself emotionally involved on the Soviet side of the US-Soviet conflict, perhaps in part because we appear to be lined up with the colonial powers on so many issues in the UN and we are allied with them militarily."[29]

Lodge even played upon the political anxieties of a presidential election year to advance his cause. In July, 1956, he suggested that the nation's negative stance on the colonial question had influenced its declining popularity with international youth. This trend could be reversed, Lodge assured Eisenhower, "without its costing us a nickel—merely a different policy position, a somewhat different line of talk." He urged the president to request Congress to establish target dates for independence for the remaining U.S. dependent territories and make an address in which he recommended that within the next ten years all nations still administering colonies set similar timetables for decolonization. Eisenhower's reply was characteristic of his conservative approach to the entire question. "Offhand I must say I like your suggestion for a statement regarding our dependent territories, even though I think there might be difficulties involved," he responded. But he dealt the proposal a fatal blow, given the difficulty of forging interdepartmental consensus, when he added, "Of course I'll have to check it out with State and Defense."[30]

Individuals serving at the UN for even a limited time often converted to the anti-colonial cause. Leonard C. Meeker, the assistant legal adviser for UN affairs and a member of the U.S. delegation to the Fifteenth General Assembly in 1960, offers one such example. After only a few months in New York, Meeker concluded that the United States was "long over-due for alter-

29. Cabinet Paper, November 6, 1959, Reel 29, HCLP, MHS.

30. Lodge to Eisenhower, June 26, 1956, Reel 29, HCLP, MHS; Eisenhower to Lodge, September 26, 1956, in folder marked "Henry Cabot Lodge: 1956 (1)," Box 24, Administration Series, EP, AWF, EL; Lodge to Eisenhower, September 19, 1956, in folder marked "Henry Cabot Lodge: 1956 (2)," Box 24, Administration Series, EP, AWF, EL.

ing fundamentally" its attitude toward the Algerian situation. Instead of abstaining, the United States should lead the effort to adopt a resolution pleasing to the African-Asian bloc and "put maximum pressure" on France. Meeker thus joined Lodge, Sears, and others at USUN and the State Department who were disappointed by the administration's refusal to espouse the anti-colonial cause or at least follow a policy of genuine moderation.[31]

A final measure of the administration's views on decolonization came in the waning months of the decade. On September 23, 1960, Soviet premier Nikita Khrushchev introduced a resolution calling for independence within one year for all colonial and non-self-governing territories. Still viewing the colonial question almost solely through the lens of the cold war, Herter spoke for the administration in denouncing the Soviet resolution as an attempt "to make the transition from colonial to independent status as difficult as possible, to encourage the emerging countries of Africa and Asia to look to the Soviet Union for leadership, and to create a maximum amount of turmoil, under which Communism can operate to best effect."[32] After prolonged debate, a more moderate Third World resolution emerged that called for "speedily and unconditionally ending colonialism in all its forms and manifestations." It declared political freedom to be a basic right for all peoples, and asserted that colonialism violated basic human rights and the fundamental principles of the UN Charter.

The State Department agonized over the decision of whether to recommend to Eisenhower that the United States vote in favor of the resolution or abstain. Newly elevated to the post of U.S. representative (after Lodge resigned to campaign for the vice presidency on the Republican party ticket), Wadsworth exerted his limited influence on behalf of the resolution. He contended that, despite its intemperate language, the United States ought to vote for this expression of support for self-determination. Although more critical of the resolution, Herter finally agreed with USUN. He reluctantly decided that the intensity of anti-colonial sentiment outweighed the potential liability of offending America's European allies. Nevertheless, Herter acknowledged "holding [his] nose with regard to much of the language," for

31. Meeker, "United States Policy and the Fifteenth General Assembly," October 4, 1960, in *FRUS, 1958–1960,* II, 390.

32. Herter, "Selected Major Issues Expected to Confront the United States at the Fifteenth General Assembly," October 6, 1960, in folder marked "1960 Cabinet (3)," Box 19, Herter Papers, EL.

although the wording was inclusive of Soviet colonialism, it slighted the Europeans' positive contributions to the development of their territories.[33]

Eisenhower set policy and determined strategy and tactics on this question. Repeatedly discussing the matter with Herter on the telephone, he remained informed of changes in the resolution throughout the debate. On December 8, he approved the recommendation to vote for the measure, but then changed his mind the next day after a telephone call from Prime Minister Harold Macmillan, who implored him to join Britain in abstaining. Eisenhower then directed USUN to explain that, while it agreed with the basic principles embodied in the resolution, it had been compelled to abstain because of the wording. The measure passed overwhelmingly, with anticolonial forces procuring 90 votes in favor, 0 opposed, and 9 abstentions. Announcement of the final tally sparked spontaneous applause in the assembly chamber. Even Zelma Watson George, a member of the U.S. delegation, rose to her feet and joined in the celebration.[34]

The anti-colonial reaction to the vote, according to Wadsworth, was "immediate, strong, sometimes emotional, and invariably negative." Fittingly, the United States ended the Eisenhower era at the UN with a vote that, once again, indicated its desire to remain neutral or aloof from the colonial controversy. The UN had evinced its explicit support for an end to colonialism, but it did so without the assenting vote of the United States—a nation proud of its history of support for self-determination and national independence.[35]

Closely related to the decolonization question was the problem of the admission of new members to the international organization. Particularly during the latter half of the Eisenhower era, the decolonization process produced

33. Memorandum, Herter to Goodpaster (Brigadier General Andrew J. Goodpaster, staff secretary to President Eisenhower), December 8, 1960, in *FRUS, 1958–1960,* II, 455; Telegram from Herter to USUN, November 1, 1960, same volume, 430–32; Telegram from Wadsworth to the Secretary of State, December 6, 1960, in folder marked "December 1960 (2)," Box 11, Dulles-Herter Series, EP, AWF, EL; Telegram from Herter to USUN, December 7, 1960, same folder.

34. Memorandum of a Telephone Conversation, Eisenhower and Herter, December 8, 1960, in *FRUS, 1958–1960,* II, 455–57; *MTCH,* Reel 11, Herter and Eisenhower, December 9, 1960, 6:15 P.M. and 10:50 P.M.; *MTCH,* Reel 11, Herter and Wadsworth, December 10, 1960.

35. Telegram from Wadsworth to the Department of State, December 15, 1960, in *FRUS, 1958–1960,* II, 460.

dozens of new states, most of which sought UN membership. Admitting them, the administration realized, would change the orientation of the UN and the dynamics of its operation.

Late in 1958, Dulles ordered a State Department report on the impact of new members. Noting that an expanded membership would disproportionately increase the size of the neutralist group, the report presaged that the General Assembly would become both more important and more unwieldy, and the United States would experience greater difficulty in obtaining a two-thirds majority on important issues. Moreover, the new members would emphasize economic and social issues, rather than the Communist threat. Consequently, the report concluded, the nation's traditional leadership role might be jeopardized and the United Nations would no longer "provide as effective a cold-war forum" for the United States.[36]

The report offered a number of recommendations. First, the United States ought not attempt to limit UN membership, which had become "the ultimate symbol of independent status." In order to retain the UN's usefulness as a cold war forum, the United States could no longer afford to dissipate goodwill by insisting that countries vote with the United States on purely symbolic matters. It would have to accept the likelihood that the underdeveloped countries' "bargaining position will be enhanced, and their support on matters of vital interest to the US can be expected to become more and more conditional on receiving our support both inside and outside the UN on matters of primary concern to them"—namely, colonial, social, and economic issues.[37]

Even these changes, however, would not be sufficient. On a more fundamental level, the United States should consider using the UN more selectively in the future. When it did work through the UN, the report advised, the United States should rely more heavily on the secretary-general, the Security Council, and smaller bodies such as the Economic and Social Council, and less on the General Assembly. Furthermore, the administration should begin to retreat from its insistence that UN members had an "over-riding moral obligation" to carry out the body's resolutions, for an occasion might arise in the future when the United States would choose not to abide by a

36. "Admission of New Members to the United Nations," Bureau of International Organization Affairs, March 4, 1959, in *FRUS, 1958–1960,* II, 110, 113.

37. *Ibid.,* 113–14.

UN resolution.[38] Clearly, the State Department had begun a slow shift toward the more defensive posture that would characterize American policy in the UN until the 1980s.

The Bureau of International Organization Affairs offered a less pessimistic assessment. It cautioned that a petulant disengagement from the organization would leave a vacuum that the Soviet Union would eagerly fill. Injecting a note of realism into the discussion, the bureau warned that the "United Nations will continue to mirror the extent of our international influence and the reactions of other governments to our over-all policy. If the mirror should ever reflect an unfortunate image, it would be folly to imagine that the image could be changed simply by smashing the mirror."[39]

Lodge also took issue with the dire tone of the State Department report. He suggested that the United States could use the broader membership to its benefit; greater universality would increase the organization's value as a forum of international opinion and propaganda. However, now more than ever, contended Lodge, the United States "cannot afford to look stuffy or pro-colonialist, or stick-in-the-mud. The United States has got to *be* for peaceful change, and it must *look* as though it is for peaceful change." If the nation took a "more evolutionary" position, it had nothing to fear from an expanded UN membership.[40]

The proliferation of new states exacerbated an already serious membership problem at the United Nations. By 1955 only nine states had been admitted as new members since the founding of the organization, and all nineteen applicants since 1950 had been rejected. The USSR had used its veto twenty-eight times to block the admission of fourteen states and five Soviet-sponsored states had been unable to obtain the required seven Security Council votes and General Assembly approval. Although the impasse arose directly from the East-West conflict, it was the newly independent states of Africa and Asia knocking on the UN door that suffered the consequences. Fully cognizant that the cold war, rather than any intrinsic lack of eligibility, threatened to prevent their entry, they and their supporters already in the UN demanded a solution. The final communiqué of the Bandung Confer-

38. *Ibid.,* 116; "The Fourteenth General Assembly and Future United Nations Prospects," Bureau of International Organization Affairs, May, 1960, same volume, 239–56.

39. "The Fourteenth General Assembly and Future United Nations Prospects," Bureau of International Organization Affairs, May, 1960, in *FRUS, 1958–1960,* II, 256.

40. Lodge to Wilcox, February 26, 1959, *ibid.,* 106.

ence of Asian and African States in April, 1955, for example, called for the admission of Cambodia, Ceylon, Japan, Jordan, Laos, Libya, Nepal, and Vietnam.

The Eisenhower administration also sought to break the membership deadlock. Greater universality of membership, it publicly and repeatedly insisted, was essential to increase the moral power of UN judgments and the overall effectiveness of the organization. Privately, the administration acknowledged that the desire to acquire the support of the African and Asian nations applying for admission provided a more powerful impetus to resolve the membership impasse. Since it was inevitable that these countries eventually would gain admission, it behooved the United States to support their applications and reap whatever goodwill was possible. Even for those opposed to admitting geographically small, economically impoverished, and politically impotent states, graceful accommodation to the new international realities proved to be the only sensible course. In 1955, therefore, the administration decided to reverse its earlier opposition to a package deal—the simultaneous admission of the sixteen candidate nations sponsored by the superpowers.[41]

The administration knew that the admission of more African and Asian states would increase the anti-colonial and neutralist forces in the UN. Eisenhower nevertheless approved the package deal. "I can't personally see any great defeat for us here," the president declared. "Those countries are small nations." While every member cast one vote in the General Assembly, Eisenhower understood that the United States and the larger states enjoyed a variety of other forms of influence and power. Too, Lodge argued that admission would help the new states. Membership in the UN, he suggested with more than a hint of paternalism, "should help in the maturing process" of the young states.[42] The United States subsequently both spoke on behalf

41. Telegram from Hoover (acting secretary) to Dulles, 310.393/11–1155, in Box 1241, RG 59, NA. For a sample of the administration's public statements, see "Admission of New Members," Wadsworth statement to the *Ad Hoc* Political Committee on November 2, 1954, *Department of State Bulletin,* November 22, 1954, pp. 786–88. On the views expressed in private, see, for example, Memorandum, Key to the Secretary of State, June 7, 1955, in *FRUS, 1955–1957,* XI, 280–81.

42. For Eisenhower's position, see Telegram from Hoover (acting secretary) to the Secretary of State, November 5, 1955, in *FRUS, 1955–1957,* XI, 327–28. For the quotation from Lodge, see Lodge to Bolton, June 18, 1957, same volume, 501. See also Memorandum, Wain-

of and voted for the admission of more than one dozen Asian and African nations from 1956 to 1960.

Partly to compensate for the changes wrought in the UN's composition by the new admissions, the State Department instituted new staffing practices at USUN by the end of the decade. The administration slowly upgraded the personnel in New York in order to ensure that U.S. interests were being pursued most effectively. By mid-decade, Lodge had begun lobbying to appoint only professionals to the U.S. delegation. Though he understood the public relations rationale for employing prominent citizens, he was deeply dissatisfied with the caliber and commitment of the "amateurs" who formed the early delegations. The ambassador sought a professional delegation and a larger, more experienced staff for USUN. He insisted that, given the influx of new members, the General Assembly would "become unmanageable" for the United States unless it staffed the delegation with men and women both knowledgeable about the issues involved and skilled in the tactics employed. Dulles, too, appeared to be increasingly willing to consider foreign service professionals. Accepting Lodge's advice, Eisenhower in 1960 broke with his tradition of seven years and chose professionals to sit on the seven committees and three political nominees who would only conduct special studies.[43]

When it came to office in January, 1953, the Eisenhower administration found itself thrust into the unwanted position of broker between the long-standing colonial claims of its European allies and the demands of the growing anti-colonial forces. Given the nation's historical traditions, it was an especially untenable position. The United States' customary sensitivity to international public opinion and its profound ideological disdain for colonialism militated against unconditional support for the European powers. At the same time, Eisenhower and Dulles feared that accelerating the decol-

---

house to the Secretary of State, August 24, 1955, same volume, 293–97; Telegram from Dulles to USUN, November 8, 1955, same volume, 327–28.

43. Lodge to Dulles, January 12, 1959, Reel 5, HCLP, MHS; Lodge to Dulles, June 16, 1955, Reel 4, *ibid.;* Lodge statement before the Senate Appropriations Committee on May 1, 1957, in folder marked "1957: Statements and Letters," Box 13, *ibid.;* Dulles to Eisenhower, April 3, 1958, in folder marked "John Foster Dulles: April 1958 (2)," Box 8, Dulles-Herter Series, EP, AWF, EL; *MTCH,* Reel 11, Message from Lodge to Herter, April 21, 1960; Memorandum of Conference with the President, April 22, 1960, in folder marked "Staff Notes—April 1960 (1)," Box 49, DDE Diary Series, EP, AWF, EL.

onization process might fan the flames of Third World nationalism and light the fires of Communist expansionism in Asia and Africa. These factors precluded extending significant assistance to the campaign to eradicate colonialism.

In the end the administration proved incapable of extricating itself from its untenable position, balancing awkwardly on the median strip in the "middle of the road." Unsure of how to proceed, it struggled, with little real success, to take a stance as a moderating, conciliatory influence. On the one hand, the administration encouraged the colonial powers to accept the demise of colonialism. Yet this was mitigated by its simultaneous urging of the anti-colonial nations to pursue their objectives more slowly.

The American policy was manifested at the United Nations in two ways. First, the U.S. delegation repeatedly insisted that UN discussion of decolonization cases would not facilitate a peaceful resolution of the situation. Instead, it pushed for direct, bilateral negotiations. Indeed, while the United States generally upheld the UN's right to debate, it questioned the wisdom of even rhetorical involvement on the part of the world organization. When the United Nations did insist on passing resolutions, the United States encouraged the anti-colonial powers to adopt resolutions on only the most general of issues, seeking mere expressions of support for fundamental principles as a standard toward which all nations should strive, rather than singling out any one nation or group of nations for condemnation. Even in the debate over the language in resolutions, the United States consistently urged adoption of the vaguest, most general, least active terms. Attention to semantics rather than active diplomacy was the centerpiece of the policy. The result was that, for example, USUN preferred the General Assembly to "take note of" rather than "recommend" that an administering authority take a particular action. Furthermore, in its attempt to dilute criticism of its European allies, the United States sought to include "the new colonialism" of Soviet imperialism under the rubric of resolutions denouncing European colonialism.

The Eisenhower administration employed a second tactic, closely related to the first, to shackle the anti-colonial forces. Led by Secretary Dulles, an expert on international law, the U.S. delegation skillfully used the legal system, an inherently conservative force, to slow the anti-colonial attack on the status quo. Legalistic reasoning, including frequent invocations of the domestic-jurisdiction clause to challenge UN jurisdiction, became a hallmark of American arguments in the General Assembly. By focusing on the legal aspects of the colonial questions, the State Department sought to evade the substantive issues.

Finally, the U.S. delegation's vote and the explanation accompanying its vote provide perhaps the clearest indications of the administration's tortured position. The U.S. delegation frequently prefaced its vote with a statement reiterating its support for the aspirations of the anti-colonial powers and the principle—though not the unqualified right—of self-determination. Although the administration tried to disassociate itself ideologically from the European colonial powers, when the time came to vote it usually did not act in accordance with its preliminary statement. The United States either abstained, perhaps the ultimate indication of the administration's desire to remain aloof from the increasingly heated conflict, or it voted with its NATO partners. Only rarely did the United States vote with the anti-colonial nations.

Clearly, the Eisenhower administration failed to devise a principled and consistent position on this admittedly complex issue. Too often, the American "policy" was one of vacillation and equivocation. This was perhaps inevitable, for as the State Department's North African expert aptly noted, the United States was "trying to sit on a fence which [was] not there."[44] What made this situation even more damaging was the apparent failure to realize that shifting back and forth from support for colonialism to support for anti-colonialism did not constitute a genuine "middle-of-the-road" policy. Moreover, attempts to travel in the "middle-of-the-road" succeeded only in exposing the United States to traffic coming in both directions. Vacillation and equivocation strained the nation's relations and credibility with both its traditional allies and the newly emerging nations. The anti-colonial nations became disillusioned by the chasm between U.S. rhetoric and action, and the European powers came to suspect that the United States sought economic advantages in the decolonizing areas.

The anti-colonial nations had more reason to complain. A variety of factors, particularly the priority placed upon NATO by Eisenhower and Dulles and the dominance of Europeanists in the State Department, consistently led the administration to veer in the direction of its European allies. "It might

---

44. Quoted in Frank Costigliola, *France and the United States: The Cold Alliance Since World War II* (New York, 1992), 111.

be that we could find a way to reconcile our verbal policies, which tend to alienate the colonial powers, with our action policies, which tend to alienate the anti-colonial powers," the Bureau of International Organization Affairs opined in 1956. But it conceded that because of the perceived exigencies of the cold war "there is not much real latitude for American policy." The State Department and the rest of the administration thus seemed resigned, halfway through the Eisenhower era, that the United States was "not going to win any popularity contests on the colonial issue within the framework of our present overall policy structure."[45] Pushed and prodded, partly by Lodge's constant reminders that the support of the nonaligned world was essential in the ongoing battle against the Soviet Union, Eisenhower only slowly and reluctantly became more responsive to the demands of the anti-colonial forces during his second term in office.

What Eisenhower, Dulles, and Herter really sought was to impose a sense of order on the decolonization process. Their efforts were in vain. Sadly, the president and his secretaries of state never fully realized or could not accept that decolonization was an inherently and unavoidably messy, chaotic, and disorderly process. It simply was not amenable to United States' control. Lodge, Wadsworth, Sears, and those who were intimately involved in the issue on a daily basis more readily grasped this fundamental truth and sought to alter the course of American policy accordingly. Although Lodge never wholly abandoned his fundamental cold war mindset and world view, he gradually came to believe through his years at the UN that the United States could impose whatever order was possible only by working with the forces of change. But the administration in Washington failed to realize that a dominant world power could not remain neutral or aloof from one of the most fundamental and far-reaching systemic changes of the twentieth century. The speed with which the phenomenon of global change traveled from Europe to the periphery, and the consequent altering of the composition, agenda, and direction of the United Nations, appeared to catch the Eisenhower administration by surprise. A more positive, active, and imaginative policy might have done more to meet the challenges at the UN posed by decolonization and the proliferation of new members in the nation-state system. However, the administration generally focused its energies on resisting

45. Bloomfield, Draft report for the assistant secretary of state for international organization affairs, February 9, 1956, in *FRUS, 1955–1957,* XI, 56.

rather than working with the fundamental changes taking place in the international system.

In January, 1953, fifty-six nations claimed membership in the United Nations. By the time Eisenhower left for Gettysburg and retirement eight years later, that number had grown to ninety-nine, largely because of decolonization. The size of the increase alone would have rendered the administration's relationship with the United Nations more complex. But the changing nature of the body's composition proved to be of even greater importance. The admission of the new nations, hailing primarily from the underdeveloped regions of Africa and Asia, made the Third World a significant factor in the world organization for the first time. Although this bloc did not achieve its maximum organization and power until late in the 1960s, the implications were already apparent midway through the Eisenhower era. It remained to be seen how President Eisenhower and his administration would respond to the different agenda of the UN's newest members.

9

Responding to the Underdeveloped World

Human Rights, Multilateral Aid, and Racial Equality

As Eisenhower assumed office, the international community was in the midst of momentous changes. The decolonization process had shifted into high gear and the newly independent nations began to insist that their collective voice be heard. Consequently, 1953 marked the beginning of "the era in which the United States fully entered the maelstrom of third-world affairs."[1] During the Eisenhower years, the United States discovered, to its sharp discomfort, that the nations emerging from decolonization had different problems, fears, priorities, goals, and ambitions.

The United States sought to tie the Third World into the capitalist economic system and its collective-security alliance structures. However, the ideological battle between capitalism and communism that was at the core of the cold war held limited appeal for many states on the periphery. At the Bandung Conference of 1955 much of the Third World had made evident its rejection of the cold war paradigm. Many of these states would not endorse the bipolar division of the world or bring themselves to join one of the opposing sides. Indeed, many of the new nations viewed the cold war and the attendant Soviet-American competition for allies as another form of imperialism. Nor did they share the strategic and geopolitical interests that often dictated American policy in the Third World.

1. Dennis Merrill, "The United States and the Rise of the Third World," in Gordon Martel, ed., *American Foreign Relations Reconsidered, 1890–1993* (London, 1994), 174.

The former colonies had a different agenda, one shaped by a compelling need to address urgent questions of social, political, and economic development. As a group, to the extent that it is possible to generalize, they sought international protection of basic human rights, a more equitable distribution of the world's wealth, and racial equality. Lacking either the military or the economic power to realize their objectives, the underdeveloped nations quickly embraced the most effective instrument at their disposal—the power of international public opinion. Since the Western nations had professed their willingness to abide by international public opinion, as articulated by the United Nations, the Third World turned to the world organization to voice their concerns and seek redress of their grievances. For the United States, navigating around and through this hazardous maelstrom of issues, both in debate at the UN and in practice in the world, constituted a seemingly endless challenge.

The new administration immediately encountered turbulent water, generated by the almost completed Human Rights Covenants. In the drafting stage since 1948, the covenants represented an attempt to further one of the principal purposes of the UN, as proclaimed in Article 1 of the Charter: to "promot[e] and encourag[e] respect for human rights and for fundamental freedoms for all without distinction as to race, sex, language or religion." They sought to codify a universal set of rights not only in the fields of civil and political liberties, but also in the social and economic realms. Education, housing, health care, and social security were all addressed by the overly ambitious authors. Given the instability of Third World governments and the frequency of constitutional changes in many Third World nations, the Latin American–Asian–African bloc sought international codification as the best way to ensure the maintenance of basic human rights. Also of central importance to these states was the fact that the first article of the Human Rights Covenants proclaimed "the right of peoples to self-determination," including "permanent sovereignty over their natural wealth and resources." This attempt to resist the continued economic dominance of the core states over the periphery was bound to provoke American concern.

The arrival of the Human Rights Covenants on the international stage collided head on with the emergence of a potentially disruptive movement on the domestic scene—an effort to amend the U.S. Constitution. On January 7, 1953, Senator John W. Bricker of Ohio had introduced Joint Resolution 1. The resolution called for a constitutional amendment that would re-

199

strict the president's power to enter into executive agreements, and limit the internal influence of treaties by making them effective only after Congress passed validating legislation. Bricker had offered his amendment unsuccessfully in the past. But in the midst of the rising tide of anti-communism, and with the new Republican majority in the Senate, it now commanded widespread support; 62 other senators, including 44 of the 47 other Republicans, cosponsored the resolution.

In addition to seeking to curb presidential power, Bricker and his supporters shared an isolationist opposition to expanding the nation's role in world affairs, and particularly in the UN.[2] The Ohio senator feared that the UN Charter and other treaties ratified by the government (and thus part of the supreme law of the land, according to Article 6 of the U.S. Constitution) would supersede state statutes that conflicted with provisions of the international treaties. The UN might thereby, according to Bricker, legally assume "jurisdiction over domestic matters within the United States." More specifically, Bricker worried that UN treaties might be used to promote liberal reforms in the United States. The UN's venture into economic, social, and cultural fields would transform the organization, he warned, into "the economic overseer of all humanity." Echoing his concerns, southern Democrats feared that treaties governing economic and social rights ultimately would destroy the southern system of racial segregation. They suspected that Senate ratification of the Human Rights Covenants could compel the federal government to enact legislation that abolished segregation in order to uphold U.S. treaty obligations.[3]

Eisenhower vehemently objected to the Bricker Amendment. He believed that it would endanger the United States' ability to conduct relations with other nations and would place undue restraints on the executive's for-

2. Cathal J. Nolan presents the best case for this argument. See Nolan, "The Last Hurrah of Isolationism: Eisenhower, the United Nations, and the Bricker Amendment" (Paper presented at Ike's America Conference, October 6, 1990, University of Kansas, Lawrence, Kansas). Other historians emphasize the human rights treaties, rather than a broader isolationist impulse, as the central factor precipitating the controversy. See Duane A. Tananbaum, *The Bricker Amendment Controversy: A Test of Eisenhower's Political Leadership* (Ithaca, 1988).

3. Tananbaum, *The Bricker Amendment Controversy,* 31; Duane A. Tananbaum, "The Bricker Amendment Controversy: Its Origins and Eisenhower's Role," *Diplomatic History,* IX (1985), 77; Herbert Brownell, *Advising Ike: The Memoirs of Attorney General Herbert Brownell* (Lawrence, 1993), 264–65.

eign policy powers. The president and his secretary of state were also deeply concerned about a potential amendment's impact on the nation's rapidly expanding alliance structure and its influence in the UN. Yet while Eisenhower was committed to promoting individual liberty, he was not very concerned about the fate of the Human Rights Covenants. He thought that the covenants were unrealistic. Legal instruments alone could not transform human behavior. Moreover, true to Republican principles, the president espoused an essentially conservative approach in seeking social and economic change. He preferred local- and state-based action to federal legislation; federal encroachment on the powers of the states was to be kept to a minimum.[4]

The Bricker Amendment placed Dulles in a difficult position, for he had a public record of support for the Human Rights Covenants. In 1948 he had written that a covenant was necessary to "translate human rights into [international] law," and as acting chairman of the U.S. delegation to the UN in 1948, he had strongly endorsed the Universal Declaration of Human Rights and the Genocide Convention. As secretary of state, however, Dulles was confronted not only with theoretical and legal questions but also with the possibility that the USSR might turn a human rights conference into a propaganda forum and the reality of congressional opposition, too. Consequently, he made what Ernest Gross, the former deputy U.S. representative to the UN, described as a "tactical" adjustment, retreating from his earlier support for codifying UN law in these controversial areas.[5]

Lodge, lacking personal expertise or credibility in this area, relied on the Legal Affairs Office of the State Department to provide him with statements. The ambassador criticized the proposed amendment while emphasizing that the UN did not threaten American sovereignty. Since the members of the UN were "free to adopt the treaty or not, as they [saw] fit," the Covenants on Human Rights and other UN treaties could not "be imposed upon" the United States. Lodge nevertheless agreed that persuasion and education, not legislation or treaties, were the appropriate means to effect domestic change. Furthermore, he believed that the UN should focus on its

4. Eisenhower, *Mandate for Change,* 278; *MTCD,* Reel 3, Dulles and Brownell, April 26, 27, 1955; The Reminiscences of Mary Pillsbury Lord, June 6, 1967, p. 31, COHP, Butler Library, Columbia University.

5. Dulles, "The Future of the United Nations," 585; Ernest Gross, interview on November 5, 1964, p. 10, Dulles Oral History Project, Princeton; Arend, *Pursuing a Just and Durable Peace,* 142–45.

primary function—the maintenance of international peace and security. Forays into economic and social reform, Lodge reassured conservative groups such as the American Legion, were inappropriate. The "United Nations has got enough to do . . . without undertaking to become a world government and a sort of super, international socialism."[6]

The final decision to withhold support from the Human Rights Covenants was not difficult. Eisenhower and his key advisers realized that only by disassociating the administration from the Human Rights Covenants could they hope to weaken support for the Bricker Amendment. Given the depth of congressional and public support for the amendment and the concurrent opposition to the covenants, the administration chose the only realistic option. It sacrificed the human rights treaties in order to achieve its first priority—the defeat of the potential threat to the president's prerogatives in the conduct of foreign relations and the nation's system of alliances.[7]

Dulles indicated that a shift in U.S. policy was imminent in a speech to the American Association for the United Nations on March 2, 1953. He informed his audience that the peoples of the world had not yet achieved "sufficient unity of judgment, of education, [and of] religion" to codify and then impose universal standards of individual rights. It therefore would be misguided and ultimately disillusioning to suggest that fundamental changes in human behavior could be effected through "a stroke of the pen."[8] Dulles left no doubt about the policy change when he announced to the Senate Committee on the Judiciary on April 6, 1953, that the United States did "not intend to become a party to any such covenant or present it as a treaty for consideration by the Senate." The administration would seek instead to promote fundamental civil and political rights through "persuasion, education,

6. Congress, House, *Hearings Before the Subcommittee on International Organizations and Movements of the Committee on Foreign Affairs,* 83rd Cong., 1st Sess., July 8, 1953, Lodge Statement, "Effect of Senate Joint Resolution 1 on United States Participation in the United Nations," p. 105; Address to the Foreign Relations Committee of the American Legion, April 16, 1953, in folder marked "Speeches and Press Releases—1953," Box 109, HCLP, MHS; Memorandum, Meeker to Phleger, July 22, 1953, Volume 9, in Box 3, Herman Phleger Papers, Mudd Library.

7. Dulles made explicit, in a cabinet meeting on February 20, 1953, the connection between the pressure of the Bricker Amendment and the decision not to support the Human Rights Covenants. See *FRUS, 1952–1954,* III, 1555n.

8. Address to the American Association for the United Nations, March 2, 1953, in folder marked "United Nations, 1953," Box 77, J. F. Dulles Papers, Mudd Library.

and example rather than formal undertakings which commit one part of the world to impose its particular social and moral standards upon another part of the world community, which has different standards."[9] This strategy appeared to work; the Bricker Amendment was defeated in February, 1954.

A number of additional international treaties, all negotiated under the aegis of the UN system, fell victim to the new policy. The administration promised in the spring of 1953 that it would not seek Senate ratification of the Genocide Convention, the Convention on the Political Rights of Women or a supplementary Convention on the Abolition of Slavery.[10]

Nevertheless, the administration did not want to abdicate leadership of the quest for individual liberties, a hallmark of the nation's post-war foreign policy. Repudiation of the covenants would cloud the United States' reputation as a champion of human rights, provide the Soviets with a valuable propaganda weapon, and strain U.S. relations with many of the developing nations that staunchly supported the international treaties. The State Department settled upon offering a constructive alternative that would appease the Bricker forces, minimize the international backlash, and permit the United States to continue to work within the UN system to promote human rights. First Dulles and then Eisenhower approved the new program, though Dulles worried that the UN still would create "new mechanisms that might give the Soviets an opportunity for prying around in human rights conditions in the United States."[11]

The State Department developed an "action program" to assist UN members in fulfilling the human rights obligations they had already assumed under the UN Charter and the Universal Declaration of Human Rights (1947). The three-part program would consist of (1) studies by the Human Rights Commission on specific, worldwide human rights problems such as freedom of religion; (2) annual reports from members on the status of human rights in their nations; and (3) advisory and technical assis-

---

9. Testimony before the Judiciary Committee of the Senate, April 6, 1953, in folder marked "Bricker Amendment 1953," Box 67, J. F. Dulles Papers, Mudd Library.

10. Brownell, *Advising Ike,* 267–68.

11. Memorandum, Sandifer to Kotschnig (Walter Maria Kotschnig, director of the Office of United Nations Economic and Social Affairs of the Department of State and deputy representative on the Economic and Social Council), February 19, 1953, in *FRUS, 1952–1954,* III, 1555; Memorandum, Hickerson to Dulles, February 9, 1953, same volume, 1542–47; Memorandum, Phleger and Hickerson to Dulles, February 18, 1953, same volume, 1549–54.

tance programs to help governments improve their adherence to human rights.[12]

The United States presented this program to the Commission on Human Rights at its annual meeting in Geneva in April, 1953. In her maiden speech to that body, on April 8, Mary Pillsbury Lord, the United States representative, announced that after four years of guiding the drafting process, the United States had decided that it would not ratify the covenants. Lord then enthusiastically presented the action program as an alternative means of advancing human rights. Questioning American sincerity and suspecting that the action program was instead a cover for inaction, the delegates received the program coolly. Their skepticism was warranted. By Lord's own subsequent admission, the State Department had developed the action program partly so that she would not arrive in Geneva "empty-handed."[13]

Despite the initial world reaction, the administration persisted with its program in 1954 and 1955. However, the American proposal received little attention until after the completed Human Rights Covenants had been transmitted to the Security Council and the General Assembly in 1955. Once the commission turned its attention to the action program, the United States finally prevailed in the spring of 1956, despite opposition from the Soviet bloc and resistance from the colonial powers. Staunch support from the Third World, which welcomed the opportunity to receive more technical-assistance funding, provided the margin of victory.

Economic development was of even greater importance and more immediate concern to the underdeveloped nations at the UN. Proposals for the establishment of a special United Nations economic development fund were first put forth in 1952, but the question of multilateral aid did not become a major issue until the mid-1950s, with the emergence of a host of new nations in Asia and Africa. Convinced that centuries of economic exploitation by the colonial powers had contributed to their poverty, the new nations turned to

---

12. Position Paper, "Commission on Human Rights," February, 1953, SD/E/CN.4/44–85, in Box 44, Lot 82 D 211, RG 59, NA; Memorandum, Hickerson and Phleger to Dulles, March 26, 1953, in *FRUS, 1952–1954,* III, 1556–58.

13. Reminiscences of Mary Pillsbury Lord, June 6, 1967, p. 31, COHP, Butler Library, Columbia University; "U.S. Policy on Human Rights," Lord statement before the Human Rights Commission on April 8, 1953, *Department of State Bulletin,* April 20, 1953, pp. 581–82.

the Western members for assistance in correcting the problems colonialism had wrought.

The administration, especially early in its first term, handled the issue of multilateral foreign aid indecisively. The problem stemmed, at least in part, from the uniqueness and complexity of the question. In contrast to the majority of foreign policy issues, foreign aid did not fit neatly within the cold war paradigm. Cold war hostility certainly fueled the debate, particularly because the Communist bloc, according to the State Department, sought to become "the Machiavellian self-styled protectors of the underprivileged." But the fundamental division, the State Department acknowledged, lay between "the have and the have-not, the progressive and the backward, the rich and the poor." In addition to the East-West conflict, sharp divisions between North and South—the developed versus the underdeveloped world—thus lay at the crux of the problem.[14]

Domestic political and economic factors also complicated the foreign aid question. Having campaigned in 1952 on the slogan of "trade not aid," Eisenhower hesitated to endorse foreign assistance programs, specifically the sort of soft loans popular at the UN. Moreover, the New Look's fiscal parsimony demanded cuts in foreign aid. Aid was to be targeted at specific, vulnerable areas, not at staunch allies or vague, all-encompassing UN multilateral programs. For political, economic, and philosophical reasons the United States thus favored short-term, low-cost projects aimed at meeting immediate needs. The Third World, in contrast, sought a long-term, financially generous American role and a fundamental restructuring of the international economy. Consequently, both sides were philosophically at loggerheads from the start.[15]

Despite rhetorical support for economic development throughout 1953

14. Memorandum by King (senior adviser to the U.S. delegation to the UN), September 9, 1954, in *FRUS, 1952–1954,* I, 98. For indispensable accounts of the Eisenhower administration's broader foreign economic policy, see Burton I. Kaufman, *Trade and Aid: Eisenhower's Foreign Economic Policy, 1953–1961* (Baltimore, 1982) and Walt Whitman Rostow, *Eisenhower, Kennedy, and Foreign Aid* (Austin, 1985). Thomas Zoumaras argues that Eisenhower gradually shifted from a policy of "trade not aid" to using public money to help Third World development. See Zoumaras, "Eisenhower's Foreign Economic Policy: The Case of Latin America," in Melanson and Mayers, eds., *Reevaluating Eisenhower,* 155–91.

15. Nick Cullather demonstrates the impact of fiscal conservatism on U.S. policy toward the Philippines. See Nick Cullather, *Illusions of Influence: The Political Economy of United States–Philippine Relations, 1942–1960* (Stanford, 1994).

and 1954, the administration often acted in a manner that led many to question whether it had a positive economic and social vision on the question of UN development programs. Clearly, the administration had not yet determined what portion of U.S. foreign, nonmilitary aid it was willing to expend through the United Nations and what programs it desired to support. As the U.S. delegation to the UN Economic and Social Council (ECOSOC) summarized the situation in August, 1953, "We profess great faith in the United Nations but we have reached the point where we must be better prepared to demonstrate that faith in concrete economic and social programs, which are not completely dwarfed by our bilateral programs, or we must temper our professions of faith."[16] Recognizing that a significant degree of its influence in the Third World came from its bilateral financial largesse, the administration hesitated to dilute this influence through multilateral aid. However, it was now time for the United States, to use one of Eisenhower's favorite phrases, "to fish or cut bait."

The attention of the underdeveloped countries focused on the effort to create a Special United Nations Fund for Economic Development (SUNFED). The State Department recognized that "SUNFED has become a symbol of their [the underdeveloped countries'] cause." President Eisenhower unwittingly sent the hopes of SUNFED proponents soaring with his "Chance for Peace" address on April 16, 1953. Calling upon the Soviet Union to join with the United States and the UN in devising a disarmament program, Eisenhower pledged to devote "a substantial percentage of the savings achieved by disarmament to a fund for world aid and reconstruction."[17]

The State Department directed the U.S. delegation to the spring meeting of ECOSOC to emphasize that the United States did not support SUNFED at the present time. Eisenhower's pledge pertained to a post-disarmament period, not the present era of cold war. Until that time, preparations for the defense of the free world must take precedence. Proposed cuts in the U.S. military budget for 1954 stemmed from a new defense strategy—the New

---

16. "Special Report of the United States Delegation to the Sixteenth Session of the Economic and Social Council, Geneva, June 30–August 5, 1953," August 5, 1953, in *FRUS, 1952–1954,* I, 277; Memorandum, Lincoln P. Bloomfield (special assistant for Charter review) to Key, August 23, 1954, same volume, 289.

17. Memorandum, Wilcox to Douglas MacArthur II (counselor of the Department of State), March 30, 1956, in *FRUS, 1955–1957,* IX, 373; "The Chance for Peace," April 16, 1953, in *Public Papers of the Presidents of the United States: Dwight D. Eisenhower, 1953,* 186.

Look. The cuts neither signaled progress toward disarmament nor portended increased contributions to economic development. Moreover, the administration viewed even this proposal as a pledge, "a multilateral declaration of intent, an earnest [show] of good faith." It was not, under any circumstances, to be viewed as "a binding contract."[18] Still, the administration was determined not to be lumped with opponents of SUNFED. Dulles therefore permitted the U.S. delegation to vote for a General Assembly resolution calling for additional preparation for SUNFED, even though he believed that an abstention would be the "most honest and appropriate position."[19]

The underdeveloped countries grew increasingly suspicious of American sincerity. Led by India, they claimed that the United States had established the precondition of disarmament with the full expectation that it would never be achieved. They urged the developed world, as a sort of token of good faith, to begin a smaller, pre-disarmament version of SUNFED with an initial capitalization of $250 million. Publicly, the administration asserted that it would be foolish to undertake such a formidable task with insufficient monetary resources. Privately, officials acknowledged the desire to delay the establishment of SUNFED for as long as possible, fearing that once operational it would become an irreversible and unproductive drain on the U.S. treasury and fuel the revolution of rising expectations.[20]

The State Department knew that the U.S. refusal to support SUNFED hurt the nation's image "as the disinterested friend and benefactor of the less developed countries." Moreover, the department worried both about the increasing solidarity of the Third World and that "the objectives of the underdeveloped countries [we]re obviously highly vulnerable to exploitation of Soviet Russia for its own ends." Internal departmental divisions, however,

18. Memorandum, Murphy to Dulles, September 24, 1953, 340/9–2453, in Box 1315, RG 59, NA; Telegram from Dulles to the American counsul in Geneva, July 6, 1953, 340/7–153, in Box 1314, RG 59, NA.

19. Telegram from Dulles to USUN, November 16, 1953, 340/11–1153, in Box 1315, RG 59, NA; Memorandum, Murphy to Dulles, September 24, 1953, 340/9–2453, same box; Telegram from Lodge to the Secretary of State, November 17, 1953, 340/11–1753, same box.

20. Memorandum, Wilcox to MacArthur, March 30, 1956, in *FRUS, 1955–1957,* IX, 372–77; "Meeting the Economic Needs of Underdeveloped Countries," Preston Hotchkis statement to the U. N. Economic and Social Committee on July 22, 1954, *Department of State Bulletin,* August 23, 1954, pp. 280–83.

made a compelling counterproposal impossible. The Policy Planning Staff, the Bureau of European Affairs, and the Bureau of Near Eastern, South Asian, and African Affairs favored SUNFED. The Bureau of Economic Affairs opposed the project as too costly and inefficient, while the Bureaus of Far Eastern and Inter-American Affairs preferred a regional rather than universal approach.[21]

By 1955 Lodge had become the primary advocate within the administration for multilateral aid. This came as a dramatic change, for as a senator he had voiced qualified opposition to even much bilateral aid.[22] Lodge's support for the unpopular cause resulted from his daily exposure at the UN to the increasingly inseparable problems of the cold war and the Third World's demand for economic development. He saw that U.S. opposition to SUNFED lent legitimacy to charges that the United States preferred imperialistic bilateral aid programs, and spurred the growth of anti-American sentiment, a potentially serious development if the United States were to retain majority support in the General Assembly. By 1955 it was apparent that a disarmament agreement was not imminent, and Lodge suspected that the United States was rapidly losing the propaganda advantage to the Soviets, who had repeatedly declared their willingness to contribute to SUNFED if joined by the other major donor nations. Moreover, traveling in Africa and Asia in the spring of 1956 with John J. McCloy, he had seen firsthand the poverty of the Third World and the potential for Soviet economic penetration.

Although Lodge still viewed the question of multilateral versus bilateral aid through the lens of the cold war, his perspective was also shaped by a fuller understanding of the sentiment in the underdeveloped world. By contributing under the aegis of the UN, the United States could avoid charges that its aid was just a cover for economic imperialism or a patronizing handout. Lodge also advocated adopting a new attitude toward aid recipients. The United States, he counseled, "should always remember that many foreign peoples would rather be told 'no' politely than 'yes' rudely. They are *not* basically materialistic; they have pride and self-respect which means more to them than material gain." Instead of acting like the "'Mother Superior' [*sic*] who is always trying to make the little boy swallow some medicine he doesn't

21. Hotchkis to Dulles, August 20, 1954, 340/8–2054, in Box 1319, RG 59, NA; Memorandum, Kotschnig to Wilcox, June 13, 1956, in *FRUS, 1955–1957,* IX, 386–90.

22. H. W. Brands, *The Specter of Neutralism: the United States and the Emergence of the Third World, 1947–1960* (New York, 1989), 67.

like," the administration should permit the recipients more discretion in spending the money.[23]

Specifically, Lodge lobbied for two types of aid. Rather ironically, at least upon first appraisal, he urged the administration to fund more "flashy," high-impact projects that clearly displayed a "made in America" label. Too often, the Soviet Union received excessive credit for its contributions, while American benevolence remained unheralded. To illustrate this problem, Lodge frequently cited an experience he had had in Kabul, Afghanistan. In the Afghan capital he had been shown an impressive silo and bakery built by the Soviet Union and serving as "a standing monument to Russian friendliness." The silo, Lodge discovered, "was full of American grain," but he complained that he had "had to dig to get this information!"[24]

At the same time, in a proposal he called "UN Multilateral," Lodge repeatedly urged the administration to channel more aid through the United Nations. UN Multilateral called for a grant fund for basic capital developments to improve the infrastructure of underdeveloped countries. In order to ensure that contributors retained principal control, the International Bank for Reconstruction and Development (in which donors enjoyed weighted votes) would approve specific requests for aid and then the UN would provide final, *pro forma* approval. The ambassador emphasized that his proposal would not entail the allocation of additional American dollars for foreign aid. Instead, it simply called for distributing 6 to 8 percent, approximately $100 to $150 million, of the funds already allocated through multilateral rather than bilateral channels. It was a proposal, Lodge stressed, that "costs us nothing and gains us much."[25]

Lodge viewed multilateral economic aid as an invaluable cold war weapon, and he pitched it to the administration and the public as such. He suggested that the United States challenge the Soviet Union to match U.S.

---

23. Remarks on Telenews, January 1, 1955, in folder marked "Speeches and Press Releases: 1955," Box 112, HCLP, MHS; Memorandum, Lodge to Eisenhower, March 5, 1956, in folder marked "Henry Cabot Lodge: 1956 (3)," Box 24, Administration Series, EP, AWF, EL. See also H. W. Brands, *Cold Warriors: Eisenhower's Generation and American Foreign Policy* (New York, 1988), chapter 3.

24. Lodge to Eisenhower, February 20, 1958, Reel 29, HCLP, MHS.

25. See, for example, Lodge to Dulles, April 13, 1956, Reel 4, HCLP, MHS; Statement to the President's Citizen Advisers on the Mutual Security Program, November 30, 1956, Reel 29, HCLP, MHS.

contributions, dollar for dollar in convertible currency, to a new development program. If the USSR participated, the Third World would benefit. If not, the United States would win a propaganda victory. In this vein, he repeatedly suggested that a presidential multilateral aid initiative could have the same propaganda benefits as the Atoms for Peace and Open Skies proposals. On a more substantive level, the diversion of even a small portion of the USSR's far more limited monetary resources would slow Soviet economic penetration in vital areas. Furthermore, it would minimize the existing auction or "blackmail" situation, in which Third World nations manipulated the superpowers to outbid each other in an effort to win their allegiance. Moreover, many neutral nations, Lodge argued, would rather accept aid from the UN than from the Soviet Union, further thwarting the Communist effort to lure the Third World into satellite status. Finally, if requests for aid had to be denied, the UN rather than the United States would be the bearer of the bad news. Immediate action was imperative. If the United States acted first it could, Lodge had been assured by Hammarskjöld, exert more control over the program.[26]

Eisenhower and Dulles gave Lodge's proposal serious consideration. Both men liked the idea of challenging the Soviet Union to match an American contribution to a UN fund. Moreover, the president hoped that using the UN might "sterilize"—eliminate the political influence of—Soviet funds. As with the theory behind the atomic-pool proposal, contributions to an international fund might deplete the USSR's cash supply, and thereby limit Soviet bilateral aid programs.[27]

At an April 25, 1956, press conference, Eisenhower announced his general approval of an economic aid plan through the United Nations. By the following week, however, a congressional outcry had forced him to retreat. Although the president reiterated his support for the theory of aid distribution

---

26. Lodge to Dulles, April 13, 1956, Reel 4, HCLP, MHS; Telegram from Lodge to the Secretary of State, February 2, 1956, in *FRUS, 1955–1957,* IX, 365–66; Lodge to Humphrey, March 19, 1956, Reel 4, HCLP, MHS; Memorandum, Lodge to Eisenhower, March 15, 1956, in folder marked "Henry Cabot Lodge: 1956 (3)," Box 24, Administration Series, EP, AWF, EL; Lodge to Eisenhower, May 11, 1956, in *FRUS, 1955–1957,* IX, 383–85.

27. *MTCD,* Reel 9, Dulles and Eisenhower, April 2, 1956, White House Telephone Calls; Dulles to Humphrey, April 16, 1956, in *FRUS, 1955–1957,* IX, 377–78; Transcript of the President's Press Conference, April 25, 1956, in Box 4, Press Conference Series, EP, AWF, EL; Eisenhower to Lodge, May 24, 1956, in folder marked "Henry Cabot Lodge: 1956 (2)," Box 24, Administration Series, EP, AWF, EL.

through the UN, he stated that "in actual practice," it was at present impossible to keep international politics out of the organization. Thus, he continued, "our efforts as we see it today must be largely done on bilateral, or let us say on some kind of an association basis, and not the major effort through the United Nations as of now." Despite their personal approval of Lodge's scheme, both Eisenhower and Dulles refused to support increased multilateral aid because of their intense apprehension that congressional antipathy might jeopardize funding for bilateral programs or the mutual security program.[28]

Lodge's proposals received mixed reactions within the administration at large. The idea of a "flashy" project met with general antagonism, with most questioning its long-term value.[29] Claiming to be "scared to death" by the consequences of pooling aid, Secretary of the Treasury George M. Humphrey led the forces against both Lodge's "UN Multilateral" proposal and SUNFED. Humphrey argued that all American foreign aid should be distributed through bilateral channels in order to maximize credit for the United States and maintain careful stewardship of taxpayer money. The United States ought not to share control of its funds with Communists or endorse soft loans. Moreover, he maintained that it would be impossible to separate economic aid from military assistance. Humphrey's fundamental objection, however, was that such a program would undermine attempts to cut the federal budget. The secretary asserted that "experience has shown us that such a scheme once started never ends and continually grows—with the great bulk of the money always coming from us." Eisenhower advised Lodge to persuade Humphrey to relent, but Lodge's efforts were in vain.[30]

28. Transcript of the President's Press Conference, May 4, 1956, in Box 4, Press Conference Series, EP, AWF, EL; Transcript of the President's Press Conference, April 25, 1956, same box; Memorandum of Conversation with William Jackson by Dulles, May 1, 1956, in folder marked "Memos of Conversation—General–J through K (1)," Box 1, General Correspondence and Memoranda Series, Dulles Papers, EL; "Two Democrats Raise Obstacles to Plans for Wider U.S. Aid," New York *Times,* April 28, 1956, pp. 1, 9.

29. Comments on the views of Ambassador Lodge, enclosed with the President's memorandum of March 9, n.d., in folder marked "Herbert Hoover, Jr.," Box 19, Administration Series, EP, AWF, EL; Memorandum, John B. Hollister (director, International Cooperation Administration) to the Acting Secretary of State, March 14, 1956, in folder marked "Henry Cabot Lodge: 1956 (3)," Box 24, Administration Series, EP, AWF, EL.

30. Minutes of a Meeting, "Possible United States Participation in the United Nations Economic Development Program," January 3, 1957, in *FRUS, 1955–1957,* IX, 408; Humphrey to Joseph Dodge (chairman of the Council on Foreign Economic Policy and former di-

Those people involved in the work in the trenches at the UN offered the most enthusiastic support for multilateral aid. In fact, the entire U.S. delegation to the Eleventh General Assembly took the unprecedented step of telegramming Dulles and imploring him to propose positive economic development initiatives. John C. Baker, the representative to the Economic and Social Council, articulated the widely held view that while the proposed SUNFED program had significant weaknesses, its objectives were valid. Paul G. Hoffman, former administrator of the Marshall Plan and a delegate to the Economic Committee of the General Assembly in 1956, sounded the same theme, arguing that economic development, second only to international peace, was the most important priority of the Third World. Neil H. Jacoby, a member of the Council of Economic Advisers from 1953 to 1955 and the U.S. representative to ECOSOC in 1957, offered an alternative to SUNFED that would involve the United States in a multilateral aid enterprise while meeting the business community's desire to rely primarily on private investment.[31] However, neither the persuasive abilities of proponents of SUNFED nor the entreaties of the underdeveloped nations altered the administration's stance.

Changing international circumstances finally compelled the White House to soften its opposition. The administration reassessed its position in light of the Soviet intention to vote in favor of the creation of SUNFED, Britain's intention to abstain, the increasing ability of other Western powers to contrib-

---

rector of the budget), April 27, 1956, quoted in Rostow, *Eisenhower, Kennedy, and Foreign Aid,* 116; Memorandum, Dulles to Eisenhower, January 10, 1957, in *FRUS, 1955–1957,* IX, 412–13; Lodge to Eisenhower, March 23, 1956, in folder marked "Henry Cabot Lodge (3)," Box 24, Administration Series, EP, AWF, EL; Humphrey to Lodge, December 5, 1955, Reel 7, HCLP, MHS; Lodge to Humphrey, December 13, 1955, in *FRUS, 1955–1957,* IX, 350–51; Humphrey to Lodge, March 5, 1956, in folder marked "U.S.-U.N.—Economic Aid," Box 91, HCLP, MHS; Lodge to Humphrey, March 19, 1956, in *FRUS, 1955–1957,* IX, 370–72; Humphrey to Eisenhower, May 7, 1956, same volume, 380–83.

31. Telegram from the U.S. Delegation to the 11th General Assembly to Dulles, February 23, 1957, in Box 1269, RG 59, NA; Baker to Wilcox, December 7, 1955, in *FRUS, 1955–1957,* IX, 345–48; Baker to Wilcox, February 16, 1956, same volume, 366–69; Hoffman to Eisenhower, December 17, 1956, same volume, 404–406; Memorandum, Jacoby to Lodge, September 23, 1956, in folder marked "United Nations (2)," Box 99, White House Central Files, Confidential Files, ER, EL; Paul G. Hoffman, "Operation Breakthrough," *Foreign Affairs,* XXXVIII (1959), 30–45; Reminiscences of Neil H. Jacoby, November–December 1970, pp. 105–109, COHP, Butler Library, Columbia University.

ute to such a fund, and the inability of trade and private investment to solve the economic problems of the underdeveloped world. Still opposed to SUNFED, the administration devised a more palatable alternative. Presented at the fall, 1957, General Assembly, the new proposal called for expanding the UN Technical Assistance program two to three times (though the U.S. portion of the total would decline from 40 percent to $33^1/_3$ percent within three years) and focusing primarily on pre-investment studies such as surveys of natural resources. Even this abridged version of SUNFED required extensive interdepartmental negotiation.[32]

The American proposal encountered stiff opposition at the UN from those loyal to SUNFED. In mid-December, Dulles finally authorized the U.S. delegation to accept a compromise resolution between the American proposal and SUNFED. The secretary did so "with reluctance and misgivings," but he conceded that "as Sputnik has taught us, we cannot safely avoid the propaganda aspects of what we do." The nation could not afford to "be a minority of practically one on the SUNFED resolution . . . at this juncture." Support for a compromise was "perhaps part of a price we have to pay for lapses in other respects."[33]

Dulles was willing and politically able to make such compromises at least partly because of the services of Representative Walter Judd (R-Minnesota), the delegate to the Second (Economic) Committee in 1957. In contrast to the progressive Republicanism of Hoffman, Judd was a conservative who had opposed channeling multilateral assistance through the existing Expanded Program of Technical Assistance (EPTA). Exposure to delegates from the developed and underdeveloped world had slowly converted him to the cause, and he played an important role in hammering out the compromise and securing congressional support.[34]

The perceived exigencies of propaganda politics and the ability of Judd to deflect conservative Republican criticism, rather than fiscal considerations or humanitarian concern, thus dictated Dulles's support. Nevertheless, under Judd's leadership, the U.S. delegation still obtained the principal American

32. Memorandum, Kotschnig to Hanes (John W. Hanes, Jr.), October 26, 1957, in *FRUS, 1955–1957,* IX, 427–31; Memorandum, Dillon to Dulles, October 31, 1957, same volume, 421–27.

33. Dulles to Anderson, December 7, 1957, in *FRUS, 1955–1957,* IX, 439.

34. Seymour Maxwell Finger, *Your Man at the UN: People, Politics, and Bureaucracy in Making Foreign Policy* (New York, 1980), 85–88.

objectives—an emphasis on technical assistance and pre-investment studies rather than capital projects, and an agreement to proceed no further with SUNFED until disarmament had freed adequate resources. Lodge assured Dulles that as a result of Judd's efforts SUNFED was "in cold storage."[35]

On December 14, 1957, the General Assembly passed a resolution that established the Special Fund. It was to be a semi-autonomous organization responsible to a governing council elected by the General Assembly and funded by the voluntary contributions of UN member nations. The resolution received unanimous support from all except the Soviet bloc, which abstained and consequently lost some of its credibility as the economic friend of the less developed countries. The United States agreed to contribute two-thirds of the total amount received from other countries, and thereby reassumed its leadership in the UN economic field.

The Special Fund began operating in 1959. As the principal donor nation, the United States was rewarded with comparable influence in its administration. Hoffman was named to head the Special Fund, and he pleased Eisenhower, Dulles, and Herter with the manner in which it functioned under his leadership. Nevertheless, Lodge's pleas to increase the U.S. contribution and expand the fund's mandate from pre-investment studies to capital projects—the "bricks and mortar" projects that, he claimed, would "make a definite and favorable impact on the mind of the man in the street"—fell on deaf ears. Eisenhower insisted that he "had no thought of expanding the use of SUNFED, where a great many countries would be making decisions on this matter when they were supplying little or none of the resources."[36]

The president shied away from using multilateral aid for a number of reasons. Philosophically, he opposed the concept of grants in aid preferred by

35. Telegram from Lodge to the U.S. embassy in France, December 14, 1957, in *FRUS, 1955–1957,* IX, 441–42; Dulles to Anderson, December 7, 1957, same volume, 439; Memorandum of a Telephone Conversation between Dulles and Anderson, December 6, 1957, same volume, 440–41; Telegram from Lodge to the Department, December 20, 1957, same volume, 442–50.

36. Memorandum, Lodge to Eisenhower, in *FRUS, 1958–1960,* IV, 414–15; Memorandum of a Conference with the President, September 14, 1959, in folder marked "Staff Notes—September 1959 (2)," Box 44, DDE Diary Series, EP, AWF, EL; Telegram from Lodge to the Secretary of State, October 21, 1959, 310.5/10–2159, in Box 1245, RG 59, NA; Cabinet meeting minutes, in folder marked "November 6, 1959 (1)," Box 14, Cabinet Series, EP, AWF, EL; Telegram from the Department of State to USUN, November 4, 1960, in *FRUS, 1958–1960,* IX, 403–404.

SUNFED proponents. True to his Abilene roots, he believed that handouts would only make a struggling nation dependent on its benefactor; it would stifle self-sufficiency. Expanded American trade and private investment, he initially believed, would be sufficient to ameliorate the economic problems. Moreover, as a fiscal conservative, Eisenhower feared that multilateral aid programs would enlarge the federal government bureaucracy and increase the budget. He was reluctant to channel U.S. aid through an organization over which the United States did not have complete control. At least to some extent, he shared the American perception that "ECOSOC always has its hand in Uncle Sam's pocket."[37] Furthermore, during the early part of the decade, when the United States was just about the only provider of funds, bilateral aid was obviously more attractive. As the largest single donor nation, the United States was able to use its *de facto* financial veto to shape SUNFED more to its liking. Finally, during the 1950s Congress preferred military aid to economic aid, reinforcing Eisenhower's natural inclination to designate as much foreign aid for "defense" purposes as possible. Energetic advocacy by high-level leadership might have overcome congressional opposition and strong presidential support would have overruled opponents within the administration, but Eisenhower did not believe strongly enough about the issue to invest his political capital in a multilateral aid venture.

Interestingly, in the final months of his administration Eisenhower offered his strongest support for multilateral aid. Certainly, the sentimental humanitarianism of a man nearing retirement may have been partially responsible. But it seems more likely that he responded to personal experiences and changing circumstances. The shift can be attributed in part to his goodwill trips to Asia, Africa, and Latin America in 1959 and 1960. Perhaps because of these trips, he came to a belated recognition that the competition to fill the power vacuum left by the withdrawal of the colonial powers could ignite World War III. Heightened superpower tensions, most notably in the Congo, provided evidence of this danger.

Addressing the General Assembly in September, 1960, Eisenhower recommended increasing UN aid for Africa. The president believed that the complexities of the political situation and the multiplicity of new states in that region made multilateral aid preferable to bilateral aid. Though he approved bilateral aid in temporary situations, he wanted the United States to

37. Memorandum by King, April 9, 1954, in *FRUS, 1952–1954,* I, 95.

encourage the African states to seek aid through the UN. Perhaps Lodge's argument that use of multilateral forums would enable the United States to refuse African entreaties for additional assistance and exert more control over the aid informed Eisenhower's decision. Moreover, by the late 1950s the United States was no longer the sole nation capable of extending sizable sums to the Third World. Having finally recovered from World War II, the nations of Western Europe and Japan were able to contribute more generously to the economic development effort. Multilateralism thus became more attractive as a means of coordinating aid from the Western world.[38]

The critical significance White House leadership might have had in the field of multilateral aid became apparent in the establishment of the world food program in 1960. Although proposals to distribute American food surpluses through the UN had surfaced repeatedly from 1953 to 1958, they had come to naught. The world food program did not get off the ground until Vice President and presidential candidate Nixon, motivated by presidential ambitions, gave the idea his full support in the spring of 1960. Key individuals, including Treasury Secretary Robert Anderson and Herter, opposed it. Herter asserted that the "whole concept, while it is noble, ha[d] him buffaloed," because it almost duplicated existing programs that permitted the government to accept inconvertible local currencies to pay for surplus agricultural products.[39]

Ultimately, the early White House approval spurred the proposal to realization. The active support of the president and particularly the vice president kept the idea from being killed by legitimate objections or lost in bureaucratic infighting. Given the general agreement that the UN could not manage a large food program, USUN devised a plan whereby the UN would serve as a "clearinghouse" for food aid agreements. The initiative became a U.S. proposal at the 1960 General Assembly. In order to highlight the

38. Memorandum of a Conference with the President, September 27, 1960, in folder marked "Staff Notes—September 1960 (1)," Box 53, DDE Diary Series, EP, AWF, EL; Memorandum of a Conference with the President on November 1, 1960, in folder marked "Staff Notes—November 1960," Box 54, DDE Diary Series, EP, AWF, EL; Robert E. Asher, "Multilateral Versus Bilateral Aid: An Old Controversy Revisited," *International Organization,* XVI (1962), 697–719.

39. *MTCH,* Reel 11, Herter and Anderson, August 10, 1960; Memorandum, Nixon to Eisenhower, May 2, 1960, in folder marked "Toothache," Box 86, Jackson Papers, EL; Finger, *Your Man at the UN,* 91–93.

resolution for political and propaganda purposes, the United States requested that it be given priority. The Soviet delegate unwittingly focused international press attention on the proposal and virtually assured its passage when, objecting to having the measure receive priority consideration, he proclaimed: "What is the hurry? People have been hungry for a long time." The General Assembly unanimously passed the resolution on October 27, 1960, and established the World Food Program at the Food and Agriculture Organization headquarters in Rome.[40]

The newly independent states of Africa and Asia also brought the issue of racial equality to the fore at the United Nations during the 1950s.[41] Beginning in 1952, they focused their efforts to eradicate racial prejudice on the apartheid policy of the Union of South Africa. Predictably, the South African government argued that Article 2(7) of the UN Charter precluded intervention in the nation's domestic affairs.

The Eisenhower administration confronted the issue for the first time in 1953, in the form of a resolution requesting the Commission on the Racial Situation in South Africa to continue its work. The administration's carefully nuanced response reflected its ardent desire to avoid alienating either of the principal antagonists. As it had on the broader question of colonialism, it attempted to stake out a "middle position" despite its recognition that "the middle-ground position which we would have wished to occupy has often been obliterated," for the African-Asian bloc now insisted upon action.[42]

In an attempt to walk the "delicate rope," the United States suggested that the General Assembly ought to "bear in mind" the jurisdiction clause. At the same time, it maintained that discussion would not constitute intervention, and it agreed that conditions in South Africa warranted UN consideration. The U.S. delegation thus supported the underdeveloped nations on the procedural point of debate. However, the United States offered not a

40. Finger, *Your Man at the UN,* 92; Herter to Leonard W. Hall (chairman of the Republican National Committee), April 11, 1960, in folder marked "Letters A–L: Official—Classified (3)," Box 19, Herter Papers, EL; Lodge to Hall, April 12, 1960, Reel 6, HCLP, MHS.

41. For more detailed accounts of the administration's policy on the apartheid question, see Thomas J. Noer, *Black Liberation: The United States and White Rule in Africa, 1948–1968* (Columbia, Mo., 1985), chapter 3; George W. Shepherd, *Anti-Apartheid: Transnational Conflict and Western Policy in the Liberation of South Africa* (Westport, 1977).

42. "The Colonial Question in the United Nations," n.d., in *FRUS, 1952–1954,* III, 103.

shred of support for the substance of the resolution. The U.S. delegate insisted that the situation was neither as bad as the anti-colonialists depicted nor unique to South Africa. The General Assembly therefore should restrict itself to restating general principles of conduct rather than singling out any one state for condemnation. Moreover, a request for South Africa to abandon its domestic apartheid policy would constitute intervention in that nation's internal affairs. Dulles wanted to vote against even extending the life of the commission, but USUN's insistence that such a vote would be perceived as evidence that the United States condoned racial discrimination persuaded him to permit an abstention. The American policy remained essentially unaltered for the next four years.[43]

Domestic and international developments gradually persuaded the administration to adopt a tougher stance against apartheid. Domestic factors included the clamor of liberals, the increasing political importance of the civil rights movement, and Nixon's awakened interest in eliminating segregation at home and abroad and improving relations with Africa. Heightened anti-colonial resentment, South Africa's refusal to moderate its behavior, and a loosening of ties to Britain and France in the wake of the Suez Canal Crisis were among the international factors encouraging a change in American policy.[44]

American votes in the UN began to reflect the impact of these factors. In 1958 and 1959 the United States voted for resolutions that chided South Africa for violating Article 55 of the Charter (which called for racial equality) and expressed increasing concern that the South African government had not mended its ways. Throughout, the U.S. delegation carefully distinguished between racial discrimination in the United States—where the federal judiciary was actively engaged in breaking down barriers to racial equality—and South Africa, where racial prejudice was sanctioned by federal law.

Ultimately, South African guns at Sharpeville precipitated a more sig-

---

43. Memorandum, Murphy to Dulles, November 30, 1953, in *FRUS, 1952–1954,* XI, 1023–24; Telegram from Dulles to USUN, December 1, 1953, same volume, 1025–26; "The Problem of Apartheid in South Africa," Wadsworth statements in the *Ad Hoc* Political Committee on December 6, 8, 1954, *Department of State Bulletin,* January 3, 1955, pp. 32–36.

44. For detailed accounts on domestic agitation on anti-apartheid, see Noer, *Black Liberation,* 48–52; James Moss, "The Civil Rights Movement and American Foreign Policy," in George W. Shepherd, ed., *Racial Influences on American Foreign Policy* (New York, 1970); Al-

nificant change in American policy. On March 21, 1960, South African police fired on a crowd demonstrating against a law that required all Africans
to carry "pass" books. Seventy-four black Africans were killed. Four days
later, twenty-nine African and Asian delegations urgently requested a meeting of the Security Council, and Herter announced the administration's support. When the council met, Ecuador introduced a resolution that deplored
the loss of life, called on South Africa to achieve harmonious racial relations,
and asserted that, if continued, the situation in South Africa might endanger
international peace and security.

Despite the massacre, Eisenhower expressed understanding of the South
African government's position. Eisenhower reminded Herter that the
United States was "not entirely in a different position ourselves," even
though the federal government was making a greater effort to improve conditions. Consequently, he warned, "if we vote for a tough resolution, we may
find ourselves red-faced—in other words concerning our own Negro problem." The president made the final decision to vote in favor only after evalu-
ating the draft resolutions and determining that the Ecuadoran proposal was
more moderate than the alternatives. Abandoning his earlier moderation,
Lodge for the first time denounced the policy of apartheid by name, though
he noted that the United States had "no false pride" about the state of its
own racial relations. Eight other members of the Security Council joined the
United States in voting to "censure" South Africa.[45]

Lodge's denunciation of the South African government reflected a consistent split within the administration. On racial as on economic issues, the former Massachusetts senator was out in front of both Eisenhower, who was
known to tell racial jokes in office, and Dulles. Lodge recognized that the
United States' racial practices constituted an international relations nightmare and, more personally, made his job infinitely more difficult. He frequently bemoaned "the immense harm done to our world position by the
emotions raised by race and color." Most of the problem, he asserted, was

fred O. Hero, "The Negro Influence on U.S. Foreign Policy, 1937–1967," *Journal of Conflict
Resolution,* XIII (1969), 220–51.

45. Eisenhower and Herter, March 30, 1960, in folder marked "Telephone Calls—March
1960," Box 48, DDE Diary, EP, AWF, EL; "Security Council Calls for Adherence to U.N.
Principles in South Africa," Lodge statement in the Security Council on March 30, 1960, *Department of State Bulletin,* April 25, 1960, p. 668; *MTCH,* Reel 10, Eisenhower and Herter,
March 31, 1960, Presidential Telephone Calls.

caused by the "obstruction by a very few of the Supreme Court decisions on segregation in schools."[46]

The violent reaction to school desegregation in Little Rock, Arkansas, in 1957 had the most negative impact on the American image at the UN. Eisenhower emphasized this point in his televised address to the nation on September 24, the day he federalized the national guard and ordered U.S. armed forces to Little Rock. "Our enemies are gloating over this incident and using it everywhere to misrepresent our whole nation," he informed the American public. "We are portrayed as a violator of those standards of conduct which the peoples of the world united to proclaim in the Charter of the United Nations." Clearly, such dire international consequences mandated a strong presidential response.[47]

Lodge concurred. "Here at the United Nations I can see clearly the harm that the riots in Little Rock are doing to our foreign relations," the ambassador reported to his chief. "More than two-thirds of the world is non-white and the reactions of the representatives of these people is easy to see." Lodge congratulated Eisenhower on his astute assessment of the situation and reported that the president's decisive response had helped minimize the negative fallout. Even Nehru, Lodge noted, had praised the federal reaction. Similarly, Lodge applauded Eisenhower's handling of opposition to school desegregation in Charlottesville, Virginia, the following fall, and passed along a complimentary letter from UN Undersecretary-General Ralph Bunche.[48] Still, when Eisenhower asked how the United States could improve its standing with the underdeveloped world in the aftermath of Little Rock, Lodge offered suggestions in keeping with the conservative racial views of the administration. His prescription—a worldwide effort by American diplomats to "extend hospitality to distinguished colored people"—was hardly radical.[49]

Lodge's emphasis on personal diplomacy as the key to changing percep-

46. Lodge to Eisenhower, November 6, 1959, Reel 29, HCLP, MHS.

47. "Radio and Television Address to the American People on the Situation in Little Rock," September 24, 1957, in *Public Papers of the Presidents: Dwight D. Eisenhower, 1957,* 694.

48. Lodge to Eisenhower, September 25, 1957, Reel 29, HCLP, MHS; Lodge to Eisenhower, October 16, 1957, same reel; Bunche to Lodge, September 29, 1958, same reel; Lodge to Eisenhower, September 30, 1958, same reel.

49. Lodge to Eisenhower, October 15, 1957, in Box 24, Administration Series, EP, AWF, EL.

tions and attitudes was not new. In March, 1956, he had urged Eisenhower to encourage high-ranking American officials to undertake goodwill trips to African and Asian countries. It was essential, Lodge insisted, for Americans to develop personal relationships with the leaders of the underdeveloped countries and convince them that the United States was interested in them as people. Lodge had also requested Dulles to see that the foreign service in South Africa invited blacks to the Fourth of July receptions. Dulles agreed with the basic principle, but maintained that it should be applied only "to the extent the traffic will bear." Noting that UN diplomats read the New York *Times,* Lodge even suggested that the newspaper be reminded to print the pictures of black Americans appointed to high professional positions.[50]

Personal diplomacy and enlightened education were thus, in Lodge's opinion, essential. "Problems, important and far-reaching though they are, are still not as vital as the *feelings* which pervade peoples and governments. . . . History is full of bad feelings which led to wars," he lectured. The goal of U.S. diplomats should therefore be to reach "the human heart . . . that is always the central target."[51] In the end, the objective at home must be to effect "new ways of thinking by our people." Until the end of his tenure, Lodge expressed his certainty that if the American people "could see what I see they would think—and act—differently."[52] Nonetheless, though certainly not for lack of effort, Lodge failed to convince the president to adopt a more liberal attitude toward racial relations at home and abroad.

Eisenhower combined a perfunctory commitment to consider the Third World's agenda with an absolute refusal to tolerate the new nations' active intervention in superpower relations. He quickly crushed an initial foray in this direction in 1960. Late in September, 1960, five heads of state—President Kwame Nkrumah of Ghana, Nehru, President Ahmed Sukarno of Indonesia, President Gamal Abdel Nasser of the United Arab Republic, and President Josip Broz Tito of Yugoslavia—submitted a resolution requesting

50. Dulles to Lodge, April 3, 1956, in folder marked "Miscellaneous Correspondence: March 3, 1956–May 7, 1956," Box 4, General Correspondence and Memoranda Series, Dulles Papers, EL; Lodge to Dulles, March 23, 1956, same box; Lodge to Eisenhower, March 26, 1956, Reel 29, HCLP, MHS: Eisenhower to Lodge, March 29, 1956, same reel; Minutes of the Cabinet Meeting, December 18, 1959, in folder marked "Staff Notes—December 1959," Box 46, DDE Diary Series, EP, AWF, EL.

51. Lodge to Eisenhower, December 28, 1959, Reel 29, HCLP, MHS.

52. Lodge to Eisenhower, November 6, 1959, *ibid.*

Eisenhower and Khrushchev to meet in an effort to reduce world tension. In appealing directly to the two men, the resolution marked a departure from the usual practice in the UN of addressing governments, rather than individuals.

The proposal infuriated Eisenhower. In public the president took the position that "it was a well-intentioned but naive proposal." In private, he angrily charged that Khrushchev had concocted the entire idea to "promote chaos and bewilderment in the world to find out which nations are weakening under this attack and to pick what he can by fishing in troubled waters." Once again, when a Third World nation took a position contrary to the United States, the administration accounted for it by suggesting that the offending countries were victims of Communist manipulation. Eisenhower fretted that it could put the United States in the awkward position of having to respond to any small nation's request. Personally involved in crafting a response, he reaffirmed his commitment to resolving international problems, but refused to meet with Khrushchev because the USSR had not indicated its desire to relax world tensions.[53]

The president also played an active role in determining American strategy at the UN. The administration sought to convince Nehru to withdraw the resolution. It simultaneously broadened the resolution to include Britain and France, and set preconditions—a Soviet apology for shooting down the U.S. RB-47 (a patrol plane downed over the Barents Sea, north of Russia), the safe return of the airmen, and a lower-level delegation meeting—for a summit meeting. The tactics successfully killed the proposal.[54]

The Eisenhower administration thus did not make proactive use of the UN to meet the challenges of development in the Third World. Despite the revolutionary changes taking place in the international system, the president made no bold initiatives through the world organization. Indeed, the American administration resisted efforts by the newly independent nations to use

53. Letter in Reply to a Proposal for a Meeting of the President and Chairman Khrushchev, October 2, 1960, in *Public Papers of the Presidents of the United States: Dwight D. Eisenhower, 1960–61,* 742–44; Memorandum of Conference with the president, October 1, 1960, in folder marked "Staff Notes—October 1960 (2)," Box 53, DDE Diary Series, EP, AWF, EL.

54. Memorandum of Conference with the President, October 5, 1960, in folder marked "Staff Notes—October 1960 (2)," Box 53, DDE Diary Series, EP, AWF, EL.

the UN to codify international human rights, redistribute the world's wealth, and achieve racial equality.

The administration recognized, understood, and, to some extent, sympathized with the goals of the Third World. Eisenhower wanted to help the developing nations, if only to win their support. However, other American foreign policy goals took precedence. Eisenhower understandably deemed the military and geopolitical goals of a nation in the midst of the cold war to be more important than the social, economic, and human rights agenda of the Third World. Moreover, the administration maintained that the UN's function in maintaining international peace and security must take precedence over its economic, social, and humanitarian endeavors. The administration also argued that, while some aspects of the general welfare were suitable for action through an international organization, most were handled best through other channels.

As a result, the United States sought to formulate and pursue different policies with regard to what it identified as the two different functions of the UN. To its consternation, however, the administration discovered that the UN's economic and social goals and programs were often profoundly political and inextricably linked to the achievement and maintenance of international peace and security. In the end, the United States' unwillingness to subordinate the ostensible demands of the cold war to the demands of economic and social development hurt the nation's leadership in the United Nations. Only when compelled by the exigencies of cold war competition with the Soviet Union did the Eisenhower government offer occasional support for Third World initiatives. Even in these instances, it did so with obvious reluctance, a fact that did not go unnoticed by this increasingly powerful bloc.

10

Trouble on Two Fronts

The Administration Responds to the Suez and Hungarian Crises

The administration's pronouncements of support for the United Nations were put to a severe test in the fall of 1956 by simultaneous crises in the Middle East and Eastern Europe. The Suez Canal situation, whose immediate causes included intense Egyptian and Arab nationalism, Islamic solidarity, Arab-Israeli hostility, and tensions in the Atlantic alliance, largely grew out of the anti-colonial Third World independence movement and for the United States served as a watershed event. The crisis occasioned by the Soviet invasion of Hungary, in contrast, arose out of and was shaped by the cold war. Though the two situations were thus fundamentally different and required different angles of approach, the administration used the UN in both cases.[1]

1. On Suez, see, for example, Isaac Alteras, *Eisenhower and Israel: U.S.-Israeli Relations, 1953–1960* (Gainesville, 1993); Herman Finer, *Dulles over Suez: The Theory and Practice of His Diplomacy* (Chicago, 1964); Diane B. Kunz, *The Economic Diplomacy of the Suez Crisis* (Chapel Hill, 1991); Keith Kyle, *Suez* (New York, 1991); Cole C. Kingseed, *Eisenhower and the Suez Crisis of 1956* (Baton Rouge, 1995); William Roger Louis and Roger Owen, eds., *Suez 1956: The Crisis and Its Consequences* (New York, 1989); W. Scott Lucas, *Divided We Stand: Britain, the United States and the Suez Crisis* (London, 1991); Donald Neff, *Warriors at Suez: Eisenhower Takes America into the Middle East* (New York, 1981); Hugh Thomas, *The Suez Affair* (Middlesex, 1970); Selwyn Ilan Troen and Moshe Shemesh, *The Suez-Sinai Crisis, 1956: Retrospective and Reappraisal* (New York, 1990); Earl Oliver Kline, "The Suez Crisis: Anglo-American Relations and the United Nations" (Ph.D. dissertation, Princeton University, 1961); Arthur McLean Stillman, "The United Nations and the Suez Canal" (Ph.D. dissertation, American University, 1965). On Hungary, see Daniel F. Calhoun, *Hungary and Suez,*

On July 26, 1956, Egyptian president Gamal Abdel Nasser announced that he had signed a presidential decree nationalizing the Suez Canal Company. Nasser's announcement outraged the British and the French. They depended heavily on the Suez Canal as a route for trade and oil shipments, and were the primary investors in the privately owned Suez Canal Company. The British feared that nationalization would drastically undermine their position in the Middle East. The French saw dire consequences for their colonial position in North Africa, given Nasser's support for the Algerian rebels. Comparing Nasser's move to Hitler's remilitarization of the Rhineland, the French government decided that since a showdown with Nasser appeared increasingly inevitable, it made more sense for it to take place in Egypt than in Algeria. They immediately demanded the return of the waterway and resolved to reverse Nasser's action.[2]

Prime Minister Anthony Eden summoned American chargé d'affaires Andrew Foster—in lieu of vacationing ambassador Winthrop Aldrich—to a British cabinet meeting convened only hours after Nasser's announcement. Foster reported to Washington that Eden was adamant on regaining the canal, by force if necessary. The British cabinet, he noted, opposed referring the matter to the Security Council because of its estimation that the UN could not handle the matter expeditiously—the question would become "hopelessly bogged down." The probability of a Soviet veto, a reluctant recognition that nationalization might well be legal, and uncertainty about the American response reinforced the British unwillingness to appeal to the UN.[3]

Nasser's announcement apparently took the American administration by surprise. Although the United States' abrupt decision to withdraw its offer of aid to construct the Aswan High Dam was at least partly responsible for precipitating Nasser's action, the State Department had not prepared for such a contingency. The Suez Canal was simply not of vital interest to the

---

1956: An Exploration of Who Makes History (Lanham, 1991); Paul Kecskemeti, *The Unexpected Revolution* (Stanford, 1961); David Pryce-Jones, *The Hungarian Revolution* (New York, 1970); Janos Radvanyi, *Hungary and the Superpowers: The 1956 Revolution and Realpolitik* (Stanford, 1972); Paul E. Zinner, *Revolution in Hungary* (New York, 1962).

2. For more detailed accounts of the British and French reaction, see Keith Kyle, "Britain and the Crisis, 1955–1956," in Louis and Owen, eds., *Suez 1956,* 103–30; Robert Rhodes James, "Eden," in Troen and Shemesh, *The Suez-Sinai Crisis, 1956,* 100–109; Maurice Vaisse, "France and the Suez Crisis," in Troen and Shemesh, *The Suez-Sinai Crisis, 1956,* 131–43; Kyle, *Suez,* 143–48; Alteras, *Eisenhower and Israel,* 189–91.

3. Telegram from Foster to the Department of State, July 27, 1956, in *FRUS, 1955–1957,* XVI, 4; Kyle, *Suez,* 136–39.

United States. Anxious about Soviet expansionism and radical Arab nationalism, the administration was, however, concerned that neither Egyptian nor European actions undercut Western dominance in the Middle East. Consequently, the administration's behavior during the first week of the crisis was essentially reactive.

Eisenhower set U.S. policy throughout the crisis. From the start, the president adhered to one fundamental principle—he opposed using force to wrest control of the canal from Nasser. Nationalization alone, Eisenhower believed, provided inadequate justification for military intervention. Indeed, nationalization was perfectly legal as long as the stockholders received just compensation. The use of force ought not even to be considered until Egypt had proved incapable of operating the waterway, all other options had been exhausted, and public opinion had been prepared for such a move. Eisenhower thus counseled Eden on July 31, "I cannot overemphasize the strength of my conviction that some method must be attempted before action such as you contemplate should be undertaken."[4]

Eisenhower believed that negotiation, not armed confrontation, was the logical first step. Frightened by the belligerent tone of communications from Eden, the president first sent troubleshooter Robert Murphy and then Dulles to London to engage in tripartite talks with the British and French. During this period, Eisenhower contemplated and eventually rejected bringing the situation to the limited multilateral forum of NATO, where all the major maritime powers would have a voice.

For a number of reasons, Eisenhower and Dulles were even less inclined than the British to bring the matter to the UN. First, they suspected that while the UN deliberated, Nasser would consolidate his control and become more difficult to dislodge. UN consideration "would surely bog down our efforts for [an] indefinite time," Eisenhower warned. Second, the administration worried that the debate would pit the anti-colonial forces against the colonial powers. Assembling a coalition of Third World votes, Nasser could prevent passage of a resolution. Since the United States simply could not manage the General Assembly in this situation, it would be better, Eisenhower concluded, to restrict participation to the principal parties involved.

4. Eisenhower to Eden, July 31, 1956, in *FRUS, 1955–1957,* XVI, 70; Memorandum of Conversation, July 27, 1956, same volume, 11–12. For Eisenhower's leadership style during the crisis, see especially Kingseed, *Eisenhower and the Suez Crisis of 1956,* and Robert R. Bowie, "Eisenhower, Dulles, and the Suez Crisis," in Louis and Owen, eds., *Suez 1956,* 189–214.

Third, even if the United States garnered enough votes for a constructive resolution, the Soviet Union would probably veto it. Fourth, given the solely recommendatory and hortatory power of resolutions, the Western alliance still would be compelled to enforce a UN decision in its favor. Explaining his broad reasoning at a press conference on August 8, Eisenhower stated, "Here was a matter that seemed to demand . . . not a hurried solution but a prompt one, and I think to get the nations, who by their maritime activities, and by the character of their economies[,] were most . . . interested, to get them together was a better method at the moment. Now the only trouble with the other one [bringing the dispute to the UN] would be I think its slowness."[5]

Finally, and perhaps most important, Eisenhower and the State Department feared that UN discussion of the status of the Suez Canal would set a dangerous precedent. The administration did not want to empower the UN, even indirectly or inadvertently, to "override treaty rights," for the organization might turn its attention to other international waterways, specifically the Panama Canal. Indeed, the prospect of a challenge to American control of the Panama Canal Zone so incensed the president that he declared that if the United States "left the Panama Zone we would take the locks with us." Eisenhower's concern was not unfounded. Early in August, Nasser considered requesting the UN to devise a set of regulations applicable to all international waterways, including the Suez and Panama Canals. Interestingly, Nasser predicted that the UN would ultimately resolve the crisis in a manner beneficial to Egypt.[6]

Seeking an alternative to force or Security Council consideration, the administration espoused conference diplomacy. A multilateral conference held the promise of pacific negotiation, without the peril of tying the United States to any specific course of action. In addition, during protracted negotiations the crisis might simply dissipate. Dulles thus proposed an international conference, associated with the UN but not held under its auspices.

5. President's News Conference of August 8, 1956, in Box 5, Press Conference Series, EP, AWF, EL.

6. Telegram from the Department of State to the U.S. embassy in the United Kingdom, July 30, 1956, in *FRUS, 1955–1957,* XVI, 49; Memorandum of a Conversation between the President and the Secretary of State, August 8, 1956, same volume, 163; Telegram from Henry A. Byroade (ambassador to Egypt) to the Department of State, August 4, 1956, same volume, 133–35; Amin Hewedy, "Nasser and the Crisis of 1956," in Louis and Owen, eds., *Suez 1956,* 171; Kyle, *Suez,* 185.

Faced with Anglo-French resistance, however, he readily agreed to abandon any connection to the UN.[7]

At the same time, the administration actively resisted pressure from other directions to bring the situation to the United Nations. A complaining Soviet premier Bulganin hinted that the USSR might raise the issue in New York. The U.S. ambassador to Moscow, Charles E. Bohlen, temporarily silenced this threat with legalistic arguments. Hammarskjöld also sought to transfer negotiations to the UN. Meeting with Dulles, Lodge, and Wadsworth in New York on August 10, he expressed his disappointment that the UN had been excluded thus far. Dulles could only somewhat disingenuously assure Hammarskjöld that he had advocated a conference not to avoid the organization, but because he believed that "the more delay there was the less likelihood there was it [force] would be invoked," and suggested that the UN might still play a role in a future canal authority.[8]

Delegations from twenty-two countries met at Lancaster House in London from August 16 to 23, 1956. Conspicuous in its absence, the Egyptian government had rejected the British invitation, charging that the effort to establish international control of the canal was "nothing but a polite form of what might be called international colonization." Dulles sought to cut through the political aspects of the dispute and focus on the technical questions of the control and operation of the canal. He proposed Egyptian ownership, but international management of the waterway. An international board "associated with the United Nations" and including an Egyptian representative would run the canal. The secretary's ideas on how the UN might be associated with the international board were vague, probably intentionally, and remained largely unexplored.[9] By a vote of 18 to 4 the conference adopted a scheme—the Eighteen-Power Proposals—to organize an international management body to control the canal.

Ironically, although the United Nations was not officially represented in London, the world organization was omnipresent in the rhetoric of the conference. References to the UN Charter abounded as delegates maintained that their proposals were in accord with the principles, objectives, and spirit

7. Telegram from Dulles to the Department of State, August 2, 1956, in *FRUS, 1955–1957,* XVI, 100–102.

8. Memorandum of a Conversation, August 10, 1956, in *FRUS, 1955–1957,* XVI, 183; Telegram from Bohlen to the Department of State, August 7, 1956, same volume, 156–60.

9. Egyptian government statement, quoted in Kline, "The Suez Crisis," 71; Memorandum of a Conversation, August 18, 1956, in *FRUS, 1955–1957,* XVI, 221–26.

of the UN Charter and accused others of violating those precepts. Thus, for example, British foreign secretary Selwyn Lloyd insisted repeatedly that Britain was acting in accord with Article 33 of the UN Charter in its attempts to achieve a peaceful settlement, while Nasser, from afar, condemned British war preparations as breaches of the "letter and spirit of the Charter of the United Nations."[10]

Obtaining wider acceptance of the Eighteen-Power Proposals proved to be impossible. A delegation headed by Prime Minister Robert G. Menzies of Australia journeyed to Cairo to meet with Nasser on September 3, but six days of discussion produced little progress. Nor did the State Department's Bureau of International Organization Affairs believe that the UN could be used to demonstrate favorable world opinion for the London conference decisions. The distrust of the African-Arab-Asian bloc would prevent a majority vote endorsing them. Coercive measures, such as blocking economic development projects and manipulating U.S. cotton exports, the State Department concluded, held a better chance of convincing Nasser to relent.[11]

Anticipating failure, Eden had begun to plan his next step. The prime minister believed that the time had almost come to compel Nasser to "disgorge" the canal by the use of force. First, however, in order to meet Britain's obligations as a signatory of the UN Charter, buttress his argument that Britain had explored and exhausted every pacific option, and satisfy the British public, Eden had to make at least a *pro forma* approach to the UN. Eden and the British cabinet, joined more reluctantly by French foreign minister Christian Pineau (who was also head of the French delegation at the UN), decided to refer the issue to the Security Council. As Lloyd admitted to Dulles, "The main object of the exercise would be to put us in the best possible posture internationally" before undertaking military action. Moreover, the British government wanted to move before Egypt, citing the British buildup of forces in the Mediterranean as a threat to peace, lodged its own complaint.[12]

Eden remained ever mindful that the Security Council could be a treach-

---

10. Nasser statement, quoted in Kline, "The Suez Crisis," 86.

11. Position Paper, "Measures to Secure Egyptian Acceptance of the Conference Decision," Stuart W. Rockwell (deputy director, Office of Near Eastern Affairs), August 13, 1956, Reel 48, J. F. Dulles Papers, Mudd Library. On Menzies' role, see J. D. B. Miller, "Australia and the Crisis," in Louis and Owen, eds., *Suez 1956*, 275–83.

12. Message from Lloyd to Dulles, August 28, 1956, in *FRUS, 1955–1957*, XVI, 326; Kyle, *Suez*, 226.

erous forum. As one of Dulles's advisers warned the prime minister, the Security Council was like quicksand: "Once in it, one did not know how deep it would prove, or whether one would ever get out." Eden was determined to limit debate and prevent the passage of damaging resolutions. Britain and France hoped that a strong majority in favor of a resolution embodying the Eighteen-Power Principles would legitimize the Anglo-French position. Even a Soviet veto, however, could provide a pretext for military intervention. If debate dragged on, Britain would simply conclude discussion by pointing to the UN's inability to resolve the dispute. Eden beseeched Dulles for U.S. cosponsorship, tactical support during the debate, and assurances that the United States would object to any resolutions limiting Anglo-French freedom of action.[13]

The administration understood the Anglo-French intent. Eisenhower and Dulles knew full well that Britain and France intended to refer the matter to the Security Council "as primarily a smokescreen, designed to cover them against charges of neglecting the UN," and they supported the idea, to an extent. Solid Security Council support for an Anglo-French resolution, the secretary had advised, might transfer some of the blame to Egypt and enhance the London proposals' moral authority. Most important, bringing the dispute to the UN might mire Britain and France in the "quicksand" of the Security Council. It might "get them into a situation from which they could not readily disengage themselves for the purpose of hostilities," Dulles suggested to Eisenhower.[14]

But Eisenhower and Dulles ultimately decided to resist such a cynical attempt to manipulate the UN. If large nations resorted to force without first exhausting all peaceful mechanisms of conflict resolution, Eisenhower feared, "the United Nations would be badly weakened and possibly destroyed." It was imperative, the president wrote in a draft message to Eden, that Britain first seek the world organization's endorsement of the Eighteen-Power Proposals. Eisenhower publicly cited the American commitment to the UN to support his opposition to the use of force in an early-September

13. Anthony Eden, *Full Circle* (Boston, 1960), 509; Memorandum of a Conversation, September 10, 1956, in *FRUS, 1955–1957,* XVI, 469–72; Telegram from Walworth Barbour to the Department of State, August 28, 1956, same volume, 312–13.

14. Memorandum of Discussion at a Department of State–Joint Chiefs of Staff Meeting, August 31, 1956, in *FRUS, 1955–1957,* XVI, 342; Memorandum of a Conversation, August 29, 1956, same volume, 315; Memorandum of a Conversation, August 24, 1956, same volume, 285–86.

press conference. Dulles too spoke out, refusing to condone blatant Anglo-French manipulation of the UN in order to legitimize what he believed to be an unwarranted use of force. He would support a move to the Security Council only as an honest means to pressure Nasser, not as an "exercise."[15]

Dulles emphasized the problems inherent in an approach to the Security Council in an effort to dissuade Britain. He asked whether the matter would be referred as a "dispute" or a "situation," noting the difficulty of getting a majority of votes in the former case and the dim prospects of obtaining an effective resolution in the latter. Furthermore, he asserted that the Anglo-French position was juridically weak, since nationalization was legal and Egypt's rejection of the Eighteen-Power Proposals did not constitute a threat to international peace and security. Without a promise of American support, Britain and France retreated.[16]

Dulles instead urged that Eden and Pineau merely inform the Security Council of the situation by letter and request no action. They finally did so on September 12, even though Dulles refused to cosign their letter, and Egypt followed suit on September 17. Anxious to involve the UN in some carefully controlled fashion, Lodge broached the idea of proposing a resolution linking U.S. recognition of Egyptian sovereignty in the canal with an opening for the use of force if Egypt blocked canal traffic. Dulles rejected the idea—at least, he told Lodge, until after a further attempt at conference diplomacy. Hammarskjöld too questioned the wisdom of using the Security Council, since neither side wanted genuine negotiations.[17]

In an attempt to forestall either an Anglo-French move to the UN or a resort to force, Dulles organized another multilateral conference to create an association of the users of the canal. The second London conference convened on September 19, 1956. Dominating the conference, Dulles proposed a voluntary association that would involve the UN only by requesting the ca-

15. Draft message from Eisenhower to Eden, September 8, 1956, in *FRUS, 1955–1957,* XVI, 432; Report prepared in the Executive Secretariat of the Department of State, September 5, 1956, same volume, 377; President's news conference of September 11, 1956, in Box 5, Press Conference Series, EP, AWF, EL.

16. Memorandum of a Conversation, September 7, 1956, in *FRUS, 1955–1957,* XVI, 420–30; Memorandum of a Conversation, September 7, 1956, same volume, 411–15.

17. Memorandum of a Conversation, September 8, 1956, in *FRUS, 1955–1957,* XVI, 438–41; Memorandum of a Conversation, September 9, 1956, same volume, 455–58; Lodge to Dulles, September 13, 1956, same volume, 494; Dulles to Lodge, September 17, 1956, same volume, 495; *MTCD,* Reel 5, Lodge and Dulles, September 11, 1956; Kyle, *Suez,* 252.

nal management's executive group to report to the world organization. In response to concerns that the dispute should be brought to the UN, Dulles, citing Article 40, insisted that the users had a right and a "duty first of all to seek a solution by means of their own choosing." Not until the users had devised a specific practical proposal would it be worthwhile to move to the UN. "We are getting the problem in shape so that it can be handled by the United Nations," the secretary assured the skeptical delegates.[18]

The meeting concluded on September 21 after agreement finally had been reached on a name and an acronym for the new organization—the Suez Canal Users Association (SCUA). As even Dulles later conceded, the plan had "no teeth." It lacked the means to compel members to pay dues or to impose sanctions if Egypt failed to cooperate. Nor did the conference make provisions to take the plan to the UN. Hammarskjöld had suggested establishing a committee on the Suez question, but Dulles opposed the idea. He was eager, however, for Hammarskjöld to serve as an intermediary in an attempt to obtain Nasser's acceptance of SCUA. Clearly, Dulles sought to use Hammarskjöld for his own purposes—on a thankless and most likely futile mission to Nasser.[19]

Nothing substantive came of SCUA. Its ostensible purpose—to keep the canal operational if the Suez Canal pilots went on strike—was quickly rendered unnecessary, as Eisenhower, experienced in the daily operations of the Panama Canal, must have anticipated. The pilots struck on September 15, but new Egyptian pilots succeeded in keeping the canal traffic flowing smoothly, belying Western claims of Egyptian incompetence.

As it became clear that SCUA would not turn out to be an effective agency, Eden and French prime minister Guy Mollet proceeded with their earlier plan to bring the dispute to the United Nations. On September 22, while Dulles was airborne from London to Washington, Eden and Mollet formally requested Security Council consideration of Egypt's termination of the system of international operation of the canal. Egypt countered the following day, requesting consideration of the threat to international peace posed by the Anglo-French military buildup in the eastern Mediterranean.

The Anglo-French action infuriated Dulles for political as well as per-

18. Dulles, quoted in Kline, "The Suez Crisis," 104–105.
19. Telegram from Dulles to the Department of State, September 18, 1956, in *FRUS, 1955–1957,* XVI, 511–12.

sonal reasons. He knew that the two U.S. allies had no constructive, long-term objectives in approaching the UN. They merely wanted "to make a big thing out of calling Egypt to the Security Council to answer for her behavior" and clear the way for hostilities once debate ended in mid-October. Moreover, Dulles considered the allies' notification—taken when he was incommunicado—to be a personal affront. Confident that he had convinced Eden and Pineau to delay indefinitely, Dulles was stunned to hear to the contrary when he deplaned.[20]

With Britain and France intent on turning to the UN, the administration first indulged in commiseration and then began distancing the United States from its allies' belligerent course. "It is a deplorable situation," Dulles grumbled. Agreeing, Lodge asserted that the Anglo-French move "indicates [their] willingness to scrap the U. N.—go through it and have a showdown." At an October 2 news conference, Dulles announced that because of their differences over colonialism, the United States, Britain, and France were not allied on all questions in all parts of the world. The president even decided against addressing the opening session of the Security Council. Politically cautious in the final month of the presidential campaign, Eisenhower felt, according to Dulles, that a speech "would overdramatize the situation and that the future program of the British and French was not sufficiently clear for him to commit his prestige."[21]

On October 5, prior to the Security Council meeting, Dulles endeavored to extract "a frank statement" of Anglo-French intentions. Complaining that the administration felt "somewhat out of touch with your thinking," Dulles warned Foreign Secretary Lloyd and Foreign Minister Pineau that the United States would not "go along blindly." Too much was at stake. "War would be a disaster for the interests of the West in Asia and Africa," he bluntly asserted. Lloyd maintained that Britain genuinely sought a peaceful settlement. But he still insisted that a settlement on the basis of the Eighteen-Power Proposals must be achieved within ten days or force might become "the lesser evil." Pineau echoed his British counterpart, warning that France would "play the game in the Security Council, but we will not get bogged down in procedure." Annoyed, Dulles reminded them again of his convic-

20. Report prepared in the Executive Secretariat of the Department of State, September 24, 1956, in *FRUS, 1955–1957,* XVI, 569–70.

21. For the conversation between Lodge and Dulles, see *MTCD,* Reel 4, September 25, 1956. For Eisenhower's views, see *FRUS, 1955–1957,* XVI, 627n.

tion that "the use of force in violation of the Charter would destroy the United Nations," and insisted that they pledge to negotiate in good faith. Only after they had done so did he agree to discuss procedure and support the resolution.[22]

The Security Council met repeatedly between October 5 and 13 in both open and closed sessions. Debate focused on the Anglo-French item that had been inscribed on the agenda late in September. Private meetings of the principal parties, however, proved to be more effective. Desirous of keeping general debate and interference by the nonprincipals to a minimum, the United States had advocated private diplomacy in conjunction with the public Security Council effort. Lloyd, Pineau, and Mahmoud Fawzi, the Egyptian foreign minister and chairman of the delegation, met six times with Hammarskjöld in the secretary-general's office on the thirty-eighth floor of the UN Secretariat. The private meetings produced agreement on six principles: free passage of the canal; respect for Egyptian sovereignty; no political influence on the canal; SCUA and Egypt to set tolls; allocation of a fair percentage for development; and arbitration between Egypt and the Suez Canal Company, mechanisms for the implementation of these principles, and arbitration procedures.

Throughout the Security Council session, the Eisenhower administration professed to be playing only a supporting role. Indeed, Dulles assured Eisenhower that "he had deliberately stayed out of" the action. But Dulles's protestations notwithstanding, the administration had, in fact, remained a central actor in the negotiations, though working largely behind the scenes. Dulles and Lodge repeatedly exhorted Hammarskjöld to play a more dynamic role. The secretary-general was not to serve as a "chaperon," Dulles advised, but as an active participant in bringing the parties together.[23] Dulles urged Lodge to "get what we can from Hammarskjold," and the secretary-general readily complied. Hammarskjöld briefed them on his private meetings with Lloyd, Pineau, and Fawzi, even sharing "confidential" information

22. Memorandum of a Conversation, October 5, 1956, in *FRUS, 1955–1957,* XVI, 639–45; Message from the Secretary of State to the President, October 5, 1956, same volume, 648–50; Vaisse, "France and the Suez Crisis," 141.

23. Memorandum of a Conversation, October 13, 1956, in *FRUS, 1955–1957,* XVI, 713; Memorandum of a Conversation, October 10, 1956, same volume, 679; Afternoon summary, October 4, 1956, Reel 93, State Department Microfilm, J. F. Dulles Papers, Mudd Library.

with them. The administration also relied on Hammarskjöld to convey the U.S. position to Egypt.[24]

Furthermore, the United States worked with Britain and France to devise tactics for the passage of the two-part resolution. On October 13, the Security Council unanimously adopted the first part (a restatement of the six principles) and voted 9 to 2 (the Soviet Union and Yugoslavia) in favor of the second part (which named the Eighteen-Power Proposals as the basis of implementation). Dulles deemed the Soviet veto "not an unmixed blessing," for Britain and France would have found it difficult to abide by a settlement approved by the USSR.[25]

As the Suez Canal dispute dragged on into the final weeks of the presidential campaign, Eisenhower became increasingly uneasy about its potential impact on the election. In an October 8 memorandum, press secretary James Hagerty advised his chief that Americans expected the president "to do something dramatic—even drastic—to prevent" a war. Ever mindful of Eisenhower's Korean pledge in the 1952 campaign, Hagerty cautioned that "I would not like to see the President lose his leadership in the fight for peace in America and throughout the world to the opposition candidate who might conceivably think of saying: 'I shall call on Nasser' or 'I shall call a summit conference on the Suez Canal.'" Spurred by this warning, and borrowing liberally from the memorandum, Eisenhower told Acting Secretary of State Herbert Hoover, Jr., that the United States "should not fail to do something about it, possibly dramatic, possibly even drastic" and made a number of suggestions, from secret Security Council meetings to using "some clandestine means [to] urge Nasser to make an appropriate public offer."[26]

As the Security Council session concluded, most participants and observ-

---

24. *MTCD,* Reel 5, Dulles and Lodge, October 11, 1956. The umlaut was omitted from "Hammarskjöld" in the original—an omission that occurs frequently in the primary source material. In all quotations I have retained or omitted the umlaut according to the form used in the original document.

25. Memorandum of a Telephone Conversation, October 14, 1956, in *FRUS, 1955–1957,* XVI, 721.

26. On Hagerty's memorandum, see Neff, *Warriors at Suez,* 327. For the quotations from Eisenhower, see Memorandum of a Telephone Conversation, October 8, 1956, in *FRUS, 1955–1957,* XVI, 661–62.

ers believed that the UN had made significant progress. It had forestalled the resort to force, and the issue remained on the Security Council agenda. Moreover, negotiations would continue in Geneva on October 29 under the auspices of the secretary-general. A heartened Dulles proclaimed confidently "that the status quo will be preserved for quite a while and there will be no use of force."[27]

An overoptimistic Eisenhower announced prematurely at a televised press conference on October 12 that "it looks like here is a very great crisis that is behind us." Motivated at least in part by a desire to dispel the prospect of war on the eve of the election, the president continued to trumpet this theme. In an October 27 address to the Dallas Council on World Affairs he claimed that the UN had prevented a war. Eisenhower noted correctly that the UN had succeeded in bringing the antagonists together and providing a framework for negotiation. But he failed to acknowledge that the organization had not resolved the central dispute—Egypt refused to accept the internationalization of the canal, and Britain and France would not accept Egyptian control or international supervision.[28]

In mid-October a new factor emerged on the international scene, sending tension to new heights. On October 19 mass demonstrations began in Poland and spread to Hungary. Demonstrators demanded greater personal freedom and the removal of pro-Soviet leaders. Thrilled by this turn of events, which appeared to vindicate its claims that democracy would prevail in Eastern Europe, the administration warily awaited the Soviet reaction. Suspecting that the Kremlin would attempt to silence the protest, the State Department prepared an appeal to the UN in the event of Soviet intervention.[29]

On October 24, the Hungarian Communist government invoked the Warsaw Treaty and appealed to the Soviet Union to suppress the disorder. Fighting broke out between freedom fighters and Soviet troops in Budapest. Concerned that in the absence of an American initiative the administration would be charged with having been "caught napping and doing nothing,"

27. Memorandum of a Telephone Conversation, October 13, 1956, in *FRUS, 1955–1957,* XVI, 713; *MTCD,* Reel 5, Lodge and Dulles, October 17, 1956.

28. Eisenhower, quoted in Finer, *Dulles over Suez,* 311.

29. Record of a Meeting of the Policy Planning Staff, Department of State, October 23, 1956, in *FRUS, 1955–1957,* XXV, 259–60; *MTCD,* Reel 5, Dulles and Lodge, October 22, 1956.

Dulles considered the options. After discarding the possibility of appeals to the Human Rights Commission or the General Assembly, he decided to bring the question to the Security Council. Lodge and Dulles agreed to send a circular letter to the Security Council to propose an observation commission, but Eisenhower wanted to wait for at least the "grudging assent" of Britain and France. The British were disinclined to participate in the Security Council, and, in light of the tenuous situation in the Suez, wanted to wait until November for a General Assembly debate. Once the violence appeared to be spreading, the administration obtained British and French agreement to inscribe the issue on the council's agenda. Security Council debate, it hoped, would generate world opinion against Soviet military intervention.[30]

October 28 marked the beginning of a chaotic period for Lodge and USUN. As Lodge recalled, "For seventeen nights, I'd just get catnaps on a leather sofa, in a little office I had over there" (at USUN). At the urgent request of the American, British, and French delegations, the first Security Council meeting on the Hungarian question finally took place on Sunday afternoon, October 28. The Soviet delegate, Arkady Sobolev, denounced the three powers for interfering in Hungary's internal affairs and contended that the United States had financed the rebellion. The following day, Lodge submitted a resolution to place the Hungarian question on the agenda. Lodge insisted that the United States wanted only freedom and human rights in Hungary and Poland; it did not seek military allies. Yet Lodge may have offered the Hungarian freedom-fighters misplaced hope when he proclaimed that "we [the UN] will not fail you." The American resolution passed by a vote of 9 to 1.[31]

---

30. Memorandum of a Telephone Conversation, October 24, 1956, in *FRUS, 1955–1957,* XXV, 273; Memorandum of a Telephone Conversation, October 25, 1956, same volume, 290; Telegram from the U.S. embassy in the United Kingdom to the Department of State, October 26, 1956, same volume, 303–304; Memorandum of a Telephone Conversation, October 26, 1956, 7:06 P.M., same volume, 306–307; *MTCD,* Reel 5, Dulles and Lodge, October 25, 1956, 11:00 A.M.; Afternoon summary, October 25, 1956, Reel 93, State Department Microfilm, J. F. Dulles Papers, Mudd Library; Calhoun, *Hungary and Suez, 1956,* 338–39.

31. Henry Cabot Lodge, interview with Philip Crowl, n.d., in folder marked "Dulles Oral History Project," Box 92, HCLP, MHS; Lodge, quoted in Calhoun, *Hungary and Suez, 1956,* 340.

Confronted by Soviet and Hungarian insistence that the UN had no jurisdiction, there was little more that the United States could do at that point. The administration had accomplished its main objective—focusing attention on Soviet aggression in Hungary. Moreover, the situation appeared to be improving, with the news on October 29 of discussions concerning Soviet withdrawal. On October 30, Imre Nagy announced the formation of a new national government, and declared that the Soviet forces had agreed to withdraw. Consequently, the Security Council adjourned without even setting a date for a future meeting on the situation. In the meantime, events in the Middle East overshadowed Hungary.[32]

Despite the president's public campaign assurances, by the end of October Eisenhower and Dulles had become increasingly concerned about the volatile situation in the Middle East. They had good reason to be worried. On October 24 Great Britain, France, and Israel had secretly agreed to a timetable for invading the Sinai on October 29. The prospect of further talks dimmed when Britain and France insisted that Egypt present an alternative means of implementing the six principles. The United States refused the secretary-general's request to press its allies to be more conciliatory. Convinced that the United States no longer had any influence over them, Dulles wanted Hammarskjöld to take the lead. As he admitted to Lodge, "We have lost control of the situation and the only fellow who can resume it at the moment is Hammarskjold." Having placed its fate in the hands of the secretary-general, the administration could only await the outcome.[33]

Three months of fervid war preparations and more desultory negotiations finally culminated in an armed attempt to secure control of the Suez Canal and depose Nasser. In accord with the October 24 agreement, Israel attacked Egypt on the evening of October 29 (as the Security Council was holding its first emergency meeting on Hungary). Furious, Eisenhower and Dulles reacted instantly to thwart the invasion. They determined to go forthwith to the Security Council, with or without Britain and France, in order to obtain the best "psychological effect" and prevent Soviet preemption of the UN. As Eisenhower lectured British chargé d'affaires John Coulson, whom

32. Dulles Staff Meeting, October 29, 1956, Reel 93, State Department Microfilm, J. F. Dulles Papers, Mudd Library; *MTCD*, Reel 5, Dulles and Lodge, October 29, 1956.

33. *MTCD*, Reel 5, Dulles and Lodge, October 24, 1956; Memorandum for the Record by the President, October 15, 1956, in *FRUS, 1955–1957*, XVI, 724–26; Memorandum of Telephone Conversations, October 23, 24, in *FRUS, 1955–1957*, XVI, 771–73.

he called to the White House, "We plan to get to the United Nations the first thing in the morning when the doors open, before the USSR gets there."[34]

Lodge was informed of the president's decision to demand Israeli withdrawal while he was attending a performance of *Norma* at the Metropolitan Opera on October 29. In what he described in his journal as "one of the most disagreeable and unpleasant experiences he had ever had," Lodge then apprised his fellow patron of the opera, British representative to the UN Sir Pierson Dixon, seated in a nearby box, of Washington's plans. A shocked Dixon protested Lodge's calling of the Security Council. Asked if Britain intended to honor the 1950 Tripartite Declaration, Dixon retorted, "Don't be so damned high-minded." Lodge reported to Dulles, "Last night it was as though a mask had fallen off, he [Dixon] was ugly and unsmiling."[35]

Eisenhower and Dulles were initially uncertain about the degree of Britain and France's involvement. The next morning, October 30, they still hoped that Britain and France might join the United States in submitting a resolution against Israel. Their hopes were in vain. "White-faced and hostile," Dixon and French representative Bernard Cornut-Gentille refused.[36]

The Security Council convened later that morning, at eleven o'clock. The rapidity with which the meeting was called caught most representatives unprepared. Undaunted, Lodge spoke at length. He asked the council to consider how to bring about an immediate cessation of hostilities, to act quickly in determining that a breach of the peace had occurred, and to insist that the Israeli army withdraw behind the armistice lines. All agreed that in conducting a large-scale reprisal raid, Israel had violated the provisions of the 1949 Armistice Agreement. But at first, few accused Israel of wider aggression. The debate assumed a more ominous tone, however, when the Soviet representative read an Associated Press bulletin reporting that Britain and

34. Memorandum of a Conversation, October 29, 1956, in *FRUS, 1955–1957*, XVI, 829; Alteras, *Eisenhower and Israel*, 225; Memorandum of a Conference with the President, October 29, 1956, in *FRUS, 1955–1957*, XVI, 833–39.

35. Journal entry, October 29, 1956, Reel 17, HCLP, MHS; Eisenhower and Dulles, October 30, 1956, 8:40 A.M., in folder marked "October 1956 Phone Calls," Box 18, DDE Diary Series, EP, AWF, EL; Lodge, *The Storm Has Many Eyes*, 130–31.

36. Telegram from the Mission at the United Nations to the Department of State, October 30, 1956, in *FRUS, 1955–1957*, XVI, 859; Memorandum of a Conference with the President, October 30, 1956, same volume, 851–55; *MTCD*, Reel 5, Dulles and Lodge, October 30, 1956, 9:41 A.M.

France had issued an ultimatum to the governments of Egypt and Israel demanding that both nations cease fighting, withdraw their forces ten miles from the Suez Canal, and permit Anglo-French troops to occupy Port Said, Ismailia, and the Suez Canal Zone.

When the afternoon session convened at four o'clock, Dixon presented the Anglo-French case. The British representative argued that intervention was necessary to separate the two sides and protect free passage through the Suez Canal. Since the United Nations itself had neither the strength nor the speed to step into the breach, Anglo-French forces would do so. They would act as the agent of the organization, as American forces had done in the early days of the Korean conflict.

Next, Lodge presented an American resolution. It called for a withdrawal behind the armistice lines and, in an effort to nullify the Anglo-French ultimatum, appealed to all UN members to assist in enforcing the armistice terms and refrain from providing military, economic, and financial assistance to the belligerents. Despite British pleas to delay, Lodge pressed forward. The U.S. resolution received 7 votes in favor and 2 abstentions, but was vetoed by France and Britain, the latter using its veto for the first time. Both nations also vetoed a subsequent milder Soviet resolution that called for a cease-fire and an Israeli withdrawal behind the armistice lines.

With the Security Council's recommendation frustrated by the vetoes, the Yugoslavian representative moved to invoke the Uniting for Peace resolution and transfer the dispute to an emergency General Assembly session. Dulles somewhat reluctantly concluded that the United States ought to support the change in forum. If the United States did not, it would be impossible to guide the General Assembly when the matter arrived in that organ. In addition, since the United States had brought the matter to the organization, it had a responsibility to "exhaust all UN possibilities." Although Dulles believed it unlikely that the General Assembly could prevent Britain and France from enforcing their ultimatum, he hoped that it might halt the further spread of hostilities.[37] When the Yugoslav resolution came to a vote on October 31, Lodge cast the deciding seventh vote in favor.

The United States faced a momentous decision prior to the meeting of the

---

37. Memorandum of a Telephone Conversation, October 31, 1956, in *FRUS, 1955–1957*, XVI, 885–86; Tentative Notes of the Secretary's Staff Meeting, October 31, 1956, same volume, 885–86.

emergency session. The National Security Council devoted its meeting on the morning of November 1 to deciding whether or not to take a leadership role in the session. The United States, Dulles asserted, could not continue walking a fine line "between the effort to maintain our old and valued relations with our British and French allies on the one hand, and on the other trying to assure ourselves of the friendship and understanding of the newly independent countries who have escaped from colonialism." If it supported its longtime allies, the new countries of Africa and Asia would turn to the Soviet Union and the United States would be "forever tied to British and French colonialist policies." Eisenhower and Dulles believed that since Britain and France would no longer be powerful enough to dominate the Middle East, the United States would have to fill their shoes. It sought to do so without strings attached to the European colonialists.[38]

Dulles thus advocated offering a resolution imposing mild sanctions on Israel, and Eisenhower seconded the idea. If the United States did not propose "soft and reasonable" sanctions, Eisenhower argued, then the Soviet Union might well propose "mean and arbitrary" measures, including a blockade of Britain and France. Moreover, if the General Assembly recommended stiff sanctions, the belligerents most likely would only defy them, thereby undermining the UN. Eager to avoid alienating Britain, and sensitive to Egypt's responsibility for numerous provocations, most of those attending the NSC meeting, including Secretary of Defense Charles E. Wilson, Treasury Secretary Humphrey, Harold Stassen, and Allen Dulles, advised waiting at least until the UN had officially branded Israel the aggressor. Eisenhower and Dulles resisted, forcefully reminding the doubters that Britain and France had vetoed the Security Council call for a cease-fire. As Eisenhower had explained in his speech to the nation the preceding night, the allies also had violated the UN Charter in using force. If they did not pull out, the United States would move negotiations to the UN. It would not be sucked into unilateral involvement, even on a diplomatic level.[39]

Unswayed by objections, Dulles and Eisenhower drafted a mild resolution and planned longer-range strategy. Committing his thoughts to paper for Dulles's guidance in New York, Eisenhower wrote that the UN should

38. Memorandum of Discussion at the 302nd Meeting of the National Security Council, November 1, 1956, in *FRUS, 1955–1957,* XVI, 906, 912.

39. *Ibid.,* 912; Richard B. Gregg, "The Rhetoric of Distancing: Eisenhower's Suez Crisis Speech, 31 October 1956," in Medhurst, ed., *Eisenhower's War of Words,* 174.

act first to achieve a cease-fire, ascertain the belligerents' objectives, and devise a resolution that would accurately allocate blame and outline future action to resolve the fundamental problems of the region. The United States had to take the lead in order to prevent the passage of "a harshly worded resolution that would put us in an acutely embarrassing position," and to keep the Soviet Union from "seizing a mantle of world leadership through a false but convincing exhibition of concern for smaller nations." The United States should not act unilaterally in condemning any of the nations involved.[40]

The General Assembly convened to consider the Suez question at 5:00 P.M. Dulles personally took charge of the situation. "It is getting so confused I just can't meet the alternatives that might arise adequately over the telephone," he explained to Lodge. Addressing the General Assembly "with a heavy heart," Dulles condemned the use of force, asserted that the Anglo-French action was not justified because a solution had been within reach, and introduced a resolution. The multipart resolution defined the Israeli invasion as a violation of the Armistice Agreement of February 24, 1949, called for a cease-fire by all involved and a withdrawal of forces, requested member nations to refrain from introducing troops, called for the canal to be reopened, and requested the secretary-general to observe and report on the situation. The resolution did not denounce Israel, Britain, or France and did not include the provision of the vetoed U.S. Security Council resolution that all members refrain from providing assistance to Israel.[41]

After a marathon twelve-hour session, the General Assembly passed the resolution at 4:20 A.M. on November 2. It was the largest majority ever assembled—64 votes in favor, 5 opposed (United Kingdom, France, Australia, New Zealand, and Israel), and 6 abstentions (Portugal, Union of South Africa, Belgium, Canada, the Netherlands, and Laos). The U.S. resolution became the basic guideline for subsequent UN action.

The administration also took steps to address the root causes of the con-

40. Memorandum by the President, November 1, 1956, in *FRUS, 1955–1957,* XVI, 924–25.

41. *MTCD,* Reel 5, Dulles and Lodge, November 1, 1956; "United States Consideration of Developments in the Middle East," Dulles' statement in the General Assembly on November 1, 1956, *Department of State Bulletin,* November 12, 1956, pp. 751–56; Dulles and Eisenhower, November 1, 1956, 11:10 A.M., in folder marked "November 1956, Phone Calls," Box 19, DDE Diary Series, EP, AWF, EL.

flict. It proposed the establishment of two committees to consider a more comprehensive, long-term settlement of the problems in the Middle East. The first committee would tackle the major problems standing in the way of permanent peace. The second committee would work on reopening the Suez Canal and would formulate a plan for its operation. The U.S. delegation circulated draft resolutions on these committees on November 3, but procuring agreement on a cease-fire was a more urgent issue and took precedence. Eisenhower and Dulles also considered the possibility of the president joining with Nehru to form "an elder statesmen 'board of appeals'" to arbitrate the dispute as a last resort.[42]

The escalating crisis in Hungary also clamored for attention. Nagy sent an unprecedented telegram to Hammarskjöld on November 1. Not trusting his own UN delegation, Nagy announced that the new government had broken with the Warsaw Pact, appealed for help from the Great Powers, demanded the removal of Soviet troops, and requested that the Hungarian question be placed on the General Assembly agenda. Preoccupied with the Suez Crisis, the Secretariat did not treat it as an urgent message and no action was taken on November 1.

The United States sought UN involvement on November 2. Since additional Soviet troops appeared to be entering Hungary, the administration decided to move to the Security Council again to request a Soviet explanation. At 4 A.M., Britain and France sought U.S. cosponsorship of a resolution condemning the USSR's actions and calling for a special General Assembly session. Suspecting that this was aimed at deflecting attention from events in the Middle East, and concerned that they lacked adequate information about what was happening in Hungary, Dulles and Eisenhower refused. After a four-hour Security Council debate yielded no resolution, Lodge supported a motion to adjourn until November 5. Lodge's vote generated widespread displeasure. At a time when the United States was insisting upon prompt UN action in the Middle East, it appeared to be siding with the USSR in postponing further consideration of the Hungarian question. A brief Security Council meeting at 8 P.M. on November 3 finally resulted in a mild resolution calling for the Soviet Union to stop its interference and peti-

---

42. Memorandum of a Conference with the President, November 2, 1956, in *FRUS, 1955–1957,* XVI, 936; Hoover and Eisenhower, November 2, 1956, 12:20 P.M., in folder marked "Phone Calls, November 1956," Box 19, DDE Diary Series, EP, AWF, EL.

tioning the secretary-general to send humanitarian aid.[43] Interestingly, the NSC had adopted a similarly conservative stance at its October 31 meeting, advocating UN pressure on the USSR to stop intervention rather than providing actual aid to the rebels. This report never reached the president, who was focused on the Suez situation, so there was no subsequent directive. Nevertheless, Lodge appears to have unknowingly responded along the same lines.[44]

The United States' response during the early days of the Suez Canal Crisis, in contrast, met with general acclaim at the UN. Hammarskjöld wrote Lodge that "this is one of the darkest days in postwar times. Thank God you have played the way you have. This will win you many friends." The secretary-general appeared to be correct, for Lodge reported that the African, Asian, and Latin American delegates applauded the American position. Concerned about the upcoming election, Eisenhower wistfully wondered if the "story can't be given to the press for all the United States to hear."[45]

Just as the administration got an initial handle on the dual crises, it encountered a complication. On the night of Friday, November 2, Dulles awoke with severe abdominal pains and was transported to Walter Reed Hospital, where doctors soon diagnosed cancer. In his absence, Eisenhower assumed the burden of setting policy without the close collaboration of his secretary of state, while Lodge took over the drafting of statements and resolutions.

Dulles's absence during the critical weeks of the conflict did not occasion a dramatic change in American policy. Throughout, Eisenhower, Dulles, and Lodge had been in basic agreement on the U.S. position. Shifts did occur, but they were shifts of degree, not kind. More than Dulles might have, Eisenhower counted on the UN, specifically the moral force generated by that organization, to resolve the crisis. The UN's success in achieving a

43. Notes on the 42d Meeting of the Special Committee on Soviet and Related Problems, November 1, 1956, in *FRUS, 1955–1957,* XXV, 359–63; Memorandum of a Telephone Conversation, November 2, 1956, same volume, 365; Telegram from Lodge to the Department of State, November 2, 1956, same volume, 368–69.

44. Calhoun, *Hungary and Suez, 1956,* 362–63.

45. Eisenhower and Lodge, October 31, 1956, in folder marked "Phone Calls, October 1956," Box 18, DDE Diary Series, EP, AWF, EL; Telegram from Lodge to the Secretary of State, October 31, 1956, in folder marked "October 1956 (1), Foster Dulles," Box 6, Dulles-Herter Series, EP, AWF, EL.

cease-fire encouraged him to continue to rely on it to effect a withdrawal of forces and the clearance of the canal. Lodge reinforced Eisenhower's predisposition in this regard. With Dulles temporarily out of the picture, the perspective from New York prevailed over that of Washington more often than it usually did. Consequently, "Let Dag Do It" became the refrain of American policy makers.[46]

Initially, the UN justified the administration's faith in it by responding in an expeditious, forceful, and innovative manner. Canadian minister for external affairs Lester Pearson, a former chairman of the General Assembly who ardently believed in the UN, led the effort. On November 3 the General Assembly considered an unprecedented step—the creation of a UN Emergency Force (UNEF) to police the Suez Canal Zone. Pearson and the Canadian Foreign Office had presented the proposal, and it was later revised and reworked in the halls of the Secretariat and the offices of the State Department. Pearson then sponsored the U.S. resolution. Dulles gave the idea his public support, but in private he believed that a UN force could not be created and deployed rapidly enough to defuse the situation.[47]

The administration nevertheless gave priority to Pearson's proposal. On November 4, the General Assembly passed the resolution creating a UN police force by a vote of 50 in favor, 0 opposed, and 19 abstentions. Eisenhower wisely decided that, in order to remove any pretext for Soviet intervention, U.S. troops would not participate, although the United States would provide military transport for other forces (and the troops even wore U.S. Army helmets that had been spray-painted blue). As Eisenhower explained to Eden, "I would like to see none of the great nations in it. I am afraid the Red boy [the Soviet Union] is going to demand the lion's share. I would rather make it no troops from the big five."[48]

46. Fasulo, *Representing America: Experiences of U.S. Diplomats at the UN,* 107–108; Reminiscences of Loy Henderson, by Don North, December 14, 1970, p. 48, Dulles Oral History Project, Mudd Library, Princeton University; Andrew Cordier, oral history, February 1, 1967, p. 18, Dulles Oral History Project, Mudd Library, Princeton.

47. Lodge, *The Storm Has Many Eyes,* 132; Urquhart, *Hammarskjöld,* 178; Michael G. Fry, "Canada, the North Atlantic Triangle, and the United Nations," in Louis and Owen, eds. *Suez 1956,* 310–11; Memorandum of a Conversation, November 2, 1956, in *FRUS, 1955–1957,* XVI, 940–42.

48. Transcript of a Telephone Conversation between Eisenhower and Eden, November 6, 1956, in *FRUS, 1955–1957,* XVI, 1026; *Legislative Meeting Series,* Reel 2, Bipartisan Legislative Meeting, November 9, 1956; Kyle, *Suez,* 493.

Meanwhile, on November 4, Soviet tanks rolled into Budapest, Hungary, crushing the opposition. The Soviet force killed fifty thousand Hungarians and silenced the resistance. Consequently, less than an hour after the General Assembly had passed the Canadian resolution establishing a UN force, the Security Council met in an emergency session at 3 A.M. Thirteen minutes later, a resolution demanding Soviet withdrawal and requesting the secretary-general to investigate the situation received 9 votes in favor, but was vetoed by the Soviet representative. Employing the Uniting for Peace procedure, Lodge then called successfully for an emergency special session of the General Assembly.

By the time the emergency session of the General Assembly convened at 4 P.M., the United States had determined to make the most of its only viable option. It would use the UN to turn international opinion against the Soviets and brand them aggressors. Lodge condemned the Soviet Union's "wholesale brutality," and submitted a resolution that had been drafted at the White House and telephoned to the U.S. delegation only an hour earlier. It demanded immediate Soviet withdrawal, requested the secretary-general to investigate, and called upon the governments of Hungary and the USSR to permit observers to enter the country. The Soviets insisted that the UN had no authority to investigate, but the General Assembly nevertheless passed the resolution by a commanding vote of 50 to 8, with 15 abstentions.[49]

Enforcing the November 4 resolution proved to be impossible. Afraid of provoking World War III, the United States was unwilling to employ the military, political, and economic pressure that might have compelled the Soviet Union to abide by the provisions. The interdepartmental Special Committee on Soviet and Related Problems contemplated and ultimately discarded a number of ideas, ranging from a UN police force for Hungary to boycotting the Olympics, in an effort to coerce Soviet compliance. As Eisenhower lamented to the NSC, the Soviet armed intervention "was indeed a bitter pill for us to swallow . . . but what can we do that is really constructive[?]"[50]

---

49. "The Hungarian Question Before the General Assembly," Lodge statements on November 4, 5, 1956, *Department of State Bulletin,* November 19, 1956, pp. 800–803, 804–805; Memorandum of Conference with the President, November 5, 1956, 1:30 P.M., in folder marked "November 1956 Diary—Staff Memos," Box 19, DDE Diary Series, EP, AWF, EL.

50. Memorandum of Discussion at the 303d Meeting of the National Security Council, November 8, 1956, in *FRUS, 1955–1957,* XXV, 419; Notes on the 44th Meeting of the Special Committee on Soviet and Related Problems, November 6, 1956, same volume, 400–404.

Within days, it became apparent that the administration would have to settle for supporting resolutions that kept the spotlight on the situation. For example, it accused the Soviet Union of interfering with the distribution of medical supplies and food. The administration strove to quiet cries for action, at least temporarily, by insisting that the UN might be able to persuade the USSR to ease its repression in Hungary. If "the United Nations is to work, Mr. Hammarskjold must act as he, and the United Nations, see fit," Eisenhower explained.[51]

Eager to deflect attention from Eastern Europe, the Soviet Union became actively engaged in the Suez Canal Crisis on November 5. First, the USSR proposed that the two superpowers join forces to halt aggression in the Middle East. Second, the Soviet foreign minister requested that the Security Council meet to discuss the belligerents' noncompliance with the resolution of November 2. Finally, they submitted a resolution that demanded a cease-fire within twelve hours and a withdrawal of all troops within three days.

The Soviet proposals reinforced Eisenhower's desire to proceed with a UN-supervised cease-fire with all due haste. The president pronounced the idea of joint, American-Soviet action "unthinkable." It was merely a transparent attempt to divert world attention from the bloody crushing of the Hungarian revolution. He reiterated American support for all UN resolutions, challenged the Soviet Union to supply similar backing, and warned that the United States would resist the introduction of new forces to the area. The Security Council rejected the Soviet resolution by a vote of 3 in favor, 4 opposed, and 4 abstentions.[52]

Tensions in the Middle East eased as the UN resolutions and American pressure began to have their desired effect. On November 5, Israel agreed to a cease-fire, and Britain and France reluctantly followed suit the next day. An immensely relieved Eisenhower, eager to treat the situation like "a family spat," hoped quickly to reestablish warm relations with the nation's oldest allies by inviting Eden and Mollet to Washington. Dulles, Hoover, and Adams

51. Eisenhower to Jackson, November 19, 1956, in folder marked "Dwight D. Eisenhower: 1956 (1)," Box 41, Jackson Papers, EL; Telegram from Hoover to the Mission at the United Nations, November 6, 1956, in *FRUS, 1955–1957,* XXV, 404–405; Notes for an Oral Report to the Operations Coordinating Board by the Chairman of the Special Committee on Soviet and Related Problems, November 7, 1956, same volume, 416–18.

52. White House News Release, November 5, 1956, in *FRUS, 1955–1957,* XVI, 1007; Memorandum of a Conference with the President, November 5, 1956, same volume, 1000–1001.

objected, arguing that tripartite talks would undermine the authority of the UN. Eisenhower conceded, postponing the meeting until Britain and France had carried out the UN resolutions. Suspecting that Israel wanted only to delay its withdrawal and create an impression of amity between the two nations, the administration also refused requests for a meeting between Eisenhower and Israeli prime minister David Ben-Gurion.[53]

During the first week of the Suez Canal Crisis, the United States and the United Nations developed a symbiotic relationship. The United Nations depended upon American support and leadership to effect an unconditional cease-fire. The insistent Americans kept the General Assembly working through late-night sessions, pushed matters to a vote even when some delegations lacked instructions, and skillfully masterminded the marshaling of international opinion in support of the UN. The United States, Hammarskjöld gratefully wrote Eisenhower, had been "the decisive factor in avoiding collapse and pointing the way to a constructive path out of the difficulty."[54]

In turn, the United States eagerly embraced the multilateral approach as a way to avoid association with its errant allies' tainted imperialist policies. It used Hammarskjöld and the UN as a front behind which the United States could advance its aims while downplaying the direct break with those allies. As a result, the administration gained a new appreciation for Hammarskjöld. Voicing a consensus opinion, Hoover condescendingly asserted that the secretary-general had "matured greatly" since July and, most important, "seemed without question to be on our [the United States'] side." This reliance on the UN also reflected a recognition that the UN stood a better chance of resolving the conflict, as well as a calculated attempt to minimize the nation's direct responsibility in the likely event that a solution to the fundamental problems in the Middle East remained elusive.[55]

The UN's next order of business was to obtain the withdrawal of foreign

---

53. Memorandum of a Telephone Conversation, November 7, 1956, in *FRUS, 1955–1957,* XVI, 1040; Memorandum for the Record, same volume, 1043–45; Memorandum of a Conversation, November 8, 1956, same volume, 1089–91.

54. Hammarskjöld to Eisenhower, November 24, 1956, in folder marked "United Nations (1)," Box 37, Administration Series, EP, AWF, EL.

55. Memorandum of Discussion at the 303d Meeting of the National Security Council, November 8, 1956, in *FRUS, 1955–1957,* XVI, 1082; Memorandum by the President, same volume, 1088–89; Acting Secretary's Staff Meeting, Tentative Notes, November 7, 1956, Reel 246, State Department Microfilm, J. F. Dulles Papers, Mudd Library.

troops from Egypt. The United States strongly backed the organization in this effort, bringing the full measure of its economic as well as diplomatic pressure to bear. In personal messages from Eisenhower to Ben-Gurion, as well as meetings between officials of the two governments, the administration warned that an Israeli failure to comply might result in strict sanctions or expulsion from the UN.[56] The U.S. diplomatic corps even shut out the British ambassadors in Washington, D.C., and New York. The administration also refused to address the questions of oil and hard currency shortages in Britain and Western Europe until its allies had withdrawn. Ultimately, it was this economic pressure that proved crucial, for Eisenhower also made it clear that generous assistance would be forthcoming following compliance with the UN resolutions. However, early on Britain and France still resisted, maintaining that the anticipated UN force of 3,500 to 4,000 troops was inadequate. Eisenhower disagreed, declaring perceptively that since "the whole UN prestige [wa]s pledged," the number of troops was not significant.[57]

Increasingly frustrated by the aggressors' recalcitrance, in mid-November the African-Arab-Asian bloc submitted a resolution that called on Britain, France, and Israel to comply with resolutions requiring them to withdraw. The State Department wanted to abstain in order to avoid subjecting Britain to additional embarrassment. Lodge, however, requested permission to vote for the relatively mild resolution. An abstention, he cautioned, would "undoubtedly cause a slow-down in the present congealed snail's pace of withdrawal," upset the African-Arab-Asian bloc, and discourage Hammarskjöld, whose opinion, Lodge asserted, was "entitled to great weight." When the resolution came to a vote on November 24, the United States joined a strong majority in favor. At the same meeting, Lodge abstained on a Belgian amendment that would have allowed Britain, France, and Israel to withdraw their troops more slowly. Protesting that the amendment implied that the UN forces would carry on the work of the Anglo-French troops, Lodge

---

56. See, for example, Message from Eisenhower to Ben-Gurion, November 7, 1956, in *FRUS, 1955–1957,* XVI, 1063–64; Memorandum of a Conversation, same volume, 1065–67.

57. Memorandum of a Conference with the President, November 19, 1956, in *FRUS, 1955–1957,* XVI, 1153; Telegram from the Mission at the United Nations to the Department of State, November 14, 1956, same volume, 1123–25; Memorandum of Discussion at the 303d Meeting of the National Security Council, November 8, 1956, same volume, 1070–78; Afternoon summary, November 14, 15, 1956, Reel 93, State Department Microfilm, J. F. Dulles Papers, Mudd Library; Kunz, *The Economic Diplomacy of the Suez Crisis,* 138–52.

had personally presented his case to Eisenhower. He must have been persuasive, for Eisenhower consented, despite Lodge's direct instructions from the State Department to vote for the amendment.[58]

Left without an alternative, Britain and France ultimately obeyed, announcing their decision to withdraw on December 3. The United States, eager to restore alliance amicability before the NATO meeting early that month, rewarded them. The administration, for example, supported a phased rather than an immediate withdrawal and pressured Hammarskjöld and Nasser to include Britain and France in the canal-clearing operation.[59]

Though the administration continued to work through the UN, the relationship soon began to deteriorate. By mid-November, Eisenhower was becoming impatient with the slow pace of UNEF's deployment, a move that he believed would "pull the rug out from under the Soviet psychological offensive."[60] Unsympathetic to Hammarskjöld's difficulties in persuading Nasser to permit the stationing of foreign troops in Egypt, Eisenhower demanded that he "take some firm action." Hammarskjöld "should be told that, after all, he is now 'Commander in Chief' and can do as he sees fit, and put the troops in."[61]

Eisenhower failed to understand, or chose not to acknowledge, that Hammarskjöld's position did not correspond to that of the American commander in chief. The secretary-general lacked the diplomatic, military, and intelligence services available to a U.S. president. Nor could Hammarskjöld act forcefully as an intermediary, for he did not represent an independently

58. Telegram from the Mission at the United Nations to the Department of State, November 23, 1956, in *FRUS, 1955–1957,* XVI, 1184–85; Memorandum of a Conference with the President, November 23, 1956, same volume, 1178–80. Aldrich maintains that the State Department had instructed Lodge to vote for the Belgian amendment and for the African-Arab-Asian resolution only if the Belgian amendment was adopted, but that Lodge then reversed his instructions. For Aldrich's account, see Winthrop W. Aldrich, "The Suez Crisis: A Footnote to History," *Foreign Affairs,* XLV (1967), 550–51.

59. Memorandum of a Telephone Conversation, December 3, 1956, in *FRUS, 1955–1957,* XVI, 1240.

60. Memorandum of Discussion at the 303d Meeting of the National Security Council, November 8, 1956, in *FRUS, 1955–1957,* XVI, 1083; Memorandum of a Conversation, November 12, 1956, same volume, 1112–14.

61. Eisenhower and Hoover, November 14, 1956, in folder marked "November 1956, Phone Calls," Box 19, DDE Diary Series, EP, AWF, EL.

powerful third force. More important, he depended upon a moral consensus to enforce his judgments. As a result, Hammarskjöld realistically chose not to act until he had acquired broad support for introducing troops. Finally, on November 15, the first UNEF contingent arrived in Egypt.

Dulles and Eisenhower also became increasingly disappointed by the UN's failure to address the problems of the operation of the Suez Canal and the Palestine question, the subject of the administration's two resolutions of November 3. As the likelihood of getting Egyptian support, the prerequisite for a two-thirds majority, declined, the administration became "less wedded to the present resolution."[62] It was determined, however, to keep the U.S. resolutions "alive and in the forefront" at the UN. But Hammarskjöld strongly advised against General Assembly involvement. The secretary-general maintained that if he were to mediate private discussions among the principal parties the dispute could be settled on the basis of the six principles agreed to in mid-October. Lodge concurred, contending that the present situation called for "sharp focus private talks" rather than "public diplomacy." [63]

By late December, Eisenhower and Dulles were losing their willingness to rely on the UN to clear the canal. Hammarskjöld persisted, but the negotiations appeared to have deadlocked. Israel refused to withdraw until it had secured assurances that UNEF would prevent a renewal of the Egyptian blockade of the Gulf of Aqaba. Egypt, in turn, held up canal-clearing operations until all Israeli troops had withdrawn. Though Eisenhower, Dulles, and Hammarskjöld insisted that Israel pull out without conditions, they placed the primary blame for the impasse on Nasser, who should not be permitted to set prerequisites for the canal clearance. Yet the United States, Dulles complained, seemed "to have very little authority and unsatisfactory, diffuse methods of asserting influence" over Nasser. "Hammarskjold is the fellow who has the titular responsibility," Dulles allowed, "but the fact of the matter is [that] the effective power behind this thing is the US." It was

---

62. Memorandum of a Conversation, November 19, 1956, in *FRUS, 1955–1957,* XVI, 1161; Secretary's Staff Meeting, November 13, 1956, Reel 93, State Department Microfilm, J. F. Dulles Papers, Mudd Library.

63. Memorandum of a Conversation, November 25, 1956, in *FRUS, 1955–1957,* XVI, 1196; Telegram from the Mission at the United Nations to the Department of State, December 10, 1956, same volume, 1289.

an awkward situation, for "most of the pressures and 'carrots' were in our [the administration's] hands whereas Hammarskjold was doing the negotiation."[64]

A thoroughly exasperated Dulles even considered having the United States appointed "agent of the UN" to handle the matter, as it had in the Korean situation. Eisenhower suggested sending Robert Anderson to Egypt to pressure Nasser in private. Dulles also promised Lodge that the United States could "put assets in [Hammarskjöld's] hands" if the secretary-general escalated his pressure on Nasser. The administration even threatened to resume action on its tabled resolution of November 3. But Hammarskjöld resisted U.S. pressure.[65]

Throughout November and December frustration with the situation in Hungary also escalated. The UN members, Lodge insisted, could not "permit ourselves to be fobbed off, to be stalled. We cannot permit the urgent recommendations of the General Assembly to be utterly disregarded." At the same time, the administration resisted the impulse to establish a deadline, for it realized that once the USSR had passed it with impunity, the effect of the resolutions "would die like a poached egg." The administration considered condemning the Soviet Union and Hungary for noncompliance, but ultimately rejected this idea because it might precipitate a similar resolution against Britain and France. A proposal to expel the Hungarian delegation was also discarded because of fears of setting a precedent for the subsequent expulsion of Nationalist China. The United States instead refused to accept the credentials of Hungary's delegation, hoping that this would force admission of the UN observers. Throughout, the administration also used the UN to maintain private contact with the Soviets.[66]

64. Tentative Notes, Secretary's Staff Meeting, December 26, 1956, in *FRUS, 1955–1957*, XVI, 1333n; Memorandum of a Telephone Conversation, December 26, 1956, same volume, 1333–34; Memorandum of a Conversation, January 17, 1957, in *FRUS, 1955–1957*, XVII, 40.

65. Tentative Notes, Secretary's Staff Meeting, December 26, 1956, in *FRUS, 1955–1957*, XVI, 1333n; *MTCD,* Reel 5, Dulles and Lodge, January 18, 1957, 1:10 P.M.; Memorandum of a Conversation, January 17, 1957, in *FRUS, 1955–1957*, XVII, 40; Telegram from the Department of State to the Mission at the United Nations, January 28, 1957, same volume, 65–66.

66. "General Assembly Calls Again for Compliance with Resolutions on Hungary," Lodge statement in the General Assembly on December 3, 1956, *Department of State Bulletin,* December 17, 1956, p. 963; Editorial Note on a Meeting of the U.S. Delegation, December 4, 1956, in *FRUS, 1955–1957*, XXV, 501; National Security Council Report, November 19, 1956, same volume, 463–69; Notes on the 53d Meeting of the Special Committee on Soviet and Re-

The administration was extremely sensitive to the charge that it was not pursuing the aggressors in Eastern Europe as vigorously as those in the Middle East. Dulles acknowledged the existence of something of a double standard, but concluded that "we cannot wipe it out for a while but must try to minimize it as far as possible and strive to maintain continuous pressure short of war on those who do not accept the United Nations standards." Lodge, too, readily conceded that the UN had been unable to drive the Soviet army from Hungary, but he maintained that the moral power of the UN resolutions had persuaded the Soviets to stop deporting the revolutionaries, strengthened anti-Soviet sentiment, and cast a worldwide pall over communism. The UN was doing all it could as swiftly as possible; stronger measures, such as economic sanctions, had to emanate from Washington.[67]

Thwarted by Soviet opposition to international observers, the United States tried a new approach early in January, 1957. The General Assembly, working with a resolution sponsored by the United States, created a Special Committee on Hungary "to investigate, and to establish and maintain direct observation in Hungary and elsewhere" and report to the assembly at its eleventh session. It passed by a vote of 59 to 8 with 10 abstentions, though USUN had to work hard to acquire a strong two-thirds vote.[68] Although the USSR denied the Special Committee entry to Hungary, the committee set to work compiling information from a wide variety of sources, including extensive interviews with Hungarian refugees.

Meanwhile, Israel's ongoing defiance of the UN resolutions generated increased pressure for a vote of condemnation. Lodge sought to soften the harsh language of a punitive resolution proposed by Egypt, while still devising a statement tough enough to compel Israel to withdraw and capable of commanding a two-thirds vote, an increasingly difficult task in the larger

---

lated Problems, November 30, 1956, same volume, 490–95; Notes on the 55th Meeting of the Special Committee on Soviet and Related Problems, December 6, 1956, same volume, 495–99; *MTCD,* Reel 5, Dulles and Lodge, December 7, 1956; Afternoon summary, November 27, 1956, State Department Microfilm, J. F. Dulles Papers, Mudd Library.

67. Dulles to Knowland, December 20, 1956, 310.1/12–1756, in Box 1234, RG 59, NA; Lodge to Knowland, December 21, 1956, Reel 9, HCLP, MHS.

68. "General Assembly Condemns Soviet Violation of U. N. Charter, Calls Again for Withdrawal of Troops From Hungary," Lodge statements in the General Assembly on December 10, 12, 1956, *Department of State Bulletin,* December 31, 1956, pp. 975–79; Lodge to Eisenhower, December 21, 1956, Reel 29, HCLP, MHS.

and more heterogeneous organization. Finally, he wrote two resolutions. The first deplored Israel's refusal to move behind the armistice lines and requested it to do so without delay. The second, taking a longer perspective, called upon both Egypt and Israel to abide by the provisions of the 1949 Armistice Agreement, placed UNEF troops along the demarcation line, and requested the secretary-general to suggest other measures to secure a permanent peace.[69]

On February 2, the General Assembly passed Lodge's two resolutions by overwhelming majorities. Once again, the refrain of "Let Dag Do It" echoed in the halls of the UN. The United States joined the chorus, but while Lodge voted for the two resolutions, the administration offered Hammarskjöld no specific suggestions as to how in fact he could promote peace in the region.

As the movement to impose sanctions on Israel gathered strength, the Eisenhower administration attempted to arrest it. Anxious to obviate the need for a resolution, it used a combination of carrots and sticks to persuade Israel to concede. Foremost among the "sticks" was the prospect of U.S. approval of sanctions. Lodge encouraged Eisenhower to back the sanctioning. He contended that the United States could not justify "abandoning our position [of support for the UN] which won us universal respect and acclaim from the Afro-Asian world." To abandon it would deliver "a body blow" to the UN. It would also render the United States vulnerable to charges that, while it had been willing to punish Britain and France, it would not "adhere to the policy of 'one law for all'" and sanction Israel, because of the powerful Jewish vote at home. Moreover, if the UN proved unable to dislodge Israel from Egyptian territory, the problem would eventually devolve solely upon the United States.[70]

Eisenhower and Dulles also offered Israel a carrot—assurances that its

---

69. Telegram from the Mission at the United Nations to the Department of State, January 15, 1957, in *FRUS, 1955–1957*, XVII, 37–38; Telegram from the Mission at the United Nations to the Department of State, January 25, 1957, same volume, 59–61; Dulles and Lodge, January 30, 1957, in folder marked "Memoranda of Telephone Conversations—General: January 1957–February 28, 1957 (3)," Box 6, Telephone Conversation Series, Dulles Papers, EL; Telegram from Lodge to the Secretary of State, February 2, 1957, 310.5/2–157, in Box 1242, RG 59, NA.

70. Telegram from the Mission at the United Nations to the Department of State, February 5, 1957, in *FRUS, 1955–1957*, XVII, 95; *MTCD,* Reel 5, Dulles and Lodge, February 12, 1957.

primary demand would be met, though outside the UN framework. Dulles did not ask Hammarskjöld's opinion of this move. Touchy about preserving the nation's freedom of action, he did not want Hammarskjöld "to feel that we [the United States] are entirely dependent on him." In a February 11 aide-mémoire, the administration informed Ben-Gurion that it was prepared to assert the right to free and innocent passage through the Gulf of Aqaba. When Israel deemed even this communication to be only a basis for future negotiation, it exhausted Eisenhower's and Dulles's patience.[71]

Frustrated, the secretary made a number of unusual, anti-Semitic comments. Complaining that it was "almost impossible . . . in this country to carry out foreign policy not approved by the Jews," he denounced Jewish control over the media and Congress, and determined to support UN sanctions against Israel. In an attempt to build support for his position, Dulles even encouraged a Protestant counterattack to offset the outcry of the Jewish lobby.[72]

The administration also unsuccessfully battled complaints that, if it was not willing to impose sanctions on the Soviet Union, it ought not to do so against Israel. Senator William F. Knowland, a member of the U.S. delegation to the Eleventh General Assembly, threatened to resign if the United States voted for sanctions. Lyndon Johnson argued that "the United Nations cannot apply one rule for the strong and another for the weak."[73] Moved by this argument against "picking on the little fellow" and cognizant of the danger of a "double standard," Eisenhower considered submitting a resolution placing sanctions on the Soviet Union before doing so on Israel. Dulles objected. He reminded the president that the USSR was already subject to U.S. sanctions, as well as the moral force of a horrified world. Lodge pro-

71. Memorandum of Telephone Conversations, February 10, 1957, in *FRUS, 1955–1957,* XVII, 119; Aide-Mémoire from the Department of State to the Israeli Embassy, February 11, 1957, same volume, 132–34; Memorandum of a Telephone Conversation, February 15, 1957, same volume, 157–58; Memorandum of a Conversation, same volume, 158–70.

72. Memorandum of a Telephone Conversation, February 11, 1957, in *FRUS, 1955–1957,* XVII, 136–37; Memorandum of a Telephone Conversation, February 12, 1957, same volume, 142–44; Memorandum of a Telephone Conversation, February 22, 1957, same volume, 239–40; *MTCD,* Reel 5, Dulles and Dr. Roswell Barnes (National Council of Churches), February 19, 1957.

73. Johnson to Dulles, February 11, 1957, in *FRUS, 1955–1957,* XVII, 139–40; Memorandum of a Telephone Conversation, February 16, 1957, same volume, 187–88; *MTCD,* Reel 5, Dulles and Luce, February 21, 1957.

fessed, though not very persuasively, that the UN's inability to achieve its objective in one case should not prevent it from doing right in another case: "The fact that a powerful law breaker escapes punishment does not mean that we suspend all the laws for all other law breakers."[74]

Continued Israeli resistance led Dulles and Lodge to confer with Eisenhower at Thomasville, Georgia, where he was vacationing at Secretary Humphrey's estate. On February 16, the three agreed that the administration could neither be put in the position of negotiating with Israel about what the UN would do nor appear to be directed by the Jewish lobby. Eisenhower reluctantly concluded that only U.S. support for a proposed Asian resolution, one that called for suspending governmental and private assistance, would force Israel to withdraw. They stood by this decision in an acrimonious meeting with congressional leaders on February 20. Addressing the nation that same day, Eisenhower explained: "If the United Nations once admits that international disputes can be settled by using force, then we will have destroyed the very foundation of the Organization, and our best hope of establishing world order.... The United Nations must not fail. I believe that—in the interests of peace—the United Nations has no choice but to exert pressure upon Israel to comply with the withdrawal resolutions."[75] Still, the administration worried about the almost total opposition of Congress and the public to sanctions on Israel.

On February 22, the non-Arab nations of Asia joined the Arab nations to introduce a resolution calling for a cessation of all military, economic, and financial aid to Israel. The State Department drafted an alternative that called upon all governments to "withhold assistance to Israel" and to assist in achieving a settlement based on the principles of international justice once Israel had withdrawn. Perhaps seeking to reassure each other in the face of vocal opposition, Lodge and Dulles deemed this resolution to be "a very good one, with justice—'a statesmanlike thing.'" Underscoring their determination, even as Israeli and American representatives met in Washington,

---

74. *MTCD,* Reel 5, Dulles and Lodge, February 11, 1957, 8:57 A.M.; Lodge to Rabb, February 14, 1957, Reel 13, HCLP, MHS; Alteras, *Eisenhower and Israel,* 260–61.

75. Radio and Television Address to the American People on the Situation in the Middle East, February 20, 1957, in *Public Papers of the Presidents of the United States: Dwight D. Eisenhower, 1957,* 147, 150; Memorandum of Conversation with the President, February 16, 1957, in *FRUS, 1955–1957,* XVII, 178–80; Record of a Bipartisan Legislative Meeting, February 20, 1957, in *FRUS, 1955–1957,* XVII, 214–24.

USUN was discussing a resolution calling for sanctions with other delegations.[76]

The administration's combination of carrots and sticks, in tandem with continued pressure from Hammarskjöld, finally prevailed. On March 1, Israeli minister of foreign affairs Golda Meir, speaking in the General Assembly, proclaimed Israel's intention to withdraw on the basis of certain assumptions regarding *de facto* UN control of the Gaza Strip. Speaking next, Lodge applauded the Israeli announcement as "a turning point," and pronounced its assumptions "not unreasonable." Once Israel had agreed to work through the UN, the administration did what it could to facilitate the process.[77]

The Israeli announcement cleared the way for a return to the uneasy *status quo ante bellum* in the Middle East. On March 8 Hammarskjöld announced that Israel's withdrawal from Gaza and Sharm al-Sheikh was complete. Moreover, on April 24, Egypt finally issued a Declaration on the Suez Canal that recognized obligations similar to those put forth by Hammarskjöld the previous October. The Suez Canal Crisis had been resolved, though the underlying conflicts raged virtually unabated.

The Special Committee on Hungary finally published its long-awaited study of the Hungarian situation on June 20, 1957. The four-hundred page report concluded that the rebellion had been "a spontaneous national uprising" that had been ruthlessly crushed by Soviet military forces. The United States Information Agency determined to "shoot the works" in saturating the media with the highlights of the report.[78]

76. Telegram from the Department of State to the Mission at the United Nations, February 21, 1957, in *FRUS, 1955–1957,* XVII, 232–33; Memorandum of Telephone Conversation, February 22, 1957, 9:45 A.M., same volume, 236; Memorandum of a Telephone Conversation, February 26, 1957, same volume, 283–84; Memorandum of a Conversation, February 26, 1957, same volume, 291–95.

77. "Israeli Withdrawal from Egyptian Territory," Lodge statement in the General Assembly, March 1, 1957, *Department of State Bulletin,* March 18, 1957, pp. 431–34; Memorandum of a Telephone Conversation, February 28, 1957, in *FRUS, 1955–1957,* XVII, 317–18; Memorandum of a Telephone Conversation, March 3, 1956, in *FRUS, 1955–1957,* XVII, 356; Telegram from the Mission at the United Nations to the Department of State, March 4, 1957, in *FRUS, 1955–1957,* XVII, 360–61; Secretary's Staff Meeting, Notes, February 28, 1957, Reel 56, State Department Microfilm, J. F. Dulles Papers, Mudd Library.

78. "Report of the Special Committee on the Problem of Hungary," General Assembly Official Records: Eleventh Session, Supplement No. 18 (A/3593), 1957; Notes on Discussion at the 327th Meeting of the National Security Council on June 20, 1957, in Box 9, NSC Series, EP, AWF, EL.

Dulles and Lodge debated reconvening the Eleventh General Assembly. On the one hand, they recognized that such dramatic action might turn world attention on the report, mollify those demanding action, and compel the neutral states to take a stand—they hoped against the Soviet Union. On the other, they fretted about obtaining a two-thirds vote for a strong resolution affirming the Special Committee's conclusions. Moreover, continued Soviet defiance of additional resolutions would only emphasize the UN's ineffectiveness. Heightened animosity on this issue also would hamper superpower negotiation in other areas, such as disarmament. Although Dulles and Lodge concluded that the disadvantages outweighed the advantages, congressional pressure for a special session dictated their response. They would be "blasted politically" if they "lobby against it in any way that will become known," Dulles warned. Hence, they decided to support, but not initiate, the call for a special session.[79]

When the Eleventh General Assembly session reconvened in September, 1957, the State Department directed the U.S. delegation to use the Special Committee's report to focus world attention on the USSR. In addition, the U.S. delegation was to take no action on Hungarian credentials, neither approving nor rejecting them, to demonstrate that the UN did not condone the new regime. The United States then mounted an intensive campaign for a tough resolution that wholeheartedly endorsed the report, took special note of the conclusion that the USSR had violated the UN Charter in depriving Hungarians of their political independence and human rights, and appointed the General Assembly president, Prince Wan Waithayakon of Thailand, to serve as the special representative on the Hungarian problem. In the September 14 roll call, Lodge garnered 60 votes in favor, while only 10 votes were registered in opposition, with 10 abstentions. There was little more the United States could do through the UN.[80]

---

79. Dulles and Lodge, June 19, 1956, in *FRUS, 1955–1957,* XXV, 638; *MTCD,* Reel 6, Dulles and Lodge, June 25, 1957; Memorandum, Walmsley (Walter N. Walmsley, Jr., deputy assistant secretary of state for international organization affairs) to the Secretary of State, June 24, 1957, in *FRUS, 1955–1957,* XXV, 639–41.

80. Report of the OCB Committee on the United Nations General Assembly Special Meeting to Consider the Report of the Special Committee on Hungary, September 4, 1957, in *FRUS, 1955–1957,* XXV, 652–55; Circular telegram from Dulles to certain diplomatic missions, September 11, 1957, same volume, 655–56; *MTCD,* Reel 10, Dulles and Eisenhower, September 16, 1957, White House Telephone Calls; Lodge to Jackson, September 18, 1957, in folder marked "Henry Cabot Lodge, Jr.," Box 56, Jackson Papers, EL.

The administration maintained a modicum of international attention on the Kadar regime by pressing for continued inclusion of the Hungarian situation on the fall, 1958, General Assembly agenda. Indeed, had it not been for a one-man campaign waged by C. D. Jackson, the administration would not have even considered additional measures. But Jackson, convinced that Communist oppression in Hungary constituted a potentially invaluable weapon in the nation's psychological warfare arsenal, urged rejection of the credentials of the Hungarian regime. "Even the dumbest truck driver," Jackson asserted, would appreciate the meaning of such an action. He persuaded Eisenhower to take a personal interest in the cause, but Dulles was unsupportive, for he had grave doubts about both the procedural legality of such a move and the probability of acquiring sufficient support.[81]

Nevertheless, by the first week in December, Dulles and Eisenhower had decided to initiate rejection of the Hungarian delegation's credentials, though Eisenhower decided against actively lobbying for it. Lodge acknowledged that such a move might be necessary for "keeping face in the world." However, he insisted that the U.S. position was of questionable legality; the Hungarian credentials were legitimate, the United States just did not like the government that had issued them. Lodge warned that the same reasoning might then be employed to vote against some of the Latin American delegations, sent by equally unrepresentative but infinitely more pro-American governments. Most important, Lodge argued that it would be impossible to obtain a two-thirds vote for denying accreditation unless Eisenhower invested personal and national political capital in the undertaking. After pressuring Eisenhower and Dulles in person over the weekend of December 6, he persuaded them to reverse their decision.[82]

81. Jackson to Allen Dulles, July 2, 1958, in folder marked "Allen Dulles," Box 40, Jackson Papers, EL; Jackson to Allen Dulles, December 11, 1957, same folder; Jackson to Eisenhower, October 30, 1958, in folder marked "Jackson: 1958–1959 (2)," Box 22, Administration Series, EP, AWF, EL; Eisenhower to Jackson, November 6, 1958, same folder; Eisenhower to Dulles, November 6, 1958, in folder marked "DDE Dictation—November 1958," Box 37, DDE Diary Series, EP, AWF, EL; Memorandum, Wilcox to Dulles, November 7, 1958, 320/11–1758, in Box 1266, RG 59, NA.

82. *MTCD,* Reel 8, Dulles and Lodge, November 26, 1958; Telegram from Herter (acting secretary) to Lodge, December 3, 1958, 310.2/12–358, in Box 1237, RG 59, NA; *MTCD,* Reel 8, Dulles and Lodge, December 5, 1958; Memorandum by J. N. Greene, Jr. (special assistant to the secretary of state), December 8, 1958, in folder marked "Greene-Boster Chronological—December 1958 (1)," Box 14, Special Assistants Chronological Series, Dulles Papers, EL; Telegram from Herter (acting secretary) to USUN, December 8, 1958, 320.11/12–858, in Box

Eisenhower assured a disconsolate Jackson that he had "lived quite constantly with this Kadar problem ever since you reminded me of its existence." He had concluded that rejecting credentials was so similar to expulsion that the United States would be misguided to expel Hungary and not the USSR. For the remainder of Eisenhower's tenure, therefore, the United States took the more moderate position of registering its displeasure with the Kadar regime by refusing to accept its credentials.[83]

The administration's continued inability to lift Soviet oppression in Hungary generated profound public dissatisfaction with the United Nations. Although there was a widespread appreciation of the UN's seminal role in arousing and sustaining moral outrage, the American public vainly sought measures of greater significance. Henry Luce's *Life* magazine articulated the prevailing sentiment in a March 4, 1957, editorial that accused Lodge of being "not prepared to do anything." In a rebuttal that Luce agreed to publish, Lodge insisted that the United States had taken "every step short of war"; it had "left no stone unturned." Noting that during the period from October 27 to December 12, 1956, the United States had sponsored nine resolutions and he had made twenty-five speeches on the subject, Lodge defied critics to suggest "a *practicable* step that we omitted to take." The ambassador then cut to the heart of the matter: "The truth is that, although the United States is powerful, it is not all-powerful. Although the United Nations is influential, it cannot make its will immediately effective against the Soviet Union— any more than it could against the United States—without their consent."[84]

The dual crises in the Middle East and Eastern Europe provided both a formidable challenge and an unparalleled opportunity for the United Nations

---

1266, RG 59, NA; Log entries, December 9, 10, 1958, in folder marked "Log—1958," Box 57, Jackson Papers, EL.

83. Eisenhower to Jackson, December 6, 1958, in folder marked "DDE Dictation—Dec. 1958," Box 37, DDE Diary Series, EP, AWF, EL; Dulles to Jackson, January 8, 1959, in folder marked "Strictly Confidential: I–K (2)," Box 2, General Correspondence and Memoranda Series, Dulles Papers, EL.

84. For the Luce editorial, see *Life,* March 4, 1957, p. 13. For Lodge's response see Lodge to Luce, March 4, 1957, in folder marked "Hungary," Box 56, HCLP, MHS, and *Life,* March 18, 1957, p. 44. On public opinion, see Main Lines of Public Comment, June 16–July 15, 1957, in folder marked "UN Monthly Reports 1957," Box 22, Office of Public Opinion Studies, 1943–1965, RG 59, NA.

and the United States. Prior to these crises, the Eisenhower administration had repeatedly voiced its faith in the UN as a pillar of American foreign policy. The Suez and Hungarian crises provided occasions to act upon its rhetoric in two very different types of situations. As Eisenhower proclaimed in the midst of the turmoil, "For the first time in history an international machinery, set up by nations for the settlement of international disputes, is receiving a truly thorough test."[85]

In fact, however, the administration initially did all it could to avoid putting the UN to the test. During the first days of the Suez Canal Crisis, Eisenhower and Dulles made a conscious decision not to bring the dispute to the UN, and they maintained this course throughout the summer and early fall of 1956. Believing that prolonged negotiations in the more controlled environment of a limited multilateral conference would postpone indefinitely or even avert war entirely, and recognizing that Britain and France viewed the UN as the final obstacle to the use of force, Dulles repeatedly dissuaded America's allies from involving the UN in mediating the dispute. Once again, he relied upon Great Power diplomacy.

Once the crisis was placed before the Security Council late in September, Dulles, though disagreeing with the action, demonstrated an impressive mastery of the organization's resources and effectively combined traditional and multilateral diplomacy to serve the nation's interests. Dulles and Lodge, with the active assistance of Hammarskjöld, prolonged negotiations in the Security Council. They encouraged private as well as public meetings, and provided for a continuing involvement of the UN in the person of the secretary-general. In a transatlantic testing of wills, Dulles valiantly used the UN to stall, while Britain and France resisted, believing, according to Eden, "that we must not allow our case to be submerged or manoeuvred into a backwater at the United Nations."[86]

Not until October 29, 1956, after active hostilities had begun, did the United States itself initiate action at the United Nations. It was a logical step, one dictated by principle as well as international politics. When faced with an international problem, Eisenhower's initial inclination was at least to evaluate the possibility of relying on a multilateral organization to solve the

85. President's news conference on November 14, 1956, in Box 5, Press Conference Series, EP, AWF, EL; Pre-Press Conference Briefing, November 14, 1956, in folder marked "November 1956 (1)," Box 8, Ann Whitman Diary Series, EP, AWF, EL.

86. Eden, *Full Circle,* 553.

problem. Only after deciding against international intervention would the president proceed with a unilateral solution. The United States had helped create mechanisms for handling international disputes, and unless the United States had good reasons not to use these mechanisms, it should use them. By late October, the reasons that had persuaded Eisenhower not to turn to the UN in July were outweighed by a new factor. Forced by the outbreak of war to choose between its colonialist allies and the emerging African-Asian-Arab bloc, the administration concluded that it would be most beneficial to exert its influence as one of the members of a collective security action. Leadership of the UN effort would improve its standing in the Third World and head off Soviet attempts to move into the Middle East. Bereft of its Atlantic-alliance partners and unwilling to play international "Lone Ranger," the United States found the world organization to be an appealing instrument through which to achieve its foreign policy goals. In addition, the British defeat had eliminated that nation as the chief force in the Middle East and left the door open for the United States. The UN helped the United States get its foot in the door, to take the first steps toward becoming the dominant Western power in the Middle East.

The administration also determined that the United Nations provided a useful forum in which to place the long-term questions underlying the dispute. It was highly unlikely that the United States could find a way to resolve the deeply rooted problems in the area. Therefore, it was easiest to entrust them to (or, critics charged, to dump them on) the UN. But Eisenhower and Dulles had no illusions about the UN's ability to resolve the Arab-Israeli conflict. The Old Testament, Dulles mused rather strangely to an assistant, had taught him "that the root of the problem could not be eradicated. . . . he could [not] solve problems which Moses and Joshua with Divine guidance could not solve." The reality was that the best the UN could do in the Middle East was to reassert and then maintain the status quo, as articulated in the Armistice Agreement of 1949.[87]

Despite its decision to "Let Dag Do It," the administration, perhaps inevitably, became frustrated with the UN. It bemoaned the secretary-general's inability to resolve the immediate points at issue and make progress in addressing the underlying conflict. Eisenhower and Dulles understood that Hammarskjöld faced formidable difficulties, and believed that he had done

87. Memorandum of a Telephone Conversation, January 12, 1957, in *FRUS, 1955–1957,* XVII, 29; Transcript of a Telephone Conversation, same volume, 30.

an admirable job. Yet they nevertheless bristled at his refusal to accept all of their advice and his determination to retain at least a modicum of independence for his office. The White House came to share Sir Pierson Dixon's sentiment of November, 1956, that "we may find it inconvenient to have to deal with a Secretary-General who will be elevated to the status of a Pope with temporal as well as spiritual powers." Hammarskjöld appreciated the United States' crucial role in the organization, but he could not let himself or the UN become U.S. puppets, either in reality or in international perception. Eisenhower and Dulles thus failed to accept that while the UN's objectives were similar to those of the United States, they were not completely identical.[88]

As a result, Eisenhower and Dulles fought the constant temptation to bully their way through the situation, railroading Israel and Egypt into returning to the *status quo ante bellum.* Only half in jest, Eisenhower suggested late in February that they simply inform Egypt and Israel "that if they want 20 million [dollars] they better get on board." Although Dulles laughed, the two men may well have wished they could handle it that way, for both had grown increasingly impatient with working through the UN.[89]

In the end, Eisenhower relied on military power to enhance American influence in the region and bolster anti-communism and anti–radical nationalism. Focused on this objective, he addressed a joint session of Congress on January 5. Cognizant of congressional susceptibility to anti–Communist rhetoric, the president asked for executive authority "to use American armed forces to support any Middle East state threatened by overt international communism" and $200 million in economic and military aid for the region. Signed into law on March 9, the Eisenhower Doctrine represented an attempt to thwart Soviet penetration and establish the United States as the dominant external power in the Middle East. It did not deal with the far more intractable Arab-Israeli conflict. The UN, Dulles told the Senate Foreign Relations Committee, "provided the best forum for solving those problems."[90]

88. Dixon, quoted in Kyle, *Suez,* 481; Memorandum of Discussion at the 312th Meeting of the National Security Council, February 7, 1957, in *FRUS, 1955–1957,* XVII, 99–101.

89. Memorandum of a Telephone Conversation, February 24, 1957, in *FRUS, 1955–1957,* XVII, 268–69.

90. Special Message to the Congress on the Situation in the Middle East, January 5, 1957, in *Public Papers of the Presidents: Dwight D. Eisenhower, 1957,* 13; Congress, Senate, *Hearings Before the Committee on Foreign Relations and the Committee on Armed Services,* 85th Cong., 1st

Ironically, in not involving the United Nations until a breach of the peace had occurred, the United States made it almost impossible for the UN to address the fundamental causes of the conflict. The organization exhausted its energy, resources, and credibility in the months-long effort to obtain a cease-fire, a withdrawal of all foreign troops from Egypt, and a restoration of the Armistice Agreement. The UN Emergency Force entered a maelstrom of violence and became an island of calm, but it could do little else. The fundamental problems producing recurrent crises in the Middle East remained unaddressed. The question of whether an earlier, more imaginative involvement of the United Nations would have been beneficial, though outside the scope of this study, remains unanswered.[91]

The administration's response during the Suez Canal Crisis constituted a critical turning point for the Eisenhower administration. As a result of its unwavering support for UN action against its closest allies, the administration earned increased goodwill and legitimacy in the Third World. "The standing of the United States—notably among the Asian powers—is at a brand new high," Lodge reported to Eisenhower in March, 1957. The United States thereby also obtained increased freedom of action in its international political relations. It had demonstrated to the world, according to Dulles, that it would no longer "be dragged along at the heels of the British and French in policies that are obsolete. This is a declaration of independence. For the first time they cannot count upon us to engage in policies of this sort." As a result of its "declaration of independence," the administration would enjoy increased latitude at the UN. Lodge concurred, noting that the United States was "no longer forced to act on a tripartite basis with the United Kingdom and France. We are now free to team up with countries of our choice whenever it suits our interest to do so. . . . Such a strategy gives us greater flexibility and influence."[92]

President Eisenhower realized, however, that heightened sensitivity to the Third World was not without potentially grave drawbacks. "In the kind of

Sess., January 14, 1957, John Foster Dulles testimony on the Eisenhower Doctrine, Part I, p. 9; *MTCD,* Reel 5, Dulles and David Lawrence, December 29, 1956.

91. For a more informed discussion of this point, see Lincoln P. Bloomfield, *The United Nations and U.S. Foreign Policy* (Boston, 1960), 168.

92. Lodge to Eisenhower, March 11, 1957, Reel 29, HCLP, MHS; Memorandum of a Telephone Conversation, October 31, 1956, in *FRUS, 1955–1957,* XVI, 884; Lodge to Eisenhower, February 4, 1957, Reel 29, HCLP, MHS.

world that we are trying to establish, we frequently find ourselves victims of the tyrannies of the weak" and "unavoidably give to the little nations opportunities to embarrass us greatly," he wrote his friend Swede Hazlett. Moreover, the local problems and conflicts of the smaller nations could even dominate the international agenda. As the president complained in February, 1957, in the midst of the negotiations with Egypt and Israel, "It seems funny the whole world is balked by 2 little countries worrying re local prestige etc. and other countries torn by troubles have to take this and make it their major business and get nothing else done."[93]

In contrast, Eisenhower and his advisers understood that the realities of power politics, as well as geographical and logistical obstacles, precluded a vigorous response to Soviet suppression of the Hungarian uprising. This was due partly to lacking complete, accurate, and up-to-the-minute accounts of the unfolding events. The absence of a chief of mission in the legation compounded the slow transmission of information from Budapest to Washington. Furthermore, neither U.S. nor UN troops had access to the territory. Most important, the administration feared that military action might prompt World War III.[94]

Lodge nevertheless felt under siege by critics. Frustrated by the United States' impotence in the Hungarian situation, many Americans turned on Lodge, for his high profile at the UN made him the embodiment of that organization, especially to the millions still unsure of, if not antagonistic toward, the American role in the post-war world. Lodge defended himself and his work strongly. He argued that the "truth is that every initiative taken in the United Nations regarding Hungary was taken by me."[95] That was little solace to a nation only recently released from the grip of McCarthyism. Indeed, to most Americans there was little that the UN could do besides rallying international opinion.

The similarities between the Suez Canal and Hungarian crises were limited to the matter of timing. Through decisive action and steadfast leadership, the United States worked with the UN to resolve the dispute in the Middle East, essentially a matter involving the nation's alliance partners and weak Third World nations. British and French responsiveness to the moral

93. Robert Griffith, ed., *Ike's Letters to a Friend, 1941–1958*, 165; Memorandum of a Telephone Conversation, February 25, 1957, in *FRUS, 1955–1957*, XVII, 273.

94. Eisenhower, *Waging Peace, 1956–1961*, 89.

95. Lodge to Dillon, November 9, 1956, Reel 4, HCLP, MHS.

force of world opinion made the UN an effective body. The crisis in Eastern Europe, on the other hand, only confirmed in stark terms what the administration had known all along—the UN could not resolve a conflict involving a superpower. Seemingly impervious to moral considerations, the Soviet Union simply ignored the body's judgments. As a result, there was little to show for a period of constant meetings and long hours.[96]

Despite the dramatically different natures and outcomes of the two cases, they also reveal that the Eisenhower administration had become adept at using the United Nations as an instrument of its foreign policy. During the Suez Canal Crisis, Dulles and Eisenhower demonstrated a masterful ability to use the organization for their purposes and prevent the Soviet Union from assuming leadership of the UN effort at this critical juncture. Even in the Hungarian situation, the administration used speeches, resolutions, and reports to provide at least a rhetorical outlet for American frustration. Denunciations and moral condemnations might have been the only available weapons wielded by the United States in this particular cold war conflict. Still, they could be wielded with greater force and in front of a larger audience at the United Nations, and the administration skillfully used the organization to the fullest extent possible in this regard.

The White House also used the UN during both crises to insulate the situations from domestic politics. By insisting that the UN orchestrate the international response, the administration was able to remove the Suez and Hungarian crises from the forefront of American concern during the presidential election season without appearing to have abdicated its international responsibilities. The UN, argued the administration, could handle the situation according to the principles of peace and justice shared by the United States. The United States was actually doing the UN a favor, Eisenhower proclaimed in his October 31 national address. It was encouraging the UN to stand firm in fulfilling its central mandate—bringing about and maintaining international peace and security. The administration's actions and rhetoric thereby revealed both an idealistic view of the UN, in the adminis-

96. Wilcox to Dulles, November 12, 1956, in folder marked "Francis O. Wilcox: 1956," Box 112, J. F. Dulles Papers, Mudd Library. For a contemporary comparison of the crises, see Stanley Hoffman, "Sisyphus and the Avalanche: The United Nations, Egypt, and Hungary," *International Organization,* XI (1957), 446–69. For a more recent comparison, see John C. Campbell, "The Soviet Union, the United States, and the Twin Crises of Hungary and Suez," in Louis and Owen, eds., *Suez 1956,* 233–73.

tration's belief that the organization could resolve the crises, and a far more pragmatic assessment of the body, in its realization that at the very least the UN provided a means by which to distance thorny issues from domestic politics.

Thus, the virtually simultaneous crises in the Middle East and Eastern Europe had spotlighted both the potential and the limits of the United Nations in the changing world. The UN's ineffectiveness in Hungary revealed that despite the changes in the world's power structure, neither the organization nor the United States, ever mindful of the threat of a third world war, could do much to offset superpower action. Judged as an American instrument in the cold war, the body appeared to be weak, if not impotent. Happily, the UN's success in ending active hostilities and restoring the status quo in the Middle East had shown that in non–cold war conflicts the UN was useful and thus continued to justify its existence, at least to a skeptical American populace.

11

Coping with Crises in Uncharted Terrain

Intervention in Lebanon and the Congo

During his final two years in office, Eisenhower confronted situations in Lebanon and the Congo that he perceived as threats to the maintenance of international peace and security. Although the circumstances differed in each situation, during both the turmoil in Lebanon in 1958 and the conflict in the Congo in 1960 Eisenhower faced the decision of whether to meet the perceived threat through the United Nations or unilaterally. His differing reactions to each situation raise a critical question: Why did the administration rely primarily on unilateral action in Lebanon in 1958, but then pursue a multilateral route in the Congo Crisis less than two years later?

In the tense aftermath of the Suez Crisis, both the United States and the Soviet Union, hoping to fill the power vacuum left by declining Anglo-French influence, had stepped up their activity in the Middle East.[1] This

---

1. On the Lebanese situation, see M. S. Agwani, ed., *The Lebanese Crisis, 1958: A Documentary Study* (London, 1965); Erika Alin, *The United States and the 1958 Lebanon Crisis: American Intervention in the Middle East* (Lanham, 1994); Wade R. Goria, *Sovereignty and Leadership in Lebanon, 1943–1976* (London, 1985); Alan Dowty, *Middle East Crisis: U.S. Decision-Making in 1958, 1970, and 1973* (Berkeley, 1984); Richard I. Miller, *Dag Hammarskjöld and Crisis Diplomacy* (New York, 1961), chapters 6 and 7; Gerald L. Curtis, "The United Nations Observer Group in Lebanon," *International Organization,* XVIII (1964), 738–65; Douglas Little, "His Finest Hour?: Eisenhower, Lebanon, and the 1958 Middle East Crisis," *Diplomatic History,* XX (1996), 27–54; Michael B. Oren, "The Test of Suez: Israel and the

growing superpower rivalry combined with a developing spirit of pan-Arabism to create a volatile atmosphere. By the spring of 1958, the Middle East was again on the brink of disaster.

A Lebanese political controversy ultimately precipitated the crisis. Civil disturbances began when rumors circulated that the pro-Western and Christian president, Camille Chamoun, intended to seek an amendment to the constitution that would enable him to serve a second six-year term when his current term expired on September 23. Chamoun's plan upset the precarious balance between Lebanon's Moslem and Christian societies, and convinced his diverse opponents to join forces against him. The Chamoun government charged that the United Arab Republic (UAR)—formed at Nasser's initiative through the union of Egypt and Syria on February 1, 1958—was instigating the rebellion in order to force pro-Western Jordan and Lebanon to join the new Arab confederation. As civil disturbances escalated, Chamoun inquired in mid-May about the nature of a possible American response if he were to petition for military assistance. Charging that the UAR was a Communist puppet, Chamoun suggested that an invocation of the Eisenhower Doctrine might be appropriate. Lebanon had been the only Arab state formally to endorse the Eisenhower Doctrine, so his request was not unexpected.

Eisenhower determined to prevent the most pro-American government in the area from falling under the control of either Communist influence or anti-Western Arab nationalism. He was ever mindful of the region's crucial importance as a source of oil and wary of Nasser's expansionist ambitions throughout the area, including in Iran, Turkey, Ethiopia, and the Sudan. The president sought to show Nasser that the United States would not permit him to take over the region. More broadly, the administration believed American credibility to be at stake. A failure to assist Lebanon in defeating a Communist threat would adversely impact the nation's alliances worldwide. The United States must demonstrate its willingness to assist its allies in stemming the spread of communism.

On the other hand, Eisenhower was acutely aware that U.S. intervention

---

Middle East Crisis of 1958," *Studies in Zionism,* XII (1991), 55–83; Ritchie Ovendale, "Great Britain and the Anglo-American Invasion of Jordan and Lebanon in 1958," *International History Review,* XVI (1994), 284–303; Robert Schulzinger, "The Impact of Suez on United States Middle East Policy, 1957–1958," in Troen and Shemesh, eds., *The Suez-Sinai Crisis, 1956,* 251–73.

might have drastic repercussions. He understood that intervention could increase anti-Americanism. Moreover, he believed that the Eisenhower Doctrine did not apply at the moment because there was no external Communist aggression. Notwithstanding these reservations, the president maintained that the situation in Lebanon provided an ideal opportunity to thwart Communist subversion legitimately, at the invitation of the Lebanese government and in accord with the principles and procedures of the UN Charter. Searching for additional grounds, Eisenhower inquired about the authority for the United States' "former so-called gun-boat diplomacy." Dulles had to explain that this was no longer "acceptable practice." Consequently, Eisenhower and Dulles concluded that, if necessary, intervention would be justified on the basis of protecting the lives and property of American citizens in Lebanon.[2]

Eisenhower decided to assure Chamoun of the United States' intention to safeguard the independence and territorial integrity of Lebanon, but he had to place conditions upon U.S. assistance. The United States would not intervene in order to secure Chamoun a second term, or unless at least one other Arab nation supported the action. Also, an appeal for U.S. intervention ought to be accompanied by a complaint to the Security Council charging that outside interference in internal Lebanese affairs constituted a genuine threat to its independence. The United States discouraged a request at that time, however, believing that the Lebanese army, aided by American arms already in its possession, could handle the situation. Taking no chances, it dispatched the Sixth Fleet to the eastern Mediterranean and also began to plan UN strategy with Britain and France in the event of unilateral, bilateral, or trilateral intervention in Lebanon.[3]

The administration believed that a UN finding in support of Lebanon's charges would be essential for the UN to sanction American intervention. However, as the State Department conceded, for Lebanon to acquire majority support in the Security Council, its "case must be airtight before it is presented and it is doubtful if such a case can be made." In addition, the ad-

2. Memorandum of a Conversation, May 13, 1958, in *FRUS, 1958–1960,* XI, 47; Stephen E. Ambrose, *Eisenhower: The President* (New York, 1984), 463.

3. Memorandum of a Conversation, May 13, 1958, in *FRUS, 1958–1960,* XI, 45–48; Telegram from Dulles to the U.S. embassy in Lebanon, May 13, 1958, same volume, 49–50; *MTCD,* Reel 7, Dulles and Lodge, May 21, 1958; Eisenhower, *Waging Peace, 1956–1961,* 265–89.

ministration questioned the wisdom of bringing a case between two Arab nations to a non-Arab body in the first instance. Consequently, during the first half of May the State Department took no position on the question of an approach to the UN. At the same time, the department directed Lodge to work with the Lebanese to help them prepare as "airtight" a case as possible.[4]

On May 22, the Lebanese representative to the UN requested an urgent meeting of the Security Council to consider the question of intervention by the United Arab Republic in the internal affairs of Lebanon. When the Arab League (to which it had addressed a similar letter the previous day) placed the item on the agenda of its May 31 meeting, Lebanon requested the Security Council to postpone consideration of the problem. Once it became apparent that the Arab League would not be able to resolve the situation to its satisfaction, Lebanon asked the Security Council to commence its deliberations.

Lebanese foreign minister Charles Malik presented his nation's complaint to the Security Council on June 6. He alleged that the UAR had supplied arms and training to subversive elements, waged a press and radio campaign against Lebanon, and participated in directing the rebellion. Omar Loutfi, the UAR representative, heatedly denied the charges. Speaking for the United States, Deputy Representative to the Security Council James Barco urged the body to take the situation under consideration. The Soviet delegate, backing the UAR, maintained that Malik had not furnished sufficient proof of external interference.[5]

A proposal for UN involvement offered a way to break the superpower deadlock. On June 10, 1958, Sweden submitted a resolution asking the Security Council to dispatch a neutral observation group to Lebanon "to ensure that there is no illegal infiltration of personnel or supply of arms or other material across the Lebanese borders," and the council adopted it on June 11. Hammarskjöld appointed three men—Galo Plaza, former president of Ecuador; Rajeshwar Dayal, former representative of India to the UN; and Ma-

---

4. Memorandum from Colonel D. J. Decker of the Joint Middle East Planning Committee of the Joint Chiefs of Staff to the Chief of Naval Operations (Admiral Arleigh A. Burke), May 19, 1958, in *FRUS, 1958–1960,* XI, 64.

5. For Malik's and Loutfi's statements, see Agwani, *The Lebanese Crisis, 1958,* 122–59. For Barco's statement, see "U. N. Security Council Sends Observation Group to Lebanon," *Department of State Bulletin,* July 14, 1958, p. 88.

jor General Odd Bull of Norway—to head the UN team, which by June 24 numbered ninety-four military observers from eleven member nations. At its height, the UN Observer Group in Lebanon (UNOGIL) consisted of 591 military personnel and 118 support staff. From the beginning, the United States urged rapid deployment and expansion of the group. Dulles even mused about the possibility of intervention by a UN multinational force, similar to the UN force in Korea.[6]

The formation of UNOGIL eased tensions somewhat. Eisenhower and Dulles shared the widespread, though unrealistic, hope that the UN team would be able to prevent further infiltration of arms and rebels across the Syrian-Lebanese border. Unfortunately, UNOGIL quickly discovered that it was impossible to seal the border completely; it had neither the authority nor the power to stop infiltration or seize supplies. The UN resolution and UNOGIL's presence marginally increased the Chamoun government's confidence, but Chamoun refused to disavow the possible need for future assistance from other nations. Peace reigned for the time being, but Dulles remained vaguely uncomfortable, feeling that "we are pawns in a political game we do not understand very well."[7]

UNOGIL introduced a new factor into the Lebanese equation. Eisenhower realized that it would be exceedingly difficult to justify unilateral intervention until UNOGIL had issued a report that corroborated the Lebanese charges of UAR penetration. As Dulles noted, the United States had at least to "pay some respect to the UN effort which Lebanon itself invoked and with the results of which it professed to be satisfied." The administration decided that, ideally, the United States would not intervene until after the USSR had vetoed a Security Council resolution to establish an armed UN force, the Uniting for Peace resolution had been invoked, and the General Assembly had approved the use of force. At a minimum, any U.S. action must await an emergency Security Council session at which the Chamoun government argued convincingly that its opponents were trying to destroy

6. "U. N. Security Council Sends Observation Group to Lebanon," Lodge statements in the Security Council on June 10, 11, 1958, *Department of State Bulletin,* July 14, 1958, pp. 88–90; *MTCD,* Reel 7, Dulles and Lodge, June 11, 1958; Dulles press conference, June 17, 1958, *Department of State Bulletin,* July 1, 1958, p. 8; Alin, *The United States and the 1958 Lebanon Crisis,* 90.

7. *MTCD,* Reel 7, Dulles and Rountree, June 15, 1958.

Lebanese independence before an adequate UN force could be introduced, thus justifying immediate intervention by nations with property and lives to protect. Recognition that Congress would be more likely to support intervention on behalf of the UN reinforced the administration's resolve to obtain UN sanction.[8]

Yet the administration's ambivalence about relying on the UN was apparent from the outset. As early as June 17, Dulles instructed State Department officials to begin planning strategy and tactics for presenting the American case at the UN in the event of unilateral intervention. Eisenhower too avoided a wholehearted endorsement of the UN effort. At a June 18 press conference, the president would pledge only that a U.S. decision to intervene militarily would be "dependent somewhat" upon conclusions reached by UNOGIL and Hammarskjöld. By June 20, less than ten days after the Security Council had passed the resolution authorizing UNOGIL's formation, John Foster Dulles was already complaining to his brother Allen that the situation was "slowly disintegrating" and that Hammarskjöld was "not bucking it up very much."[9]

Still, Dulles opposed taking the next step within the UN framework. When the British government proposed asking Chamoun to request a UN military force for Lebanon, Dulles demurred, citing the uncertainty of Hammarskjöld's response and the possibility that Chamoun might conclude that the Western powers were vacillating on their commitment to him. Dulles thus gradually concluded that, if requested by Chamoun, the United States would have to intervene, with or without UN approval. A larger issue—the credibility of the American commitment to its allies, from Pakistan to Vietnam and China—was at stake.[10]

---

8. Telegram from Dulles to the U.S. embassy in Lebanon, June 15, 1958, in *FRUS, 1958–1960,* XI, 129; Memorandum of a Conversation, June 15, 1958, same volume, 130–32; Memorandum of a Conversation, June 15, 1958, same volume, 133–37; Memorandum for the Record by the Secretary of State's Special Assistant (Greene), June 17, 1958, same volume, 148–49.

9. President's press conference of June 18, 1958, in Box 7, Press Conference Series, EP, AWF, EL; Memorandum of a Telephone Conversation, June 20, 1958, in *FRUS, 1958–1960,* XI, 163; Memorandum for the Record by the Secretary of State's Special Assistant (Greene), June 17, 1958, same volume, 148–49.

10. Memorandum of a Conversation, June 20, 1958, in *FRUS, 1958–1960,* XI, 164–65; Little, "His Finest Hour?," 42.

Painfully aware of the distrustful atmosphere at the UN, Lodge warned about the drawbacks of such action. Unilateral intervention would gravely jeopardize the nation's post-Suez prestige, particularly in the Arab world. He suggested that the United States instead step up its effort to achieve a political compromise within Lebanon. Taken aback, Dulles expressed concern that he and Lodge were "working a little bit at cross-purposes." Lodge maintained that he was carrying out the secretary's instructions, but Dulles nevertheless condescendingly reminded him that a refusal to intervene would have worldwide ramifications. Lodge could only insist that he would need access to all the administration's information in order to build a compelling case for the U.S. charge of Communist subversion.[11]

UNOGIL's leaders reached a preliminary conclusion when the group held its first formal meetings with Hammarskjöld in Beirut on June 19 and 20. They concluded, in the words of Plaza, that "the world is being taken for a ride." Finding little evidence of substantive UAR involvement, they asserted that the situation was one of internal strife generated by Chamoun's insistence on seeking another term as president. UNOGIL's official report on July 3 took the same stance. The administration realized that, if made public, the report would "explode the whole government case" and make it difficult, if not impossible, to obtain UN legitimation of unilateral intervention. It was useless to press the matter at the UN for the moment, since the United States would not get the necessary seven votes in the Security Council as long as Hammarskjöld claimed that the UN effort might succeed.[12]

Buoyed by the observers' report, Hammarskjöld opposed Chamoun's desire to strengthen the UN position with military forces. The secretary-general explained that he could not form an adequate force from among the smaller countries to patrol the border, and he did not want to call upon the larger ones. More important, he insisted that a military force was unnecessary. The UN observers could produce a stalemate in the civil conflict and gradually immobilize the agitators by depriving them of outside backing. The Lebanese would then have to settle the political situation themselves. Although recognizing the somewhat precarious health of the Lebanese re-

11. *MTCD*, Reel 7, Dulles and Lodge, June 20, 1958; Memorandum of a Conversation, June 22, 1958, in *FRUS, 1958–1960*, XI, 166–68; Lodge to Dulles, June 23, 1958, same volume, 168–69.

12. Memorandum, Lodge to the Secretary of State, June 26, 1958, in *FRUS, 1958–1960*, XI, 175–76.

public, he expressed his hope to Lodge "that anxious friends will stay out of the sickroom" and permit the patient to recover on its own.[13]

The administration split in its reaction to UNOGIL's report and Hammarskjöld's assessment. Lodge agreed with Hammarskjöld's diagnosis and his prescription for recovery in Lebanon. The secretary-general's cautious optimism was encouraging, Lodge reassured Eisenhower at a breakfast meeting on June 27. His efforts to calm the president notwithstanding, Lodge must have known that Chamoun would reject UNOGIL's conclusions. Indeed, Chamoun and Malik asserted that the UN team had not detected significant infiltration because it did not work at night, when border crossings were most frequent.[14]

Dulles shared Chamoun's skepticism. Convinced that Hammarskjöld was "getting out of step" with the United States, Dulles invited him for lunch in Washington on July 7. At the meeting, Hammarskjöld informed Dulles that during his recent week of shuttle diplomacy between Beirut and Cairo both sides had indicated a willingness to compromise. He suggested extending UN protection to a permanent basis by stationing a small group of UN observers in Beirut. Dulles and William M. Rountree (assistant secretary of state for Near Eastern, South Asian, and African affairs) were interested, but they perceived the measure to be useful only after the present crisis had passed. In the meantime, they agreed at least to enlarge the observation force. Hammarskjöld left persuaded that "American policy has become almost parallel to the UN."[15] Within the week, however, the United States and the United Nations would be working at cross-purposes.

The administration's ambivalence about intervening without UN sanction disappeared in the aftermath of a violent coup in Iraq. On July 14 a group of army officers assassinated Iraqi king Faisal II and his pro-Western prime minister. Fearing that the coup would spark disorder in Lebanon, President Chamoun officially and urgently asked the U.S. government for

13. Urquhart, *Hammarskjöld,* 269; Telegram from Lodge to the Secretary of State, June 25, 1958, 310.5/6–2258, in Box 1243, RG 59, NA.

14. Diary entry, June 27, 1958, in folder marked "June 1958 (1)," Box 10, Ann C. Whitman Diary, EP, AWF, EL.

15. Eisenhower and Dulles, July 2, 1958, in folder marked "Telephone Calls—July 1958," Box 34, DDE Diary Series, EP, AWF, EL; Hammarskjöld, quoted in Little, "His Finest Hour?," 43; Memorandum of a Conversation, July 7, 1958, in *FRUS, 1958–1960,* XI, 200–201; Memorandum of a Conversation, July 7, 1958, same volume, 202.

military assistance. The situation, Dulles informed Hammarskjöld at 1:30 P.M. on July 14, had been "radically altered" by the new events.[16] Invoking the Eisenhower Doctrine, the president quickly determined to intervene. The U.S. Sixth Fleet sailed for Beirut, and the first detachment of an ultimate contingent of almost fifteen thousand Marines splashed ashore on July 15, to the surprise of sunbathers on Ouzai Beach.

Despite Eisenhower's repeated declaration of his belief in multilateral diplomacy, the administration acted without consulting the UN. Indeed, the president intervened fully cognizant that, as he confided to Macmillan, he was "opening a Pandora's Box." He had decided that if the UN condemned the intervention, then the United States would simply withdraw. Until then, it had to act.[17] Dulles wished that action could have awaited UN approval, but he concluded that "the losses from doing nothing would be worse than the losses from action." With his finger ever on the nation's political pulse, Nixon concurred, asserting that there would be "nothing worse internationally or domestically than waiting for the UN."[18]

The administration moved quickly to determine its strategy at the United Nations. Eisenhower ordered an immediate radio search to pick up Lodge, cruising in his boat off the coast of Maine. Dulles requested Lebanon to call an urgent meeting of the Security Council for Tuesday at 10:30, shortly after the landing of the first battalion of U.S. Marines. The U.S. delegation was directed to report on U.S. actions and, Eisenhower insisted, to emphasize that the United States had gone in "to stabilize the situation until the United Nations can act." Second, the delegation was to deter any Security Council action that "might inhibit military efforts." Finally, it was to persuade the Lebanese delegate to express appreciation for the efforts of UNOGIL, state its hope that the UN would send military forces to bolster the observer group, and explain that the increased tumult in the region had compelled it to request U.S. assistance.[19]

16. Memorandum of a Telephone Conversation, July 14, 1958, in *FRUS, 1958–1960,* XI, 217.

17. *Ibid.,* 233; Memorandum of a Conference with the President, *FRUS, 1958–1960,* XI, 226–28.

18. Memorandum of a Conference with the President, July 14, 1958, in *FRUS, 1958–1960,* XI, 213; *MTCD,* Reel 7, Dulles and Nixon, July 15, 1958.

19. Memorandum of a Conference with the President, July 14, 1958, in *FRUS, 1958–1960,* XI, 227; Telegram from Dulles to the Mission at the United Nations, July 14, 1958, same volume, 236; *MTCD,* Reel 7, Dulles and Lodge, July 14, 1958.

The United States took immediate precautions to defuse the anticipated UN outrage. Relying particularly heavily on legal arguments, the administration implied that it was acting in accord with Article 51 of the UN Charter, under which member states can act on an emergency basis pending UN action (though many questioned whether Article 51 could be applied to indirect aggression) and would defer to the UN once that body had acted. Clearly, it still hoped that the UN could provide an "umbrella" to cover the U.S. intervention and minimize comparisons with British intervention in the Suez.[20]

Recognizing that Hammarskjöld provided the key to much of the uncommitted sentiment in the UN, the administration sought to convince the secretary-general of the necessity of short-term American intervention. Lodge faced a difficult task. He later recalled that when he informed Hammarskjöld at a 9:30 A.M. meeting on July 15 that American troops were landing in Lebanon, Hammarskjöld's face "first became pink and then flushed to red," and he condemned the action as legally indefensible. Although he described the private meeting as "memorable," Lodge reported to Dulles that Hammarskjöld had not reacted as badly as he had expected. The State Department authorized Lodge to provide the secretary-general with information indicating that the UAR was providing military assistance to the Lebanese opposition, but Hammarskjöld remained unpersuaded.[21]

The administration closely coordinated its strategy in the UN with Britain, which had undertaken similar action in Jordan on July 17. Still wounded by the Suez Canal incident and eager for even indirect retribution against Nasser, Britain sought assurances of U.S. support in the UN and logistical assistance in Jordan. Eisenhower and Dulles pledged their backing in the UN, but they wanted to keep the matters of intervention in Lebanon and Jordan separate in the world body.[22]

In addressing both the domestic and international audiences, the administration emphasized that it intended to cooperate with the United Nations. President Eisenhower released a statement on July 15 at 9:00 A.M., timed to

---

20. Memorandum for the Record of a Meeting, July 14, 1958, in *FRUS, 1958–1960*, XI, 211; Alin, *The United States and the 1958 Lebanon Crisis,* 111–12.

21. Lodge, *The Storm Has Many Eyes,* 138; *MTCD,* Reel 7, Dulles and Lodge, July 16, 1958, 1:16 P.M.; Telegram from Dulles to the Mission at the United Nations, July 16, 1958, in *FRUS, 1958–1960,* XI, 258.

22. Memorandum of a Telephone Conversation, July 16, 1958, in *FRUS, 1958–1960,* XI, 316; Memorandum of a Conversation, July 17, 1958, same volume, 317–18.

coincide with the initial landing, in which he announced that the Marines were in Lebanon only until the UN could take over. Expounding on his statement in an address to the nation that night, Eisenhower insisted that the "United States does not, of course, intend to replace the United Nations" in ensuring Lebanon's security. Its prompt action on the military front was matched, the president contended, by its efforts at the United Nations. Once again, he invoked the UN to provide legal sanction.[23]

Lodge bore the burden of explaining and defending American intervention at the UN, this despite having been provided with no hard evidence to make his case. And a burden it was. As he recalled in his memoirs, he was "more perplexed than I had ever been at the United Nations—before or since—on just how to deal with the problem. I had no proof of interference. I decided to base my case on generalities." Lodge echoed the president's central theme in an address to the Security Council later that morning. The UN observer group had achieved at least limited success, but it had not obviated the need for stronger action, particularly in light of the violent coup in Iraq. The United States thus had intervened only "to stabilize the situation . . . until such time as the United Nations can take the steps necessary to protect the independence and political integrity of Lebanon," Lodge notified the skeptical Security Council. American intervention was not a departure from its stated position of support for a UN solution, but was designed only as a stopgap measure, until UNOGIL could be sufficiently strengthened to make an American withdrawal possible.[24]

Not satisfied with Lodge's apprehensive support, Dulles sought to bolster the U.S. mission to the UN. He repeatedly called Lodge, whom he believed needed "bucking up," and he became intimately involved in determining strategy and even tactics in the UN. Despite Lebanese fears that the United States was moving too precipitously to turn over military control to the UN, Dulles proceeded with a plan to preserve Lebanese independence by having a "UN mantle cast over Lebanon." He even contemplated creating a separate

23. Statement Following the Landing of United States Marines at Beirut, July 15, 1959, in *Public Papers of the Presidents: Dwight D. Eisenhower, 1958,* 553; Dowty, *Middle East Crisis,* 63–65.

24. Lodge, *The Storm Has Many Eyes,* 139; "The Lebanese Complaint in the Security Council," Lodge statement in the Security Council on July 15, 1958, *Department of State Bulletin,* August 4, 1958, p. 186; Afternoon Summary, July 15, 1958, Reel 100, State Department Microfilm, J. F. Dulles Papers, Mudd Library.

and independent status for Lebanon, unconnected to the UAR, and making it a ward of the UN.[25]

The first step was to reassert UN control over the situation. On July 17, the United States, with Hammarskjöld's prior approval, introduced a draft resolution to the Security Council that requested UNOGIL to continue its work and called on the UN to take additional measures, including the use of military contingents, to defend Lebanon. Lodge warned that a UN failure to halt indirect aggression might lead to the breakup of the organization. Also on July 17, the Soviet Union introduced a draft resolution that demanded a cessation of Anglo-American armed intervention and a withdrawal of foreign forces. The Security Council defeated the Soviet resolution by a vote of 8 to 1, with 2 abstentions. The American resolution then received 9 votes in favor, but was vetoed by the USSR.[26]

Eisenhower and Dulles next considered requesting an emergency session of the General Assembly. The British government and Hammarskjöld opposed a meeting. But the administration decided that taking the initiative in moving the debate to the General Assembly, might, as a "bucked up" Lodge shrewdly suggested, help sustain the "look of sincerity" presently enjoyed as a result of the nation's pledge "to lay down our burden when the UN takes over."[27]

On July 18 the U.S. delegation thus presented a resolution calling for an emergency special session of the General Assembly to consider the Lebanese complaint of aggression by the UAR. The Soviets countered with a resolution calling for an emergency session to consider the intervention of the United States and the United Kingdom in Lebanon and Jordan. The council deferred a vote on both resolutions until it had considered a Japanese compromise that requested the secretary-general to strengthen UNOGIL in order to facilitate the withdrawal of American troops.

25. *MTCD,* Reel 10, Dulles and Eisenhower, July 17, 1958, White House Telephone Conversations; Memorandum of a Conversation, July 19, 1958, in *FRUS, 1958–1960,* XI, 336.

26. "The Lebanese Complaint in the Security Council," Lodge statements in the Security Council on July 16, 17, 1958, *Department of State Bulletin,* August 4, 1958, pp. 189–96.

27. *MTCD,* Reel 7, Dulles and Lodge, July 16, 1958, 9:45 A.M.; Notes of a Telephone Conversation, July 16, 1958, in *FRUS, 1958–1960,* XI, 252; Afternoon summary, July 16, 1958, Reel 100, State Department Microfilm, J. F. Dulles Papers, Mudd Library; Telegram from Dulles to the U.S. embassy in the United Kingdom, July 18, 1958, in *FRUS, 1958–1960,* XI, 325–26.

The Japanese compromise attempt failed. On July 22 the Security Council voted 10 to 1 in favor, but the sole opposing vote, a Soviet veto, produced a stalemate. According to a plan prearranged with Lodge, Hammarskjöld then announced that he would exercise his authority to expand the activities of UNOGIL and take other steps under the provisions of the Charter and the resolution of June 11. Grateful for his efforts, Dulles arranged a transfer of $8 million from Mutual Security Act funds to help finance the expanded operation.[28]

On July 19, Khrushchev attempted to make the most of the unsettled situation by issuing another of his periodic calls for a summit meeting. Khrushchev proposed that the heads of government of the USSR, the United States, Britain, France, and India, and the secretary-general meet in Geneva on July 22 to consider the threat to the peace in the Near and Middle East. The idea sparked intense discussion within the Western alliance. Dulles and Eisenhower opposed Indian inclusion as well as the broader concept of a summit that would provide another forum for Soviet charges of illegal U.S. aggression in Lebanon. They insisted that they would attend a summit meeting only if the Middle East was simply one of many problems discussed. Eisenhower justified his opposition on the grounds that the five nations should not arrogate to themselves the power to make decisions that were the prerogative of the entire UN membership. The administration reluctantly proffered the alternative, already gaining currency because of British acceptance and growing public support, for a Security Council meeting attended by the heads of government.[29]

On July 23, 1958, Khrushchev sent Eisenhower a second letter, in which he agreed to hold a summit within the framework of the Security Council. Eisenhower initially approved this plan, hoping that it would "terminate the exchange," which was "giving him [Khrushchev] the center of the stage, and

28. Dulles and Lodge, July 19, 1958, 4:09 P.M., in folder marked "Memoranda of Telephone Conversations—General: June 2, 1958 to July 31, 1958 (2)," Box 8, Telephone Conversation Series, Dulles Papers, EL; Staff Notes, July 19, 1958, in folder marked "Toner Notes—July 1958," Box 34, DDE Diary Series, EP, AWF, EL.

29. Memorandum of a Conference with the President, July 20, 1958, in *FRUS, 1958–1960*, XI, 347–50; Dulles and Lodge, July 21, 1958, 9:07 A.M., in folder marked "Memoranda of Telephone Conversations—General: June 2, 1958 to July 31, 1958 (2)," Box 8, Telephone Conversation Series, Dulles Papers, EL; Letter to Nikita Khrushchev, July 22, 1958, in *Public Papers of the Presidents: Dwight D. Eisenhower, 1958*, 560–64.

... a large voice in Mid-East affairs." Dulles cautioned his chief, however, that since "the United Nations approach tends so much to be one of compromise and 'trimming,'" it would not be wise to "trust everything to them [the UN], or give them carte blanche." On the defensive and eager to put to rest the notion that the Soviet Union was a major player in Middle Eastern diplomacy, the administration now sought additional changes in both the format and the subject matter of the meeting.[30]

On July 28, Khrushchev wrote again, reiterating his call for a meeting to be held under the auspices of the secretary-general. Lodge urged Dulles to accept the challenge and use a conference to respond positively to the constructive elements of Arab nationalism, perhaps by proposing an economic development plan for the region. Eisenhower replied on August 1. He insisted that the United States would not participate in a Great Power conference that bypassed the UN. The president agreed, however, to discuss the problem of indirect aggression in the Middle East at a Security Council meeting attended by the heads of government, beginning as early as August 12.[31]

Khrushchev sent Eisenhower a final missive regarding a summit meeting on August 5. The Soviet premier dropped his demand for a meeting of the heads of government and called instead for an emergency session of the General Assembly to discuss the immediate withdrawal of Anglo-American troops from Lebanon and Jordan. Charging that the Security Council had not demonstrated sufficient independence, he urged that the venue be shifted to the General Assembly.

Khrushchev's August 5 letter convinced the administration to seize the initiative in the General Assembly. From the beginning of the crisis, the United States had anxiously sought to avoid a meeting without giving the impression that it doubted its ability to obtain assembly support for its actions in Lebanon. Since Khrushchev's proposal made a resort to the General Assembly appear inevitable, the administration decided to launch the movement. A preemptive maneuver might provide an aura of legitimacy, however illusory, for its actions, preserve American world leadership and

30. Memorandum of a Conference with the President, July 24, 1958, in folder marked "Staff Memos—July 1958 (1)," Box 35, DDE Diary Series, EP, AWF, EL.

31. *MTCD,* Reel 7, Dulles and Nixon, July 29, 1958; *MTCD,* Reel 7, Dulles and Lodge, July 31, 1958; Letter to Nikita Khrushchev, August 1, 1958, in *Public Papers of the Presidents: Dwight D. Eisenhower, 1958,* 577–79.

prestige, and demonstrate that the administration did not fear a General Assembly meeting. Despite British reluctance, Eisenhower released a statement on August 5 in which he welcomed Khrushchev's agreement to proceed to the General Assembly.[32]

On the following day both Lodge and the Soviet representative presented resolutions in the Security Council calling for an emergency special session of the General Assembly. In a skillful parliamentary maneuver, Lodge insisted that his resolution, introduced on July 18 but not pressed to a vote at that time, had priority. The council adopted the U.S. resolution, which simply called upon the General Assembly to assume responsibility for the maintenance of peace and security in light of the Security Council's lack of unanimity.

The emergency General Assembly session convened on August 8; fifteen meetings were held over the next two weeks. Attesting to the importance placed on the session, Eisenhower resolved to deliver an address to the assembly—his first since the Atoms for Peace speech in December, 1953. A consensus was quickly reached that the president should deliver a lofty and wide-ranging speech. But the specific content became the subject of intense intra-administration debate. C. D. Jackson was brought in at Eisenhower's request to assume command of the effort, but most of the president's advisers participated in the drafting process, and the administration even consulted Hammarskjöld. Concerned uppermost with the domestic audience, Jackson led a group that desired to take the offensive, denouncing the indirect aggression masterminded by the Communists. He advocated a strong speech, "projected with a force that reaches down to the last bedouin, the last impassioned Arab egghead." Ever conscious of the UN audience, Lodge, supported most staunchly by Allen Dulles, urged the president to take the high road—defending U.S. intervention, but focusing primarily on outlining a constructive program for the Middle East.[33]

32. *MTCD,* Reel 7, Dulles and Lodge, July 21, 1958; Dulles and Lodge, July 21, 1958, in folder marked "Memoranda of Telephone Conversations—General: June 2, 1958 to July 31, 1958 (2)," Box 8, Telephone Conversation Series, Dulles Papers, EL; Memorandum of Conference with the President, August 5, 1958, in folder marked "August 1958—Staff Notes (3)," Box 35, DDE Diary Series, EP, AWF, EL; *MTCD,* Reel 8, Dulles and Herter, August 5, 1958.

33. Jackson, quoted in Alin, *The United States and the 1958 Lebanon Crisis,* 128; Memorandum of a Conversation, August 8, 1958, in *FRUS, 1958–1960,* XI, 444; *MTCD,* Reel 8, Lodge and Dulles, August 8, 1958, 8:44 A.M. and 6:40 P.M.; Log: July 24 to August 13, 1958—Near

Eisenhower took a middle position in his August 13 address. Although he denounced regional subversion, he highlighted the legal and political justification for intervention, outlined a six-point peace plan, proposed an economic development plan, and announced that U.S. troops would be withdrawn if Lebanon so requested. The General Assembly debate was remarkably moderate and nonpolemical. The atmosphere was due in large part to the fact that a political settlement had already been arranged in Lebanon by Deputy Undersecretary of State Robert Murphy. According to the three-part settlement (ironically, quite similar to one proposed by Nasser in June), Chamoun agreed not to seek a second term, the Lebanese parliament elected a new president—General Fuad Chehab, a moderate nationalist acceptable to all factions—and the opposition to Chamoun was granted amnesty. Nevertheless, the General Assembly pressured the United States to agree to a formula for removing its troops.

For much of the session, Dulles personally orchestrated the negotiations, engaging in unceasing behind-the-scenes diplomacy. It was an uncomfortable position, for as he admitted to Jackson, he was "fighting a defensive rather than an offensive battle."[34] Still, Soviet foreign minister Gromyko's relatively conciliatory attitude, dictated by the Soviet Union's desire to ameliorate superpower tensions over the test-ban treaty negotiations in Geneva, made a compromise solution possible.

Dulles and Lodge persuaded Hans Engen, the head of the Norwegian delegation, to lead the compromise effort. Engen introduced a general resolution that called upon all states to protect Lebanon's independence and asked the secretary-general to make arrangements to uphold the principles of the UN Charter in Lebanon and Jordan. It did not explicitly mention the withdrawal of American forces, though all involved understood that the United States intended to pull out as soon as the UN had established some sort of semi-permanent presence in Lebanon. Indeed, on August 18 the

---

East Crisis, in folder marked "Log: 1958," Box 57, Jackson Papers, EL; *MTCD,* Reel 10, Dulles and Eisenhower, August 9, 1958, White House Telephone Calls; *MTCD,* Reel 8, Dulles and Hammarskjöld, August 10, 1958; *MTCD,* Reel 8, Dulles and Lodge, August 11, 1958, 1:07 P.M. and 5:24 P.M.; Memorandum of a Conference with the President, August 11, 1958, in folder marked "August 1958—Staff Notes (2)," Box 35, DDE Diary Series, EP, AWF, EL; Memorandum of a Conference with the President, August 12, 1958, in folder marked "August 1958: Staff Notes (2)," Box 35, DDE Diary Series, EP, AWF, EL.

34. *MTCD,* Reel 8, Dulles and Jackson, August 19, 1958.

United States and Britain announced that they would withdraw their troops if the UN took steps to maintain peace in the region. The Norwegian resolution was thus primarily a way for the United States to save face.[35]

After all of Dulles's work, at the last moment the faction-ridden Arab bloc temporarily united to prepare an alternative resolution. The Arab proposition requested all members to respect each others' territorial integrity and petitioned the secretary-general to make arrangements to uphold the Charter and facilitate U.S. withdrawal. Although Dulles did not want to strengthen the Arab bloc or the Arab League, which he criticized as "a bad organization," he reluctantly decided to vote for the resolution. In an address to the assembly on August 21, he admitted that the United States preferred the language and form of the Norwegian resolution (because it had not explicitly called for American withdrawal and had implicitly endorsed the Anglo-American action), but noted that the substance of the two resolutions was similar. Privately, the administration realized that Arab sponsorship of the final resolution actually might be beneficial, since the Arab nations might be more willing to abide by self-imposed conditions. Moreover, since the United States planned to withdraw anyway, it had no substantive impact. Later that day, the General Assembly unanimously adopted the Arab resolution and transferred the burden of implementation to the secretary-general.[36]

On September 29, Hammarskjöld reported to the General Assembly on his progress in achieving the goals of the August 21 resolution—political stability and the withdrawal of Anglo-American military forces. He noted that Lebanon had agreed to a temporary expansion of UNOGIL to speed the withdrawal. In regard to Jordan, an agreement had been reached to station a personal representative of the secretary-general there to report on implementation of the resolution.

35. *MTCD*, Reel 8, Dulles and Herter, August 13, 1958; Memorandum of a Telephone Conversation, August 14, 1958, 12:54 P.M., in *FRUS, 1958–1960*, XI, 474; *MTCD*, Reel 10, Dulles and Eisenhower, August 17, 1958, White House Telephone Calls; *MTCD*, Reel 8, Dulles and Herter, August 18, 1958, 9:40 A.M.; Telegram from Dulles to the Department of State, August 18, 1958, in *FRUS, 1958–1960*, XI, 488–91; Memorandum of a Conversation, August 18, 1958, same volume, 495–501.

36. *MTCD*, Reel 10, Dulles and Hagerty, August 21, 1958, White House Telephone Conversations; "General Assembly Emergency Session Adopts Arab Resolution on the Middle East," Dulles statement in the General Assembly on August 21, 1958, *Department of State*

Throughout the secretary-general's negotiations, the United States had effectively used the Arab resolution to disengage cautiously from the situation. The administration had, for example, insisted that any new evidence uncovered of UAR penetration be presented to the secretary-general, not the United States, and it denied Jordanian requests for U.S. financing of the addition of two new brigades to the nation's army.[37] The United States sought to remove its remaining forces without leaving the impression that it was doing so at the behest of either the UN or Lebanon. On October 24, 1958, it finally withdrew, and UNOGIL ceased its operation on December 9, 1958.[38]

As it had in Guatemala in 1954, the Eisenhower administration had once again charged Communist subversion in its public rhetoric, despite private acknowledgment that the revolutionary nationalism of Nasser posed a larger threat. Similarly, the administration's intervention in Lebanon ultimately redounded to the discredit of the United States, for Arab nationalism bristled at this stark display of anachronistic "gunboat diplomacy." But once again, the administration relied on skillful and superior parliamentary maneuvering to justify its actions and prevent the UN from passing a resolution of condemnation or even criticism. In fact, it adroitly used the UN to ratify U.S. intervention. The United States chose not to use the UN more substantively because it was convinced that it could manage the situation more expeditiously on its own, without danger of Soviet intervention.

But at the same time, the United Nations had become an important enough arena that the administration could not bypass the organization entirely. Instead, it astutely used the UN to extricate itself from the Lebanese tangle. Operating on the maxim that the best defense is a good offense, it launched initiatives in the Security Council and the General Assembly. As Lodge later recalled, the Lebanon situation was the "most complicated, arduous, the most difficult thing" because "we had no facts we could use there. It involved tactics, technique, what in the Senate you would call filibus-

---

Bulletin, September 15, 1958, pp. 409–11; *MTCD,* Reel 10, Dulles and Eisenhower, September 16, 1958, White House Telephone Conversations.

37. Memorandum of a Telephone Conversation, August 23, 1958, in *FRUS, 1958–1960,* XI, 519; Telegram from Dulles to the U.S. embassy in Jordan, October 2, 1958, same volume, 592.

38. Dulles and Herter, September 17, 1958, transcript of telephone conversation, in *FRUS, 1958–1960,* XI, 571 n. 4; Memorandum of a Telephone Conversation, September 19, 1958, same volume, 574–75.

tering."[39] Dulles, employing his expertise in the legal technicalities, and Lodge, displaying his mastery of verbal damage control, devised essentially face-saving resolutions and mustered majority votes for their passage that enabled the United States to withdraw after having accomplished its objectives by means of unilateral action.

The American response to a similar situation of unrest in the Congo provides an illuminating counterpoint to the nation's reaction in Lebanon.[40] In contrast to the United States' close involvement in the Middle East and in Lebanon in particular, the Congo existed on the periphery of the region courted by the superpowers. Yet the situation combined, at least potentially, the problems and perils of both decolonization and the cold war.

The Congo problem arose during the final months of the Eisenhower era, a period in which the formation of American policy toward the UN altered considerably. Dulles's resignation and death in May, 1959, had fundamentally changed the White House–State Department–USUN relationship in this regard. While Dulles's successor, former undersecretary of state Christian A. Herter, was eminently qualified and had Eisenhower's confidence, there was not sufficient time left to develop the working, not to mention the personal, relationships that had existed at the highest levels of the foreign policy decision-making apparatus among the president, his first secretary of state, and his ambassador to the UN. Moreover, Lodge's nomination for the vice presidency in 1960 undermined his ability to focus on UN matters. His subsequent resignation at the start of the fall campaign brought another player, Wadsworth, to the forefront of the policy-making debate. Thus, the lack of a coordinated, comfortable team put even more pressure on the oldest president ever (up to that time) as he tried to formulate a coherent policy

39. Interview with Richard D. Challener, in folder marked "John Foster Dulles—Oral History Project," Box 92, HCLP, MHS.

40. For secondary accounts, see Madeline G. Kalb, *The Congo Cables: The Cold War in Africa—From Eisenhower to Kennedy* (New York, 1982); Stephen R. Weissman, *American Foreign Policy in the Congo, 1960–1964* (Ithaca, 1974); Ernest W. Lefever, *Crisis in the Congo: A United Nations Force in Action* (Washington, D.C., 1965); Conor Cruise O'Brien and Feliks Topolski, *The United Nations: Sacred Drama* (New York, 1968); George Abi-Saab, *The United Nations Operation in the Congo, 1960–1964* (Oxford, 1978); Arthur H. House, *The U.N. in the Congo: The Political and Civilian Efforts* (Washington, D.C., 1978); D. Katete Orwa, "Responses of the United Nations and the United States to the Congo Crisis: Events and Issues" (Ph.D. dissertation, University of Akron, 1979); James Edward Winkates, "The Influence of

in the waning months of his time in power. Further complicating the effort, this struggle occurred in the midst of the battle over who would exercise that presidential power in the future. All of this, combined with the differences inherent in the Congo Crisis, made that situation unlike virtually any other the administration had previously faced. The resulting lack of resolve and intra-administration coordination became increasingly apparent as the crisis deepened.

The Congo problem had developed during the early months of 1960. In response to rising nationalism throughout the Congo and bloody riots in Léopoldville, Belgium promised its colony full independence on June 30, 1960. Before that time, the United States had had little interest in the region. Viewing the central African region as falling within the European sphere of influence, the Eisenhower administration had lacked a detailed and well-formulated policy toward the Belgian territory. In fact, the State Department did not establish a separate Bureau of African Affairs until July, 1958, and even then it was staffed primarily by people with European experience. As Eisenhower conceded in September, 1960, the administration had been caught in a difficult position because it "had always said to Britain and France and Belgium that those governments were the ones who would have to look after African situations. . . . Therefore we in the United States are comparatively ignorant about the African situation except for academic reports we have had." The administration knew that the political situation was potentially volatile on the eve of independence, with dozens of small parties still in their infancy. Nevertheless, the administration still lacked a plan of action to handle possible disorder.[41]

The new nation enjoyed only a brief period of celebration. On July 5, but five days after the inaugural ceremony, units of the Congolese army rebelled against their Belgian officers. In violation of the Belgian-Congolese Treaty of Friendship of 1960, Belgium sent paratroopers into the Congo—most of them going to the mineral-rich province of Katanga—in a supposed attempt to quell the civil strife and protect Europeans and foreign investments. The following day, Katanga, led by Moise Tshombe, announced its secession and

---

the United Nations on National Policy: The United States in the Congo Crisis" (Ph.D. dissertation, University of Virginia, 1972).

41. Pre-press conference notes for September 7, 1960, in Box 10, Press Conference Series, EP, AWF, EL; Editorial note, in *FRUS, 1955–1957,* XIV, 274; Weissman, *American Foreign Policy in the Congo, 1960–1964,* 43, 50.

requested Belgian military assistance. The central government of Prime Minister Patrice Lumumba, the former head of the independence movement, and President Joseph Kasavubu, Lumumba's chief rival and a more moderate nationalist, protested Katanga's secession. Congo officials approached the U.S. ambassador, Clare M. Timberlake, for military assistance in repulsing Belgian aggression. Timberlake refused. Believing that a UN role would keep out the Soviets, he advised an appeal to Ralph Bunche, UN undersecretary-general, who was then in the Congo. "This should keep bears out of the Congo caviar," he predicted.[42]

Eisenhower and Herter fully backed their ambassador. The United States, Herter assured Hammarskjöld, did "not want to do a single thing which we do not do under UN auspices." As a solely precautionary measure, the United States had dispatched an aircraft carrier to stand by off the coast, but the U.S. government expressed its strong desire to avoid introducing American or any other "white troops not speaking French" to the region. The United States would place its anticipated technical and financial assistance programs on hold, and channel all aid through the UN. Only requests for food aid would be met unilaterally, but even in that case UN distribution would be preferred.[43]

The absence of a well-formulated policy toward the newly independent Congo allowed the administration significant latitude and flexibility in determining its response to the situation. At a meeting at the summer White House in Newport, Rhode Island, on July 13, Eisenhower and a few key advisers discussed the three broad options available. First, the United States could choose not to respond. The group quickly eliminated this option, fearing that it would enable the USSR to create a Communist stronghold in the strategically important heart of the continent and bring the cold war to Africa. Second, the United States could intervene unilaterally. This option too was discarded, since all present concluded that it ran an unacceptable risk of provoking a superpower conflict in the Congo. Moreover, intervention in a

42. Timberlake, quoted in Kalb, *The Congo Cables,* 7; Telegram from Burden (William A. M. Burden, ambassador to Belgium) to the Department of State, July 10, 1960, in *FRUS, 1958–1960,* XIV, 286–88; Telegram from Herter to USUN, July 11, 1960, in *FRUS, 1958–1960,* XIV, 292–93; Memorandum of Telephone Conversation, July 12, 1960, in *FRUS, 1958–1960,* XVI, 295–96.

43. Memorandum of Telephone Conversation, July 12, 1960, in *FRUS, 1958–1960,* XIV, 297; Memorandum of Telephone Conversation, July 12, 1960, same volume, 296.

black, underdeveloped country experiencing a surge of nationalism would render the United States vulnerable to charges of neo-colonialism and would alienate the new and emerging African nations (sixteen of which were candidates for UN membership in 1960 and would become crucial swing votes). Finally, the administration recognized that given its sheer size and its economic and ethnic diversity, the Congo might prove to be simply ungovernable.

Eisenhower therefore chose the third option available—constructive intervention through the UN to facilitate Belgian withdrawal and establish political stability. The advantages inherent in a multilateral initiative were numerous. The United States could neutralize the Soviet Union without angering the African-Asian bloc or engaging in unilateral military action on a continent with which it was unfamiliar. A multilateral response would improve the peacekeeping credibility and capability of the UN, thereby strengthening its ability to handle future disorders in other newly decolonized areas. By operating as merely one member of a larger group, the administration would minimize American political liability and financial expenditures. In addition, as on other essentially colonial issues, the UN provided the best means of not alienating either the European powers or the increasingly powerful Third World bloc. Perhaps most important, Eisenhower appears to have concluded that, given the variety of pressing foreign policy problems, the question of the Congo was best consigned to the UN. Khrushchev's ultimatum over Berlin, the civil war in Laos, Fidel Castro's overthrow of the Batista regime in Cuba, the shooting down of Gary Powers' U-2 plane, and the breakup of the May, 1960, Paris summit all demanded the president's personal attention and a unilateral American response.[44]

Eisenhower's willingness to rely on the UN was reinforced by a pragmatic recognition that the United States, though by 1960 no longer wielding virtually unchallenged power, still had considerable influence in the organization. The pro-Western bloc controlled four of the five permanent seats on the Security Council and three of the six elected seats. Even in the General Assembly, the United States would need the votes of only twelve of the African-Asian states to obtain a two-thirds majority. Moreover, during the previous

44. Winkates, "The Influence of the United Nations on National Policy," 36–39; "U.S. Rejects Request of Congo for Troops to Quell Uprisings," New York *Times,* July 13, 1960, p. 13; The Reminiscences of Francis O. Wilcox, April 3, 1972, pp. 41–50, COHP, Butler Library, Columbia University.

seven years, and particularly as a result of Hammarskjöld's crisis management during the Suez affair, the administration had gained increased confidence in the Secretariat and the ability and intentions of its leader. The Secretariat had demonstrated that it could be innovative in exercising its mandate to maintain peace and security. In addition, the United States held a significant minority of the senior positions in the Secretariat. The three top Secretariat officials on the issue—Bunche, Andrew Cordier (the secretary-general's executive assistant) and Heinrich Weisschoff (the African affairs expert)—were all Americans. Almost half of the top one hundred positions in the Secretariat were held by American, British, or French nationals. On a more personal level, Wadsworth and Hammarskjöld had developed a close friendship.[45]

Furthermore, Eisenhower, bereft of Dulles's wisdom and experience, had become increasingly dependent upon Lodge. With Lodge championing a dominant role for the UN, the lame-duck president was more willing to entrust the organization with the problem. Reflective of these changes, the less experienced Herter gave Lodge more "leeway." And Lodge, despite receiving the Republican nomination for vice president in June, remained at his post until the end of August. The administration continued to rely on USUN even after Lodge, increasingly involved in the campaign, had delegated most responsibility to Wadsworth and Barco.[46]

Eisenhower quickly sought to inject the calming presence of the UN into the increasingly chaotic situation. He suggested that Hammarskjöld bypass the Security Council, because of the possibility of a Soviet veto, and deploy the troops offered by African nations without the council's approval. The secretary-general should simply "go there and take charge." Questions of finance could be resolved later; if necessary, the United States, Britain, and France would guarantee financing for the emergency force. Herter tamed the president's impulsiveness, pointing out that while UN consideration would mean a delay of a few hours, it would establish a firmer legal and financial basis for action.[47]

Invoking Article 99 of the UN Charter, on July 13 Hammarskjöld re-

45. Weissman, *American Foreign Policy in the Congo, 1960–1964,* 60; The Reminiscences of James J. Wadsworth, April 24, 1967, pp. 193–94, COHP, Butler Library, Columbia University.

46. *MTCH,* Reel 11, Herter and Wilcox, July 20, 1960.

47. Memorandum of a Telephone Conversation, July 13, 1960, 1:00 P.M., in *FRUS, 1958–1960,* XIV, 301.

quested an immediate Security Council meeting. The secretary-general believed that the UN could fill an important role by stepping into the power vacuum in the Congo and averting a Great Power confrontation. Herter instructed USUN to give its full support to Hammarskjöld's plan. The U.S. delegation should agree with his decisions to use UN troops to restore order, and to exclude troops from the Great Powers in a UN force. It should volunteer American assistance with transportation, communications, and logistics.[48]

The Security Council met on July 13, 1960. Lodge rose immediately to Belgium's defense, maintaining that under international law Belgium had the right to protect its nationals, and advocated speedy action by the UN. Predictably, the Soviet Union charged Belgium with aggression. Debate focused on a draft resolution prepared in the State Department and introduced by the representatives of Tunisia and Ceylon that asked the UN to provide military and technical assistance until Congolese forces could maintain internal order.[49]

The Security Council passed the resolution in the early hours of the morning of July 14, recording 8 votes in favor, 0 opposed, and 3 abstentions. The only addition to the State Department's draft resolution, though an important one, was the first operative paragraph that called for the withdrawal of Belgian troops. In a rare display of superpower unity, both the United States and the USSR voted for the resolution despite sharp differences over Belgian culpability and the timing of the UN arrival. Britain and France abstained, anxious that the resolution's implicit advocacy of rapid decolonization might have untoward ramifications in their remaining colonies, particularly nearby Rhodesia and South Africa. Acting on the authorization to provide the necessary military force, Hammarskjöld formed a UN operation (Opération des Nations Unies au Congo, or ONUC) composed of two branches—civilian operations and an international armed peace force, the United Nations Force in the Congo.[50]

48. Memorandum of Telephone Conversation, July 13, 1960, 5:35 P.M., in *FRUS, 1958– 1960,* XIV, 302; Telegram from Herter to the Mission at the United Nations, July 13, 1960, same volume, 303–304; *MTCH,* Reel 11, Lodge and Herter, July 13, 1960, 11:10 A.M.

49. "Security Council Considers Situation in Republic of the Congo," Lodge statements in the Security Council on July 13, 1960, *Department of State Bulletin,* August 1, 1960, pp. 159–61.

50. Herter call to USUN, n.d. (probably July 12 or 13, 1960), in folder marked "Telephone Calls: 7/1/60 to 8/31/60 (3)," Box 13, Telephone Conversation Series, Herter Papers, EL;

The United Nations thereby undertook its most formidable peacekeeping operation, but fundamental questions about its objectives and the participation of the superpowers remained unanswered. Eisenhower supported Hammarskjöld's intentions of employing the force to restore order without taking sides in the internal political struggle while working toward Belgium's eventual withdrawal. In addition, he backed Hammarskjöld's decision to restrict superpower involvement to logistical support (though in response to concerns that the United States would not receive due credit, Eisenhower suggested that perhaps American vehicles should be painted red, white, and blue). In contrast, the Soviets, who viewed Belgium as the aggressor, expected UN support of Lumumba, the head of the new Congolese government. They insisted that the UN troops maintain the territorial integrity of the Congo by suppressing the secessionist forces in Katanga and expelling the Belgian troops.[51]

This latent difference of opinion surfaced dramatically during a July 20 Security Council debate. The Soviet representative accused the United States of maintaining a military presence in the region, and warned that if the UN did not remove all Belgian troops within three days, Soviet troops would be sent to bolster Lumumba's forces. At the direction of Herter and Eisenhower, who viewed this Soviet threat as a potentially grave danger, Lodge reminded the Soviets that the United States was only providing transportation and communication assistance. Furthermore, he proclaimed that the United States would do whatever was necessary "to prevent the intrusion of military forces not requested by the U. N." Herter reiterated Lodge's warning the following day. In an attempt to avert Soviet intervention, the council called upon all states to refrain from interfering and requested Belgium to hasten its withdrawal.[52]

Though the administration trod as carefully as possible by means of the

---

Memorandum of Telephone Conversation, July 14, 1960, 9:05 A.M., in *FRUS, 1958–1960,* XIV, 306–307; Telegram from Lodge to the Department of State, July 14, 1960, 3:00 A.M., in *FRUS, 1958–1960,* XIV, 305.

51. Memorandum of a Conference with the President, July 19, 1960, in folder marked "Staff Notes: July 1960," Box 51, DDE Diary Series, EP, AWF, EL; Memorandum of Discussion at the 454th Meeting of the National Security Council on August 1, 1960, in Box 12, NSC Series, EP, AWF, EL; Kalb, *The Congo Cables,* 17–24.

52. "Security Council Calls for Cooperation of All States in Resolving Situation in Republic of the Congo," Lodge statement in the Security Council on July 20, 1960, *Department of State Bulletin,* August 8, 1960, p. 223; *MTCH,* Reel 11, Lodge and Herter, July 20, 1960, 5:20 P.M.; Telegram from Herter to USUN, July 20, 1960, in *FRUS, 1958–1960,* XIV, 334–36;

UN, it still had difficulty walking the fine line between Belgium, its NATO ally, and the Congo. The administration's predicament intensified when Lumumba journeyed, uninvited, to both New York (where he met with Hammarskjöld and Lodge, among others) and Washington (where he visited the State Department) in late July. The administration resented the diplomatic dilemma and confusion presented by his appearance. In its uncertainty about what to make of the entire situation, it even speculated that Lumumba's visit might be a blessing in disguise if his absence from the Congo brought about the collapse of his government. Eisenhower humorously offered to provide a "3 weeks tour of the U.S. on a modest basis" for Lumumba if anyone could be sure that his departure from the Congo would help stabilize the situation.[53]

The administration carefully resisted Lumumba's importunings for military and financial resources to regain control of Katanga. Maintaining that the United States would operate only under UN auspices in order to head off cold war competition in the Congo, both Herter and Undersecretary of State C. Douglas Dillon refused to promise the prime minister either military or bilateral financial aid. Yet simply by meeting with Lumumba, the administration incurred the wrath of the Belgians.[54] At the same time, despite Hammarskjöld's personal request and the realization that Belgium's continued presence might provoke a belligerent response from the USSR, the administration at first moved hesitantly to encourage Belgium to leave Katanga.[55]

Bowing to pressure from Lodge, the administration virtually reversed its position on August 9. In a report to the Security Council, written partly by Lodge, Hammarskjöld criticized Belgium for not complying with the resolutions and insisted that ONUC must maintain its neutrality. The adminis-

---

Secretary Herter's News Conference of July 21, 1960, in folder marked "Secretary's Press Conferences: July 9, 1959 to September 14, 1960 (1)," Box 17, Herter Papers, EL; Kalb, *The Congo Cables,* 24–33.

53. Editorial note, in *FRUS, 1958–1960,* XIV, 354.

54. *MTCH,* Reel 11, Memorandum of Telephone Conversation with Ambassador Burden, July 27, 1960; *MTCH,* Reel 11, Memorandum of Telephone Conversation with Mr. Eugene Black, July 28, 1960; *MTCH,* Reel 11, Herter and Labouisse (UN Secretariat), August 4, 1960; Memorandum of Conversation, July 27, 1960, in *FRUS, 1958–1960,* XIV, 359–66; Memorandum of Conversation, July 28, 1960, in *FRUS, 1958–1960,* XIV, 367–70.

55. *MTCH,* Reel 11, Herter and Burden, August 2, 1960, 9:00 A.M., 1:35 P.M., and 6:35 P.M.; *MTCH,* Reel 11, Herter and Whitney, 10:35 A.M.; Telegram from Herter to the embassy in Belgium, August 2, 1960, in *FRUS, 1958–1960,* XIV, 381–83; Telegram from Merchant to USUN, August 6, 1960, in *FRUS, 1958–1960,* XIV, 392–94.

tration, pushed by Lodge, supported a draft resolution to this effect. Belgium no longer had any reason "to postpone speedy withdrawal from Katanga," Lodge contended during the debate. On August 9, the Security Council unanimously adopted the resolution. The behind-the-scenes lobbying that yielded such a strong majority for the American position had been "spectacular," Lodge informed Herter. Eisenhower too applauded the Security Council resolution, expressing confidence that it would further a peaceful solution to the conflict. And indeed, by the end of August most of the Belgian troops had evacuated from the Congo. However, Eisenhower's optimism was premature. This was to be the last occasion on which the United States, the USSR, and African neutrals joined in support of Hammarskjöld's efforts.[56]

Unhappily, the Belgian evacuation did not mark the end of the crisis. An ominous cold war confrontation was brewing. The more pressing concern as summer turned into fall was that Lumumba was facilitating Soviet penetration in the Congo. The administration concluded that Lumumba was not simply a left-leaning African nationalist, but an irrational Communist. In Eisenhower's opinion, he was "radical and unstable . . . a Communist sympathizer if not a member of the Party." Lumumba's acceptance of Soviet assistance in violation of the Security Council resolutions of July 14 and 22, 1960, reaffirmed such fears. The NSC and Eisenhower determined that the UN must step up its enforcement of restrictions on external aid and continue its presence in the heart of Africa even if such action provoked a superpower confrontation. If the UN could not keep out Great Power troops and remain in the Congo, Eisenhower warned, its very reason for being would be called into question.[57]

The administration still believed that it shared mutual objectives with the

56. "Security Council Considers New Difficulties in Congo," Lodge statement in the Security Council on August 8, 1960, *Department of State Bulletin,* September 5, 1960, p. 385; *MTCH,* Reel 11, Memorandum of Telephone Conversation with Lodge, August 9, 1960, 12:55 P.M.; *MTCH,* Reel 11, Herter and Lodge, August 8, 1960, 1:15 P.M.; Synopsis of State and Intelligence Material Reported to the President on August 8, 1960, in folder marked "Briefings—August 1960," Box 52, DDE Diary Series, EP, AWF, EL; President's News Conference of August 10, 1960, in *Public Papers of the Presidents: Dwight D. Eisenhower, 1960–1961,* 619–20.

57. Eisenhower, *Waging Peace, 1956–1961,* 572, 574; Memorandum of Discussion at the 456th Meeting of the National Security Council on August 18, 1960, in Box 13, NSC Series,

United Nations. Specifically, it remained willing to rely upon the UN because Hammarskjöld desired to see Lumumba "broken." The administration thus pledged its full support for any action he took to prevent further Soviet intervention. Herter personally placed a call to the secretary-general assuring him that the United States supported him "1000 percent" and exhorting him to act even more decisively.[58]

The collapse of the Congolese government early in September and the subsequent constitutional crisis destroyed the remaining remnants of superpower consensus. On September 5, 1960, President Kasavubu dismissed Prime Minister Lumumba. Lumumba responded in an emotional radio address, declaring that Kasavubu was no longer chief of state and requesting the people and army to rise in his support. On September 14, Colonel Joseph Mobutu, chief of staff of the Force Publique, proclaimed himself dictator, closed the Soviet embassy and ordered all Soviet diplomats to leave the nation. Four national governments—three Congolese governments, led by Kasavubu, Lumumba, and Mobutu, plus the Katangan government of Tshombe—now existed in the Congo, with the United States openly supporting Kasavubu.

Fearing that Lumumba's fall from power and the UN's support for Kasavubu might provoke a belligerent Soviet response, the United States took the offensive at the UN. On September 15, Wadsworth presented a draft resolution in the Security Council that accused the USSR of seeking to create a "Soviet satellite state in the heart of Africa," requested members to cease all unilateral aid to the Congo and contribute to the financial support of ONUC, and urged the secretary-general to act vigorously to implement Security Council resolutions. The Soviets responded by demanding that the UN stop its intervention in the internal affairs of the Congo. Ceylon and Tu-

---

EP, AWF, EL; Orwa, "Responses of the United Nations and the United States to the Congo Crisis," 151–52, 158–59; Kalb, *The Congo Cables,* 50–55.

58. Synopsis of State and Intelligence Material Reported to the President, August 30, 1960, in folder marked "Briefings—August 1960," Box 52, DDE Diary Series, EP, AWF, EL; Memorandum of Telephone Conversation, September 10, 1960, 1:30 P.M., in *FRUS, 1958–1960,* XIV, 478; *MTCH,* Reel 11, Herter and Wadsworth, September 8, 1960; *MTCH,* Reel 11, Herter and Wadsworth, September 10, 1960, 1:20 P.M.; Telegram from Lodge to the Department of State, August 19, 1960, in *FRUS, 1958–1960,* XIV, 432–33; Telegram from Dillon to USUN, August 16, 1960, in *FRUS, 1958–1960,* XIV, 413; Telegram from Herter to USUN, September 3, 1960, in *FRUS, 1958–1960,* XIV, 455–57.

nisia proposed a slightly milder version of the American resolution, one that requested that no military assistance be sent to the Congo except as part of the UN action, appealed for contributions to a UN Fund for the Congo, and reaffirmed the ONUC's mandate. The Ceylon-Tunisia resolution obtained a majority vote, but was defeated by a Soviet veto. Stalemated, the Security Council adjourned, but not before the United States, invoking the Uniting for Peace resolution, called for an emergency session of the General Assembly.[59]

The emergency special session (only the fourth in the history of the UN, after the crises in the Suez and Hungary in 1956 and Lebanon in 1958) convened on September 17, 1960. The United States welcomed the opportunity to put the Soviets on the defensive, charging them with hindering a UN effort supported overwhelmingly by the Third World. The United States threw its influence behind a seventeen-nation African-Asian resolution that imposed a ban on all external military assistance, expressed approval of Hammarskjöld's policies, authorized Hammarskjöld to appoint a Conciliation Commission of African-Asian representatives to help in forming a Congolese government acceptable to all factions, and generally increased his mandate to conduct operations in the Congo. On September 20, 1960, the assembly recorded an impressive majority of 70 votes in favor of the African-Asian resolution, with 0 opposed and 11 abstentions.

Domestic politics reinforced the administration's drive in late summer to use the UN to thwart Soviet penetration in the Congo. As the presidential campaign heated up, the Democratic nominee, Senator John F. Kennedy, had made the situation an election issue. Asserting that Communists were infiltrating central Africa, and using NATO airfields to do so, the junior senator from Massachusetts blamed the situation on the Republican administration's indifference toward African affairs and its lack of initiative in waging the cold war. The president complained that such politically motivated statements were precisely why he did "not want to permit the injection of the campaign into the conduct of foreign policy." Although Eisenhower claimed to be angry because Kennedy's comments made the situation more

---

59. Draft resolution, quoted in Kalb, *The Congo Cables,* 88. On the U.S. objectives see, for example, Telegram from Herter to USUN, September 12, 1960, in *FRUS, 1958–1960,* XIV, 481–83.

difficult for the UN, he was undoubtedly infuriated by this challenge to his policies.[60]

Hailed by the New York *Times* as constituting "the most spectacular cast in the history of the UN," the regular session of the General Assembly opened only days after the conclusion of the special session. When it became evident that Khrushchev would attend, world and national leaders flocked to New York City. After prolonged intra-administration debate about the sagacity of a presidential appearance, Eisenhower led the pilgrimage to the glass house on the East River and spoke on the opening day, September 22, 1960. Eager to establish a dignified tone for the session and contrast U.S. support for the UN with Soviet attacks, the president called for noninterference in the domestic affairs of African nations, support for ONUC, and economic assistance for Africa.[61]

If Eisenhower seized the high road, Khrushchev burrowed a path that gave new meaning to the term "low road." Speaking on the following day and again on October 3, he accused Hammarskjöld of supporting the colonialists rather than executing the Congo mandate. In an increasingly virulent series of attacks, accompanied by shoe banging on the table and shouts from the floor, the Soviet premier urged Hammarskjöld to resign and proposed that the secretary-general be replaced by a tripartite executive representing the Communist states, the United States and its allies, and the neutralists. The Soviet assault only invigorated the American defense of the UN and its embattled head. Outraged, the usually circumspect Herter denounced the troika proposal as "a declaration of war" against the UN, while Eisenhower railed against the idea of an additional Soviet veto at the "operational level" of the secretary-general.[62]

60. Memorandum of a Conference with the President, September 6, 1960, in folder marked "Staff Notes—September 1960 (4)," Box 53, DDE Diary Series, EP, AWF, EL; *MTCH,* Reel 11, Hagerty and Herter, September 7, 1960.

61. "Fateful Assembly," New York *Times,* September 18, 1960, Section 4, p. 4; *MTCH,* Reel 10, Memorandum of Telephone Conversation with Ambassador Cabot Lodge, August 9, 1960, 12:55 P.M.; *MTCH,* Reel 11, HTCS; Herter and Hagerty, September 12, 1960, 11:35 A.M.; Memorandum of Conference with the President, September 12, 1960, in folder marked "Staff Notes—September 1960 (4)," Box 53, DDE Diary Series, EP, AWF, EL.

62. Eisenhower, quoted in Orwa, "Responses of the United Nations and the United States to the Congo Crisis," 195; Memorandum of Conference with the President, September 27,

Eisenhower and the secretary-general agreed that the Congo needed an effective government, legitimately elected by the people, that could be neutral between the superpowers. But as the situation continued to defy resolution, the administration increasingly questioned the Secretariat's tactics in its effort to achieve these shared objectives. Most specifically, the two differed on the legality and wisdom of arresting Lumumba and removing him from power, the handling of pro-Lumumba African states, and the withdrawal of Belgian troops. In August, 1960, Hammarskjöld had appointed Rajeshwar Dayal to serve as his special representative in the Congo. Arriving on September 6, in the midst of the constitutional crisis, Dayal had to decide between the Lumumba and Kasavubu rival governments in Léopoldville, as well as manage a variety of separatist governments. When Dayal, trying to retain the support of African and Asian neutrals who supported Lumumba, took a position that Timberlake viewed as too pro-Lumumba, he incurred the animosity of the increasingly autonomous ambassador, Wadsworth, and the upper levels of the State Department. In fact, Herter was so troubled that he met with Hammarskjöld late in September to express his concern.[63]

Tensions increased further after Dayal submitted a report on November 2 in which he criticized Mobutu for retaining Belgian advisers and recommended reconvening the Congolese parliament. Fearing that such actions might further harm the United States' relations with Belgium and might strengthen Lumumba, the Eisenhower administration opposed Dayal's suggestions and pressed its case for the Kasavubu regime in the General Assembly credentials committee. The debate was heated and intense. The United States emerged victorious, but only after it had exerted considerable pressure on selected embassies worldwide. From that point on, Lumumba's influence waned.[64]

1960, in folder marked "Staff Notes—September 1960 (1)," Box 53, DDE Diary Series, EP, AWF, EL.

63. See, for example, Memorandum of Conversation, September 26, 1960, in *FRUS, 1958–1960,* XIV, 506–508; Memorandum of Discussion at the 464th Meeting of the National Security Council, October 20, 1960, same volume, 539–41; Telegram from Barco to the Department of State, October 22, 1960, same volume, 542–46; Telegram from Wadsworth to the Department of State, October 29, 1960, same volume, 556–60.

64. Telegram from Herter to the USUN, November 4, 1960, in *FRUS, 1958–1960,* XIV, 566–67; Telegram from Wadsworth to the Department of State, November 16, 1960, same volume, 589–91.

The complicated situation took a new twist in early December. For the previous two months the United States had implored Hammarskjöld to release Lumumba from UN protective custody in the prime minister's mansion, where the U.S. government believed he was too prominent a symbol of the opposition to Kasavubu. In November, Mobutu and Kasavubu reached an agreement in which Kasavubu resumed control of the government. On November 27, 1960, Lumumba left Léopoldville for Stanleyville, in order to be where his forces were in control. On December 2, while en route, he was arrested by Mobutu's forces at the behest of Kasavubu, and with at least the implicit blessing of the Eisenhower administration.[65]

The Security Council met on December 7, at the USSR's request, to discuss this latest crisis. Soviet representative Zorin charged the United States with manipulating events against Lumumba and accused Hammarskjöld of complicity with the West in not using UN soldiers to defend Lumumba. Zorin demanded Lumumba's release, the disarming of Mobutu's soldiers, and the expulsion of Kasavubu's Belgian advisers. Wadsworth and Barco angrily denied the charges. They insisted that since Lumumba's arrest was a matter that fell within the internal jurisdiction of the Congo, it was not subject to a UN resolution. The council defeated the Soviet resolution and the Soviet delegate, in turn, vetoed a Western resolution simply calling for Lumumba's humane treatment and reaffirming support for Hammarskjöld's actions in the Congo.[66]

The General Assembly picked up where the Security Council had left off, renewing debate on the Congo on December 16, 1960. An African-Asian resolution proposed liberating all political prisoners, reconvening the Congolese Parliament, and giving the secretary-general a stronger mandate. Their position grew closer to that of the USSR on this issue. The United States and Britain cosponsored a resolution calling upon all involved to ob-

65. See, for example, Memorandum of Discussion at the 463rd Meeting of the National Security Council on October 13, 1960, in Box 13, NSC Series, EP, AWF, EL; *MTCH,* Reel 11, Herter and Barco, October 22, 1960. On the assassination of Lumumba, see, for example, Kalb, *The Congo Cables,* 189–96; H. W. Brands, *The Devil We Knew: America and the Cold War* (New York, 1993), 63–64.

66. "Security Council Debate on Congo Results in 92d Veto," Wadsworth statements on December 9, 1960, and Barco statement on December 14, 1960, *Department of State Bulletin,* January 9, 1961, pp. 51–56; Editorial note, in *FRUS, 1958–1960,* XIV, 621–22; Kalb, *The Congo Cables,* 161–64.

serve international human rights standards, requesting the Red Cross to check on the safety and treatment of Lumumba and other prisoners, and renewing calls for an end to external military aid, in light of the recurrent rumors of Soviet planes landing laden with weapons. The Anglo-American resolution, however, did not call for Lumumba's release. It therefore implied that Kasavubu had the right to arrest and detain him. The General Assembly defeated the African-Asian resolution on December 20 by a vote of 42 opposed (including the United States and its Western allies) to 28 in favor (including the USSR), with 27 abstentions. The U.S. draft resolution failed by a single vote, compiling totals of 43 for, 22 against (including most of the African-Asian states), and 32 abstentions. One can only suspect that under the more dynamic leadership of Lodge, USUN would have succeeded in obtaining the two votes necessary to pass the measure. In its final days, the administration simply did not invest the necessary effort in the increasingly laborious task of lining up a two-thirds majority.[67] The United States continued to foot the bill for much of the operation in the Congo, but the Eisenhower administration remained unhappy with the direction in which things appeared to be heading under Dayal's leadership during January, 1961.

Lumumba, who had been targeted by the CIA for assassination, was handed over by the Kasavubu government to the Katangan rebels on January 17. He was assassinated by the Katangans and Belgians probably almost immediately.

Thus, the final chapter in the administration's involvement in the Congo ended on a dismal note. Reflecting this distress, Herter asserted at the final NSC meeting of the Eisenhower presidency that "he had the strong feeling that our interests have not been advanced by the way the UN operation in the Congo had been conducted." He held Hammarskjöld and Dayal responsible. Equally dissatisfied with the current state of affairs, particularly the nasty tenor of the fall General Assembly session, and reflecting the ambivalence that had marked his eight years of dealing with the UN, Eisenhower suggested that the time had come to reappraise the nation's relationship with

67. Editorial note, in *FRUS, 1958–1960*, XIV, 635–36; Telegram from Wadsworth to the Department of State, December 18, 1960, same volume, 636–38.

the body. Apparently frustrated by the increasing difficulty of obtaining UN majorities in support of American resolutions, the president noted specifically that the nation should reconsider its policy of supporting the admission of every newly independent state to UN membership.[68]

Overwhelmed as well by the domestic press attention and the security requirements during the fall session, Eisenhower asserted that the UN should not have been established in the United States. Help with its balance of payments was the only benefit that the United States derived from having the UN located on American territory, the president bitterly claimed. Eisenhower even directed the State Department to study the possibility of relocating the organization. At the top of his list of alternative sites was Berlin, since he suggested that an international presence might lessen Soviet threats to the city. The State Department concluded, however, that the disadvantages of a move far outweighed the advantages.[69]

Eisenhower's dissatisfaction can be traced at least partly to his ambivalence about having abdicated a commanding position on the Congo situation in favor of UN control. In light of the chaotic internal conditions in the newly independent nation, the president had made a conscious decision to leave "the whole sorry mess," as he described it in his memoirs, to the UN. Unable to identify a more attractive alternative, the administration, for the first time during the Eisenhower era, permitted Hammarskjöld to take the initiative. But Eisenhower and the State Department never appeared confident that they had made the correct decision, particularly when the secretary-general went so far as to restrict the United States' involvement in the field, insisting that American suggestions, like those of every other nation, go through the ONUC chain of command. Their perception that the UN took American support (particularly financial) for granted heightened their displeasure. Herter, for example, complained in mid-August that he

---

68. Memorandum of Discussion at the 474th Meeting of the National Security Council on January 12, 1961, in Box 13, NSC Series, EP, AWF, EL; Weissman, *American Foreign Policy in the Congo, 1960–1964,* 110.

69. Memorandum, Dillon (acting secretary) to Eisenhower, August 29, 1960, in folder marked "Christian Herter: August 1960 (2)," Box 11, Dulles-Herter Series, EP, AWF, EL; Memorandum of Conference with the President, September 19, 1960, in folder marked "Staff Notes—September 1960 (3)," Box 53, DDE Diary Series, EP, AWF, EL; Memorandum of a Conference with the President, October 2, 1960, in *FRUS, 1958–1960,* II, 379.

was "getting a little fed up with the US being treated as though we were a bottomless well."[70]

The administration also experienced mixed feelings about the UN's assertion of independence. Eisenhower, Dulles, and Lodge were not quite sure what to make of Hammarskjöld's response to the situation. They loudly insisted that he take the reins and act assertively. Yet at the same time they expected him to feel daunted and overwhelmed. Instead, Hammarskjöld jumped at this opportunity for the UN to demonstrate its usefulness and was "intrigued by [the] creative role thrust upon [the] UN." At least until late in 1960, he relished the challenge of exerting UN authority in a nation lacking an effective government, and the additional hurdle of doing so without compromising UN integrity by taking extra-constitutional actions. A tired administration in its final months in office was taken aback by, and perhaps even somewhat envious of, the enthusiasm with which Hammarskjöld set out to make the United Nations a force for resolving the crises generated by colonial devolution that were increasingly at the center of international affairs.[71]

Nevertheless, the administration accepted these conditions because it shared interests and objectives with the UN. Both the UN and the United States were willing to see the Congo emerge as a nonaligned nation, and thus Eisenhower, at least on an intellectual level, recognized the UN's utility in handling this conflict at the periphery of superpower relations. Moreover, Hammarskjöld operated within broad parameters of which he knew the United States approved. Indeed, since the UN was literally in the United States' debt for the operation (at a cost of $3.9 million in 1960), Hammarskjöld could not afford to ignore the U.S. government's advice.[72]

Ultimately, of course, the United States discovered that relying on the United Nations could not keep the cold war out of central Africa. For while both the United States and the USSR initially supported UN intervention in the Congo, each nation sought to use the organization to serve its national

70. Eisenhower, *Waging Peace, 1956–1961,* 574; *MTCH,* Reel 11, Herter and Wilcox, August 15, 1960.

71. Telegram from Lodge to the Department of State, July 18, 1960, in *FRUS, 1958–1960,* XIV, 320; Telegram from Cook to the Department of State, September 7, 1960, same volume, 465.

72. Orwa, "Responses of the United Nations and the United States to the Congo Crisis," 204.

interests and to achieve diametrically opposed objectives in the region. Given that situation, the UN could not possibly satisfy both parties and in all likelihood its performance was bound to disappoint instead.

Thus, a variety of factors shaped the administration's respective responses in Lebanon and the Congo. The location and timing of the crisis, the personnel changes in the foreign policy team, the international and domestic political situations, the administration's estimate of the diplomatic ability of Secretary-General Dag Hammarskjöld, the military capability of the UN Emergency Force, and the political ability of the UN to prevent the Third World from becoming enmeshed in the ongoing cold war and falling under Soviet influence all contributed to the administration's decision to pursue different approaches to the similar but distinct problems.

The result, in Lebanon, was unilateral intervention, though conducted with rhetorical nods to the UN's involvement in the situation. The United States was simply lucky that its reputation at the UN incurred only minimal damage. Lodge's skillful defense of American intervention, his friendship with Hammarskjöld, and the fact that no Marines or Lebanese were killed contributed to the rapid waning of tension and the absence of lasting ill effects at the UN.

Different circumstances and factors produced a markedly dissimilar approach to the use of the UN in the Congo. The result in the African situation was a delegation of authority, perhaps even power, to the UN that revealed some of the weaknesses inherent in letting that body operate on its own, without the tight leash the United States had generally held. Still, it is interesting to note that the American Marine landing in Lebanon cost $200 million. In comparison, the United States' share of the cost of the UN effort in the Congo amounted to $168 million for a four-year operation in a less-accessible region and a more complex situation. Hence, the multilateral rather than the unilateral approach to peacekeeping had monetary rewards for the United States when the administration chose to employ it.[73] Both situations underscored the limits of the Eisenhower administration's willingness to use the United Nations while, somewhat paradoxically, also attesting to how the United Nations had become an integral arena of United States foreign policy.

73. Finger, *American Ambassadors at the UN*, 102.

CONCLUSION

The Unfulfilled Promise of the United Nations

In his first inaugural address, Dwight D. Eisenhower proclaimed his desire to transform the United Nations from "an eloquent symbol" into "an effective force."[1] Throughout his two terms in office, administration officials repeatedly referred to the UN as a "pillar" or even the "cornerstone" of American foreign policy. Despite this noble rhetorical commitment, the UN remained only one among many, and hardly *primus inter pares,* of the instruments with which the United States sought to achieve its foreign policy goals.

As Eisenhower assumed the presidency in 1953, a variety of signs suggested that the United Nations might play a more prominent role in American foreign policy. Most important, Eisenhower believed that the UN Charter reflected American principles and aspirations and that the United States and the United Nations shared a common goal—the maintenance of peace and security. Indeed, the organization had been created largely in the American image. Despite this apparent confluence of positive factors, the Eisenhower administration never developed a coherent and clearly articulated long-range strategy toward the United Nations. It demonstrated little foresight in formulating long-term plans for the role the UN could play in creating the kind of world order that the administration desired. Instead, the

1. *Public Papers of the Presidents: Dwight D. Eisenhower, 1953,* 6.

United States handled most questions at the UN on an *ad hoc* basis, focusing on achieving immediate objectives. In the end, the United Nations was less an instrument of aggressive foreign policy than a shield the administration used, generally with success in the short term, to defend itself against unforeseen events and developments.

Apart from this basically consistent but reactive approach, it is possible to identify two distinct periods in the administration's relationship with the United Nations. During the first period, from 1953 to 1955, the administration was concerned with acquiring the domestic support essential to implementing a strong and consistent internationalist foreign policy. An immediate task was to rebuild public confidence in the UN, gravely damaged by the attacks of McCarthy and his followers. In its first months in office, the administration sought to quiet charges and calm fears that the UN had become a hotbed of Communist subversion. Anxious to expend as little domestic political capital as possible in this effort, the administration shamelessly used its virtually unchallenged influence to manipulate the organization, imposing standards of ideological purity on the international civil service. Political expediency, rather than an attempt to conform to its rhetorical platitudes, dictated policy.

At the same time, the administration also used the UN pragmatically and effectively to publicize and legitimize its cold war policies. It even occasionally displayed creativity and initiative in using the organization to thwart its Soviet rival. The president and his key foreign policy advisers, Dulles and Lodge, appreciated the UN's unique potential both as an international stage for refuting Soviet propaganda and as a forum for presenting their own policies to an international audience. The administration moved immediately to maximize its use of the organization in this manner, launching a psychological warfare project against the Soviet Union and the Communist bloc. UN vote tallies backing U.S. positions provided evidence of the effectiveness of the administration's efforts in the international arena. Public opinion polls and State Department surveys of editorial reaction brought reassurance that the strategy was also bolstering domestic support for the UN and the administration's use of that body. The emphasis on psychological warfare, however, gravely undermined concurrent arms control negotiations. Lacking trust in the Soviet Union and therefore unable to develop a coherent long-range policy, the administration careened back and forth between UN-sponsored efforts to achieve arms control and bilateral or Four Power efforts. In both cases, U.S. policies were, more often than not, designed to establish propaganda primacy at the United Nations.

Throughout this first period, the administration made only minimal use of the UN in resolving threats to international peace and security, the primary purpose of the organization. After the inconclusive and unsatisfying settlement of the Korean situation in 1953, the United States turned its attention away from the UN as a collective defense arrangement and focused instead on regional security organizations such as NATO, the OAS, and SEATO. As a result, the administration failed to transform its rhetorical commitment into actual reliance upon the UN's procedures for resolving threats to the peace in Guatemala and Indochina. In Indochina it used the UN only indirectly, attempting to acquire support for the U.S. position in order to pressure the Communists to negotiate outside the organization. It worked assiduously to bypass the UN entirely in Guatemala, preferring to operate through the regional mechanism of the OAS, over which it had tighter control. Only when the United States could find no better alternative, as in the conflicts with Communist China over the release of American prisoners of war and the status of the offshore islands, did it request the UN's assistance in mediating a dispute to which the United States or one of its allies was a party. Through the early part of the decade, the United States hence embraced the multilateral forum when it was perceived to best serve American interests, but ignored it with virtual impunity when it chose to act unilaterally.

The administration's relationship with and use of the United Nations changed somewhat during Eisenhower's second term. The progress of world events, more than specific actions of the U.S. government or the UN itself, accounted for these changes. To a large extent, the United States was subject to forces—rising nationalism, decolonization, the proliferation of new states, and the economic recovery of Europe and Japan—beyond its control, even though it was the world's most powerful nation. These systemic changes, combined with a slight reduction in superpower hostility, broadened the narrow focus on the struggle with the Soviet Union that had characterized the administration's relationship with the UN from 1953 to 1955. Its involvement expanded to encompass the growing Third World, while exhibiting a renewed interest in the UN's potential in maintaining international peace and security.

Nevertheless, during the second period, from 1956 through 1960, the administration's relationship with the UN was still characterized by a marked ambivalence, restraint, and caution. These hallmarks of American policy were nowhere more apparent than in the administration's participation in UN consideration of colonial issues. The United States resisted the movement to bring disputes over colonialism to the UN. When further avoidance proved impossible, it attempted to use the body to moderate the views of the anti-colonial extremists, while privately pressuring the colonial powers to bend to the inevitable.

It demonstrated even less willingness to use the UN to come to grips with the consequences of decolonization and the attendant demands of the underdeveloped world. Skeptical about the propriety of UN involvement in such matters as multilateral aid, human rights, and racial justice, the administration offered only qualified and limited support for UN endeavors in the economic and social realms. No doubt with an eye to the increasing domestic turmoil over racial issues at home, the administration conveniently maintained throughout that the UN's mission in the social, economic, and humanitarian fields was secondary to securing and maintaining international peace and security. Too, the administration recognized, most obviously on the question of multilateral aid, that the problems of the Third World, particularly those of an economic nature, simply defied American or even UN resolution, barring a dramatic redistribution of the world's wealth. This was a solution it (and even more vocally, Congress) could not and would not countenance. Consequently, it sought to avoid UN consideration of such issues.

This restraint and lack of imagination in managing the problems arising from colonial devolution and the growing North-South divide present a distinct contrast to the enthusiasm with which Eisenhower, in particular, explored new ways to use the UN in 1953 and 1954 to meet the Soviet challenge. Yet it represented a conscious choice by the White House and the State Department. The immediate danger to American national security posed by the Soviet Union, with its nuclear arsenal and expansive ambitions, far exceeded any challenges emanating from the Third World. As a result, efforts to defeat its avowed foe and retain the allegiance of its closest NATO allies in this struggle took precedence over the Third World's needs and claims. This immediate and eminently more potent threat provided something of an excuse for Eisenhower and Dulles, men who were the embodiments of their backgrounds in the military and the corporate boardroom, to postpone and ultimately avoid even serious contemplation of the longer-range challenges posed by the Third World and the ways in which American action at the United Nations might begin to facilitate those countries' social, political, and economic development.

Nevertheless, during this second period, the administration retained its interest, albeit gingerly and selectively, in the UN's potential in the field of peace and security. The United Nations proved particularly appealing when the administration faced the prospect of acting alone against its Atlantic alliance partners during the Suez Canal Crisis. Moreover, UN involvement, the administration wisely perceived, might insulate the Middle East conflict from the superpower struggle and provide an ideal place to deposit and perhaps defuse the seemingly intractable Arab-Israeli problem. In such cases, one subordinate noted, Dulles viewed the UN as "a receptacle where almost any stormy problem could be unloaded and stored away for a year or longer."[2] Enforcement action under Chapter VII of the UN Charter was impossible because of the veto power of the permanent members of the Security Council, but the advent of peacekeeping forces modeled on the UN Emergency Force in the Middle East provided a limited alternative that had at least modest success during the remainder of the decade.

Although the UN remained virtually impotent in resolving military conflicts at the heart of the superpower struggle—most notably the Hungarian revolution—the organization's new emphasis on peacekeeping served the United States well in managing the Congo Crisis in 1960. In theory, then, the administration preferred to follow the multilateral, collective route because of its greater international legitimacy. But here too, confronted by a situation in which it deemed unilateral action preferable, the administration did not hesitate to act without UN support or even approval. In Lebanon, as it had during the Indochina situation, the United States first advocated only a limited role for the UN as neutral observatory body and then bypassed it almost completely, engaging in a unilateral military venture.

Adapting only slowly and reluctantly to changing international realities, the United States still, somewhat surprisingly, continued successfully to advance its foreign policy goals at the UN during this second period—this despite wielding less influence as the decade progressed. The changing inter-

2. Finger, *American Ambassadors at the UN,* 75.

national scene meant that the frequently blatant manipulation and financial largesse that it had used to command large majorities during the first years of the Eisenhower era had to give way to more intense lobbying for votes, more astute use of parliamentary procedure, and occasionally greater sensitivity to the Third World to obtain the necessary support.

The Eisenhower administration thus used the United Nations in decidedly different ways during both the height of the bipolar world and the latter half of the decade, when the alliance structure altered somewhat under the influence of decolonization and neutralism. During the early years of the Eisenhower era, American interests generally coincided with those of the UN, and the organization served American interests, particularly in the cold war battle with the Soviet Union. Although the United States could never control the Security Council because of the Soviet veto power, it enjoyed a commanding influence over a General Assembly, which was composed overwhelmingly of nations friendly to the West and willing to follow American direction. Consequently, the UN, created largely in the image of the United States, did America's bidding, as most Americans expected it should.

This situation changed with the admission of several-score African and Asian nations from 1955 to 1960. The resulting changes in the UN's composition not only made the General Assembly far less amenable to American control, but also altered the organization's priorities. By the late 1950s, the UN was in the process of being re-created, many believed, in the image of the Third World, and was primed to do its bidding. For the first time, many of the goals of the UN, as now voiced by the emerging Third World majority in the General Assembly, deviated from those of the Eisenhower administration. As it became increasingly difficult to make the UN serve American interests, the United States became less enamored of the organization.

During both periods, however, the administration considered the UN to be sufficiently important not to act without at least considering how its actions would be viewed by the organization. It had concluded that the UN, in spite of its many weaknesses, provided the vocabulary for and the context within which international disputes ought to be debated and military action justified. The UN Charter provided an accessible and widely accepted statement of principles with which the United States had publicly and repeatedly proclaimed its agreement. It therefore behooved the United States to justify its actions and even alter its behavior, to the extent consonant with the national interest, in order to act in accord with the Charter. Consequently, when the administration did use or sanction the use of force, it went to great lengths to stress that it did so under Article 51 of the Charter—the right of individual or collective self-defense (Guatemala, Indochina) or at the invitation of a legitimate government (Lebanon). Indeed, both secretaries of state judged the United States' role in strengthening the UN to be among the their top accomplishments.[3]

But there were clear limits to the administration's willingness to use the UN. Eisenhower was neither a starry-eyed idealist nor an unprincipled practitioner of realpolitik. Far from viewing the organization as an idealistic attempt at world government, the president considered it to be a useful instrument for protecting the national interest and advancing American foreign policy objectives, particularly in the traditional superpower conflict. Under Eisenhower's leadership, the United States adopted a pragmatic approach to the body and demonstrated a willingness to use all available options to achieve what the administration deemed to be in the best interests of the nation. It displayed an impressive ability to utilize the UN's resources as well as effectively to combine traditional and multilateral diplomacy to achieve its ends. The results satisfied Eisenhower. His rhetoric notwithstanding, he had limited expectations for what could be accomplished through the UN and he had met these narrow goals.

The United States succeeded in achieving its objectives at the UN to the extent that it did largely because Lodge and Dulles worked out a *modus vivendi* that permitted USUN to operate effectively and efficiently. Dulles insisted from the beginning that the State Department and not USUN be the locus of policy-making authority, and Lodge realized that Eisenhower too wanted control to reside in one place—the State Department. Familiar with the importance that the former general placed upon an orderly chain of command, Lodge was willing to abide by that arrangement as long as Dulles took the time to keep him informed about the broader policy ramifications of decisions at the UN, which he did. As a result, the State Department provided its ambassador with the substance of the U.S. position, Lodge crafted

3. Memorandum, "United States Foreign Policy Under the Eisenhower Administration, 1953–1959," April 10, 1959, in folder marked "Foreign Policy—Eisenhower Administration," Box 140, J. F. Dulles Papers, Mudd Library; Memorandum from Herter to Eisenhower, "United States Foreign Policy Under the Eisenhower Administration," January 6, 1961, in folder marked "White House Correspondence (1)," Box 20, Herter Papers, EL.

it into a compelling presentation, and, on matters of importance, Dulles approved, and frequently even participated in writing, the final version. Although Lodge quickly learned to work more closely with State Department staff and less with Dulles, it was not unusual for him to speak with the secretary four or five times a day.[4] Not surprisingly, after Lodge's six years on the job and because of his and Christian Herter's shared roots in Massachusetts politics, he enjoyed slightly greater autonomy under Dulles's successor, but the central lines of authority remained the same.

Although Dulles and Lodge developed an effective professional partnership, the relationship between the two remained somewhat strained. Wadsworth observed diplomatically that while there was "a very strong mutual admiration" between the two men, it never "flowered into a very great warmth." Herman Phleger sensed a "constant irritation" between them. David Wainhouse, too, noted that their relations "on the surface were correct, but neither friendly nor warm," for Lodge felt that Dulles "was talking down to him" and Dulles "felt that Cabot was a politician, grinding the Presidential axe, and somewhat of an upstart using the post of Ambassador to the UN to further his ambitions."[5]

For the most part, Dulles and Lodge succeeded in suppressing any latent hostility. They had a healthy respect for each other's abilities and, perhaps more important, for Eisenhower's regard for the other individual. Dulles never ceased to be aware of his own lack of independent domestic political power. He knew that Eisenhower both believed he owed Lodge a political debt and valued Lodge's political counsel. Eisenhower was more than satisfied with Lodge's work. In fact, he considered him for secretary of state upon Dulles's retirement. Only Dulles's urgings to promote Herter from the deputy post in order to maintain greater continuity convinced the president

4. Lodge to Dulles, October 26, 1957, in folder marked "Henry Cabot Lodge, Jr.: 1957," Box 118, J. F. Dulles Papers, Mudd Library; Lodge interview with Richard D. Challener, February 16, 1965, p. 12, in Box 92, HCLP, MHS; John Wainhouse, interview with Philip Crowl, August 24, 1965, pp. 35–36, Dulles Oral History Project, Mudd Library, Princeton University.

5. Wadsworth interview with Philip Crowl, June 21, 1965, p. 8, Dulles Oral History Project, Mudd Library, Princeton University; Phleger interview with Philip Crowl, July 21, 1964, p. 71, Dulles Oral History Project, Mudd Library, Princeton University; Wainhouse interview with Philip Crowl, August 24, 1965, p. 36; Murphy interview with Richard D. Challener, May 19, 1965, pp. 30–32, Dulles Oral History Project, Mudd Library, Princeton University; Roderic L. O'Connor interview with Philip Crowl, April 2, 1966, pp. 168–69, *ibid.*

to leave Lodge in New York. Again, early in 1960, when Eisenhower advocated creating a new position, "secretary of government," similar to that of the prime minister under the parliamentary system, he suggested that Lodge would be ideally suited for this post or for secretary of state in a Nixon administration.[6] Lodge, in turn, respected Dulles's "encyclopedic" knowledge, tremendous diplomatic experience, and remarkable legal background. The ambassador was not simply fawning when he wrote the secretary that he had "read and re-read and carefully annotated" Dulles's latest book.[7] Neither Dulles nor Lodge wanted to be placed in the position of asking the president to choose between them.

The administration's success at the UN produced a gradual change in public opinion. Despite the fact that the influx of new nations and the emergence of troubling issues made the UN increasingly impervious to United States control as the 1950s progressed, public support increased steadily during the Eisenhower era. By 1960, 80 percent of those queried in a Gallup poll expressed support for the UN, up from 74 percent in 1955 and 55 percent in 1953. In the years after the formation of UNEF, increasing numbers of Americans also believed that the UN should have a permanent armed force.[8]

A variety of factors was responsible for the UN's improved standing among the American people. Lodge repeatedly attributed it to Eisenhower's "successful efforts in the foreign policy field" in his frequent letters keeping Eisenhower apprised of the latest polling results. Yet the rising support was also due in no small measure to Lodge's endeavors both at the UN and through the national media. Lodge's success at thwarting the Soviet Union, at least in televised debate, had earned him and the UN the gratitude of an

6. Memorandum of Conversation, January 13, 1960, Reel 29, HCLP, MHS; Eisenhower to Lodge, September 29, 1959, same reel; Journal entry, spring, 1959, same reel; *MTCH,* Reel 11, Lodge and Herter, March 9, 1960.

7. Lodge to Dulles, November 16, 1954, Reel 28, HCLP, MHS; Lodge to Dulles, March 9, 1953, in folder marked "Henry Cabot Lodge, Jr.: 1953," Box 72, J. F. Dulles Papers, Mudd Library.

8. See, for example, The Gallup poll of March 11, 1953, in George H. Gallup, ed., *The Gallup Poll: Public Opinion,* II, 1127–28; *ibid.,* 1341–42 (June 19, 1955); *ibid.,* 1459 (December 9, 1956); *ibid.,* 1478–79 (April 7, 1957); *ibid.,* 1518–19 (October 13, 1957); *ibid.,* 1544 (March 12, 1958); *ibid.,* 1679 (August 3, 1960); National Opinion Research Center poll—Current Popular Attitudes Toward the United Nations and UNESCO, August 26, 1955, in folder marked "U. N. Special Reports: 1950–1957," Box 24, Office of Public Opinion Studies, 1943–1965, RG 59, NA.

American people eager for even an oratorical triumph over communism. The ambassador also wrote numerous articles about his position and the good work being performed in multiple ways by the UN. Most important, both the administration's continued ability to prevent the UN from taking a stand against the United States on an important issue and its skill in obtaining UN backing on a host of matters of significant concern to the nation rightfully persuaded Americans that the United Nations was continuing to serve U.S. interests.[9]

Nixon's selection of Lodge as his running mate further attests to the salience of the United Nations during the Eisenhower administration. Lodge's prominence at the organization, especially during events such as the U-2 incident and the Congo rebellion, had brought him into the homes of millions of TV viewers as a powerful and vigorous advocate of American policy. Both political parties acknowledged Lodge as one of the key people who understood the Russians and how to handle them. With the exception of the secretary of state, the UN ambassador was arguably the nation's best-known diplomat and the most popular figure in the administration after the president.

Ambassador Lodge may have been the administration's photogenic point man in the television age, but President Eisenhower was indisputably the central figure in setting policy toward the United Nations. The president determined the broad direction of U.S. policy and provided essential directives for the State Department and USUN. Dulles, who headed an elaborate staff system, usually outlined the options. Lodge always had an open line to the president and frequently offered suggestions. But Eisenhower made the final decisions on important matters. Although he generally eschewed day-to-day involvement in the implementation of policy, during major international crises he always took charge of the situation and provided strong, forceful leadership.

9. Lodge to Eisenhower, October 16, 1957, Reel 29, HCLP, MHS; Lodge to Eisenhower, October 7, 1954, in folder marked "Henry Cabot Lodge: 1954 (4)," Box 24, Administration Series, EP, AWF, EL; Lodge to Eisenhower, August 26, 1955, Reel 29, HCLP, MHS; Eisenhower to Lodge, August 31, 1956, same reel. On Lodge's role, see, for example, Henry Cabot Lodge, Jr., "An Answer to Critics of the U. N.," *New York Times Magazine*, April 22, 1953, pp. 12–14; "Don't Sell the U. N. Short," *Newsweek*, October 12, 1953, p. 42. For a more detailed study of public opinion, see William A. Scott and Stephen B. Withey, *The United States and the United Nations: The Public View, 1945–1955* (New York, 1958).

As a result, the United States' interaction with the UN reflected the character of the president. While Eisenhower was capable of using the UN to propose innovative U.S. programs, such as the Atoms for Peace plan, more often his use of the organization mirrored his more fundamental outlook on American foreign policy. This general approach, stressing cautious and conservative pragmatism, produced accomplishments that even the president's admirers concede were mostly "negative in nature."[10] As he did elsewhere, Eisenhower counseled moderation, caution, and restraint. He sought to use the UN to prevent the spread of communism, to resist the disorderly movement toward decolonization, to impose order on an increasingly unsettled world, and to preserve a status quo that largely had benefited American national interests in the post-war world. Given this ambitious agenda, the Eisenhower administration could claim a remarkable degree of success.[11]

Eisenhower's use of the United Nations generally advanced American national interests. Even the limited and qualified support provided on decolonization and issues of importance to the Third World yielded benefits. Participation in debate on these questions heightened awareness of the extent and nature of the growing discontent in many underdeveloped nations. Moreover, the African–Asian–Arab–Latin American bloc's use of the UN as a forum to discuss these issues, and even a moderately sympathetic American response, permitted these nations an opportunity to vent their frustrations in a peaceful and ostensibly meaningful manner. Finally, the constant exposure over time to such arguments encouraged the United States gradually to distance itself from its colonial allies and to support some of the Third World's more reasonable measures.

In the final analysis, however, Eisenhower failed to use the United Nations to its fullest possible potential even given the restraints imposed by the cold war. To make the most of the UN as an instrument of U.S. foreign policy, Eisenhower would have had to take a far more activist approach to the organization. Little evidence exists to suggest a hidden-hand approach to his

10. Robert A. Divine, *Eisenhower and the Cold War* (New York, 1978), viii.

11. Eisenhower's fiscal conservatism also influenced his view of the UN. In March, 1962, the ex-president discouraged Kennedy from providing the UN with a long-term loan of $100 million. While he insisted that he wanted the UN preserved, he argued that "a deliberate resort to deficit spending in these matters would finally destroy the whole institution." Eisenhower to Herter, March 25, 1962, Folder 179, bMS Am 1829, Herter Papers, Houghton Library Harvard University; Herter to Eisenhower, March 29, 1962, *ibid.*

use of the UN. Eisenhower was at most a moderately activist president in this area. Given the UN's existence outside the scope of traditional bilateral diplomacy, a strong and unwavering presidential commitment would have been necessary to ensure that all possibilities for UN action were explored in full. Moreover, creative and innovative thinking, never watchwords for the Eisenhower presidency, would have been necessary to discover the most effective means for working through the UN to achieve international peace and facilitate responsible economic and social development in the midst of the cold war. Eisenhower demonstrated these qualities only on occasion, most notably with arms control in his Atoms for Peace and Open Skies proposals and in his steadfast support of UN intervention during the Suez Crisis. As a result, his administration's policies were neither as wise nor as effective as they might have been had the president provided more "hands-on" leadership and forcefully articulated a more positive vision of the role the United Nations could serve in achieving the United States' foreign policy goals.[12]

Unfortunately, Eisenhower chose not to invest his presidential prestige in any sort of follow-through on his proposals. Consequently, both Atoms for Peace and Open Skies languished in UN committees, where the former plan was even truncated beyond recognition. Similarly, once the immediate crisis in the Suez had been resolved, there was no multilateral follow-up to deal with the fundamental problems of the region. Indeed, the next time tensions rose in the Middle East, the United States resorted to a unilateral response in Lebanon. Only by being visibly engaged might the president have realized his rhetorical goal—a strengthened UN actively working in partnership with the United States in the quest for peace.

Eisenhower's approach prevailed not only because he was the president, but also because of the absence of a strong countervailing view within the administration. Dulles was preoccupied with the cold war struggle against communism, essentially satisfied with the international status quo as it per-

---

12. Interestingly, in retirement, Eisenhower voiced a strong and far more idealistic hope that the UN could acquire a military force. He asserted that the organization should be equipped with a peace force, armed with conventional and nuclear weapons, to enforce compliance with UN law and force nations to settle their disputes through recourse to the International Court of Justice in The Hague. Mary Kersey Harvey, "Of War and Peace and the United Nations: An Exclusive Interview with General Dwight D. Eisenhower," *Vista*, IV (January-February, 1968), 18–20.

tained to the Third World, ever wary of the response of a conservative Congress, and reluctant to surrender any authority to USUN or the UN. Secretary Dulles hence reinforced Eisenhower's proclivity to use the UN in a reactive and unimaginative fashion. Ambassador Lodge, a strong proponent of the UN, might have served such a purpose had he enjoyed greater policy-making influence. Though he could be as staunch a cold warrior as either the secretary or the president, Lodge was a flexible, pragmatic politician and he had a more keenly developed understanding of the importance of style as well as substance at the UN. As Eisenhower perceptively observed, Lodge was generally most concerned with altering "the wrappings of the packages that we have to sell" rather than seeking to change the substantive policy being sold. The ambassador thus consistently pressured the State Department to advance an agenda at the General Assembly that was "positive, constructive, and ha[d] sex appeal."[13] This was a request beyond the ken of those— Eisenhower and Dulles included—who personified the decade of the man in the gray flannel suit.

Ultimately, the Eisenhower administration's use of the United Nations represented, at least potentially, a missed opportunity. The United States possessed a degree of leverage in the United Nations that it would never have again, but it did not take sufficient advantage of this, especially in meeting the challenges posed by decolonization and the Third World. Using the UN as it had been intended to be used would have required a far different set of Soviet responses, but the administration also failed to explore all of the possibilities of using the UN in circumstances not directly involving the superpowers. While confronted with a new world scenario—two Great Powers engaged in an unprecedented cold war—Eisenhower and his chief foreign policy lieutenants drew upon experiences in traditional alliance and foreign policy situations to craft a policy that did not fully utilize a new and unique forum.

In the end, the best of intentions could not take the place of thoughtfulness, consistency, and a coherent policy. While it is true that creativity was not a hallmark of the administration's approach to problem solving in the foreign policy arena, it is often unclear whether the administration even realized that unprecedented circumstances offered the possibility of using

13. Eisenhower to Lodge, January 3, 1958, Reel 29, HCLP, MHS; *MTCH,* Reel 11, Herter and Lodge, June 9, 1960.

this new organization to help shape the post-war world order. A developing Third World in the midst of a never-before-seen cold war left the former general, the secretary of state who traced his lineage and ambition back to late-nineteenth-century diplomacy, and an ambassador brought up at the knee of America's most famous opponent of international organization in a confused state. They responded by pursuing a pragmatic and reactive path that most often used the UN to maintain a status quo that, in fact, was no more than an outdated memory.

As the first Republican administration in a generation, as the first group to confront the reality of an established cold war and an emerging Third World, and as the first administration to inherit an operating UN, Eisenhower and his men had an unparalleled opportunity to revamp the United States' role in world affairs. But the administration faced formidable constraints—its preoccupation with the cold war, its own partisan charges during the election of 1952, the burden of McCarthyism, divisions within the Republican party, the lingering isolationism manifested in the still-prevalent specter of the UN as a frightening, or at least suspect, usurper of American sovereignty. Consequently, it proved unwilling to venture wholeheartedly into new diplomatic arenas and its actions never approached the level of its rhetorical commitment to the UN. As a result, the Eisenhower administration left the world little safer and relegated the UN to a symbol of international impotence, a forum to be used only when it served the Great Powers' interests.

BIBLIOGRAPHY

PRIMARY SOURCES

Manuscripts

Baker Memorial Library, Dartmouth College, Hanover, New Hampshire
    Adams, Sherman. Papers.
Dwight D. Eisenhower Library, Abilene, Kansas
    Adams, Sherman. Papers.
    Brownell, Herbert, Jr. Papers.
    Dulles, John Foster. Papers.
    Eisenhower, Dwight D.
        Pre-Presidential Papers, 1916–1952.
        Papers as President of the United States, 1953–1961 (Ann Whitman File).
            Administration series.
            Cabinet series.
            Campaign series.
            DDE Diary series.
            Dulles-Herter series.
            International series.
            International Meetings series.
            Legislative Meeting series.
            NSC series.
            Presidential Transition series.
            Press Conference series.
            Ann Whitman Diary series.

Records as President, White House Central Files, 1953–1961.
    Confidential File.
    Official File.
    Pre-Inaugural File.
Eisenhower, Milton S. Papers.
Hagerty, James C. Papers.
Hanes, John W., Jr. Papers.
Harlow, Bryce N. Papers.
Herter, Christian A. Papers.
Jackson, C. D. Papers, Records.
Jacoby, Neil H. Papers.
Lord, Mary Pillsbury. Papers.
Smith, Walter Bedell. Papers.
White House Office, Cabinet Secretariat: Records, 1953–1961.
White House Office, National Security Council Staff: Papers, 1948–1961; Records, 1948–1961.
White House Office, Office of the Special Assistant for Disarmament: Records, 1955–1958.
Houghton Library, Harvard University, Cambridge, Massachusetts
    Herter, Christian A. Papers.
Massachusetts Historical Society, Boston, Massachusetts
    Lodge, Henry Cabot, II. Papers.
National Archives, Washington, D.C.
    Record Group 59. Records of the Department of State.
Seeley G. Mudd Library, Princeton University, Princeton, New Jersey
    Dulles, Allen W. Papers.
    Dulles, John Foster. Papers.
    Hughes, Emmet J. Papers.
    Phleger, Herman. Papers.
United Nations Archives, New York, New York
    The Executive Office: Office of the Executive Assistant (1946–1961), Office of the Secretary-General. Records.

Interviews and Oral Histories
Columbia University Oral History Project, Butler Library, Columbia University, New York, New York
    Dumont, Donald A., by John T. Mason, December 28, 1972.
    Hagerty, James C., by Ed Erwin, January 31, 1968.
    Jacoby, Neil H., by James V. Mink, November–December 1970.
    Lord, Mary Pillsbury, by John T. Mason, June 6, 1967.

Wadsworth, James J., by John T. Mason, April–June 1967.

Wilcox, Francis O., by John Luter, April 3, 1972.

John Foster Dulles Oral History Project, Seeley G. Mudd Manuscript Library, Princeton University, Princeton, New Jersey

Cordier, Andrew W., by Richard Challener, February 1, 1967.

Dulles, Allen W., by Philip Crowl, June 3, 1964.

Gross, Ernest, by Richard D. Challener, November 5, 1964.

Hanes, John W., Jr., by Philip Crowl, January 29, 1966.

Henderson, Loy, by Don North, December 14, 1970.

Munro, Leslie Knox, by Spencer Davis, September 10, 1964.

Murphy, Robert, by Richard D. Challener, May 19, 1965.

O'Connor, Roderic L., by Philip Crowl, April 2, 1966.

Phleger, Herman, by Philip Crowl, July 21, 1964.

Wadsworth, James J., by Philip Crowl, June 21, 1965.

Wainhouse, John, by Philip Crowl, August 24, 1965.

Newspapers, Magazines, and Journals

Foreign Service Journal, 1953–1961.

Newsweek, 1952–1961.

New York *Times,* 1952–1961.

Time, 1952–1961.

United Nations Bulletin, 1953–1954.

United Nations Review, 1954–1961.

U.S. News & World Report, 1952–1961.

Microfilm

Kesaris, Paul, and Joan Gibson, eds. *Minutes of Telephone Conversations of John Foster Dulles and Christian Herter, 1953–1961.* Washington, D.C., 1980. 11 reels.

Legislative Meeting Series, 1952–1960. Frederick, Md., 1980. 2 reels.

Government Publications

Codification of Presidential Proclamations and Executive Orders: April 13, 1945–January 20, 1989. Washington, D.C., 1989.

Congressional Record, 1953–1961.

Department of State Bulletin, 1953–1961.

Foreign Relations of the United States, 1952–1954.

Vol. I, *General Economic and Political Matters* (1983).

Vol. II, *National Security Affairs* (1984).

Vol. III, *United Nations Affairs* (1979).

Vol. IV, *The American Republics* (1983).

Vol. XI, *Africa and South Asia* (1983).

Vol. XIII, *Indochina* (1982).

Vol. XIV, *China and Japan* (1985).

Vol. XV, *Korea* (1984).

Vol. XVI, *The Geneva Conference* (1984).

Foreign Relations of the United States, 1955–1957.

Vol. II, *China* (1986).

Vol. III, *China* (1986).

Vol. IX, *Foreign Economic Policy; Foreign Information Program* (1987).

Vol. XI, *United Nations and General International Matters* (1988).

Vol. XIII, *Near East: Jordan-Yemen* (1988).

Vol. XVI, *Suez Crisis: July 26–December 31, 1956* (1990).

Vol. XVII, *Arab-Israeli Dispute, 1957* (1990).

Vol. XX, *Regulation of Armaments; Atomic Energy* (1990).

Vol. XXV, *Eastern Europe* (1990).

Foreign Relations of the United States, 1958–1960.

Vol. II, *United Nations and General International Matters* (1991).

Vol. IV, *Foreign Economic Policy* (1991).

Vol. IX, *Berlin Crisis, 1959–1960; Germany; Austria* (1993).

Vol. XI, *Lebanon and Jordan* (1992).

Vol. XIV, *Africa* (1992).

Public Papers of the Presidents of the United States: Dwight D. Eisenhower, 1953–1961. 8 vols. Washington, D.C., 1989.

U.S. Congress. House. 83rd Cong., 1st Sess. *Hearings Before the Subcommittee on International Organizations and Movements of the Committee on Foreign Affairs* (1953).

―――. 83rd Cong., 2nd Sess. *Hearings Before the Subcommittee on International Organizations and Movements of the Committee on Foreign Affairs* (1954).

―――. 85th Cong., 2nd Sess. *Hearings Before the Subcommittee on International Organization and Movements of the Committee on Foreign Affairs on House Res. 367 and House Res. 373* (1957).

U.S. Congress. Senate. 83rd Cong., 1st Sess. *Hearings Before the Committee on Foreign Relations on Nomination of Henry Cabot Lodge to Be United States Representative to the United Nations* (1953).

―――. 83rd Cong., 1st Sess. *Hearings Before the Committee on Foreign Relations on Nomination of John Foster Dulles, Secretary of State-Designate* (1953).

―――. 83rd Cong., 1st Sess. *Hearing Before the Committee on Foreign Relations; Testimony of Ambassador Henry Cabot Lodge, Jr., the United States Representative to the United Nations, and Representative in the Security Council* (1953).

―――. 83rd Cong., 1st Sess. *Preventing Citizens of the United States of Questionable*

Loyalty to the United States Government from Accepting Any Office or Employment in or under the United Nations. Presented by Sen. Pat McCarran (1953).

———. 82nd Cong., 2nd Sess. *Hearings Before the Subcommittee to Investigate the Administration of the Internal Security Act and Other Internal Security Laws; Activities of United States Citizens Employed by the United Nations* (1952).

———. 83rd Cong., 1st Sess. *Hearings Before the Subcommittee to Investigate the Administration of the Internal Security Act and Other Internal Security Laws of the Committee on the Judiciary—Activities of United States Citizens Employed by the United Nations* (1953).

———. 83rd Cong., 2nd Sess. *Hearings Before the Subcommittee to Investigate the Administration of the Internal Security Act and Other Internal Security Laws of the Committee on the Judiciary—Activities of United States Citizens Employed by the United Nations* (1954).

———. 84th Cong., 2nd Sess. Report No. 2118 of the Committee on the Judiciary, *Preventing Citizens of the United States of Questionable Loyalty to the United States Government from Accepting Any Office or Employment in or under the United Nations* (1956).

———. 85th Cong., 1st Sess. *Hearings Before the Committee on Foreign Relations and the Committee on Armed Services on S. J. Res 19 and H. J. Res. 117* (1957).

Documents of the United Nations

Economic and Social Council. Doc. E/2397, VII Sess., April 10, 1953.

General Assembly. "Report of the Special Committee on the Problem of Hungary." Doc. A/3593, Supplement No. 18, XI Sess., 1957.

Secretariat. "Report of the Secretary General to the General Assembly." Doc. A/2364, VII Sess., January 30, 1953.

UN Doc. A/L 146, VII Sess., March 28, 1953.

Diaries, Memoirs, and Other Published Primary Sources

Adams, Sherman. *Firsthand Report: The Story of the Eisenhower Administration.* New York, 1961.

Association of the Bar of the City of New York. *Report of the Special Committee on the Federal Loyalty-Security Program.* New York, 1956.

Benson, Ezra Taft. *Cross Fire: Eight Years with Eisenhower.* Westport, 1962.

Boyle, Peter G., ed. *The Churchill-Eisenhower Correspondence, 1953–1955.* Chapel Hill, 1990.

Brownell, Herbert, with John P. Burke. *Advising Ike: The Memoirs of Attorney General Herbert Brownell.* Lawrence, 1993.

Chandler, Alfred D., *et al.,* eds. *The Papers of Dwight David Eisenhower.* Baltimore, 1970–1989. 13 vols.

Cordier, Andrew Wellington, and Wilder Foote, eds. *Public Papers of the Secretaries-General of the United Nations: Dag Hammarskjöld.* 8 vols. New York, 1969–1977.

Cutler, Robert. *No Time for Rest.* Boston, 1966.

Dayal, Rajeshwar. *Mission for Hammarskjöld: The Congo Crisis.* Princeton, 1976.

Dulles, Allen W. *The Craft of Intelligence.* New York, 1963.

Dulles, John Foster. *War or Peace.* New York, 1950.

―――. *War, Peace, and Change.* New York, 1939.

Eban, Abba. *The New Diplomacy: International Affairs in the Modern Age.* New York, 1983.

Eden, Anthony. *Full Circle.* Boston, 1960.

Eisenhower, Dwight D. *At Ease: Stories I Tell to Friends.* Garden City, 1967.

―――. *Crusade in Europe.* Garden City, 1949.

―――. *Mandate for Change, 1953–1956.* Garden City, 1963. Vol. I of Eisenhower, *The White House Years.* 2 vols.

―――. *Peace with Justice: Selected Addresses of Dwight D. Eisenhower.* New York, 1961.

―――. *Waging Peace, 1956–1961.* Garden City, 1965. Vol. II of Eisenhower, *The White House Years.* 2 vols.

Eisenhower, John S. D. *Strictly Personal.* Garden City, 1974.

Eisenhower, Milton S. *The President Is Calling.* Garden City, 1974.

Ferrell, Robert H., ed. *The Diary of James C. Hagerty: Eisenhower in Mid-Course, 1954–1955.* Bloomington, 1983.

―――, ed. *The Eisenhower Diaries.* New York, 1981.

Gallup, George H., ed. *The Gallup Poll: Public Opinion, 1935–1971.* 3 vols. New York, 1972.

Griffith, Robert, ed. *Ike's Letters to a Friend, 1941–1958.* Lawrence, 1984.

Hughes, Emmet John. *The Ordeal of Power: A Political Memoir of the Eisenhower Years.* New York, 1963.

Lie, Trygve. *In the Cause of Peace: Seven Years with the UN.* New York, 1954.

Lodge, Henry Cabot. *As It Was: An Inside View of Politics and Power in the '50s and '60s.* New York, 1976.

―――. *The Storm Has Many Eyes: A Personal Narrative.* New York, 1973.

Murphy, Robert. *Diplomat Among Warriors.* Garden City, 1964.

Nixon, Richard M. *The Memoirs of Richard Nixon.* New York, 1978.

Rozek, Edward J., ed. *Walter H. Judd: Chronicles of a Statesman.* Denver, 1980.

Stassen, Harold, and Marshall Houts. *Eisenhower: Turning the World Toward Peace.* St. Paul, 1990.

Strauss, Lewis L. *Men and Decisions.* Garden City, 1962.

Taylor, Allan, ed. *What Eisenhower Thinks.* New York, 1952.

Treuenfels, Rudolph L., ed. *Eisenhower Speaks: Dwight D. Eisenhower in His Messages and Speeches*. New York, 1948.

Wadsworth, James J. *The Glass House*. New York, 1966.

SECONDARY SOURCES

Books

Abi-Saab, George. *The United Nations Operation in the Congo, 1960–1964*. Oxford, 1978.

Accinelli, Robert. *Crisis and Commitment: United States Policy Toward Taiwan, 1950–1955*. Chapel Hill, 1996.

Agwani, M. S., ed. *The Lebanese Crisis, 1958: A Documentary Study*. London, 1965.

Alexander, Bevin. *Korea: The First War We Lost*. New York, 1986.

Alexander, Charles C. *Holding the Line: The Eisenhower Era, 1952–1961*. Bloomington, 1975.

Alger, Chadwick F. *United States Representation in the United Nations*. New York, 1961.

Aliano, Richard. *American Defense Policy from Eisenhower to Kennedy: The Politics of Changing Military Requirements*. Athens, 1975.

Alin, Erika. *The United States and the 1958 Lebanon Crisis: American Intervention in the Middle East*. Lanham, 1994.

Allen, Craig. *Eisenhower and the Mass Media: Peace, Prosperity, and Prime Time*. Chapel Hill, 1993.

Alteras, Isaac. *Eisenhower and Israel: U.S.-Israeli Relations, 1953–1960*. Gainesville, 1993.

Ambrose, Stephen E. *Eisenhower: Soldier, General of the Army, President-Elect, 1890–1952*. New York, 1983.

————. *Eisenhower: The President*. New York, 1984.

Anderson, David L. *Trapped by Success: The Eisenhower Administration and Vietnam, 1953–1961*. New York, 1991.

Arend, Anthony Clark. *Pursuing a Just and Durable Peace: John Foster Dulles and International Organization*. New York, 1988.

Beichman, Arnold. *The "Other" State Department: The United States Mission to the United Nations—Its Role in the Making of Foreign Policy*. New York, 1967.

Billings-Yun, Melanie. *Decision Against War: Eisenhower and Dien Bien Phu, 1954*. New York, 1986.

Bischof, Günter, and Stephen E. Ambrose, eds. *Eisenhower: A Centenary Assessment*. Baton Rouge, 1995.

Blair, Anne. *Lodge in Vietnam: A Patriot Abroad*. New Haven, 1995.

Bloomfield, Lincoln P. *The United Nations and U.S. Foreign Policy.* Boston, 1960.

Boyd, Andrew. *Fifteen Men on a Powder Keg: A History of the UN Security Council.* New York, 1971.

Brands, Henry W. *Cold Warriors: Eisenhower's Generation and American Foreign Policy.* New York, 1988.

————. *The Devil We Knew: America and the Cold War.* New York, 1993.

————. *The Specter of Neutralism: The United States and the Emergence of the Third World, 1947–1960.* New York, 1989.

Brendon, Piers. *Ike: His Life and Times.* New York, 1986.

Broadwater, Jeff. *Eisenhower and the Anti-Communist Crusade.* Chapel Hill, 1992.

Brown, Ralph S., Jr. *Loyalty and Security: Employment Tests in the United States.* New Haven, 1958.

Bundy, McGeorge. *Danger and Survival: Choices About the Bomb in the First Fifty Years.* New York, 1988.

Burk, Robert F. *Dwight D. Eisenhower: Hero and Politician.* Boston, 1986.

Calhoun, Daniel F. *Hungary and Suez, 1956: An Exploration of Who Makes History.* Lanham, 1991.

Caridi, Ronald J. *The Korean War and American Politics: The Republican Party as a Case Study.* Philadelphia, 1968.

Caute, David. *The Great Fear: The Anti-Communist Purge Under Truman and Eisenhower.* New York, 1978.

Claude, Inis L., Jr. *Swords into Plowshares: The Problems and Progress of International Organization.* New York, 1984.

Cogan, Charles G. *Oldest Allies, Guarded Friends: The United States and France Since 1940.* Westport, 1994.

Cook, Blanche Wiessen. *The Declassified Eisenhower: A Divided Legacy.* New York, 1981.

Cooper, Chester L. *The Lion's Last Roar: Suez, 1956.* New York, 1978.

Costigliola, Frank. *France and the United States: The Cold Alliance Since World War II.* New York, 1992.

Craig, Gordon A., and Frank Loewenheim, eds. *The Diplomats, 1939–1979.* Princeton, 1994.

Cullather, Nick. *Illusions of Influence: The Political Economy of United States–Philippine Relations, 1942–1960.* Stanford, 1994.

Cumings, Bruce. *The Origins of the Korean War.* Princeton, 1981.

Divine, Robert A. *Blowing on the Wind: The Nuclear Test Ban Debate.* New York, 1978.

————. *Eisenhower and the Cold War.* New York, 1981.

Dowty, Alan. *Middle East Crisis: U.S. Decision-Making in 1958, 1970, and 1973.* Berkeley, 1984.

Duiker, William J. *U.S. Containment Policy and the Conflict in Indochina.* Stanford, 1994.

Fasulo, Linda M. *Representing America: Experiences of U.S. Diplomats at the UN.* New York, 1984.

Finer, Herman. *Dulles over Suez: The Theory and Practice of His Diplomacy.* Chicago, 1964.

Finger, Seymour Maxwell. *American Ambassadors at the UN: People, Politics, and Bureaucracy in Making Foreign Policy.* New York, 1988.

————. *Your Man at the U. N.: People, Politics, and Bureaucracy in Making Foreign Policy.* New York, 1980.

Foot, Rosemary. *A Substitute for Victory: The Politics of Peacemaking at the Korean Armistice Talks.* Ithaca, 1990.

————. *The Wrong War: American Policy and the Dimensions of the Korean Conflict, 1950–1953.* Ithaca, 1985.

Freedman, Lawrence. *The Evolution of Nuclear Strategy.* New York, 1981.

Fried, Richard M. *Nightmare in Red: The McCarthy Era in Perspective.* New York, 1990.

Gaddis, John Lewis. *Strategies of Containment: A Critical Appraisal of Postwar American National Security Policy.* New York, 1982.

Gardner, Lloyd C. *Approaching Vietnam: From World War II Through Dienbienphu, 1941–1954.* New York, 1988.

Garthoff, Raymond L. *Assessing the Adversary: Estimates by the Eisenhower Administration of Soviet Intentions and Capabilities.* Washington, D.C., 1991.

Gleijeses, Piero. *Shattered Hope: The Guatemalan Revolution and the United States, 1944–1954.* Princeton, 1991.

Goodrich, Leland. *Korea: A Study of U.S. Policy in the United Nations.* Westport, 1979.

Goria, Wade R. *Sovereignty and Leadership in Lebanon, 1943–1976.* London, 1985.

Gray, Robert K. *Eighteen Acres Under Glass.* Garden City, 1971.

Greenstein, Fred I. *The Hidden-Hand Presidency: Eisenhower as Leader.* New York, 1982.

Griffith, Robert. *The Politics of Fear: Joseph R. McCarthy and the Senate.* Lexington, 1970.

Guhin, Michael A. *John Foster Dulles: A Statesman and His Times.* New York, 1972.

Hadwen, John G., and Johan Kaufmann. *How United Nations Decisions Are Made.* Leyden, 1960.

Harding, Harry, and Yuan Ming, eds. *Sino-American Relations, 1945–1955: A Joint Reassessment of a Critical Decade.* Wilmington, 1989.

Hatch, Alden. *The Lodges of Massachusetts.* New York, 1973.

Herring, George C. *America's Longest War: The United States and Vietnam, 1950–1975.* New York, 1986.

Hewlett, Richard G., and Jack M. Holl. *Atoms for Peace and War, 1953–1961: Eisenhower and the Atomic Energy Commission.* Berkeley, 1989.

Hoopes, Townsend. *The Devil and John Foster Dulles.* Boston, 1973.

House, Arthur H. *The U. N. in the Congo: The Political and Civilian Efforts.* Washington, D.C., 1978.

Huss, Pierre J., and George Carpozi, Jr. *Red Spies in the UN.* New York, 1965.

Immerman, Richard. *The CIA in Guatemala: The Foreign Policy of Intervention.* Austin, 1982.

————, ed. *John Foster Dulles and the Diplomacy of the Cold War.* Princeton, 1990.

Kahin, George McT. *Intervention: How America Became Involved in Vietnam.* New York, 1986.

Kalb, Madeline G. *The Congo Cables: The Cold War in Africa—From Eisenhower to Kennedy.* New York, 1982.

Kaplan, Lawrence S., Denise Artaud, and Mark R. Rubin, eds. *Dien Bien Phu and the Crisis of Franco-American Relations, 1954–1955.* Wilmington, 1990.

Kaufman, Burton I. *The Korean War: Challenges in Crisis, Credibility and Command.* Philadelphia, 1986.

————. *Trade and Aid: Eisenhower's Foreign Economic Policy, 1953–1961.* Baltimore, 1982.

Kecskemeti, Paul. *The Unexpected Revolution.* Stanford, 1961.

Kingseed, Cole C. *Eisenhower and the Suez Crisis of 1956.* Baton Rouge, 1995.

Krieg, Joann P., ed. *Dwight D. Eisenhower: Soldier, President, Statesman.* Westport, 1987.

Kunz, Diane B. *The Economic Diplomacy of the Suez Crisis.* Chapel Hill, 1991.

Kyle, Keith. *Suez.* New York, 1991.

Lefever, Ernest W. *Crisis in the Congo: A United Nations Force in Action.* Washington, D.C., 1965.

Louis, William Roger, and Roger Owen. *Suez 1956: The Crisis and Its Consequences.* New York, 1989.

Love, Kenneth. *Suez: The Twice-Fought War.* New York, 1969.

Lowe, Peter. *The Origins of the Korean War.* New York, 1986.

Lucas, W. Scott. *Divided We Stand: Britain, the United States and the Suez Crisis.* London, 1991.

Lyon, Peter. *Eisenhower: Portrait of the Hero.* Boston, 1974.

McCormick, Thomas J. *America's Half-Century: United States Foreign Policy in the Cold War and After.* Baltimore, 1995.

MacDonald, Callum. *Korea: The War Before Vietnam.* New York, 1986.

Melanson, Richard A., and David Mayers, eds. *Reevaluating Eisenhower: American Foreign Policy in the Fifties.* Chicago, 1989.

Medhurst, Martin J. *Dwight D. Eisenhower: Strategic Communicator.* Westport, 1993.

————. *Eisenhower's War of Words: Rhetoric and Leadership.* East Lansing, 1994.

Miller, Richard I. *Dag Hammarskjöld and Crisis Diplomacy.* New York, 1961.

Miller, William J. *Henry Cabot Lodge.* New York, 1967.

Mitrany, David. *The Progress of International Government.* New Haven, 1933.

————. *A Working Peace System.* Chicago, 1966.

Neff, Donald. *Warriors at Suez: Eisenhower Takes America into the Middle East.* New York, 1981.

Noble, G. Bernard. *Christian A. Herter.* New York, 1970.

Noer, Thomas J. *Black Liberation: The United States and White Rule in Africa, 1948–1968.* Columbia, Mo., 1985.

O'Brien, Conor Cruise, and Feliks Topolski. *The United Nations: Sacred Drama.* New York, 1968.

Pach, Chester J., Jr., and Elmo Richardson. *The Presidency of Dwight D. Eisenhower.* Rev. ed. Lawrence, 1991.

Parmet, Herbert S. *Eisenhower and the American Crusades.* New York, 1972.

Pickett, William B. *Dwight David Eisenhower and American Power.* Wheeling, Ill., 1995.

Plummer, Brenda Gayle. *Rising Wind: Black Americans and U.S. Foreign Affairs, 1935–1960.* Chapel Hill, 1996.

Pruessen, Ronald W. *John Foster Dulles: The Road to Power.* New York, 1982.

Pryce-Jones, David. *The Hungarian Revolution.* New York, 1970.

Radvanyi, Janos. *Hungary and the Superpowers: The 1956 Revolution and Realpolitik.* Stanford, 1972.

Rees, David. *Korea: The Limited War.* New York, 1964.

Reichard, Gary W. *The Reaffirmation of Republicanism: Eisenhower and the Eighty-Third Congress.* Knoxville, 1975.

Reinhard, David W. *The Republican Right Since 1945.* Lexington, 1983.

Riggs, Robert Edwin. *Politics in the United Nations: A Study of United States Influence in the General Assembly.* Urbana, 1958.

————. *US/UN: Foreign Policy and International Organization.* New York, 1971.

Rostow, Walt Whitman. *Eisenhower, Kennedy, and Foreign Aid.* Austin, 1985.

————. *Open Skies: Eisenhower's Proposal of July 21, 1956.* Austin, 1982.

Rotter, Andrew J. *The Path to Vietnam.* Ithaca, 1987.

Schlesinger, Stephen, and Stephen Kinzer. *Bitter Fruit: The Untold Story of the American Coup in Guatemala.* Garden City, 1982.

Scott, William A., and Stephen B. Withey. *The United States and the United Nations: The Public View, 1945–1955.* New York, 1958.

Shepherd, George W. *Anti-Apartheid: Transnational Conflict and Western Policy in the Liberation of South Africa.* Westport, 1977.

————, ed. *Racial Influences on American Foreign Policy.* New York, 1970.

Stoessinger, John G. *The United Nations and the Superpowers: United States–Soviet Interaction at the United Nations.* New York, 1965.

Stueck, William. *The Road to Confrontation: American Policy Toward China and Korea, 1947–1950.* Chapel Hill, 1981.

Tananbaum, Duane A. *The Bricker Amendment Controversy: A Test of Eisenhower's Political Leadership.* Ithaca, 1988.

Thomas, Hugh. *The Suez Affair.* Middlesex, England, 1970.

Troen, Selwyn Ilan, and Moshe Shemesh. *The Suez-Sinai Crisis, 1956: Retrospective and Reappraisal.* New York, 1990.

Urquhart, Brian. *Decolonization and World Peace.* Austin, 1989.

————. *Hammarskjöld.* New York, 1972.

Weissman, Stephen R. *American Foreign Policy in the Congo, 1960–1964.* Ithaca, 1974.

Young, John W., ed. *The Foreign Policy of Churchill's Peacetime Administration, 1951–1955.* Leicester, England, 1988.

Zacher, Mark W. *Dag Hammarskjöld's United Nations.* New York, 1970.

Zinner, Paul E. *Revolution in Hungary.* New York, 1962.

Articles

Accinelli, Robert. "Eisenhower, Congress, and the 1954–55 Offshore Island Crisis." *Presidential Studies Quarterly,* XX (1990), 329–48.

Aldrich, Winthrop W. "The Suez Crisis: A Footnote to History." *Foreign Affairs,* XLV (1967), 541–52.

Alger, Chadwick F. "United Nations Participation as a Learning Experience." *Public Opinion Quarterly,* XXVII (1963), 411–26.

Anderson, David L., and Daniel P. O'C. Greene. "John Foster Dulles and the End of the Franco-American Entente in Indochina." *Diplomatic History,* XVI (1992), 551–71.

Appathurai, E. R. "Permanent Missions to the United Nations." *International Journal,* XXV (1970), 287–301.

Asher, Robert E. "Multilateral Versus Bilateral Aid: An Old Controversy Revisited." *International Organization,* XVI (1962), 697–719.

Beckhoefer, Bernard G. "The Disarmament Deadlock, 1945–1955." *Social Education,* XXVI (1962), 375–82.

Bloomfield, Lincoln. "American Policy Toward the UN—Some Bureaucratic Reflections." *International Organization,* XII (1958), 1–16.

————. "China, the United States, and the United Nations." *International Organization,* XX (1966), 653–76.

————. "How the U.S. Government Is Organized to Participate in the U.N. System." *Department of State Bulletin,* September 17, 1956, pp. 435–42.

————. "The United States, the United Nations, and the Creation of Community." *International Organization,* XIV (1960), 503–13.

Boutros-Ghali, Boutros. "Empowering the United Nations." *Foreign Affairs,* LXXI (1993), 89–102.

Brands, H. W. "The Age of Vulnerability: Eisenhower and the National Insecurity State." *American Historical Review,* XCIV (1989), 963–89.

————. "Testing Massive Retaliation: Credibility and Crisis Management in the Taiwan Strait." *International Security,* XII (1988), 124–51.

Chang, Gordon H. "To the Nuclear Brink: Eisenhower, Dulles, and the Quemoy-Matsu Crisis." *International Security,* XII (1988), 96–122.

Chang, Gordon H., and He Di. "The Absence of War in the U.S.-China Confrontation over Quemoy and Matsu in 1954–1955: Contingency, Luck, Deterrence?" *American Historical Review,* XCVIII (1993), 1500–24.

Claude, Inis L., Jr. "The Management of Power in the Changing United Nations." *International Organization,* XV (1961), 219–35.

————. "The Symbolic Significance of the United Nations." *The Virginia Quarterly Review,* XXVII (1971), 481–504.

Combs, Arthur. "The Path Not Taken: The British Alternative to U.S. Policy in Vietnam, 1954–1956." *Diplomatic History,* XIX (1995), 33–57.

Cory, Robert H., Jr. "The Role of Public Opinion in United States Policies Toward the United Nations." *International Organization,* XI (1957), 220–27.

Curtis, Gerald L. "The United Nations Observer Group in Lebanon." *International Organization,* XVIII (1964), 738–65.

Dingman, Roger. "Atomic Diplomacy During the Korean War." *Diplomatic History,* XIII (1989) 50–91.

Dulles, John Foster. "Challenge and Response in United States Policy." *Foreign Affairs,* XXXVI (1957), 25–43.

————. "A First Balance Sheet on the United Nations." *International Conciliation,* CDXXVIII (1946), 177–82.

————. "The Future of the United Nations." *International Conciliation,* CDXLV (1948), 579–90.

————. "Policy for Security and Peace." *Foreign Affairs,* XXXII (1954), 353–64.

————. "A Policy of Boldness." *Life,* May 19, 1952, pp. 149–60.

————. "Thoughts on Soviet Foreign Policy and What to Do About It." *Life,* June 10, 1946, pp. 119–27.

————. "What Shall We Do with the U.N.?" *Christian Century,* September 3, 1947, p. 1041.

Fedder, Edwin H. "United States Loyalty Procedures and the Recruitment of UN Personnel." *Western Political Quarterly,* XV (1962), 705–12.

Finger, Seymour Maxwell. "United States Policy Toward International Institutions." *International Organization,* XXX (1976), 347–60.

Frye, William R. "Press Coverage of the United Nations." *International Organization,* X (1956), 276–81.

Gordon, Leonard H. D. "United States Opposition to Use of Force in the Taiwan Strait, 1954–1962." *Journal of American History,* LXXII (1985), 637–60.

Griffith, Robert. "Dwight D. Eisenhower and the Corporate Commonwealth." *American Historical Review,* LXXXVII (1982), 87–122.

Gross, Leo. "Immunities and Privileges of Delegations to the United Nations." *International Organization,* XVI (1962), 483–520.

Harvey, Mary Kersey. "Of War and Peace and the United Nations: An Exclusive Interview with General Dwight D. Eisenhower." *Vista,* IV (January-February, 1968), 14–21.

Hero, Alfred O. "The Negro Influence on U.S. Foreign Policy, 1937–1967." *Journal of Conflict Resolution,* XIII (1969), 220–51.

Herring, George C., and Richard H. Immerman. "Eisenhower, Dulles, and Dienbienphu: 'The Day We Didn't Go to War' Revisited." *Journal of American History,* LXXI (1984), 346–63.

Hoffman, Paul. "Blueprint for Foreign Aid." *New York Times Magazine,* February 17, 1957, p. 9.

———. "Operation Breakthrough." *Foreign Affairs,* XXXVIII (1959), 30–45.

Hoffman, Stanley. "Sisyphus and the Avalanche: The United Nations, Egypt, and Hungary." *International Organization,* XI (1957), 446–69.

Holsti, Ole. "The 'Operational Code' Approach to the Study of Political Leaders: John Foster Dulles' Philosophical and Instrumental Beliefs." *Canadian Journal of Political Science,* III (1970), 123–57.

Hyde, James N. "United States Participation in the United Nations." *International Organization,* X (1956), 22–34.

Immerman, Richard H. "Confessions of an Eisenhower Revisionist: An Agonizing Reappraisal." *Diplomatic History,* XIV (1990), 319–42.

———. "The United States and the Geneva Conference of 1954: A New Look." *Diplomatic History,* XIV (1990), 43–66.

Kaufmann, Johan. "The Capacity of the U. N. Development Program." *International Organization,* XXV (1971), 938–49.

Keefer, Edward C. "President Dwight D. Eisenhower and the End of the Korean War." *Diplomatic History,* X (1986), 267–89.

Lear, John. "Ike and the Peaceful Atom." *Reporter,* XII (1956), 11–21.

Little, Douglas. "His Finest Hour?: Eisenhower, Lebanon, and the 1958 Middle East Crisis." *Diplomatic History,* XX (1996), 27–54.

Lodge, Henry Cabot. "Eisenhower and the GOP." *Harper's,* CCIV (May, 1952), 34–39.

————. "Modernize the G. O. P." *Atlantic Monthly,* March 23, 1950, pp. 23–28.

Luck, Edward C. "Making Peace." *Foreign Policy,* LXXXIX (1993), 156–74.

Meers, Sharon. "The British Connection: How the United States Covered Its Tracks in the 1954 Coup in Guatemala." *Diplomatic History,* XVI (1992), 409–28.

Merrill, Dennis. "The United States and the Rise of the Third World." In Gordon Martel, ed. *American Foreign Relations Reconsidered, 1890–1993.* London, 1994.

Nelson, Anna Kasten. "The 'Top of Policy Hill': President Eisenhower and the National Security Council." *Diplomatic History,* VII (1983), 307–26.

Oren, Michael B. "The Test of Suez: Israel and the Middle East Crisis of 1958." *Studies in Zionism,* XII (1991), 55–83.

Ovendale, Ritchie. "Great Britain and the Anglo-American Invasion of Jordan and Lebanon in 1958." *International History Review,* XVI (1994), 284–303.

Pedersen, Richard F. "National Representation in the United Nations." *International Organization,* XV (1961), 256–66.

Pemberton, Gregory James. "Australia, the United States, and the Indochina Crisis of 1954." *Diplomatic History,* XIII (1989), 45–66.

Richardson, Channing B. "The United States Mission to the United Nations." *International Organization,* VII (1953), 22–34.

Riggs, Robert. "The United Nations as an Influence on United States Policy." *International Studies Quarterly,* XI (1967), 97–109.

Rochester, J. Martin. "The Rise and Fall of International Organization as a Field of Study." *International Organization,* XL (1986), 777–89.

Rosenberg, David Allan. "The Origins of Overkill: Nuclear Weapons and American Strategy, 1945–1960." *International Security,* VII (1983), 3–71.

Rubinstein, Alvin Z. "Soviet and American Policies in International Economic Organizations." *International Organization,* XVIII (1964), 29–52.

Rushkoff, Bennett C. "Eisenhower, Dulles and the Quemoy-Matsu Crisis, 1954–1955." *Political Science Quarterly,* XCVI (1981), 465–80.

Sanders, William. "Assignment to the United Nations." *Foreign Service Journal,* XXX (November, 1953), 24–27, 62–64.

Snyder, William. "Dean Rusk to John Foster Dulles, May–June 1953: The Office, the First 100 Days, and Red China." *Diplomatic History,* VII (1983), 79–86.

Soapes, Thomas F. "A Cold Warrior Seeks Peace: Eisenhower's Strategy for Nuclear Disarmament." *Diplomatic History,* IV (1980), 57–71.

Suri, Jeremy. "America's Search for a Technological Solution to the Arms Race: The

Surprise Attack Conference of 1958 and a Challenge for 'Eisenhower Revisionists.'" *Diplomatic History,* XXI (1997), 417–51.

Tananbaum, Duane A. "The Bricker Amendment Controversy: Its Origins and Eisenhower's Role." *Diplomatic History,* IX (1985), 73–93.

Wall, Irwin M. "The United States, Algeria, and the Fall of the Fourth French Republic." *Diplomatic History,* XVIII (1994), 489–511.

Wilcox, Francis O. "The Atlantic Community and the United Nations." *International Organization,* XVI (1963), 683–708.

Unpublished Secondary Sources

Appleby, Charles Albert, Jr. "Eisenhower and Arms Control, 1953–1961: A Balance of Risks." Ph.D. dissertation, The Johns Hopkins University, 1987.

Binder, Norman E. "The United Nations as a Learning Experience for Congressional Delegates." Ph.D. dissertation, University of Arizona, 1974.

Davis, Zachary Shands. "Eisenhower's Worldview and Nuclear Strategy." Ph.D. dissertation, University of Virginia, 1989.

Habiby, Raymond N. "Problems of Loyalty of United Nations Personnel." Ph.D. dissertation, University of Minnesota, 1965.

Kingseed, Cole Christian. "Eisenhower and Suez: A Reappraisal of Presidential Activism and Crisis Management." Ph.D. dissertation, Ohio State University, 1983.

Kline, Earl Oliver. "The Suez Crisis: Anglo-American Relations and the United Nations." Ph.D. dissertation, Princeton University, 1961.

Landenburger, John F. "The Philosophy of International Politics of John Foster Dulles, 1919–1952." Ph.D. dissertation, University of Connecticut, 1969.

Levin, Aida Luisa. "Regionalism and the United Nations in American Foreign Policy: The Peace-Keeping Experience of the Organization of American States." Ph.D. dissertation, Columbia University, 1971.

Nolan, Cathal J. "The Last Hurrah of Isolationism: Eisenhower, the United Nations, and the Bricker Amendment." Paper presented at Ike's America Conference, October 6, 1990, University of Kansas, Lawrence, Kansas.

Orwa, D. Katete. "Responses of the United Nations and the United States to the Congo Crisis: Events and Issues." Ph.D. dissertation, University of Akron, 1979.

Stillman, Arthur McLean. "The United Nations and the Suez Canal." Ph.D. dissertation, American University, 1965.

Williams, Robert Edward, Jr. "The Evolution of Disarmament and Arms Control Thought, 1945–1963." Ph.D. dissertation, University of Virginia, 1987.

Winkates, James Edward. "The Influence of the United Nations on National Policy: The United States in the Congo Crisis." Ph.D. dissertation, University of Virginia, 1972.

Index